# Trading Places

# TRADING PLACES

*How We Are Giving Our
Future to Japan and
How to Reclaim It*

## CLYDE V. PRESTOWITZ, JR.

### With a Major New Introduction

*Basic Books, Inc., Publishers*

NEW YORK

Library of Congress Cataloging-in-Publication Data

Prestowitz, Clyde V., 1941–
  Trading places.

  Bibliography: p. 543.
  Includes index.
  1. Japan—Industries—1945–      . 2. United States—
Industries.     3. Japan—Commerce—United States.
4. United States—Commerce—Japan.     I. Title.
HC462.9.P69  1988     338.0952     87–47775
ISBN 0–465–08680–2 (cloth)
ISBN 0–465–08679–9 (paper)

To Carol and Lillian,

the two women in my life.

# CONTENTS

---

# PART II
## *What Makes Japan Run*

# PART IV
## *A Look toward the Future*

# LIST OF FIGURES

# PREFACE

---

I FIRST saw Japan in January 1964 from the deck of the passenger liner *President Wilson* as it steamed up Tokyo Bay early on a cold morning to dock at Yokohama. A graduate student at the East-West Center at the University of Hawaii, I was on my way to complete the Japanese-language requirement of my degree, accompanied by my wife and our infant daughter, Anne.

Japan was not a particularly popular destination for graduate students in those days. Although the "economic miracle" had recently been announced by *The Economist*, many thought of Japan as a small, somewhat exotic country whose people spoke an impossible language and devoted themselves to what was seen as the rather quaint task of trying to catch up to the United States. The action for those interested in geopolitics seemed to be in Europe and it was there that most students flocked. It was not any special clairvoyance that took me to Japan, but rather a combination of a quest for adventure and a practical father. Having lived briefly in Europe as an exchange student while in high school, I thought, upon finishing my undergraduate work, that it would be fun to go the other way to the mysterious Orient.

For the United States at that time, China was still public

enemy number two, after the Soviet Union; and the Vietnam conflict was just getting under way. I was interested in foreign policy and felt that Asia would loom larger on America's horizon in the future. The East-West Center at that time was offering full scholarships to graduate students to spend a year in Honolulu followed by a year in Asia studying an Asian language. Fortunate enough to receive the scholarship, I planned initially to study the Chinese language, but my practical father—a skilled chemist who developed coatings for stainless-steel welding electrodes—urged me to study Japanese because "they [the Japanese] make things." Thus, it was his advice that led me to Yokohama that cold January morning and to a lifelong interest in Japan.

My wife and I had no idea of what awaited us. Friends and relatives had advised us not to go. They spoke of Japan as if it were an underdeveloped country, and emphasized particularly that we should not go with a newborn baby. We weren't sure about any of that, but it seemed to us that the Japanese had babies, too, and most of them seemed to survive. So we persisted and, as a result, were fortunate enough to enjoy many memorable experiences. Our first Japanese friends, Mr. and Mrs. Kozo Hattori, the owners of a small bakery in Tokyo, spoke no English and my Japanese was rather primitive, but we became fast friends. They helped us find an apartment and took us under their wing. Our brand-new "luxury" apartment had no hot running water, no central heating, no stove, and no bath. We cooked with a kind of Bunsen burner and heated with two kerosene stoves. I will never forget the kerosene dealer and his family coming to pay their respects one night. Later I concluded that I was his best customer.

The *sento*, the neighborhood public bath, has almost disappeared today, but in those days it was where most people went before going to bed at night. I still remember my first experience. I was a bit surprised to find that although there were separate baths for men and women, there were female attendants in the men's bath to take their clothes and give them towels. We traveled all over Japan with Hattori-san and our young daughter and made friendships that have now endured for over twenty years. It was a wonderful experience that I was privileged to have and shall always treasure.

I have been involved with Japan in business and government ever since. There have been many changes. The action is now obviously in Asia and not in Europe, and everyone knows now that Japan is much more than a small, exotic nation with quaint notions. And yet as this metamorphosis has taken place, the understanding that Japan and the United States have of each other has not advanced far beyond the misperceptions I encountered in the early 1960s. Today, a little over forty years after the end of the Second World War, Japan and the United States are again being drawn into increasingly rancorous confrontations reminiscent of the past, stemming from the same misunderstandings, and carrying some of the same dangers. It is to make some small contribution to a better understanding and to avoiding further friction between the two countries that I have written this book. I hope also that it will repay in some small way the many debts I owe to those who contributed to my education.

Authors often begin their acknowledgments by mentioning the patience and understanding of spouses and family during the writing. I must admit I often thought this rather silly, but the experience of writing my first book has taught me that it is not. And so I want to begin by thanking my wife and children for putting up with my moods, for turning the TV off and the stereo down when I demanded it, and for bringing me continuous pots of hot tea. To my son Brian, let me say that "Daddy's story" is finally done.

I am deeply indebted to the Woodrow Wilson International Center for Scholars and the U.S.-Japan Program of Harvard University for supporting me as a fellow in their programs while I was engaged in writing. Jim Billington and Ron Morse at the Wilson Center and Dick Finn at Harvard made invaluable suggestions regarding the manuscript. Professors Chalmers Johnson of the University of California at Berkeley and Ezra Vogel and Bruce Scott of Harvard prodded me to do this book; I learned a great deal from them and owe them a large vote of thanks. I am grateful also to professors Kozo Yamamura of the University of Washington, Richard Samuels of the Massachusetts Institute of Technology, and Shumpei Kumon of the University of Tokyo.

The people I worked with at the Commerce Department all deserve thanks. In particular, I am indebted to the former secretary, the late Malcolm Baldrige, and to the former undersecretary Lionel Olmer. Special thank yous must go to Maureen Smith, the director of the Office of Japan and a truly outstanding public servant without whose counsel and indefatigable effort most of the things mentioned in this book could not have been accomplished; and to Herb Cochran, the commercial attaché at the U.S. embassy in Tokyo, who taught me much and upon whom I could call at any hour of the day or night. Others who were of much assistance included my secretary, Dolores Buckley, Frank Vargo, Phil Agress, Noriko Nakano, Glenn Fukushima, and Joe Massey.

In the business world, I was able to learn much about Japan thanks to Egon Zehnder International, which sent me to Tokyo as vice president of the Far Eastern office. I am also greatly indebted to William Norris of Control Data Corporation, to Robert Galvin of Motorola, and to Robert Noyce and Andy Grove of Intel for their aid and encouragement. Richard Heimlich, whom I first knew as an assistant U.S. trade representative and who later went to Motorola, gave me added insight into Washington and provided constant support, as did Bill Krist, Travis Marshall, and John Calhoun. Alan Wolfe and Tom Howell, two of Washington's most talented trade lawyers, were invaluable in collecting and interpreting data on the semiconductor industry, as was Dick Copaken for the machine tool industry.

In Japan, I am particularly grateful to Kazuhiko Otsuka

and Tomio Tsutsumi of the Ministry of International Trade and Industry and Yo Takeuchi of the Ministry of Finance for arranging study trips to Tokyo for me in 1986 and 1987. I owe a great deal to the interpreters at Linguabank, headed by Ken Yokota, who have been great teachers and friends; and to Taiji Kohara, Yoshihisa Komori, Karel van Wolferen, and Yoichi Funabashi for their useful suggestions. I would also like to thank those who agreed to be interviewed and gave freely of their time and knowledge.

I am indebted in countless ways to my friends Bill Finan and Henry Marini for reading the many drafts, making suggestions, and offering moral support at all times; to my good neighbor, the writer Edward Biehl, for the donation of his time, talents, and, occasionally, his home; to my good friend Henry Scott Stokes, correspondent for *Harper's* magazine in Tokyo; and to Fred Praeger, for his guidance and advice from the beginning to the end. To the many others who so kindly responded to my urgent requests for information and insights, and to my speed typists Suzi Maybee and Ursula Nebiker, I extend much thanks. And last but not least, I am indebted to one of the world's great editors, Phoebe Hoss, who in a short time taught me a lot about writing.

## Introduction to the Paperback Edition

# JAPANESE POWER TODAY

---

*Japan can change the whole world balance of power.*
—AKIO MORITA AND SHINTARO ISHIHARA

**D**URING his last term as the president of France, the imperious Charles de Gaulle once dismissed the Japanese as nothing more than peddlers of transistor radios. Twenty-five-odd years later, in the spring of 1989, the greatest peddler of them all, Sony Corporation's co-founder and chairman Akio Morita told the world just how far a country can go with transistor radios. In a book entitled *A Japan That Can Say No*,[1] he and his co-author and Diet member, Shintaro Ishihara, say it can and, indeed, has gone all the way to the top. Their viewpoint is best captured in the paragraph from which the epigraph above is taken. In it they assert that ballistic missiles cannot be targeted accurately without the use of Japanese semiconductors; and that as a result, Japan could change the world balance of power if it began selling semiconductors to the Soviet Union while denying them to the United States. In other words, by dint of its economic virtuosity and the dependence of other nations upon it, Japan has become a full-fledged superpower with political and military as well as economic influence.

While this bald assertion of ultimate power by one who in the West is the quintessential symbol of a Japan devoted to purely economic ambitions would shock most Americans,* it is fully justified. For it is nothing more than the confirmation that the American Century is over and that the trading of places by Japan and the United States described in this book has become a *fait accompli*.

In the nearly two years since this book was first published, Japan has, as I predicted it would, become the undisputed world economic champion with all the geopolitical power that implies. Desperate, but classically conventional measures aimed at salvaging the U.S. position have, as foreseen, not worked. Frantic demands for a "level playing field," and admonitions against the evils of governments "picking winners and losers," have not prevented the growing dependence on a Japanese technology that is systematically promoted as a matter of high national priority. A halving of the value of the dollar against the yen and stimulation of Japan's domestic economy were supposed to reduce the U.S. trade deficit and the Japanese surplus. They did not. After plateauing for a while in the $52-billion range, both are rising again. Meanwhile Japan's enormous capital accumulation has made it the world's largest aid donor and its primary financier, with the U.S. Treasury, the World Bank, the International Monetary Fund, and the Third World heavily dependent upon it.

As this inexorable trading of places increasingly demonstrated the bankruptcy of the conventional wisdom, there arose in the United States a reaction and a degree of rethinking. This was most dramatically demonstrated in the winter and spring of 1989 when a dispute over Japan's new fighter, the FSX, became the first foreign policy crisis of the new Bush administration, to be followed immediately by the unusual

---

*I say "would" because few Americans will read Morita's book. It is so far unpublished in English, and requests to Sony USA for copies of the Japanese version have to date yielded none. Reports from Tokyo say the book is intended only for a Japanese audience.

formal listing of Japan as a priority unfair trading nation under the super-301 provision of the new U.S. trade law.

The FSX dispute revolved around a proposed agreement between the U.S. and Japan to cooperate in jointly developing the new fighter. In what follows I have given what I believe is the most comprehensive account to date of the FSX story. I have done so for three reasons. The first is that the FSX debate subsumed more completely, and demonstrated better than any other single incident, the fundamental inconsistencies, misperceptions, mixed motives, bureaucratic struggles, conflicting objectives and ambitions, fallacies, and evolving dynamics that bedevil the U.S.-Japan relationship. In particular, the debate brilliantly highlighted a major theme of this book—namely, the conflict between U.S. security and economic interests.

Secondly, as a major protagonist of the debate, I was constantly frustrated by the superficial reporting of it and the ignorance in which it was conducted. For instance, the press and leading U.S. officials constantly reiterated that Japan would never buy a U.S. plane—when, in fact, it had preliminarily budgeted to do exactly that in the early 1980s. The press reported the issue as if it had no history, and what actually originated as an attempt by some Japanese to thwart introduction of U.S. planes into their Air Self Defense Force was transposed into American protectionism. I hope this account makes the record more complete.

Finally, the FSX debate was important because it suggested a potentially revolutionary change in U.S. attitudes and policies in the direction of responding directly to the Japanese challenge.

That such a change was actually occurring seemed to be confirmed by the super-301 action. The United States had long avoided any firm response to Japan under U.S. trade laws, fearing to upset the overall relationship and preferring endless negotiation instead. In frustration, Congress strengthened section 301, which deals with unfair trade, to become super 301 in the trade act of 1988. When the U.S. trade representative took advantage of the new powers to move against certain Japanese trade activities, the action was unprecedented. In the end, however, neither the FSX debate nor the super-301 action represented much more than a last gasp of protest in the face of the apparently inexorable culmination of the historic reverse of positions of the United States and Japan. Old habits and attitudes proved difficult to change. The kneejerk priority of geopolitical interests over economic concerns seemed immutable. In the words of the immortal New York Yankee catcher Yogi Berra, it was "déja vu all over again."

Beyond this was an even more important fact. The situation has by now changed to such an extent and the U.S. become so dependent that any actions conceived on the premise of the old relationship are bound to be futile. Japan has become the latter-day Midas with a wealth creating juggernaut that gives it the power of capital. This development is epochal. As the indispensable source of other capabilities, capital represents a kind of ultimate power, and Japan's enthronement as the world's banker marks a watershed. No longer must Japan sweat a living from cheap labor or desperately license or re-verse-engineer foreign technology, or worry that foreign protectionism will close markets to its mass manufactures. It now controls the source of wealth, and others must come to it as they came to the United States in the past. The implications are profound. For despite the continued insistence of many on dismissing Japan as a mere economic superpower without the political skills or military power to match the United States, Morita and Ishihara are correct. There is no such thing as economic power without geopolitical influence. Industrial and financial leadership is national security.

This all leaves Americans facing historic questions. What is their vision of the future? Will they be content with second-class status? Does leadership really matter? Does America have to be number one? What happens if it is not? To these big questions I attempt in the last part of this chapter to give an answer based on the responses I have heard from lecture audiences all over the country in the past two years.

## Foreign Policy Crisis: The FSX Fighter

As a fighting machine the F-16 Fighting Falcon has few equals and none at the price. From engine start to takeoff is fifty-two seconds. The radar is operational forty seconds later; and twenty-eight seconds after that, the plane has reached 30,000 feet and is moving at the speed of sound on its way to over mach two. It can fight at treetop levels and at over 60,000 feet and can maneuver while withstanding nine times the force of gravity. By the end of the century, the U.S. Air Force will have acquired nearly 3,000 of these planes and allied air forces an additional 2,000. At $15 million a copy, the F-16 gives more bang for the buck than any other fighter and in various upgraded versions will be the backbone of U.S. and allied air defenses well into the twenty-first century.

That neither this example of what U.S. technology can still achieve nor any other U.S. plane was deemed suitable for introduction into Japan's Air Self Defense Force was what triggered the FSX crisis and a far-reaching national debate in the winter of 1988–89. The immediate issue was whether the new administration and the Congress should effectuate a memorandum of understanding (MOU) negotiated with Japan in the waning days of the Reagan administration to use the F-16 as the basis for joint development of the FSX. Hailed at its signing as a triumph of cooperation between the two countries in pursuit of common goals, the proposed agreement was, in fact, a political compromise between those in Japan who had wanted to foster Japanese industry by developing an indigenous plane, and certain U.S. officials who feared the political consequences if Japan did not in some fashion adopt a U.S. model. The agreement quickly raised a number of serious questions under the glare of public scrutiny.

Although theoretically a joint development, it seemed to many observers that the work and technology flow would be largely to Japan. The cost would be two to three times that of the F-16 or of other U.S. alternatives and the entry into service much later and without obviously superior performance. In view of the enormous U.S. trade deficit with Japan, the U.S. responsibility for Japan's defense, and the unquestioned U.S. lead in aircraft technology, U.S. officials increasingly began to wonder why Japan would not simply buy, or at least license-produce, U.S. planes. Was Japan more interested in building up its industry and in achieving technological autonomy than in defense or the principles of free trade and comparative advantage? If so, was the United States helping to create an eventual industrial rival through this and similar deals? These questions led to the real issue and the real debate.

For most of the past forty-five years, the main international objective of the United States has been to contain the Soviets and the Chinese. Well into the 1960s, the United States was so powerful economically relative to other nations that it had no need to worry about being able to compete in international markets. This situation led to a U.S. mentality that attributed America's economic prowess to factors peculiar to the American character. These, it has been assumed, will inevitably keep the United States in the lead. Buttressing this view has been the belief (certainly true in the early postwar years) that military technology leads civilian technology; and that by dint of its huge military R&D spending, the United States will always remain far ahead. U.S. foreign policy leaders, focusing on matters of grand strategy and high politics, came thus to believe that economics could be made to serve their ends at no cost. They could make economic concessions in order to achieve geopolitical objectives, and the peculiar genius and creativity of the American system could be counted upon to maintain the competitive strength of the U.S. economy.

Thereby was born the fundamental Pax Americana doctrine of the decoupling of trade and defense matters, wherein U.S. defense supply arrangements were conducted entirely separately from other trade negotiations and by different people.

As a result, the United States, otherwise the leader of the forces pushing for freer world trade, has only rarely insisted on selling the military aircraft in which its comparative advantage with the rest of the world is indisputably the greatest. Rather, we have actually fostered a system in which the standard operating procedure in any deal is to negotiate for offsets (we agree to import goods equivalent to the value of the military sale), technology transfer, and co-production. We do this because, on the one hand, of the insistence of our allies that their citizens get defense jobs, and, on the other hand, our own concern that our allies have the most modern defense equipment on the grounds that their defense is integral to our own. Our allies use this concern of ours to obtain jobs and technology because they know that in the end it will outweigh any fear we may have of the adverse economic consequences of a deal. The best example of this occurred when the United Kingdom actually obtained a 125-percent offset for buying the AWACS airplane from the United States. In effect, we exported jobs to Great Britain in order to persuade it to buy airplanes that it needed and that were superior to anything it had or could make.

The casual attitude toward transfer of U.S. technology fostered by this system permeates the whole U.S. military-industrial complex owing to the movement of personnel between industry and the Pentagon, and has been exacerbated by the U.S. view that U.S. companies dealing with foreign governments should, as private companies, compete against each other for contracts. As a result, U.S. companies frequently bid against each other to see who can give away the most technology, and do so with the blessing—nay, the active encouragement—of their government.

All of this has, of course, been predicated upon the assumption that our allies have more or less the same defense priorities as we and share our views regarding the primacy of security over economics. The FSX saga both highlights the hollowness of the American premises and may yet provide the seeds of a new mentality and a new policy.

## JAPAN RE-CREATES ITS AIRCRAFT INDUSTRY

In 1952 after five years of war and seven of occupation, Japan had no aircraft industry, and its technological capabilities in this area seemed behind those of the United States. In the language of Western economists, Japan had no comparative advantage in aircraft. Yet within five years the groundwork for the industry's re-creation had been laid.

As soon as the Occupation ended, Japan's leaders began to lay plans to get back into aircraft. In July 1953, the Ministry of International Trade and Industry (MITI) directed Japan's big four heavy industrial companies—Mitsubishi, Kawasaki, Fuji, and Ishikawajima Harima—to form the Japan Jet Engine Consortium to begin research and development of an indigenous jet engine. In 1954, the First Aircraft Industry Promotion Law was written by MITI and passed by the Diet. This law and its successors provided the legal basis for MITI to develop extensive "elevation plans," provide subsidies, suspend antitrust laws, and otherwise foster development of the industry.[2]

In 1957, Japan established the Nippon Aircraft Manufacturing Company, a consortium of the big four plus related components manufacturers in which the government of Japan took a 50-percent equity share and guaranteed full subsidization of the development costs (at a time when Japan's GNP was about one tenth that of the United States, and most observers thought it would be lucky to survive as a manufacturer of cheap textiles).

Why this great attention to the aircraft industry? Because, as the Allied authorities who banned it in postwar Germany and Japan recognized, it is the ultimate strategic industry. Militarily, aircraft provide control of the high ground. Economically, they are the vehicle for development of some of the most advanced technologies in materials, electronics, manufacturing, and systems integration. Aerospace vehicles are knowledge-intensive, high-value-added products that justify high-wage employment. From the beginning, this was the kind of industry upon which postwar Japan, with its emphasis on industrial development as a strategic rather than a consumer matter, set its sights. While Western economists prattled on about trade being the result of comparative advantages that arise naturally from the resource endowments of each nation, the Japanese, with none of the apparently requisite resources, only intensified their striving to create the conditions for a competitive industry.

In developing the aircraft industry, Japan's planners concentrated on military aircraft, where profitability was not a consideration, and on participating, as ever more important suppliers and eventually partners, in the commercial aircraft programs of U.S. and European manufacturers. Over the next decades, Japanese companies gained knowledge and experience through coproduction* and participation in the projects of foreign producers as well as through domestic development of relatively simple planes such as trainers. U.S. cooperation, spurred by the desire of the Defense Department to enhance Japan's defense capabilities, dovetailed with this strategy to help make it a success. Technology and knowhow were liberally provided to Japanese aircraft makers, greatly speeding their progress along the learning curve.[3]

*The Vision of MITI Policies in the 1980s* (published in 1980) emphasized the importance of moving Japan's whole industrial structure to the highest levels of technology (see page 105). Mindful of Japan's dependence on foreign oil supplies —a vulnerability all too apparent in the oil crises of the 1970s—the *Vision* stressed technological leadership as the road to economic independence and called for "technological

---

*Under coproduction, the original manufacturer licenses a foreign producer to assemble, or even to manufacture parts or all of, an airplane, but the licensee does not participate in its design and development.

autonomy" as a way for Japan to acquire "bargaining power" in the community of nations. Stress was laid, as it had been for a decade, upon aerospace technology as one of the most important keys to opening the door on these goals, and new projects followed old ones unabated. The military continued to be the backbone of the industry, buying over 80 percent of its production; but increasing emphasis was put on commercial projects. MITI organized and subsidized Japanese participation in the International Aero Engine consortium with Rolls Royce to develop a new jet engine and at the same time put up $1 billion to $2 billion to ensure not only that Japanese industry could participate in Boeing's next generation 7J7 (J for Japan) but that Japanese industry would be recognized by Boeing as a full risk-bearing partner with participation in every aspect of the program from initial design to after service. Finally, in the middle to late 1980s, the Japanese government established programs parallel to those of the United States to develop a space shuttle and a hypersonic plane, known as the Orient Express, that could fly from Washington, D.C., to Tokyo in two to three hours.

The enormous cost of these programs by no means discouraged the Japanese from their commitment to developing their own aerospace industry. By the early to mid-1980s, Japanese industry was beginning to believe it had not much left to learn through coproduction. In view of Japan's increasing capabilities, the United States was already showing less enthusiasm for technology transfer (see page 271), and would, the Japanese believed, become increasingly stingy as its lead continued to diminish.

The FSX was born out of the conjunction of this view and the debate within Japan's defense establishment over how eventually to replace the F-1, the aging, domestically developed support fighter plane whose retirement was planned for the early 1990s.* In 1981, Japan Defense Agency planners identified a need for twenty-four airplanes that would have to be put

---

*Although theoretically an all-weather fighter, the F-1 does not perform well in bad weather or at night. It has a blind spot and poor maneuverability and is considered

in the budget by the end of 1987. In view of the small numbers involved, it was expected that these planes would be foreign-built (probably U.S.). Accordingly, JDA initiated discussions about procuring the new planes from U.S. aircraft makers. The most likely candidates were thought to be the General Dynamics F-16, already on duty with the U.S. Air Force in Japan at Misawa airbase, and the F-18 of McDonnell Douglas.

These plans caused great unease among an informal but closely knit group of officials and executives in the Technical Research and Development Institute (TRDI) of the JDA, the Japanese aircraft makers led by MHI, and particular bureaus at MITI, which always supplies the head of procurement of the JDA and has review power over Japan's military equipment buying. And in the winter of 1982, these men began to consider how to make the F-1 replacement a purely indigenous airplane. They were motivated partly by MITI's recent call, in its *Vision of Japan in the 1980s*, for the achievement of both technological autonomy and a leadership position in aerospace, and partly by the fact that MHI and the other Japanese producers were facing the end of major projects with nothing new coming to keep the production lines humming. At the same time, the success of Japan's electronics companies had fired national pride in Japanese technology and created confidence that Japan could succeed in any industrial undertaking. Linked with this attitude was Japan's old sense of inferiority toward the West and consequent need to prove that it could do anything America could do. Finally, there was the deep-seated Japanese reluctance to be dependent on foreign suppliers.

Between 1982 and 1985, the strategists of the indigenous-development faction worked cleverly and tenaciously to overcome several formidable obstacles, not the least of which was a general lack of confidence, outside the aircraft in-

unlikely to emerge from any dogfight alive.[4] Japanese pilots do not like to fly it because they consider it inadequate.[5] This is all the more the case in view of the massive Soviet deployment of advanced aircraft in Asia in the past decade. Although defense plans in 1976 called for an eventual one hundred F-1s to be placed in service, only about eighty were actually produced between 1977 and the mid-1980s. With a planned service life of 3,500 hours, they were slated for retirement beginning in the late 1980s.

dustry and particularly among the air staff, that Japanese producers could build a world-class fighter. There were also the problems of time—that is, the impossibility of building the FSX before it would be necessary to replace the aging F-1s with the twenty-four foreign planes, whose relatively low cost would undoubtedly cause the hard-eyed Ministry of Finance (MOF) to look unfavorably on the high cost of any future domestic development. And the United States had to be considered: the Americans were sure to see Japanese domestic development as duplication of effort and an indirect increase of the U.S. defense burden, and would pressure for sale or coproduction of another U.S. plane.

To solve these problems, these strategists seized upon an American technology to try to extend the life of the F-1 and thus gain time to accomplish domestic development. Indeed, the campaign to overcome the objections, and to prove that Japanese industry could stand alone, took on the overtones of a crusade for the future of Japan. The head of the air staff himself, General Hitoshi Omura, was reported to have said that the mission requirements and specifications for what was now being called the FSX were, in part, purposely developed so that no existing U.S. plane could meet them.[6] Thus, a two-engine requirement apparently shut out the one-engine F-16, while a long-operating radius requirement seemed to exclude the relatively short-legged F-18.

By the fall of 1984, the first battle was won. U.S. makers were told that no foreign airplanes would be procured, although certain key components might still be welcome; and in December, *Wing* magazine reported that the life of the F-1 would definitely be extended by 550 hours.[7] In January 1985, a formal query was made by the air staff (always unhappy with the F-1 and still skeptical of a domestic FSX) of TRDI about the feasibility of a domestically developed FSX. Since TRDI was at the center of the all-Japan faction, no one was surprised in April when its interim report concluded in the affirmative.

Thus far, throughout the debate in Japan, there had been no real discussion of the Soviet threat, of coordination with U.S.

forces, of the desirability of interoperability with U.S. aircraft, or of the fact that an already-inadequate airplane would be made to soldier on for four more years in the face of increasingly superior Soviet capabilities. For Japan in contrast to the United States, defense appears to have been a minor consideration compared with building a Japanese airplane and industry.

## A CRACK IN THE U.S. HEGEMONY

By 1983, some Pentagon officials were beginning to question the conventional wisdom that military technology leads civilian technology, with the growing realization that the United States was becoming dependent on Japan for a certain number of high technology components. But while Japan had ready access to U.S. technology through military coproduction deals, the United States could not as easily obtain Japanese technology because of Japan's policy ban on the export of weapons and military-related technology. In an effort to reverse this unbalance, negotiations were carried on through much of 1983 to achieve a mechanism for licensing so-called dual-use technology from Japan to the United States. After extremely difficult negotiations—with MITI and much of Japanese industry being very reluctant—an agreement was finally reached. Although the arrangement agreed to is bureaucratically cumbersome—to date, hardly any technology has found its way to the United States—it is important as a prelude to some U.S. thinking during the FSX talks and because it supported Japan's growing confidence in the superiority of its own technology and fed the view, now widely held in Japan, of the United States as a supplicant for whom Japan was doing a favor.

Also important as background music to the FSX saga was the increasing trade friction with Japan in such high-technology areas as telecommunications satellites, supercomputers, and semiconductors—during a period when the bilateral U.S. trade deficit was soaring toward $50 billion. Thus, the United States first became aware of the FSX at a moment when the foundation of its effortless industrial superiority, and of the attitudes it fostered, was beginning to crack. Although there was no revolution in attitude, Americans started to raise questions and to propose new courses of action very different from those of the past. There was, for example, the renewal in 1983 of the MOU under which Japan was coproducing the U.S. F-15. For the first time with Japan, the United States insisted on a technology flowback clause (standard in MOUs with other allies), under which the United States receives free access to any technology derived from U.S.-supplied technology. Another example was the SH-60 helicopter: the United States insisted that the JDA sign an MOU and build under license from the United States rather than simply buying key components and combining them with Japanese avionics and weapons.

It was shortly after this, in early 1984, that U.S. officials first began to discuss the FSX among themselves as the movement to extend the life of the F-1 gathered steam. The key players were Gregg Rubinstein in Tokyo and Commander James Auer then in the Pentagon, both of whom are fluent in Japanese and long-time students of Japan. Rubinstein, a career Foreign Service officer in the Mutual Defense Assistance Office in Tokyo, was responsible for the technology flowback clause in the new F-15 MOU as well as for the SH-60 arrangement. Now retired from the Navy and head of a Japanese studies institute at Vanderbilt University, Auer has been a key figure in all of the security talks between the United States and Japan over the past fifteen years. Rubinstein and Auer began to learn of the FSX situation from the Japanese press, from talks with officials at JDA and other Japanese ministries, and from information gathered from U.S. aircraft executives who were now being informed that procurement of the twenty-four foreign fighters was increasingly unlikely. (Significantly, neither the Commerce Department nor the U.S. Trade Representative were informed or aware of the situation.)

The responses of these two men reflected a transition in U.S. thinking. Rubinstein saw the FSX as a repeat of the helicopter experience. He doubted that Japanese industry could do an entirely domestically developed plane, and concluded that, under the rubric of domestic development, the Japanese would contract to buy key parts and technology from U.S. firms. He was prepared to sell but did not want simply to license technology with no provision for broader two-way cooperation and with no discussion of the desirability of interoperability between Japanese and U.S. aircraft likely to operate in the same theater. As with helicopters, Rubinstein wanted a government-to-government MOU. He saw the FSX as an opportunity to flesh out the concept of cooperation that underlay the just-completed military technology agreement. Auer shared these views, but was also concerned that the project could become what he termed a "political disaster. How would it look to the Congress," he asked, "if Japan is developing its own plane and industry with an infusion of U.S. technology while the trade deficit is soaring?"[8]

Here was a mixture of old and new views. On the one hand, the concern that the United States have some role beyond that of candy store to Japanese industry represented a change from past practice, a change engendered by recognition of the new U.S. need to think about economic competition. On the other hand, behind the fear of political disaster lay more traditional attitudes which were, ironically, now for the first time linking trade and defense in an effort to keep them decoupled. The Defense Department prefers for Japan to have limited military means, to assure the primacy of the United States in the Pacific and simplify peacekeeping by reassuring other Asian nations that are still suspicious of Japan. Moreover, as long as Japan's means are limited, the DOD enjoys a mentor-protégé relationship with Japan. This situation is sustained by our willingness to emphasize the security relationship with Japan while downplaying the concerns of economic competition—a willingness undermined by any perception that Japan is taking economic advantage of us under the U.S. defense umbrella. Nothing could engender such a perception faster than Japanese manipulation of defense needs to promote an effort to catch up with the United States in aircraft, the undisputed bastion of U.S.

leadership. Both concerns led to opposition to Japanese domestic development and to a push for some cooperative agreement, but for different reasons. One wanted cooperation to get something. The other was not opposed to getting something, but wanted cooperation at all costs for the sake of appearances in order to avoid disturbing the comfortable, overall relationship on the old basis.

The result of these lines of thought was a series of discussions, formal and informal, in which U.S. officials gently suggested to their Japanese counterparts that domestic development was not a good idea, and that some alternative based on a U.S. plane would be more appropriate. Whether the alternative would be the classic one of coproduction or something else was not clear or even much discussed.

In view of later developments, one might well wonder at this point why the United States was not more assertive, as it had a rationale for being. Japan's F-1 was already inadequate; and yet for purposes of proving its technological manhood and achieving a competitive position in the aircraft industry, Japan was proposing to extend the F-1's life in the face of a massive Soviet buildup. This would further burden the already tightly stretched U.S. forces, and moreover, it was likely that the plane Japan was proposing to build would be inferior to U.S. alternatives when it eventually came into service. The cost of the FSX would be two to three times that of procurement from the United States. In view both of Japan's dependence on free trade and the U.S. defense shield, and of the mounting trade deficit, it could be argued that the United States should early on have strongly insisted that Japan simply buy a U.S. plane or, in deference to the history of coproduction, at least coproduce a U.S. plane. Some high Japanese officials claim that had the United States taken a vigorous course, Japan would have agreed.*

The United States did not react vigorously for several reasons. At the time the FSX was a relatively minor issue com-

---

*This view was expressed to me in interviews in Tokyo and Washington, D.C., with officials of MITI and the Ministry of Foreign Affairs.

pared with others on the table. The United States was in the habit of agreeing to offsets, coproduction, and technology transfer. It was not in the habit of linking trade and defense. Indeed, there was a fear that such linkage could damage security relationships if the Defense Department came to be seen as merely a shill for U.S. defense industries. Japan is a sovereign nation, and the United States cannot just order it about. Indeed, any attempt to do so could easily prove counterproductive—especially because the United States is not so firm toward Europe. Why should Japan be singled out for special treatment, even if the Europeans do contribute much more to their own defense than the Japanese do. Finally, Auer believed the decision would ultimately be a political one: he thought that in spite of the strong drive to go indigenous at the lower levels of the bureaucracy, cooler heads would prevail once the issue got to the policy level. He knew that Japanese officials have a large stake in the primacy the United States puts on the security relationship. As long as the United States focuses primarily on the geopolitical relationship rather than on trade, it can be counted upon to maintain the open-market, free-trade policies that have so benefited Japan. Thus, Japanese officialdom wants to keep the U.S. focus on security and the overall relationship and to avoid the appearance of taking economic advantage of the relationship. And, of course, many Japanese officials simply and sincerely want to build more cooperative ties with the United States. These, Auer felt, could be counted on to overcome the narrow views of lower-level bureaucrats.

Indeed, in Auer's view, the most effective kind of pressure would be no pressure. To justify avoiding an inconvenient course of action, Japanese bureaucrats often use the excuse that they cannot be seen to be bowing to foreign pressure. If no pressure was applied, there could be no excuse; and the policy adopted would be seen to reflect the true nature of Japan which, if in conflict with the United States, could have serious consequences. While there was some justification for this view, it ignored the fact that the Japanese had often demonstrated that they interpret lack of pressure as lack of concern. This view also rested on the assumption that policy-level officials would control their underlings—an assumption that ignored the fact that some powerful politicians and policy-level officials were getting behind the all-Japan faction.

Be that as it may, throughout the rest of 1984 and 1985, the U.S. policy rested on the gentle persuasion of Auer's nonpressure-pressure approach. During this time, the Air Self-Defense Force directed many questions to the U.S. Air Force about the F-16 and the F-18 and how they could meet the requirements being developed for the FSX. Because those requirements were only vaguely defined at this point and were being at least partly developed with the idea of disqualifying foreign aircraft, the Air Force could not respond positively in a concrete manner. Some seeds of future distrust were sowed at this time, as the U.S. analysts sensed that the Japanese requirements were partly designed to justify domestic development.

As Rubinstein recalled later, "They didn't want to hear about the capabilities of the new versions of the U.S. planes. They were bent on building their own plane and only wanted to hear that existing U.S. models did not meet their requirements. They closed their ears to anything else."[9] Thus, in Tokyo, Rubinstein listened and worried. But in Washington, Auer remained confident that the policy level would handle the problem, and no particular action was taken as the all-Japan team gained momentum.

Others in Washington were not so sure. After the TRDI's interim report of April 1985, urging the feasibility of the domestic development, the Pentagon asked the C.I.A. for an analysis. The conclusion was that the Japanese were set on going it alone, but that their ability to do so was limited unless the United States was willing to make technology available. The C.I.A. paper questioned the wisdom of the project, noting that its cost would be astronomical without substantial U.S. technology transfer. The C.I.A. recommended against such transfer because of the tremendous push along the learning curve it would give Japanese industry. This report had little effect at the time. As a key C.I.A. official explained to me later, the Pentagon wanted the Japanese to have an interoperable up-to-date airplane, and was not concerned about the effects on industrial competition between the United States and Japan. This explanation was confirmed later in the summer when Michael Smith, the deputy U.S. trade representative, wrote, to Secretary of Defense Casper Weinberger and Secretary of State George Shultz, a letter expressing his fear that U.S. commercial interests were not being adequately considered. The letter seems never to have received a response. A letter at this time from the U.S. aircraft manufacturers to the secretaries of commerce, defense, and state asking for help did result in some industry-government discussions, but no significant changes ensued.

The Japanese cabinet's adoption in September 1985 of the new Mid-Term Defense Plan, including the option of indigenous development of the FSX, was a small shock and did stimulate a response. Rubinstein sent a cable from Tokyo in early October, pointing out that the Japanese did not want simply to coproduce an off-the-shelf U.S. plane, and that conversion of the existing F-4E, an option that had been suggested as a theoretical possibility, was not likely. That left domestic development, which carried the risk that the Japanese would produce another inferior aircraft like the F-1. To avoid that and to obtain some U.S. participation, Rubinstein suggested that the United States offer the Japanese the possibility of some kind of collaboration on an advanced version of a U.S. plane.

This important communication reflected implicit mental parameters that came to govern U.S. policy thinking. In particular, it was axiomatic in the Pentagon and the State Department that the Japanese would not buy or coproduce a U.S. airplane. Whether this was, in fact, the case is open to question. Not only did the U.S. president trumpet the benefits of his "Ron–Yasu relationship" with Japan's prime minister, but the U.S. ambassador to Japan, Mike Mansfield, was reported to be revered by the Japanese. Would Japan have been prepared to buy U.S. if these men and other high U.S. officials had attempted to get Japanese understanding of the desirability of that course of action? We will never know, because none of these officials ever tried. But top Japanese officials in the Foreign Ministry say that an expression of high-level U.S. interest at this point would have changed the course of Japanese decision making.*

As it was, over the next two years there was played out a grand Kabuki drama in which the all-Japan faction gave the appearance of judiciously weighing all the options while driving hard for domestic development, and the Pentagon repeatedly "solved" the problem at the policy level only to have it revert to the technicians of the all-Japan faction, who never wavered from their chosen course. Meanwhile, on the American side the ball bounced back and forth between those concerned with maintaining the U.S. industrial and technological lead and those who emphasized cooperation for the sake of the relationship.

## THE FIGHTING FALCON BEATS THE ODDS

Although the JDA's mailing of a questionnaire in December 1985 to McDonnell Douglas and General Dynamics, pursuant to a cabinet directive to complete a study of the options by summer 1986, appeared to indicate that the U.S. companies were back in the running, virtually all observers saw the mailing as a pro-forma effort by a JDA strongly in favor of domestic development—a view later confirmed by General Omura.

Indeed, in early April 1986, five of Japan's top defense officials—including the JDA's director—met secretly in a room of the Ichigaya Kaikan to discuss what to do about budgeting. Time was pressing. If domestic development of the FSX was to proceed, it had to get into the budget soon. The all-Japan faction wanted to do it now. But Nishihiro had been

---

*For obvious reasons these officials wish to remain anonymous, but they are men who were intimately involved in the whole course of the debate.

warned, at a meeting with Assistant Defense Secretary Richard Armitage and Auer in Hawaii in January, that the United States had concerns about Japan's domestic development plans and would prefer some cooperative arrangement. As a result, Nishihiro explained to his colleagues that things were no longer so simple, but said that if the ASDF could get an OK from the United States, then he himself would certainly agree to go ahead with self-development. In view of the fact that Nishihiro knew very well that there would be no OK from the Americans, this statement indicates some justification for the Pentagon view that the policy level would straighten everything out in Japan. On the other hand, Nishihiro was certainly not vigorously opposing self-development. In another example of classic Japanese negotiating style, he avoided the burden of opposition by making *gaiatsu* (foreign pressure) the bogeyman of domestic development. In any case, in what Auer and other Pentagon officials saw as a great victory, the decision was taken to delay budgeting FSX development for one year.

This led to speculation in Japan that Nakasone would agree to co-development as a kind of gift to President Reagan during his forthcoming trip to the United States. In fact, however, Nakasone made no commitments, perhaps because he was not asked. Because their own attitude would have been very different, Japanese officials were flabbergasted that no American official prodded Nakasone to make a decision for a U.S. plane. In this instance, the nonpressure-pressure strategy seems to have led to the perception on the Japanese side that the Americans at the "policy level" were really not interested or, at best, ambivalent.

This impression was apparently reinforced when Defense Secretary Weinberger visited Japan later in the spring. He was quoted by Japan's *Nihon Keizai* newspaper as saying that while the United States would welcome joint development, it opposed any link between trade and defense.[10] Though it would be nice if Japan purchased a U.S. plane, Weinberger emphasized that the most important thing was for Japan to obtain the most modern, cost-effective fighters to meet its needs. While pointing out that interoperability was important, he stressed that the U.S. purpose was not to reduce its trade deficit by selling weapons. Some Pentagon officials thought that this statement increased the pressure on the Japanese to go with a U.S. plane because interoperability and cost effectiveness both favored such a decision. But Japanese officials now say that this statement led them to think that top American officials would be happy no matter what Japan did, and note that it left the definition of needs and thus the calculation of cost effectiveness entirely in their own hands—that is, in practice, the very hands that were most strongly pushing domestic development.

Thus, the all-Japan faction took the initiative. As a sop to the United States, it accepted the term *co-development* but began to define it in terms of self-development, with Japan procuring from U.S. suppliers the engines, and any other parts it could not make. At the same time, this faction re-emphasized development of special-mission requirements and specifications that existing U.S. planes could not match. In May a team from JDA visited Washington to brief Pentagon officials on these requirements, by now refined into what became known as the "sixty-four parameters." The U.S. team was partly amused and partly dismayed. The requirements were based on a mission and tactical doctrine that U.S. officials thought would leave few Japanese planes flying after a dust-up with the Soviets. Furthermore, many of the specifications were so extreme that it was obvious that they were primarily intended to disqualify U.S. planes from consideration. Before leaving, the Japanese team, in an apparent effort to make things more difficult for the U.S. manufacturers, enjoined the Pentagon not to inform them of the sixty-four parameters.

During this maneuvering, the trade frictions that had long plagued U.S.-Japan relations were becoming more intense. Despite several "market-opening packages," the U.S. trade deficit with Japan was approaching $60 billion. The telecommunications agreement of 1985, which had purportedly opened the Japanese market, resulted in few new sales of U.S. equipment. U.S. supercomputers continued to be shut out of any Japanese government purchases, while U.S. car telephones were excluded from the lucrative Tokyo market. No technology had been transferred to the United States as of the 1983 deal; and discussion of Japanese participation in Star Wars development was proceeding slowly because of Japanese demands for access to sensitive U.S. technology, combined with reluctance to grant access to their own technology. The bitterest dispute of all, and the one that came to symbolize trade friction, was over semiconductors (see pages 147–73).

At this juncture, Kevin Kearns, who was to play an important later role in the FSX debate, arrived at the Mutual Defense Assistance office of the U.S. embassy in Tokyo in August 1986 to replace Rubinstein who was being rotated back to Washington. A career Foreign Service officer, Kearns had had long experience in political/military affairs, having worked on military assistance problems in Latin America, the Philippines, Korea, and the State Department's political/military bureau. His arrival in Japan coincided with the start of a series of events that forced the issue to a head in the spring of 1987.

One was the appearance in the Japanese press of a series of articles questioning the motivation and wisdom of the FSX. The articles emphasized that industrial objectives and not defense were the project's primary motivation, and noted that it was difficult to understand why Japan should develop a domestic fighter when it could buy an American plane for half the cost of domestic development. Similar questions were being asked at the ministries of Finance and Foreign Affairs as well as in some bureaus of MITI. Realizing that it would have to overcome these doubts and in some way gain at the least the tacit acquiescence of the Americans, the all-Japan faction took steps to prove that no U.S. plane could fulfill Japan's requirements.

In October it invited General Dynamics and McDonnell Douglas to come to Tokyo to make a formal presentation of

their proposed aircraft.* Then in December, the JDA coun-
cilor and all-Japan faction leader, Tsutsui, was dispatched to
Washington to obtain the Pentagon's understanding of why
Japan had to go with domestic development. In a presentation to all the key U.S. officials, he went through a cost-ben-
efit analysis and explained that none of the candidate aircraft
presented in Tokyo in October could meet Japan's requirements as well or as inexpensively as the homegrown FSX.
The meeting quickly became heated. While the Japanese
present have attributed this to American irritation with Tsutsui's flawless performance in nearly perfect English, all the
Americans who were there say the problem was simply that
his explanation did not make any sense. They note that
Tsutsui gave no insight into the reasoning of the JDA and
bridled at technical questions from the U.S. team.

General Phil Gast, then the head of the Pentagon's FSX
working group, was appalled. Tsutsui was claiming that
Japan could develop the FSX for $1.2 billion, whereas the
cost of a similar program in the United States or Europe
would be $3 billion to $4 billion. To Gast and the other Americans, it seemed obvious that the numbers were skewed.
Moreover, it was clear to Gast that the perfect plane was the
new F-15E which, for reasons that are still unclear, had never
been proposed as a candidate. With no modification at all, it
could easily both meet sixty-one of Japan's sixty-four parameters and be adjusted to meet the other three, which in the
opinion of the Americans were not important anyhow. Gast

---

*This was Kearns's baptism in the FSX game, and he was appalled by what he saw.
It seemed that the U.S. companies had not been informed of what was expected of
them, and were just now learning of the JDA's sixty-four parameters and being asked
to respond to them in detail overnight. Although others remember these meetings a bit
differently—some finding them useful and constructive and others saying they did not
agree with or fully comprehend the Japanese requirements—there is no dispute that
GD presented its one-engine F-16, which immediately stopped the presentation because Japan had established an absolute two-engine requirement. The show was saved
by the timely arrival of GD's Charles Anderson, the lead engineer on a two-engine
version of the F-16, who ad-libbed a presentation of that plane. Virtually all participants reported feeling that the meeting was pro forma and that the Japanese participants really were not interested in a U.S. plane. This feeling was confirmed by *Sekai
Orai*, which reported afterward that the Self-Defense Forces had decided on domestic
manufacture of the FSX.[11]

thus proposed taking the whole discussion back to square one, and Armitage suggested creation of a joint government steering group, including representatives of the military and industry from both countries, for the purpose of thoroughly analyzing the mission, the requirements, and the options. Tsutsui, however, rejected all U.S. objections and proposals, saying things were already too far along, and returned to Tokyo.

It was at this meeting, according to Rubinstein, that U.S. officials finally became fully aware of the strength of the Japanese drive for self-development and hardened their own attitudes. Their alarm was exacerbated when Kearns reported from Tokyo that Tsutsui had announced, upon his return there, that he had gotten the American OK which Nishihiro had referred to at the secret meeting nearly a year before.

Armitage and Auer tried to correct Tsutsui's misreport at a meeting with Nishihiro in Hawaii in January. Auer says that he and Armitage left the meeting convinced that Nishihiro would see to it that Japan went with either licensed production or improvement of an existing U.S. plane.

In Tokyo, however, it quickly appeared that the two sides had been talking past each other again. Kearns went to see Nishihiro himself and was told that there was no problem in Washington; and that having postponed the decision a year, JDA was proceeding to put the indigenous FSX in its budget. Kearns proceeded to draft a strong cable to Washington pointing out the discrepancy between what he was hearing in Tokyo and the optimistic reports circulating in the Pentagon. This led to a dispute within the embassy over whether to send the cable, with one official commenting, "What if Weinberger should read it? We have to manage the U.S. response." Such was his concern for the overall relationship. In the end, however, the cable was duly sent.

The U.S. companies—which feeling there was no real interest on the Japanese side, had moved slowly to reply to their questions of October—were now asked by JDA and directed by the Pentagon to make their final proposals. Thus in March 1987, General Dynamics and McDonnell Douglas teams traveled once again to Tokyo and explained how their planes, the two-engine F-18 of MD and the F-16 of GD, could be modified and improved to meet the sixty-four parameters. This time the sessions went smoothly with the companies responding concretely to all questions. Again, GD felt it had given an advanced aeronautics seminar. The U.S. companies would have been even more annoyed had they known that their presentations were turned over to MHI to aid it in making its final presentation to JDA.

With misperception apparently rampant, a now-aroused Pentagon decided on the definitive step of sending what came to be known as the Sullivan mission in April. This team, headed by Assistant Deputy Undersecretary of Defense Gerald Sullivan, included officials from all concerned parts of the Pentagon, although as usual there were no representatives from other concerned parts of the U.S. government. The task was to attempt to come to a meeting of the minds on the mission, requirements, and basis of development of the FSX. It was also to review Japanese technology. MHI and TRDI had been publicly arguing that Japanese technology was superior to that of the U.S. planes. Much was made in the press of the lower repair rate for MHI-produced F-15s as opposed to those imported from the United States. In particular, it was said that the FSX would incorporate Japanese avionics, a phased-array radar, and a single piece, cocured composite wing, none of which could be done in the United States. Sullivan was to ascertain the truth of this claim. Thus, despite Auer's nonpressure-pressure strategy, this visit, which had been arranged with the ever-vague Nishihiro, represented a major increase in U.S. pressure.

The peculiar specifications of the FSX were derived from a certain definition of mission and tactics. In two days of presentations, the Sullivan team agreed with the basic Japanese mission of securing the Soya Strait between Sakhalin and Japan's northern island of Hokkaido by using the FSX to attack Soviet missile firing and troop-carrying ships. On tactics, however, there was great disagreement. Whereas the Japanese focused on attacking ships once they had breached Japan's twelve-mile sea limit, the U.S. doctrine was to strike at a greater distance. JDA, focusing almost entirely on the anti-ship role, planned to load the FSX with maximum weaponry and fuel for this role. The U.S. team pointed out that secondary roles can be awfully important, and that the FSX would certainly need dogfight, counter-air, and air-support capabilities in addition to counter-ship ability. Noted one team member, the most difficult thing the FSX may be called upon to do is to dogfight with Mig-29s. U.S. doctrine is to design the plane to perform its most difficult as well as its primary task. This tactical difference had great implications for the airplane's requirements. Thus, the Sullivan team explained its view that the planned basing mode for the FSX was too narrow and many of the JDA requirements excessive while, on the other hand, some requirements were not being addressed at all.

Beyond matters of mission and tactics, the Sullivan team also emphasized the importance of cost, rapid-delivery potential, and interoperability of equipment between the U.S. and the Japanese forces in Japan. Sullivan stressed, in his wrap-up and subsequent report to the Pentagon, that any one of four U.S. alternatives—F-15, F-14, F-18, or F-16— could do the job sooner, cheaper, and better than the domestically developed FSX. His own favorite was the F-15E which, in his view as in Gast's, was clearly the superior airplane for the mission. Sullivan believed the Japanese should choose a U.S. plane as soon as possible and then cooperate on "tweaking" it with the U.S. producer. He was not enthusiastic about elaborate co-development proposals—largely because of the time involved, and because his team was not, on the whole, impressed with the Japanese aircraft technology. In general, the conclusion was that nothing justified designing a whole new airplane. Sullivan reported these conclusions to MOFA and to the Ministry of Finance, which were quite interested because they had been getting very different evaluations from the JDA. Both agencies said, however, that the decision was really in the JDA's hands.

Of great significance is what these discussions revealed about the state of defense planning in Japan and between Japan and the United States. Rarely, if ever, was the FSX discussed in Japan in the context of how best to defend Japan or to mesh with U.S. defense efforts. Indeed, the decision to extend the life of the already inadequate F-1 ran exactly counter to those considerations. Discussion of the mission and tactics during the Sullivan visit revealed that the Japanese ASDF had had no discussions with the Japanese naval and ground forces with regard to coordination and the mission of the FSX. The situation was best described by a high MOFA official who said that JDA had no strategy and was governed by business and the fear that if it missed this chance Japanese technology would be lost. As a result, there was not only little coordination between U.S. and Japanese forces; there was no desire for any. The U.S. forces were already defending Japan with F-16s based in Misawa and performing the same mission as that for which the FSX was to be designed. It was well known that these planes were the envy of the poor F-1 pilots, and there was no complaint that they were inadequate to the mission. Yet there was no heart-to-heart discussion between the U.S. and the Japanese air forces with regard to either the mission or the airplane.

Sullivan later said he left Tokyo believing that Japan would not go for an indigenous plane—an optimism that was, again, not necessarily justified.[12] While Sullivan was in Tokyo, Prime Minister Nakasone was again in Washington. That the President did not raise the FSX issue with the Prime Minister not only surprised him but led some Japanese officials to think that top U.S. officials were not concerned about the FSX. The Japanese press reported continued pressure for the domestic FSX. MHI stated that the rapidly appreciating yen should not affect the decision because it could build the plane for Y5 billion to Y6 billion per plane, a cost that would

be competitive with imported models (this was an unbeliev-
able figure to virtually all experts). The JDA completed its
long-running evaluation and concluded that the U.S. planes
would be unsatisfactory. Nishihiro made a hurried visit to
Washington to make what has been described as a last-ditch
effort to convince U.S. officials to go along with domestic
development. At this point, Armitage openly abandoned
Auer's nonpressure-pressure strategy and confirmed the
view of Japanese cynics by telling Nishihiro that neither domestic development nor joint development of a completely
new airplane would be acceptable to the United States.

Armitage had no choice. By this time, notwithstanding
professions and devout wishes to the contrary, defense and
trade were linked. In January 1987, a team of top-level U.S.
negotiators seeking to open Japan's supercomputer market
had been rebuffed and, according to some participants, told
that if the United States wanted to save Cray Research, its
leading producer, it might have to nationalize the company.
In March, the President had announced the imposition of
sanctions against Japan for noncompliance with the semiconductor agreement of 1986. A myriad of other trade issues
remained unsolved, and the deficit continued to soar despite
the now rapidly devaluing dollar. Congress was aware of the
FSX and could not understand why Japan could not contribute to improving relations and the trade deficit by buying
U.S.-made airplanes that the leading experts had now said
were better, less expensive, and more appropriate to Japan's
defense needs than the proposed Japanese-made FSX.
Added to all this was the recently revealed Toshiba Machine
incident (see page 374)—a major blow to the U.S. Navy
which caused great bitterness in a Congress already frustrated by what it perceived as unfair Japanese trade.

In June, Secretary of Defense Weinberger traveled to Japan
and made the FSX an issue of the first moment by telling
Defense Minister Kurihara that the matter "went to the heart
of the U.S.-Japan relationship."[13] Weinberger proposed co-
development by saying that the U.S. planes were very good,

and the best U.S. technology should be married with the best Japanese technology to make the best possible airplane. All U.S. participants agree that Weinberger had no concrete idea of exactly what the content of co-development would be. His proposal was general and really a reiteration of earlier U.S. positions. Japanese officials began to believe, however, that the United States was now serious about the FSX. Particularly at MOFA there was agreement that the issue went to the heart of the relationship because of article 2 of the U.S.–Japan Security Treaty which calls for economic co-operation in addition to military arrangements. Could the United States argue that Japan was not abiding by the treaty?

In August, in the wake of the Toshiba Machine affair and a U.S. Senate vote of 96 to 0 that Japan should buy its next fighter from U.S. producers, a team from MHI and the Japanese consortium was dispatched to meet with GD and MD about possible joint activity. It was a strange visit. The Japanese told their hosts that they did not really understand why they were there. They said they had come only because their government had forced them to do so. While visiting GD, they continued to insist that two engines were absolutely necessary. GD told them bluntly that it had decided not to make a two-engine F-16; and that if they had to have two engines, they should deal with MD. GD believed at that moment that it had taken itself out of the running.

Nevertheless, things moved quickly. In September, Japan decided to go ahead with a deal calling for modification of a U.S. plane. On 2 October, on a visit to Washington, Defense Minister Kurihara informed Weinberger of this decision. On 5 October, Prime Minister Nakasone made a public announcement of it; and on 12 October, both GD and MD were told to dispatch teams to Tokyo to make their final offers. On 22 October, GD was astounded to learn that Japan had chosen its F-16 as the plane to be modified and developed into the FSX. In the end, it seemed the two-engine requirement and many others the Japanese had said were absolute, were, in fact, not—as U.S. officials had been saying all along. In

Japan, the decision was presented as a great concession made in order to preserve good relations with the United States. In the United States, the announcement was hailed as a great victory that would result in a sale of American airplanes and equipment that would contribute to reducing the trade deficit while enhancing the policy of deterrence through greater interoperability of U.S. and Japanese forces. Auer and Armitage saw it as the confirmation of their faith that the policy level would take care of things, although in the end nonpressure pressure had given way to enormous pressure. Kearns was pleased because in his view any deal based on putting together the best technology of both countries in the aircraft industry would wind up mostly American.

Overlooked in the euphoria of the moment in the United States was the reason for choosing the F-16, which all observers had thought much less compatible with the Japanese requirements than the other candidates. It is still something of a mystery. Some Japanese cite the fact that the F-16 was less expensive. Others say McDonnell Douglas was arrogant and overconfident and angered the JDA by inciting Congress to become involved in the issue. Some say that MHI which already had experience of working with McDonnell Douglas on the F-15 wanted to gain experience with another U.S. manufacturer. A final explanation, which bears significantly on what followed, is that the F-16 was more susceptible to extensive redesign and modification into what would, in effect, become domestic development of the FSX.

## SNATCHING DEFEAT FROM THE JAWS OF VICTORY

Throughout nearly four years of debate over various modification and co-development options, there was never any analysis within the Pentagon or among the concerned U.S. government agencies of exactly what the United States wanted. No one had thought seriously about crucial issues:

the degree and desirability of potential modification; the methods, means, and location of any joint design effort; how to obtain any interesting Japanese technology; the sharing of development and production work; or the extent to which U.S. designs, new materials, and systems technology were to be transferred to Japanese producers—or the impact on U.S. competitiveness of any of these issues. The emphasis had been almost entirely on just getting Japan to say it would use an American plane in order to avoid the "political disaster" of the U.S. Congress's discovering Japan's drive for autonomy. The actual content of a deal was far less important than just getting one.

Indeed, the whole U.S. approach militated against a substantively advantageous arrangement. Minimum modification was clearly the best deal from a U.S. viewpoint. Yet the two U.S. producers were encouraged to compete against each other to get an order from a customer who desired maximum modification. Only the U.S. government could coordinate or set guidelines on the U.S. side to prevent the bidding from becoming a competition to see which U.S. company could best assist the Japanese toward their goal of maximum domestic development. But the U.S. government did not think that way. In the view of most U.S. officials, once Japan had made its basic decision, the rest was a matter of private business competition.

Modern fighters are, of course, constantly improved and modified from the day of their introduction. The F-16 being produced today has been through several modifications in two series and is now in the fourth improvement of the third. At the time of these negotiations, GD was also planning an advanced version, to be called the Agile Falcon, for introduction in the late 1990s. In response to Japanese rejection of these versions, GD had made several different proposals, including ever further modification. All such proposals, being concepts rather than actual airplanes, were open to further change. When called to Japan on 12 October, GD decided to use its highly modified SX-3 version as the baseline proposal. The failure of anyone in the Pentagon to object to this virtually guaranteed a degree of modification and technology transfer that would be less than optimum for the United States. Of course, the argument can be made that the customer is always entitled to what he wants; but in this case the United States had already pressured the customer into taking something he really didn't want. So it is difficult to understand why U.S. officials should have balked at pushing further to get the best deal for the United States. Their failure to do so in the latter days of October led some experts to see the victory as hollow almost as soon as it was announced.

The two weeks of discussion in Tokyo that preceded the F-16 announcement can only be described as chaotic from the U.S. viewpoint. Simple business logic demanded that a memorandum of understanding between the two governments with regard to such issues as technology transfer, work share, and degree of modification be concluded prior to any negotiation between the U.S. companies and the JDA and certainly prior to any competitive bidding situation. Otherwise, the companies, operating under pressure and being unsure of any guidelines, would be in an extremely weak position. Of course, they could always make concessions conditional on future U.S. government approval, but then the government would put itself under pressure to go along with concessions in order not to upset the smooth relationship with Japan. Logic to the contrary notwithstanding, the Pentagon sent the companies to negotiate with the JDA without an MOU and accompanied by a low-level Pentagon team headed by Captain Andrew Button, a former Navy pilot with no negotiating experience in Japan.

On the Japanese side, the matter had gone from the policy level back into the hands of the technicians, and they knew exactly what they wanted—maximum modification and technology transfer to Japan. By the time of the 22 October announcement, it had been agreed that the plane would have a stretched fuselage, a new and larger nose, a larger wing to be made of co-cured carbon fibers cast in a single piece, vertical canards, CCV fly-by-wire capability, a new cockpit, stealth technology, a more powerful engine, completely new avionics, and new weaponry. Thus, to call it the F-16 was really a misnomer. It would be pretty close to a new airplane. If the Japanese could do all the work, it would be as good if not better for them than pure domestic development. They would be able to pursue all their pet technologies and gain the systems integration experience they desired and have GD to help them over the rough spots.

Discussion of the MOU and of terms and conditions between either GD or MD and JDA overlapped, with three separate sets of meetings occurring simultaneously. As the outmanned U.S. team rotated members from meeting to meeting, Masaji Yamamoto, a MITI official then acting as the head of JDA procurement who had formerly participated in the semiconductor talks, made it clear that Japan wanted all the work. He immediately presented the outline of a proposed MOU, which called for, among other things: all funds to be spent in Japan; retention of all patents by the JDA; a Japanese company to be the prime contractor; any technology flow to the United States to be negotiated on an item-by-item basis under the 1983 agreement machinery; all development and production to be done in Japan; unrestricted transfer of all F-16 technology, present and future, to Japan; and assignment of several U.S. company engineers to the project. For this Japan agreed to pay a licensing fee of $500,000 per plane ($60 million for 120 planes), the same amount paid by other countries that coproduced the F-16 without benefit of technology transfer.

Thus forced into discussions for which it was unprepared, Button's team, which included Kearns and a young State Department officer named Craig Richardson, improvised and frantically faxed Washington for instructions. At one point, the GD representative, Charles Anderson, appeared to yield to the adamant Japanese position by agreeing to accept the $60 million and to send twelve engineers and the blueprints.

When Kearns asked how he could agree to such a poor deal, Anderson said he had called GD's headquarters in St. Louis, and those were his instructions. GD later denied this, saying that Anderson's remark was only made in frustration, and that the company had always insisted on a significant share of the work. Whatever the case, it is a fact that Kearns and Richardson objected that, even if GD was prepared to accept that kind of deal, the U.S. government was not. They denied Anderson's ability to make a commitment and cabled Washington for help. The result was an instruction, dreamed up literally over night, that directed them to ask for 40 percent to 60 percent of the work in the development phase of the project and 30 percent to 70 percent in the production phase. In presenting this the following day, the U.S. team leader told the Japanese that, while the U.S. range was 40 percent to 60 percent, he was sure the United States would accept 40 percent. Thus was the key point of later political dispute casually and ineptly established.

And so it went. With the Japanese remaining adamant, the U.S. team finally called a halt to the talks and went home to regroup. At the end of October, Japan's noted aerospace analyst Eiichiro Sekigawa remarked, "Japanese industry got most of what it wanted. In the end 80 percent of it will be Japanese."[14]

This was exactly the conclusion of Kearns and Richardson after a series of conversations with Japanese industry executives and JDA officials. The two Americans began writing cables from the Tokyo embassy to Washington warning that the Japanese were attempting to transform the FSX co-development back into what effectively would be domestic development, and that so far GD seemed willing to go along. These cables had to be cleared through the embassy's senior officials, whose views were reflected in the actions of Christopher LaFleur, the head of the political/military bureau. At one point Richardson commented in a cable that Japanese industry was determined to go its own way rather than to cooperate in co-development. LaFleur, who is married to the daughter of Japan's then finance minister, ordered the comment to be struck. He is reported to have said, "There is bad blood on both sides. Our job is to referee as objective a process as possible between the two governments"—implying that somehow the embassy was divorced from the U.S. government and U.S. interests.

Upon returning to the United States from temporary assignment in the embassy, Richardson went over Button's head and arranged to brief General Charles Brown, director of the Defense Security Assistance Agency (DSAA) and his deputy, Glenn Rudd. In this important meeting, for the first time in the whole process Richardson, a junior management intern, articulated comprehensively U.S. objectives and evaluated the current situation with regard to them. He pointed out that the United States wanted, or should have wanted, maximum interoperability, cost effectiveness, rapid introduction of the new plane into service, and minimal contribution to Japan's efforts to develop a competitive aircraft industry. He then explained that as things were going there would be little interoperability, high costs, slow introduction of the new plane, and a substantial contribution to Japan's industrial efforts. Although Brown fell asleep in the briefing, Rudd was visibly upset and screamed at the chagrined Button, "We have to get smarter."

As a result of this briefing, Rudd decided to take over responsibility for leading the U.S. negotiating team himself, and thus sat down to confront the old pro Yamamoto during the next round of talks in late November. Rudd's position was that the United States had to get 40 percent of the development work and a similar share of the production. He also insisted that a distinction had to be made between technology developed as a derivative of technology provided by the United States and technology wholly developed in Japan. While the latter could be licensed to the United States under terms of previous agreements, the former, he insisted, must flow back automatically to the United States free of charge. This was a standard provision of all U.S. MOUs with allies and, indeed, was contained in the F-15 MOU Rubinstein had negotiated with the Japanese. Nevertheless, the Japanese were shocked by the technology as well as by the work-share requests. Rudd's position was considered extremely tough, and Yamamoto responded by insisting on the original Japanese position.

Over the next year, the two governments held numerous meetings to try to complete the MOU. At the same time, MHI and GD negotiated continuously to complete a company-to-company licensing agreement. The talks were arduous, and the positions essentially unchanging. In January 1987, Deputy Undersecretary of Defense Steve Bryen wrote a memo urging a stronger U.S. position:

> While the current program is called joint development, it provides Japan with complete authority for design and configuration decisions. Since the Japanese have already decided that most major components will be Japanese (apparently forgetting years of U.S. industry assistance) there may not be much left for our defense industries.[15]

He urged a stronger U.S. voice in design and configuration in order to achieve better interoperability. Others in the Pentagon, however, thought it was already too late for this; and in June, Secretary of Defense Frank Carlucci met with Japanese Defense Minister Tsutomu Kawara in an attempt to overcome the difficulties. They reached a verbal agreement that the U.S. share of the development work should be 35 percent to 45 percent. It was expected that formal completion of the MOU would follow quickly. In fact, however, it dragged on for another five months.

During this time, three developments of later significance took place. The publication of this book revealed the existence of the secret side letter to the 1986 semiconductor agreement (see page 172). In response, MITI denied that there was a side letter. Only after a Japanese magazine actually obtained a copy of the letter and published it did MITI acknowledge its existence—but then said that the letter had

actually made no commitment.[16] This episode greatly undermined the credibility of agreements negotiated with Japan.

The second event was Kearns's reassignment to the Senate
Foreign Relations Committee staff. Extremely upset with the
course of the MOU talks and knowing that any MOU would
eventually have to be passed by the Congress, Kearns managed to get a State Department intern slot on the congressional staff with the intention of creating congressional pressure
against the FSX agreement. At the same time, Maureen
Smith at the Commerce Department, Joseph Massey at the
U.S. Trade Representative's office, and officials at the C.I.A.
were watching FSX developments with increasing alarm. Excluded from the talks themselves, they watched from afar
and connected the FSX talks with others taking place regarding Japanese participation in Star Wars, the space station,
and other weapons development. They became increasingly
concerned that the Department of Defense was becoming the
pipeline for transfer of the most advanced U.S. technology to
Japan.

Finally, in late November, the MOU was concluded. Four
prototypes of the FSX would be built by 1993. If they were
satisfactory after testing, production of 120 airplanes would
begin in 1997. U.S. companies were to get $440 million of the
development expenditures, which represented 40 percent of
the budgeted $1.2 billion cost. At the time of production, a
second MOU was to be negotiated, and the United States
was to receive a work share similar to that in the development phase. It was further agreed that technology "essentially" derived from U.S. technology would flow back to the
United States free of charge, while Japanese-origin technology could be licensed to U.S. firms under the onerous 1983
agreement procedures. (This meant that if Japanese companies wanted to license the technology they could, but there
was no requirement.) Even after the signing of the MOU, a
dispute over the work share for the prototype wings delayed
signing of the company-to-company licensing agreement
until 12 January 1989.

At that point, the State Department was ready to notify the Congress, which would then have thirty days to vote an objection. If it did not do so, the MOU would go into effect. Had the Japanese not taken such a tough attitude and allowed conclusion of the agreement in the summer, there is little doubt that it would have sailed through the Congress unscathed. Delay until the end of January meant the matter came before a new U.S. administration and a new Congress.

## CRISIS IN A NEW ADMINISTRATION

The Defense Authorization Act of 1988 provides that as of October 1988 the Pentagon should provide more information than in the past to the Commerce Department with regard to coproduction and co-development arrangements. As the MOU moved to conclusion in the fall of 1988, concern grew at the C.I.A., the Commerce Department, and the U.S. Trade Representative's office. These officials believed that the agreement would greatly aid Japan's drive toward world-class status in aircraft and related technologies while achieving none of the U.S. objectives as articulated by Richardson. Maureen Smith and John Richards, director of Commerce's strategic industry matters, began to request copies of the draft MOU and supporting documents from the Pentagon under the new act—but were persistently rebuffed.

In October, Smith called Richardson, who was now in the Intelligence and Research (INR) arm of the State Department, and they reviewed FSX developments. Becoming ever more concerned, Smith began to convene meetings in her office at which concerned C.I.A. and NASA officials briefed key representatives of the departments of Commerce, Energy, Labor, and Treasury and of the Office of the President's Science Adviser and the U.S. Trade Representative. These meetings complemented similar internal gatherings Massey had organized within the USTR's office. Both the C.I.A. and NASA explained their belief that the FSX deal would greatly contribute to making Japan a competitor in both commercial and military aircraft and related technologies while contributing little to the United States. Their assessment of Japanese aircraft technology was the same as that of the Sullivan mission: while there were some bright spots, in general it was of limited interest; and thus any co-development deal would almost inevitably lead to a one-way transfer of technology. The briefers noted the link between military and civilian technology and pointed out that while military and civilian aircraft are quite different, the key to both is systems-integration knowledge and design philosophy, which are easily transferable. Furthermore, there are spinoffs into electronics, materials, and so on.

Meanwhile on Capitol Hill, Kearns was quietly explaining his doubts to any staffers, congresspersons, and reporters who would listen. He found great ignorance. Only senators Danforth and Byrd seemed to be knowledgeable, and they had abandoned the field the year before after the F-16 announcement. Gradually this situation changed. Charles Smith, a key staffer for Senator Alan Dixon of Illinois, became interested, as did Ed McGaffigan of New Mexico Senator Jeff Bingaman's staff, Jim Lucier of Senator Jesse Helms's staff, and Marjory Chorlins of the Senate Armed Services Committee staff. Since the briefings being given by the Pentagon inevitably cast the deal in a positive light, Kearns called in representatives of General Dynamics to brief these and other staffers on the real difficulty of the negotiations.

After the signing of the MOU in late November 1988, Commerce finally succeeded in obtaining a copy. It confirmed the department's worst fears. To the unpracticed eye, the MOU looked balanced and innocuous; but to a seasoned negotiator with Japan, it appeared full of pitfalls. The U.S. objective had been 40 percent of the work share: the MOU said the United States would get this in the development phase, and that the objective would be to achieve a similar share in the production phase, but that would be subject to another negotiation. Old Japan hands who have experience with side letters and other agreements, usually cringe at indefinite words like *objective* and *similar* as subject to change and interpretation. Having the objective of a 40-percent work share is not the same thing as getting it. In this case, once the development phase was over, it seemed obvious that U.S. negotiators would be in a weaker position in a second round of MOU talks for the production phase, and therefore unlikely to get anything like 40 percent. Moreover, even in the development phase, the U.S. negotiators had agreed to 40 percent of $1.2 billion. But most analysts thought the Japanese budget was far too low. What if the actual cost was $3 billion? No one seemed to know for sure. The provision that called for flowback to the U.S. of technology "essentially" derived from the United States was also troubling. The word *essentially* could be the object of endless debate and negotiation, particularly in view of the unfriendly and uncooperative nature of the whole MOU negotiation. Finally, the MOU committed the United States to provide everything necessary to make the project a success. Some observers believed that this could be used by MHI to bail itself out of any difficulty by tapping into U.S. technology, all the while maintaining the fiction of its own superiority.

The delay in the signing of the company-to-company agreement after conclusion of the MOU was not encouraging. The dispute involved development work on the airplane's wings. Although it had been agreed that GD would share responsibility for development of the wings, the Japanese insisted that all test wings be built in Japan. GD emphasized that it would have to build six of the fourteen test sections in order to ensure adequate transfer of any interesting carbon-fiber technology Japan might have. It took a special trip by Karl Jackson, now on the National Security Council staff, to Japan to arrive at a compromise of four sections for GD. To many Japan hands in Washington, it seemed the MOU had failed its first test before even going into effect. Their concern was greatly heightened when the agreement between MHI and GD was finally signed and made known on 12 January 1989. It provided for transfer of virtually everything GD had, including critical software-source codes that had never been made available even to allies as close as the British, with whom the United States shares almost everything. Although, as some argued afterward, this deal was subject to later elimination of sensitive items by the Pentagon, the Pentagon was not then organizing any review, and the data began to transfer almost as soon as the agreement was signed.

The State Department, the Pentagon, and the Japanese were anxious to move the agreement through the Congress as fast as possible before opposition could coalesce. But Congress was out of session until after the inauguration, thus setting in place the key element in the latter part of the drama. To get his administration off to a quick start, President-elect Bush had asked the Senate to hold a special confirmation hearing for James Baker, his nominee for secretary of state. On the panel that quizzed Baker was Jesse Helms, with whose staff Kearns had planted a question for Baker. As the hearing was drawing to a close, the veteran senator from North Carolina popped it: Would Baker delay notification of the FSX MOU to the Congress and conduct a thorough review of its provisions in the new administration? Baker, obviously unaware of the details of the issue, said he would have to consult with the President-elect and get back to Helms. It was a pro's answer, accommodating but noncommittal. But it was just committal enough that Baker's sensitive political antennae told him this was an issue on which to be careful.

The issue mushroomed quickly and unexpectedly. Bush's nominee for secretary of commerce, Robert Mosbacher, appeared before the Senate hearing committee shortly after Baker. Already aware of the issue as a result of his transition-period briefings, Mosbacher also said he would look into it. Shortly afterward, a small article in *Newsweek* by John Barry pointed to the FSX as the first foreign policy crisis of the new administration.[17] This was followed within a few days by an article I wrote for the *Washington Post* of 29 January.[18] While warning that the aircraft industry could go the way of television and VCRs, I urged the Congress carefully to review the FSX deal. I noted the report of the Sullivan mission and the agreement of all observers, both pro and con, that with regard to meeting defense, cost, and interoperability objectives, the FSX would not be as good as a more lightly modified U.S. plane. I further explained that the United States would be turning over technology that had cost between $4 billion to $8 billion to develop while receiving perhaps only as little as $440 million in return. While proponents claimed that Japanese technology such as the cocured wing and phased-array radar would become available to the United States, I explained that the Pentagon had never checked with its own experts who thought the United States was ahead in these technologies. The only justification for the FSX project, I said, was to promote development of Japan's aircraft industry. The only reason for the United States to go along with the deal was to avoid difficulty in the overall relationship. I did not condemn Japan, but suggested that the United States should be as interested in its own industry as Japan is in its, and that the United States should not be more concerned for harmonious diplomatic relations than Japan is. I closed by suggesting that all objectives could be better met if Japan would buy fifty lightly modified U.S. planes immediately, while putting the FSX co-development on a fifty-fifty basis. This article attracted a lot of attention, and the FSX quickly became a major issue.

Upon arriving at his desk on his first day as secretary of state, Baker had found a review of the FSX project already written by Assistant Secretary of State Gaston Sigur, Deputy Assistant Secretary of State William Clark, and the State Department's Japan desk. Not surprisingly, the paper said the project was a good deal. Shortly thereafter, Mosbacher had his first briefing as secretary of commerce. The FSX issue was included; and Smith and Richards, warning that the deal was disadvantageous to the United States, urged review and revision. What conversations took place between Baker, Mosbacher, and the President in late January are unclear, but it is a fact that, on 30 January, Assistant Secretary of State for INR Morton Abramowitz called Richardson and asked him to do a paper on what the Japanese reaction to a review and delay would be. Richardson, assuming the assignment was in response to a request from the secretary, only later discovered that the request had come from Undersecretary of State Michael Armacost. Whether Armacost, who later became the U.S. ambassador to Japan, asked for this paper at Baker's behest or for his own purposes is not clear.

In any case, the next day Richardson delivered a memo to Abramowitz. Addressed from Abramowitz to the secretary of state, the memo said that the Japanese would be unhappy but restrained, that too much was at stake for the Japanese, and that they are extremely well versed in the idiosyncrasies of U.S. congressional-approval procedures. In particular, the memo pointed out that the Japanese themselves had delayed things by four months (which they would later regret) in the summer of 1988 while the JDA and MOFA wrangled over legal details. In conclusion, the memo said that the United States could take three to six months for a review without real risk.[19]

Abramowitz took a copy of this memo to a meeting with Armacost, leaving the original behind with his staff assistants. Not realizing that it was not necessarily intended to reach the secretary, they noted that it was addressed to him, and sent it on its way, probably assuming that Abramowitz was just showing an advance copy to Armacost. All department papers on East Asia go through the East Asia Bureau on their way to the secretary of state except those from INR, which go to the secretary's office directly. Had Richardson's paper passed through the bureau, it would surely have been delayed and altered. But it didn't pass that way. Thus Baker took it with him that afternoon to a White House meeting where, to the astonishment of the uninformed State Department bureaucrats, Baker presented it to the President. Cognizant of the pressure from the Hill, Baker stressed that three to six months would be no problem, and Bush then directed that a review be done.

When this became known back at the East Asia Bureau, the whole office, in the words of one observer, "went ballistic," with the deputy assistant secretary for East Asia threatening to "get" Richardson. Richardson's phone rang off the hook with demands from the Japan desk to explain himself. The desk, along with Armitage at the Pentagon, had been telling the Japanese not to worry. The last thing it wanted was a long review. To avoid one, it tried a clever bureaucratic finesse.

Japan's Prime Minister, Noboru Takeshita, was due in Washington on 2–3 February for a meeting with the President. Such meetings require briefing books filled with suggested talking points prepared by the Japan desk at the State Department. For this meeting the desk suggested that the President tell the Prime Minister of his appreciation of the FSX deal and his commitment to push it through. It is likely that this kind of talking point will pass unchecked into the President's hands, and that he will make such a statement almost subconsciously in the course of a formal meeting. This in itself then becomes a commitment. In effect, the desk laid a potential trap for the President. In this case, the National Security Council, which reviews all such papers on their way to the President, appeared willing to go along because Jackson, its top East Asia staffer, had negotiated the deal while at the Pentagon. To prevent such a development, Kearns drafted a letter from Senator Alan Dixon to the President urging him not to make any commitment before reviewing the deal. The letter quickly got twelve senatorial signatures and reached the President on 2 February. In the meantime, Commerce Secretary Mosbacher had learned of State's maneuver and called National Security Adviser Brent Scowcroft to urge him not to allow it. Finally, on 3 February, Scowcroft received a call from Senator Jeff Bingaman warning him of the growing firestorm over the issue in the Congress and urging that a full review be undertaken. As a result, State's talking points never passed the President's lips, and the stage was set for a full-scale showdown within the administration.

On one side was the alliance forged by Smith and Massey in the fall of the departments of Commerce, Energy, Labor, and Treasury along with NASA, the USTR, and the Office of the President's Science Adviser—all now under the vigorous leadership of Mosbacher, the President's friend and chief fund raiser. This group believed the deal would enhance Japan's aircraft-manufacturing capability while returning little to the United States and providing a less than best defense for either Japan or the United States. Indeed, it would indirectly increase the U.S. defense burden. These agencies did not believe that Japanese technology in this area was as good as U.S. technology, and had no confidence in the willingness of Japan to cooperate in true co-development or to transfer technology to the United States. Their immediate objective was to delay notification of the deal to the Congress while carrying out a rigorous review. For the longer term, they wanted, at a minimum, to tighten the arrangement and make it more enforceable, and some in this group believed that Japan should actually buy and/or coproduce a lightly modified U.S. plane.

The primary proponent of the deal was the Defense Department, with support from the bureaucracy of the State Department and the NSC. Of course, the Japanese embassy, an important player in the internal battles of any U.S. administration, was supporting the Pentagon. This group— never, of course, greatly concerned with the industrial and trade aspects of the deal—had all along chiefly aimed to avoid the potential political disaster to the relationship that Auer had expressed as a primary matter long ago. Since in the climate of Washington at this time, this group could not admit as much, it had to attempt to show that the deal was good from a trade point of view. It therefore emphasized the importance of Japan's co-cured carbon fiber wing, phased-array radar, and other advanced technologies and argued that transfer of these technologies would greatly enhance the capabilities of U.S. industry. At the same time, the proponents also played down the value of U.S. technology, arguing that it was already twenty years old, and that military aircraft technology is not readily transferable to civilian aircraft. The objective of this team was to avoid a review. Or, if a review was necessary, to make it as brief as possible and then to push the deal through the Congress quickly in order to avoid any possible damage to the relationship from Japanese suspicion that the new administration was trying to back out. Urgency was lent the desire for speed by the Japanese argument that the deal needed to be completed by 31 March in order to be in time for the Diet to put it in the following year's budget.

The first skirmish occurred on Friday 3 February, when Sigur called an interagency meeting to discuss what kind of a review to do pursuant to the President's comments to Baker. State's hope to call this meeting the review, or to get agreement to a short process, quickly foundered on the Pentagon's continuing reluctance to make copies of the secret MOU (while MOUs with other allies are open, those with Japan are classified at Japan's request) available to the other agencies. These said that they could not be expected to review what they had not seen. The Pentagon agreed to send copies, and another meeting was scheduled a week hence.

The following Monday, the NSC's Jackson faxed a list of questions to the participating agencies with the instruction that they be answered by the time of the next meeting now scheduled for Friday, 10 February. This maneuver served only to anger many of the agencies that had not yet received their copies of the MOU. Moreover, the questions seemed to the Commerce team to be slanted in such way as to lead to a conclusion in favor of the deal. While the Commerce team was preparing its response, the Senate weighed in again. On 9 February, Dixon drafted a sense-of-the-Senate resolution for a full review of the deal. The next morning Baker called and asked Dixon not to introduce the resolution until after the upcoming Senate recess, and said, "I am looking into it." Dixon at first agreed, but later called back to say that there were already twenty-one co-sponsors, and that the pressure was too great for him to delay.[20] Baker now knew that trouble was well and surely afoot. Any doubt was removed a few hours later, after the second interagency meeting.

This so-called deputies meeting was supposed to be an interagency coordinating group at the subcabinet level. Because the administration was new and had filled few senior slots, however, the meeting was chaired by Deputy Assistant Secretary of State Clark and was attended mostly by career officials at the deputy assistant secretary and office director level, including Smith and Richards from Commerce and Massey from USTR. Again, the question was what to do; and by all accounts, the meeting was an absolute donnybrook, breaking at several points into a shouting match. Accompanied by a dozen uniformed officers, the DSSA deputy, Glenn Rudd, apparently made a poor presentation. He admitted that the Pentagon had not read the licensing agreement between GD and MHI and thus did not have a clear idea of exactly what technology GD had proposed to transfer. When the Pentagon tried to argue that Japan's carbon-fiber technology would be extremely valuable to GD, Jack Simon of the Office of the President's Science Adviser spoke up. A composite materials expert himself, Simon explained that U.S. industry is far in advance of the Japanese in composites for aircraft. He further noted that the Pentagon's MOU negotiators had never discussed the matter with the Air Force's materials experts who had looked at the Japanese technology and given it low marks. When the Pentagon argued that the F-16 is old technology, the opponents pointed out that the airplane has been continuously upgraded. Further, they said, it may be old here but not necessarily in Japan. The meeting ended with a definition of the points at issue, but with no agreement on what to do about them. Commerce wanted to do a full ninety-day industrial assessment, while the Pentagon wanted nothing of the kind.

The following Monday, Jackson and Scowcroft are reported to have met with the President and urged him to move ahead with the agreement. Whether Mosbacher was in the meeting is unclear, but his influence was reflected in the response of the President that he wanted a review. The next day, another interagency deputies meeting was held, chaired this time by Deputy National Security Adviser William Gates. It concluded that a study to be completed by 10 March should be done, and that it should be led by the Pentagon with other agencies contributing. Given the NSC's and Gates's leanings, this was no surprise; but while Mosbacher may have been new to Washington, he obviously was no greenhorn. He called Scowcroft and said that there should be joint leadership or Commerce would do its own study. With the backing of the President and Baker, Mosbacher got his way, and the review was finally begun.

Meanwhile, Baker and the President prepared to travel to Tokyo for the funeral of Emperor Hirohito. While boning up for possible discussions of the MOU, Baker remarked that "this deal may or may not be good policy, but it is really a bad deal." (Not recorded was his comment upon being told that his new nominee for assistant secretary of state for East Asia, Richard Armitage, was largely responsible for it; Armitage later withdrew as the nominee.) In Tokyo, Baker raised the issue during a meeting with then-Foreign Minister Uno and asked for a commitment that Japan allocate to U.S. producers 40 percent of the work in both the production as well as the development phases. Baker obviously hoped to dispose of the issue quickly and smoothly by being able to report back to the Senate that he had gotten such a commitment while in Tokyo. Because the MOU already called for something similar, he no doubt assumed that such a commitment would represent nothing more for Uno than a mere tightening of language on a concession essentially already given. Thus, his apparent surprise and anger when Uno sharply rejected the request. Japanese participants say Uno replied out of surprise and not out of anger. Whatever the case, from that moment Baker seems to have become dedicated to a 40-percent U.S. work share.

As the Commerce-Pentagon study proceeded, the C.I.A. delivered two papers that neatly bracketed the dilemma of the administration. One, dealing with the impact of collapse of the FSX deal on Japan, said there was a danger of causing the fall of Prime Minister Takeshita, of strengthening the objections of the opposition parties in Japan to the U.S.-Japan security treaty while at the same time giving ammunition to rightest elements that want Japan to remilitarize. Alarmist because crafted in response to a doomsday scenario, the paper nevertheless underscored the fact that revision of the deal at this point would entail a diplomatic cost.

The second paper analyzed the technological and competitive impact of various FSX development options. It concluded that the FSX deal would significantly enhance Japan's ability to develop military aircraft on its own and to become an important competitor of U.S. industry in commercial aircraft. It confirmed Simon's view that Japan is ten years behind U.S. manufacturers in aircraft-related composite materials, and noted that most Japanese components are nonstructural and layed up by hand, and that, while their materials are older thermoset resins, U.S. producers have moved on to thermoplastics. The C.I.A. refuted Japanese claims to leadership in phased-array radars, noting that Mitsubishi Electric Company was having serious difficulties. The C.I.A. also reported that the number of transmit/receive modules in MELCO's radar was about one third that in U.S. radars, and that MELCO engineers were approaching U.S. firms for assistance. The paper explained that, through the FSX deal, Japan hoped to obtain U.S. technology with regard to design and development, systems integration, composite materials, and engines. It doubted the ability of Japan to develop the plane in time or at an affordable cost without U.S. help.[21]

While the administration debated privately, the Congress held hearings, and the press debated publicly. Former secre-

taries of defense Carlucci and Weinberger were rolled out by
their old agency to defend the deal. Carlucci told the Senate
Armed Services Committee that trade should not drive defense, and waxed poetic about the technology we would get
from Japan. Either the Pentagon had not bothered to inform
either former secretary of the C.I.A. report or, if it had, they
ignored it. The most interesting statement was made by U.S.
Trade Representative Carla Hills. Noting that U.S. officials
are always concerned about hurting the U.S.-Japan relationship, she pointed out what a boost Japan could give to the
relationship if it would just buy some airplanes from the
United States. Far from hurting Japan, she noted that such a
step would immediately improve its defense capabilities
while reducing its costs and improving relations with its only
ally. How, she asked, could you get a better deal than that?

Some Japanese were thinking the same thing. High officials of the Foreign Ministry were, in fact, urging the Japanese government to consider a purchase of twenty to thirty
airplanes. With Prime Minister Takeshita preoccupied with a
serious domestic scandal, it fell to Deputy Chief Cabinet Secretary Ichiro Ozawa to lead the Japanese response to the FSX
crisis. For some time he is reported to have seriously considered following the advice simply to buy a few airplanes.

Ironically, while he was thus considering, the tide was
shifting the other way in the United States. An argument
repeated over and over by the Pentagon, the State Department, and proponents of the deal ignorant of the original
Japanese plan to buy twenty-four foreign aircraft, was that
Japan would never buy a U.S. plane or even any longer simply coproduce one. Japan, it was said, would increasingly
insist on developing its own planes, and the best the U.S.
could hope for was some piece of the Japanese project. If the
United States didn't like that, Japan would simply turn to the
Europeans for whatever help it needed. Implicit in this view
was the questioned proposition that any deal was better for
the United States than no deal. The argument also ignored
the fact that its defense umbrella and enormous imports

from Japan entitle the United States to some degree of reciprocity. Nevertheless, it gained a certain currency. Coupled both with concern over the political impact of cancellation of the deal in Japan and with Commerce's political desire to be seen as a team player rather than as an extremist, Mosbacher's views began to change toward tightening up the MOU rather than drastically changing it.

Rather than two papers for the President, Commerce proposed a joint effort which the Pentagon accepted. In essence, the deal was that Commerce would push to improve the existing agreement but would not call for drastic changes. In exchange, the Pentagon would have to agree to a major Commerce role in this and all future co-development MOUs. This separated Commerce from its own alliance of agencies and caused bitterness at USTR and elsewhere over Commerce's submission to Pentagon seduction. But the wooing was not easy. An agreed joint paper, painfully patched together over the weekend of 4–5 March, was rejected the following week by Armitage, who was now being mentioned as a candidate for secretary of the army rather than assistant secretary of state. He objected to too much Commerce participation in what he considered the Pentagon's business. The original 10 March deadline for the study was missed as the two departments wrangled.

Finally a joint paper was submitted, and the President chaired a full NSC debate on 15 March. Three options were presented: go ahead with no changes; scrap the MOU and negotiate a new deal; go ahead with the MOU with the addition of certain safeguards. Hills and White House Chief of Staff John Sununu favored scrapping, while the Pentagon and Scowcroft argued for no change. Baker and Mosbacher came down for the middle position. All the old arguments were regurgitated. Of particular significance was Sununu's position. An MIT engineer, he had been concerned for some time about the transfer of U.S. technology entailed in the deal. When the Air Force chief of staff, General Larry Welch, argued that there was no danger because the F-16 was old technology, Sununu cut him off at the knees: "We've been spending millions every year to upgrade that plane; if it is only old technology what have you been doing with the money?"

Bush postponed a decision, and further meetings continued into the weekend. Finally on 20 March the President opted to ask the Japanese for "clarifications" of the MOU. Though presented as confirmation of the deal, this was in fact a call for renegotiation. Baker called the Japanese ambassador, Nabuo Matsunaga, to the State Department to receive an aide-mémoire. In a highly unusual move, Matsunaga at first refused to go, saying he was unprepared. Finally on 21 March, Baker handed the mémoire to Matsunaga. It called for: restriction of the transfer of critical software source codes and certain other technologies to Japan; clarification of provisions for flowback of technology to the United States; and a commitment for a U.S. work share of 40 percent in both the production and the development phases. The stage was set for the last act.

The Japanese were deeply divided and disorganized as well as perplexed and hurt by the Bush administration's handling of the FSX deal. The Japanese public and high officials and politicians had been told by the JDA and the press for a long time about superior Japanese technology. Japan was better in VCRs and television, and so it was easy to believe the assertions of MHI and JDA that it was also better in aircraft. Indeed, many Japanese thought the United States was insisting on the deal in order to steal advanced Japanese technology. From this point of view, the agreement to yield to U.S. pressure and use the F-16 as the basis of FSX development had been seen by Japanese leaders and public alike as a great concession for the sake of good relations with the United States. This view was strengthened by the assertions of the U.S. proponents who emphasized how much technology the United States would get from the deal. Thus, many Japanese felt bitter resentment. Having already made a great concession, it now seemed that the United States was backing out of a deal Japan had never wanted in the first place in order to mollify a few far-out senators and promote U.S. industry at the expense of Japanese industry. All Japanese believed that the real problem was the trade deficit, and that Japan was once again being made the scapegoat for America's competitive failings.

Many, such as the popular Diet member Shintaro Ishihara, called on the government to scrap the deal and go ahead with domestic development. Kichiro Tazawa, the new head of the JDA, was outraged and insisted that Japan not yield to any changes in the MOU or company-to-company agreement. On the other hand, Ambassador Matsunaga, one of Japan's outstanding diplomats, and other officials of MOFA feared the political fallout of a break with the United States on this issue. They knew that Japan was likely to be featured in the report on unfair foreign trade barriers that Hills had to present to the Congress at the beginning of May. They knew the firestorm brewing in the Congress. And they urged compromise. But the political situation in Tokyo did not augur well for easy resolution of the problem. With Prime Minister Takeshita's approval rating down to about 3 percent, the fall of his government was imminent.

Nishihiro was dispatched to Washington to attempt to obtain U.S. understanding. In a meeting with Baker, Mosbacher, and Scowcroft, he insisted that the deal be maintained unchanged. As talks continued, several U.S. officials realized that there had never been a concrete commitment to a U.S. work share in the production phase, and their attitude hardened. Meanwhile, opposition to the deal grew in the Senate, where Kearns's efforts had resulted in thirty-five co-sponsors for the resolution of disapproval. The credibility of the Japanese and the deal's U.S. proponents was further undermined when 31 March came and went and the contract was awarded to MHI. Obviously all the talk of the budget deadline had been merely a tactical ploy. Nishihiro went home empty-handed and feeling somewhat abused.

In Tokyo, the standoff between the JDA and the MOFA

continued. In early April, however, JDA's argument for domestic development was undercut by the cancellation of the Asuka program: the prototype of this Japanese-developed vertical takeoff plane had apparently performed poorly while costs escalated. Shortly thereafter, the *Economist* magazine estimated that development of the FSX would cost Y400 billion not the Y165 billion budgeted.[22] At length, Ozawa and the MOFA forced JDA to agree to some compromise; and Ryozo Kato of the Japanese embassy in Washington began a series of intense discussions with Robert Kimmit, a top aide to Baker. Although the Japanese had long argued that they could make no commitment on production work share before prototypes were evaluated, it was well known that the Japanese companies already had agreements among themselves on production work share. Kato now indicated that Japan might be able to make the United States a commitment of around 35 percent. Through Kimmit, Baker insisted on 40 percent, but progress was made on the technology issues.

By mid-April, enough progress had been made that Yamamoto traveled to Washington to try to wrap things up. He confirmed that a commitment on production work share could be made, although he still did not offer 40 percent. He also introduced a new wrinkle: he wanted a U.S. commitment that Japan would coproduce the bulk of the engine. This, of course, is the area of greatest technical weakness in Japan, and Yamamoto's ploy was an effort to shore it up. Baker, annoyed with introduction of a politically troublesome element, only insisted the harder on his original requests.

It began to look as if Yamamoto, too, would go home empty-handed. Then, on 24 April, Takeshita announced he would step down as prime minister—a move that, ironically, strengthened the Japanese negotiating hand. U.S. officials realized that, in Japan's currently chaotic politics, a new prime minister would have little ability to bring this issue to a conclusion, and that it might therefore grow into a really serious rift between the two countries. They softened their position somewhat by agreeing to accept a commitment for "approximately 40 percent production work share" and to somewhat convoluted language, which said that "co-production of the engine is a viable method of production."[23] Transfer of software-source codes for the fire-control system was agreed to, but transfer of codes for other key systems was restricted. A time limit of 1990 was put on the U.S. obligation to transfer approved, upgraded technology, and the United States was guaranteed access to all Japanese technology, while the terms of flowback for derivative technology were clarified and strengthened. On 28 April, President Bush announced that he was satisfied with the clarifications, and prepared to ask the Congress to approve the deal.

On the Hill, Kearns and his allies, feeling the new deal was better but still not good, redoubled efforts to defeat it in the Senate. They were aided by publication of a General Accounting Office report that had been requested earlier by the Senate Armed Services Committee. The report concluded that the United States is ahead of Japan in composite technology for aircraft as well as in phased-array radar, and further maintained that the deal would contribute to promoting Japan's ability to become a significant competitor in aerospace. This report coincided with an article in *Nihon Keizai* on Japan's aircraft industry strategy. The article said that Japan's objective was to become a world-class aerospace competitor, a position it planned to achieve by learning through co-development arrangements: "Those in the United States who oppose transfering technology to Japan have pierced through to the true root of Japanese intentions."[24]

At further hearings before the Congress, the Bush administration now presented a united front, with Commerce joining Defense and State in arguing that the "clarified" agreement was the best thing for the United States. The vote took place on 16 May after a long debate. Just before the balloting started, Minority Leader Robert Dole walked out of the cloakroom and remarked that he thought the vote would go against the administration. It was close. A swing of only three votes would have defeated the deal. But by 52 to 47, it went through. But the game was not entirely over. A resolution by Senator Robert Byrd calling for the United States to get not less than 40 percent of the production as well as of the spare parts carried overwhelmingly and was subsequently passed by the House. Bush was forced to veto it in order to avoid another renegotiation with Japan. This veto was later upheld by one vote in the Senate.

Thus, in the end the traditional view triumphed again. The FSX will be co-developed; and Japan's industry will be strengthened as a result, although probably less so than if there had been no "clarifications." Indeed, already there are reports from Tokyo that because MHI will not get the technology it had counted on from America, the project will be delayed by two more years. Nonetheless, Kearns—along with Smith, Massey, Richards, and others who were aware of the deal's potential adverse effect on U.S. interests—had forced the United States and Japan to confront as never before the facts and long-standing contradictions of their relationship. The fundamental conflict between Japan's industrial policy drives and its defense needs and free-trade principles were more clearly demonstrated than ever before. So, too, was the long conflict between U.S. national security and geopolitical concerns and the exigencies of industrial strength. Of great significance was the demonstration for the first time of the fact that the professional Japan handlers in the United States have often exacerbated relations by misleading the Japanese about realities in order to avoid being perceived as hard-liners or bashers. Finally, the link between trade and defense—which, despite desperate denial, has long been in the background of U.S.-Japan relations—was forced into the open in a way that will be impossible to ignore in the future.

Indeed, even now in the summer of 1989, the FSX debate

is having far-reaching consequences. In imitation of Japan, Korea has been negotiating for new fighters. Again, the F-16 and F-18 are candidates, and General Dynamics and McDonnell Douglas are being pitted against each other to see who will give away the most. The Korean proposal is for an off-the-shelf buy of twelve planes, followed by assembly of thirty-six knockdown kits in Korea, and then by coproduction of seventy-two planes in Korea. In addition, the two U.S. companies have offered 150-percent offset arrangements; that is, the United States will give Korea work equivalent to 150 percent of the value of the airplanes and parts that nation buys from the U.S. producers. When this offer came to light in the summer of 1989, the new secretary of defense immediately stated that he would try rather to sell airplanes to the Koreans.

The linkage of trade and defense in the FSX affair signaled a potentially new American attitude.

## Listing Japan as "Unfair": Super 301

The seemingly endless U.S.-Japan trade friction came to a crescendo immediately after conclusion of the "clarified" FSX deal. The new trade law of 1988 required the U.S. trade representative to make an extensive report to Congress on the trade barriers of major U.S. trading partners by the beginning of May 1989. The trade representative was then empowered, under the so-called super-301 section of the law, to identify priority countries and practices that would become the object of U.S. market-opening negotiations or, failing success after eighteen months, retaliation. At the same time, separate provisions required a review of market-opening progress under previous telecommunications trade agreements and possible retaliation if sufficient progress was not found.* Thus, just as President Bush was notifying the Congress of his desire to go ahead with the FSX, the trade representative was making her report. It was not good news for Japan.

The comprehensive report on trade barriers showed that impediments to foreign penetration of Japan's markets were more numerous (over thirty citations) and more pervasive than in any other country. In addition, the report noted the dampening effect on imports of Japan's industrial policies, which aim for world leadership in key industries such as semiconductors, supercomputers, and satellites. In a truly bold departure, the report also identified as unfair barriers to trade Japan's *keiretsu* relations, multitiered, manufacturer-controlled distribution systems, and other informal business practices. This was the first time the Japanese economic system had come under broad official criticism, and the way seemed open to a radical departure for U.S. trade policy.

The publication by the trade representative of the barriers report had set the clock ticking for a decision by the end of May: that is, any countries listed under super 301 as unfair traders might ultimately be retaliated against by the United States if the offending practices were not removed after the prescribed negotiations. To list or not to list Japan became the touchstone question for all those involved in trade issues in Washington. Everyone knew that the law had been written by the Congress with Japan specifically in mind. Thus, not to list Japan could only create trouble for the President in the Congress. On the other hand, listing would inevitably be taken by Japan as a slap in the face and thereby possibly harm the overall alliance. Moreover, it could lead to restrictions on Japanese access to the U.S. market, which many economists viewed as protectionist. Finally, there was the problem of other countries that had barriers similar to those of Japan. If Korea or France were listed, it would be

*Although the so-called M.O.S.S. (market-oriented, sector-specific) talks aimed at opening Japan's market for telecommunications and radio equipment and services had been declared a major success in 1985 (see pages 480–82), now it was reported that major obstacles continued to hamper the efforts of U.S. companies to penetrate the Japanese market.

difficult not to list Japan and vice versa. But the United States could not afford to pick a fight with ten or twenty countries at the same time, particularly while trying to push forward the Uruguay round of General Agreement on Tariffs and Trade (GATT) negotiations. In view of the contents of the barriers report, however, not to list any country would clearly amount to subversion of the law and call forth more draconian measures from Congress.

The debate followed a well-worn path. Phalanxes of officials from Japan, Korea, Taiwan, and elsewhere descended upon the USTR's office where they hoped that frantic last-minute negotiations would elicit a USTR statement that, in view of recent progress, listing would be unnecessary and even perhaps counterproductive. At the same time, the powerful Japanese lobby explained to officials and to the press that American discoveries of barriers in the Japanese market were misperceptions. The lobby also pointed out the growing U.S. financial and technological dependence on Japan, the danger of Japanese retaliation, the risk to the political and security relationship, and, of course, the dangers of rampant protectionism and economic nationalism.

Within the administration, the old divisions lined up. The bureaucracies of the departments of State and Defense opposed any listing, lest the overall relationship be harmed. The economists' agencies—which include the Office of Management and Budget, the Council of Economic Advisers, and the Treasury—tended to see any U.S. action as protectionist; while the USTR's office and the Commerce Department leaned toward listing. Even here, however, the issue was not clear-cut, the USTR itself being deeply divided. In late May, when it seemed that the administration might be swinging against listing, several key senators—including Robert Byrd of West Virginia, John Danforth of Missouri, and Lloyd Bentsen of Texas—called Trade Representative Carla Hills to their offices and warned that if she did not list Japan, the administration would face an extremely angry Congress. From that point, the debate within the administration swung from whether to list to how to list in the least offensive way. Here the law provided a help. For it required that the offending practices of each offending country be listed and negotiated. If the administration listed the structural barriers of Japan—such as *keiretsu*, tied distribution, relationship-based business dealings, and industrial policy—it had described in its earlier report, it would, in effect, be taking on the essence of Japanese economic organization. On the other hand, if the administration listed only narrow technical violations of GATT rules or of earlier trade agreements, it would be on more easily defined ground and could, it thought, contain the potential damage to the relationship. Thus, at the end of May, the USTR listed Japan for three "unfair" practices: its policy of banning the procurement of foreign-made satellites by government entities if such purchase interferes with "indigenous development objectives"; its effective exclusion of U.S.-made supercomputers from the Japanese public-sector market despite a 1987 agreement to the contrary; and its use of high tariffs and technical standards unrelated to performance of the material to exclude U.S. forest products from the Japanese market in violation of the GATT agreement on "technical barriers to trade."

The administration was wrestling with an acute dilemma posed by the moral framework of U.S. trade law. Section 301 gives a president broad power to deal with trade problems, but only if they are deemed to arise from the "unfair" practices of other nations. Because the law assumes that American-style capitalism and laissez-faire international trade are not only good but morally right, it implicitly defines deviations from such a system as "unfair." There is no provision for the possibility of a different system or for dealing with problems that arise not out of unfairness but from the grinding together of systems that simply do not mesh well. But, as I describe in this book, the Japanese system is quite different —not necessarily unfair, but different. Faced with the profound implications of labeling the whole Japanese system unfair, the administration shied away and found shelter in narrow technicalities. But it realized that this straddle would not really change the distorted structure of U.S.-Japan trade, but that it would very likely call forth criticism from those who would recognize the maneuver for what it was—an attempt to deal with the politics of the issue rather than with the issue itself.

To escape this dilemma, the administration came up with a potentially revolutionary proposal that, properly executed, could be the escape from the dead-end moralism of U.S. trade law. While announcing the listing of Japan, the administration also announced that it was proposing negotiations with Japan on structural impediments to trade—such as bid rigging, rigidity in the distribution and pricing systems, and market allocation. Here was an attempt to deal pragmatically with the Japan issue outside the fair-unfair dichotomy. Hallelujah! said many veteran trade negotiators who sensed the possibility of a truly new departure.

But habit quickly reasserted itself. Japan announced that it would refuse to negotiate on forest products, satellites, and supercomputers under the threat of potential U.S. retaliation. Privately it told U.S. negotiators it was always willing to discuss issues, but only outside the framework of super 301. What the result would be was unclear, but the whole process ever more resembled the years of previous trade discussions between the United States and Japan.

Nowhere was this more true than in the case of the "structural impediments" talks. Japan said it would gladly talk about structural impediments, but only on the condition that U.S. structural impediments to trade adjustment also be discussed. This creation of pseudo parity is an old and powerful Japanese tactic. The main U.S. issue is the different nature of the Japanese economic system and how to deal with it and in particular how to achieve reasonable entry into it. Although it is often sloppily discussed in terms of the trade deficit, the issue is not really the size of the deficit: that is a symptom. The question is how to mesh the Japanese and U.S. systems on a basis that is not disadvantageous to the United States. By referring to the problem of reducing the deficit and asking for discussion of U.S. structural phenomena, Japan changes the nature of the debate. This new debate is based on the old implicit assumption of the similarity of the two systems. The question then becomes what both sides should do to reduce the deficit—on the implicit assumption that responsibility and blame as well as structural phenomena are equivalent. Thus, the U.S. government budget deficit is defined as a structural impediment to trade equivalent to bid rigging, tied distribution, and industrial policy. That a country with a $120-billion trade deficit is unlikely to have effective barriers to entry is lost in the camaraderie of the task of trying to find how both sides can work together to reduce the deficit, as is the fundamental U.S. concern with the different nature of the two systems. The inevitable outcome is an agreement that Japan must stimulate its domestic economy while the United States reduces its budget deficit—in other words, pure pablum.

But the apparent requirements of fairness make it difficult for the United States to foil the Japanese maneuver. No American wants to insist that there is only one side to the story or that we have no faults. So the United States usually accepts the Japanese gambit and immediately loses the game. The new structural discussion has already taken on the character of two little-known preceding rounds of talks. The 1983–84 series of bilateral negotiations called the Industrial Policy Dialogue (see pages 251–52) took place pursuant to the administration's denial of the Houdailles petition. Sparked by concern with the trade-impeding effect of Japan's industrial policies, it became a debate over the similarities and dissimilarities of U.S. and Japanese economic policies. This dialogue was followed by the so-called Structural Dialogue which followed completion of the M.O.S.S. negotiations in 1986. Another attempt to get at the problem of different systems, the Structural Dialogue, too, descended into boring discussion of macroeconomics. Current negotiators argue that the present situation is different, that the ac-

ceptance of the Japanese request to discuss U.S. impediments is only a maneuver to cover the real gist of the
talks. And it may well be. But the fact that the talks are
being carried on at the subcabinet level, by more or less
the same people who participated in earlier rounds of the
same discussion, does not give rise to optimism. Serious
purpose by the United States would call for the engage-
ment of cabinet officers as well as senior members of the
Congress and perhaps leading business and labor figures
as well. The current situation resembles nothing so much
as the M.O.S.S. talks which preceded it.

## The New Midas: Japanese Capital

### THE U.S. TRADE DEFICIT

The final power of Japan was greatly enhanced as a result
of the United States's desperate attempts to reduce its trade
deficit by promoting dollar devaluation and the opening of
Japan's financial markets. This effort was begun in 1984 as
the U.S. budget and trade deficits soared. In an effort to
drive up the value of the yen by making it more of a reserve
currency and to obtain more business for U.S. financial institutions, the U.S. Treasury pressed Japan to deregulate its
financial markets. The hidden agenda was to tap a new current of capital to fund the gigantic budget deficit. Because
the U.S. pressure coincided with changes in the Japanese
financial world, including the need to invest a growing surplus of capital outside the country, Japan acceded to U.S.
wishes—but, of course, in its own way. The result was no
immediate strengthening of the yen and no significant in-

crease in the participation of U.S. financial institutions in the Japanese market, but a growing flow of Japanese capital to the United States. In 1985, with the twin deficits still out of control, the new secretary of the treasury, James Baker, tried again. Demonstrating the hollowness of earlier assertions by former Treasury Secretary Donald Regan that the dollar would be strong to the end of the decade because it reflected the strength of the American economy, Baker called on the world's major countries to orchestrate a devaluation of the dollar. In truth, the dollar had already begun to fall in February 1985 in response to the enormous U.S. trade deficit. But in September at the Plaza Hotel in New York, Baker and his colleagues launched a policy of leaning with the wind which had the objective of reducing the trade deficit by encouraging the continued downward trend of the dollar.

The basis of all this effort was, of course, the neoclassical economic theory that currency devaluation would reduce U.S. imports by increasing their prices and spur exports by reducing theirs. Five years later, it is clear, as I and others predicted at the time, that the theory does not work—or at least not with regard to Japan and the newly industrializing countries of Asia. After a temporary decline from $150 billion to $120 billion, the trade deficit is now rising again. While devaluation turned a deficit of $30 billion with Europe into a surplus, it had virtually no effect with Japan, where the deficit fell only from $55 billion to $51 billion and is now rising rapidly back toward $55 billion. What application of the theory did do, however, was to reduce the value of the United States and enhance that of Japan. As the dollar fell from Y240 in 1985 to Y120 at its bottom in early 1988, the value of all American assets was halved relative to Japan while relative to the United States the value of all Japanese assets was doubled.

That the United States actively promoted developments with such perverse results was due to the colossal misperceptions of neoclassic economics. The expectation that devaluation of the dollar would raise the price of Japanese exports, and thereby reduce them while inducing increased U.S. exports, failed to account for several factors. First, although Japan has deregulated many of its financial markets, it has not allowed the yen to become a true reserve currency. This means that most of Japan's raw material inputs and particularly oil are priced in dollars. Thus, the falling dollar actually reduced a substantial portion of Japanese costs. For example, at the height of the oil crisis of the late 1970s, oil imports amounted to 5 percent of Japanese GNP. By 1989, the combination of falling oil prices and a falling dollar had reduced that to 1 percent of GNP.

Second, we underestimated the ability of Japanese industry to react with rapid rationalization. Responding as if to a wartime crisis, Japanese industry launched frantic cost-cutting efforts and moved manufacture of many labor-intensive, low-value added components to Southeast Asia. The ability to make this investment was, of course, facilitated by the automatic increase in the amount of Japanese capital relative to the rest of the dollar-based world, an increase engendered by the dollar devaluation. Third, while Japanese imports rose, the home market remained virtually impervious to disruptive invasions of cheap foreign goods that could challenge the dominance of domestic manufacturers. This was mainly due to the control of Japanese producers over their own market. This is best demonstrated by a recent MITI report which shows that, between 1985 and 1988, consumer prices rose about 5 percent in Japan while wholesale, import, and export prices were falling by 15 percent, 25 percent, and 50 percent, respectively. The same report shows that prices of well-known Japanese goods are from 30 percent to 60 percent less expensive in major overseas markets than in Japan. Japanese control of the domestic market meant that sales of competitive U.S. goods, such as supercomputers, satellites, and telecommunications gear, rose not at all. Finally, there was the fact that the United States simply no longer makes a large number of items such as VCRs, ceramic chip packages, radios, and cameras. With these products, the value of the dollar does not matter. If you want them, you have to import them. Indeed, devaluation simply caused Americans to pay more for them.

## JAPANESE INVESTMENT IN THE UNITED STATES

Thus, the insistence of American policy makers in the face of mounting evidence to the contrary, on the similarity of the two economies and the equal efficacy of neoclassical economic prescriptions, led to the creation of a true colossus. Japan is now generating a current account surplus of $90-plus billion annually, greater than OPEC at its height. This is all in the hands of Japanese industry and financial institutions organized to invest it around the world. Last year the value of all the shares listed on the Tokyo Stock exchange surpassed that of those listed on the New York exchange and came to account for nearly 60 percent of the world's stock values. The value of all the real estate in Japan, a nation the size of California, surpassed that of all the real estate in the United States. One Japanese company, Nippon Telegraph and Telephone, became far and away the most valuable in the world with a market price of over $250 billion. By comparison, IBM, the most valuable American company had a market value of less than a tenth of NTT's. Of the twenty-six companies in the world with more than $1 billion in cash in their coffers, Japan has nineteen, which hold a total of $60 billion in search of overseas acquisitions. Of the world's top one hundred banks by asset value, twenty-eight are Japanese; if deposits are counted, the number mounts to thirty. Indeed, the assets of the top twenty Japanese banks exceed those of the entire American banking system. In the same way, the value of U.S. companies, office buildings, hotels, country clubs, and technology shrank relative to Japan; and the ability of the United States to compete was reduced by the very policies that were supposed to enhance it.

The new position of the United States was best perceived in Japan. There, Makoto Utsumi, the director general of international finance at the Ministry of Finance, warned that devaluation won't sell more U.S. goods; it will sell only assets. Here, a great wave of Japanese capital is washing up on American shores. In 1988, Japanese companies spent about $10 billion acquiring over eighty U.S. companies. In addition, they spent $4 billion to $6 billion on new plants while investment in U.S. real estate hit close to $17 billion. Japanese investors now hold over twenty of the prime properties in Manhattan, including Citicorp Center, the Exxon building, the ABC building, Tiffany's, and Tower 49. When added to their holdings of about 50 percent of downtown Los Angeles commercial real estate and substantial positions in Washington, D.C., and other major metropolitan centers, this means that Japan owns much of the prime property in key U.S. markets. As this movement has continued in 1989, Japan has vaulted past the Netherlands as the second largest foreign direct investor in the United States after the United Kingdom and if current trends continue, will pass that nation in another three years. Japan also plays a major role in transactions on the New York Stock Exchange, but where it is really king is in government bonds. The U.S. Treasury is thoroughly addicted to the flow of Japanese capital on which it depends for placement of nearly 40 percent of its bonds. All in all, the annual flow of Japanese capital into the United States is on the order of $70 billion.

The power of this capital has overwhelmed the retardant effect of dollar devaluation and actually accelerated the Japanese penetration of U.S. markets. Ten percent of the U.S. manufacturing base is already controlled by Japanese producers. By the end of 1990, over one million cars will be produced by Japanese manufacturers in the United States and Canada as a result of direct investment in new plants. When added to the roughly two million units of annual imports, the result will be expansion of the Japanese share of the North American market to close to 30 percent from the present 23 percent. A similar phenomenon is occurring in the construction industry. A study by the Center for Strategic Studies in Construction at Britain's University of Reading has recently concluded that developments in Japan will change the whole shape of the world construction industry.[25] The study notes that Japanese construction companies can do everything from financing the projects to running the completed facilities for the owners. Beyond that they are able to spend over 1 percent of sales on research and development, something unheard of in the rest of the world construction industry. Noting the tendency of Japanese manufacturers to rely on Japanese construction companies for building their new overseas plants, the study forecasts substantial expansion of the Japanese construction industry world market share. This trend is already evident in the United States where Japanese projects have gone from virtually zero to over $6 billion in the last several years.

Perhaps more important is the way this financial power has facilitated Japan's continued penetration of what most nations consider the twin keys to economic vitality in the twenty-first century—finance and technology. Japanese banks now account for over 10 percent of U.S. bank assets and about 13 percent of the loan market, and these proportions are expected to double in the next few years. In California, which so far has been the focus of Japanese activity, the figures are larger. Five of the ten largest banks in the state are controlled by Japanese interests, and the probability is that this proportion will increase because California law currently allows foreign banks to merge with California banks but bars non-California U.S. banks from doing the same until 1991. Perhaps the most significant clue I had to the future, however, was what key executives of one of the top three U.S. banks said over lunch in the winter of 1989: They noted that their cost of funds and of total capital was higher than that of their Japanese competitors and admitted that they could not match the Japanese in ordinary lending. They agreed that they could not make up this disadvantage by buying a Japanese bank. When I then asked how they were going to compete in the future, they said they would do so by being faster on their feet and more innovative with new products and services. They would make it in the sophisticated niches, they said.

Not a reassuring answer, I thought, because that is exactly where the Japanese are also heading—with a great deal of help from their American competitors. Money management is one of the most sophisticated areas of finance, and the *Wall Street Journal* reported in August 1989 that the "Japanese want to do in investment what they did to the floor of auto plants."[26] As a start, there are now at least eight joint ventures between Japanese banks and securities firms and U.S. money management firms. In the world of investment banking, it is increasingly difficult to do a deal without Japanese money. Kohlberg, Kravis & Roberts, upon completing the leveraged buyout of RJR Nabisco, promptly turned to Tokyo to place a third of the junk bonds. But Japan wants to do more than just buy junk bonds, and to learn the ways of Wall Street. Japanese firms have bought into Goldman Sachs; Shearson Lehman; PaineWebber; and Wasserstein Perella. These deals always entail the dispatch of a number of bright, young Japanese executives to learn the new technology. As with the entrepreneurs of Silicon Valley before them, the stars of Wall Street tend to be dismissive of Japanese capabilities. Joseph Perella told the *New York Times* in the spring of 1989 that M&A is a high-margin, brain-power kind of business.[27] Arguing that this kind of service is not mass-produced, but is done on the basis of an arcane set of rules, he concluded that it will always be done on an Anglo-Saxon standard world-wide. But Horoki Harada of Mitsui had a somewhat different view. Commenting on how he was learning, he stressed his surprise at the openness of his American colleagues who were free with information that in Japan would be considered confidential. And Koji Nakatani of Nippon Life Insurance Company made another important point when he pointed out that his American colleagues seemed to be working primarily for themselves while Japanese work for their organization. Where these developments could be leading was succinctly outlined by Simon Pyuwer, a financial analyst and long-time resident of Tokyo. With the Japanese already dominating the bidding for U.S. Treasury bonds, he was asked whether Japan could come to dominate U.S. capital markets by gaining dominance in other key areas as well. "Yes," said Pyuwer, "within two years."[28]

## FUNDING HIGH TECHNOLOGY

Because of its already strong position, Japanese financial power has even greater impact in the area of high technology than in finance. It has long been thought that Japan's weakness in technology is lack of creativity, which could slow down its rapid advance as it reaches the leading edge. While this view is open to dispute, recent developments make it a moot point. Japan does not really need to be creative because it can buy American creativity. Today Japanese money is flooding into U.S. universities and high-tech startups at an astounding rate. At last count, sixteen chairs at MIT were being endowed by Japanese industry, and it is a major backer of a research program that provides information to backers in advance of publication. Indeed, Japanese funding is so important to MIT that it has a director for Japanese gifts and a single program, the Media Lab, receives 25 percent of its funding from Japan. Similarly, Stanford receives major Japanese funding for computer research, Princeton for Diesel engine research, and the University of Arizona for digital radiography. Georgia Tech has signed a deal with Nissho Iwai to sell its technology in Japan; and Gene D'Amour of Tulane says, "We want Japan to take our technology and turn it into products."[29]

By the same token, small U.S. companies with interesting

technology and a need for cash are the source of continuing transfusions of technology to Japan. A good example is Kubota, an old-line Japanese manufacturer of tractors trying to diversify into supercomputers and engineering work stations. By taking a 25 percent stake in Dana corporation, Kubota obtained all of Dana's technology, marketing rights in Asia, and knowledge of manufacturing. Further investments in Ardent, MIPS, and Akashic Memories gave it minisupercomputer graphics, high-speed RISC, and thin-film magnetic-disk technology. It has been able to get into business quickly and for a total investment of a little over $100 million. Kyocera has made nineteen such investments, while Canon has become a major investor in Steve Jobs Next workstations. And the list grows as such deals proliferate every day. To those who saw the U.S. industry lose valuable technological leads through past licensing deals, the new equity investment vehicle has great significance. Says John Stern, vice president of the American Electronic Association's Tokyo Office, "Japanese investment is used as a vacuum cleaner for acquiring technology and porting it home. If America intends to win the race based on innovation, it must stop selling its running shoes to the competitors."[30]

### THE CREATION OF JAPANESE WEALTH

In fact, the power behind the Japanese juggernaut is much greater than most Americans suspect, and the juggernaut cannot stop of its own volition, for Japan has created a kind of automatic wealth machine, perhaps the first since King Midas. For much of the postwar period, Japan had insufficient capital to fund the rapid growth it desired. To remedy this deficiency, the Japanese government directed the banks to overloan: that is, to make loans for which there was no capital base. The banks had an implicit guarantee that if trouble developed, the government would bail them out. In effect, the Japanese government created capital by fiat. Later as Japanese industry grew and prospered, and as Japanese savings supplied increased capital to the banks, such measures were no longer necessary, and the banks stopped overloaning.

At this point, however, the stock market began to play a role. In the early 1970s, Tokyo's first bull market doubled the value of the Nikkei index (Tokyo's Dow). Since then there have been only a few gentle stops as the market has soared to stratospheric levels. Even during the crash of 19 October 1987, the Tokyo market fell far less and recovered far more quickly than the other world markets. The reason is that the Japanese government, in conjunction with leading business and financial circles, is continuing to create wealth by fiat—a process described by *Business Week* on 25 July 1988: "In fact, Tokyo is nothing less than a smoothly functioning private club run for the benefit of Japan, Inc. This powerful association hums along on ceaseless rounds of mutual back scratching among big brokers, banks, corporations, and government bureaucrats all bent on three goals: sky high savings rates, lofty stock prices, and cheap funds for economic growth."[31] To these goals Simon Pyuwer would add the desire to avoid foreign participation in the Japanese market.[32] As he notes, a major factor in the rise of stock prices is the fact that only 20 percent to 30 percent of listed shares ever trade because of the *keiretsu* system of corporate cross shareholders who never trade their shares. Originally stimulated by the Japanese government as a way of barring foreign investment in Japanese industry, the system now works to make Japanese corporations off limits by driving up prices as a result of scarcity of supply in comparison with the great amounts of investment money in Japan. Government officials also ensure rising prices with appropriate tax and monetary policy adjustment and through extensive "administrative guidance," which is facilitated by the routine lending of employees back and forth between the ministries and the major financial institutions.

The workings of real estate markets are similar and overlap with those of the stock market. Today there are more billionaires in Japan than in any other country because of continuously rising real estate values. While usually attributed to overcrowding in a small country with increasing wealth, the fact is otherwise. The prices rise because of a scarcity of available land. But the scarcity is artificial. Japanese land use and tax laws along with subsidization and protection of rice growing operate to keep most land off the market. The resultant upward spiral of prices greatly enriches both the government and large corporations. Sapporo Breweries, for example, carries one plot of central Tokyo land on its books at $2.5 million while the current market value is $9 billion. Hidden assets of this proportion have led to heavy borrowing to invest in the stock market's ever-rising shares. Investment drives stock prices even higher, thereby reducing what is already the world's lowest cost of capital and leading to more of the investment that drives up real estate prices as well as to further investment in expanding shares of foreign markets.

Some observers argue that recent losses by Japan's ruling Liberal Democratic Party may lead to political changes that will alter this system and make it more like that of the United States. Nonetheless, during a year of the worst political turmoil in Japan since 1955, the stock and real estate markets have not blinked. Significant change in the system seems unlikely because all the major power centers of the country have a stake in it and it so obviously magnifies Japanese wealth and power. The outlook for the rest of the world in dealing with Japan is thus more of the same. A recent agreement by Japan to remove its quota on beef imports was supposed to result in a spurt in U.S. exports. In fact, it resulted in Japanese importers and distributors buying a number of U.S. ranches and packing houses. Exports increased—but under the continued control of the same people who have always controlled it. The juggernaut rolls on because it is successful and no one in Japan has the power or desire to change it.

Change engendered from the outside also seems unlikely —indeed increasingly so as another result of the growing power of Japanese capital. Tremendous political support can now be generated to protect the system. The governors of the various U.S. states fight among themselves to see who can give away the most benefits to lure Japanese investment. Kentucky even offered driving lessons to Japanese employees and their families; while Michigan's governor, James Blanchard, with the U.S. big three auto makers in his backyard, told potential Japanese investors that a strategy of investing in the Midwest could produce less trade pressure in Congress. In Washington, D.C., the already long list of lobbyists and consultants for Japanese interests has only continued to grow and now includes two former USTRs along with a majority of former high-ranking trade officials. One U.S. company president with a trade complaint told me recently that it had been extremely difficult to find legal counsel who did not have conflict of interests because of Japanese clients.

More subtle, but in the long run more powerful, is the growing influence on opinion makers in the United States. Current estimates are that Japanese interests spend about $310 million annually on influencing the U.S. debate, by means of corporate philanthropy, lobbying, public relations, and other promotional activities. Its effect is seen in the comment of an executive at the Center for Strategic International Studies, one of Washington's premier foreign policy think tanks. In staffing, this man said the institute would not hire anyone who was likely to be seen as critical of Japan. A similar influence was demonstrated at a seminar in which I recently participated. Of three seminar leaders, two were consultants to Japanese interests in Washington. But of their real role the audience was never informed, these men being presented to it as experts on trade. Thus is the American agenda being influenced by a largely unseen foreign power.

## CONSEQUENCES FOR THE UNITED STATES

U.S. industry has long been blamed for the inability of the United States to compete with Japan. And there surely is much truth in the criticism. But the fact is that our industry's situation is difficult in the extreme. Suppose, for example, that you are the president of Goodyear Tire and Rubber, the world's largest tire company. Your company, an old and proud one, has long dominated the world tire industry which it invented. Recently you took on enormous debt and spent most of the better part of a year trying to avoid a take-over by a British raider. Now, in a weakened state, your company faces a major attack by the Japanese tiremaker Bridgestone. With over half the Japanese market, Bridge-stone has just acquired Firestone, thereby achieving a signifi-cant position in the U.S. market. Your company cannot enter the Japanese market: acquisition there is very difficult as a practical matter even if you could afford it; and with the prices of shares in Japan these days, you can't afford it. Sell-ing directly to Japanese auto makers is not likely to be pro-ductive because of their close ties to traditional Japanese suppliers. For all practical purposes, your major competitor has a protected home market. He also has a much lower cost of capital and profit requirement. He can afford to invest in new plants and processes; you cannot. As the Japanese car makers increase their share of world markets, your competi-tor's share of the tire business automatically increases while yours declines, thus cutting his costs and raising yours. He can acquire more of your domestic competitors and even some of your distributors. In fact, he can probably acquire you—an outcome that might be the best thing for your em-ployees and shareholders. Once in Japanese hands, the former will probably have secure jobs, and the latter will get a premium price for their shares. At home you will get no help. The states in which you operate will offer your compet-itor financial incentives to put in new plants to compete with you. Of course, they say they would offer you the same—but, because of your competitor's onslaught, you are not likely to open plants. Rather, you are faced with having to close a few, and his incentives will only hasten the process. The federal government only makes matters worse. It requires you to make a quarterly report. Your Japanese competitor does not have to make such a report to his government. Everyone chastises you for being short-sighted, but the fact is that if your quarterly earnings are not where the analysts think they should be, your share price will fall. As a result, your cost of capital will rise even further above your competitor's, and your ability to invest for the long term will be further weakened. You might even become vulnerable to another debilitating takeover battle. If your competitor wants to make life really difficult, he can dump a few tires into the U.S. market at cut-rate prices and cause you to lose money. The U.S. government probably will not help you; or if it does try, it will be too late. In fact, a clever competitor who wanted to acquire you might dump in order to force your earnings and share prices down and thus pick you up at a cheaper price. It really makes no sense to be in this business. Why not sell to him now while the getting is good?

The fact is that much of U.S. industry really doesn't have a chance. But so what? Many argue there is no cause for alarm because Japanese and other foreign investment will take up the slack by creating new jobs and bringing new technology and better management techniques. This will be just the tonic, it is said, that will make everything right with America again, and the best part is that we don't have to do anything except let it happen. The trouble with this argument is the element of truth in it. Certainly, as long as the United States is unwilling or unable to generate its own capital, it is better to have foreign capital than no capital at all. And clearly Japanese competition has forced many American industries to become more efficient and pay more attention to quality. So the Japanese challenge is not necessarily a bad thing in itself. Indeed, some observers have said that if the Japanese had not happened along, it would have been necessary to invent them. Nevertheless, not responding to the competition is costly.

As I write this, I am sitting in Hawaii looking at a headline in the *Honolulu Advertiser* that says: "Foreign Investment in

Isles Debated."[33] With over 80 percent of its hotels, 70 percent of its golf courses (including all eight nonmunicipal courses on the island of Oahu), and large chunks of prime residential as well as commercial real estate in Japanese hands, Hawaii has more experience with the impact of Japanese investment than any other region. Hawaii has found that while this investment does create jobs, it also has adverse effects. One is the closed-circle effect mentioned in the first edition of this book, where Japanese tourists stick with Japanese hotels, airlines, tour buses, and so on. Another is the rapid rise in real estate prices which tends to price local residents out of their own market, as well as increase rents and taxes for all local businesses. In effect, Honolulu real estate prices have become a captive of Tokyo's artificial shortage of property and are indirectly dictated by Japanese bureaucrats. Furthermore, evictions of native Hawaiians from land destined to become Japanese golf courses has given rise to the formation of several associations of local protestors. For local golf players, not only have fees risen dramatically, reflecting the unreal prices in Japan, but some courses are open to Japanese only. The simple problem of disclosure, of actually knowing who is investing in what, has turned out to be troublesome. Then there is the issue of money. In Japan, money talks in politics more than anywhere else; and in Hawaii, politicians running for local office have become the target of contributions from Japanese who want their assistance with real estate and business problems. In sum, many Hawaiians feel the islands are being colonized, and legislation has been proposed to ban or strictly regulate foreign investment.

Beyond the islands, the real estate question is less pressing because the weight of investment is less concentrated. And, of course, sellers and owners of property are usually happy when values rise. But prime metropolitan real estate has traditionally been where insurance and trust companies put much of their money. With much of this property in foreign hands, the domestic insurance companies will have less high-quality investment and therefore riskier portfolios, meaning higher costs for them and those they insure.

The employment issue is also problematic. Japanese investment may create employment, but such an outcome is not automatic. While a governor or a mayor may look only at the local factory and be pleased, the only proper measure is net employment on a national basis. In their 1989 book, *The New Competitors*, Norman Glickman and Douglas Woodward explain that over the past ten years foreign investment in the United States has resulted in a net loss of about 56,000 jobs.[34] Much foreign investment is acquisition of existing businesses, creating little, if any, new employment.

The auto industry will be the major battleground of the 1990s as Japanese production in the United States expands rapidly. These new plants will create employment in the area of their location, but the General Accounting Office has estimated that the net effect of Japanese auto production in the United States will be a loss of 45,000 jobs.[35] The United Auto Workers has calculated that it could be as high as 200,000.[36] The reason is that this new production probably will not displace current imports, and Japanese plants produce cars with only about 38-percent U.S. content. It is important to note that industrial structures reflect the values of those who build them. Much has been made, and rightly so, of the strength of the long-term view and relationships of the Japanese. But this job loss is also related to those values, because as the GAO notes, the ties between Japanese auto producers and their *keiretsu* suppliers make it extremely difficult for U.S. suppliers to get in the door with the new investors.

Then there is the nature of the employment. In their study, Glickman and Woodward found that the foreign firms in the United States have about half as many workers in research and development as domestic firms, and that high technology parts and processes are imported twice as much by foreign as by domestic companies.[37] A survey by Japan's Ministry of International Trade and Industry shows that senior executive jobs in Japanese U.S. subsidiaries are virtually always held by Japanese.[38] Indeed, even in the case of sales and personnel managers, jobs usually held by locals in most foreign subsidiaries, over 50 percent were Japanese nationals in the case of Japanese operations in the United States. By comparison, U.S. affiliates in Japan are almost entirely staffed by Japanese. Moreover, in their book *Selling Out*, Douglas Frantz and Catherine Collins note the Japanese practice of placing advisers in their U.S. subsidiaries.[39] Ostensibly there to help the local U.S. managers, they in fact hold the real power of decision and burn the night telephone lines to Tokyo. In an article in the *New Republic*, Robert Reich described the emerging pattern of production and employment in the United States: U.S. universities and venture companies develop technology, which is then taken to Japan for conversion into products, which are then assembled and sold by Americans in the U.S. market.[40] And after a while, as a Japanese executive recently told me, even the ability to advance the technology is lost. Said he, you begin by giving up the little things and eventually wind up losing the big ones, too.

Then there is the trade deficit. Despite dollar devaluation and massive Japanese investment in U.S. plants, the University of Michigan has recently completed a study that indicates that the U.S. trade deficit in automobiles could double in the next five years as a result of growing imports of parts, higher priced cars, and the capital equipment used in the auto plants.[41] This is consistent with the projections of the GAO. A good example of this kind of structural deficit is the machine tool industry: despite the capital spending boom of the past several years, the industry's domestic orders in 1988 were one third the level of 1979, also a boom year. As the world moves into a new age of electronics, high-definition television, flat panel displays, and fiber-optic-based communications will create whole new industries. Just as the United States is not in VCRs, so it is likely not to be in these new markets. The deficit in electronics will thus also rise despite the weak dollar and the flow of foreign investment.

Today, as a result of its great and growing economic strength, Japan has become the world's largest donor of aid. In contrast, the United States, after meeting its obligations to Israel and Egypt, has almost nothing left for the rest of the world. Increasingly, U.S. influence in the world is based on raw military power. In this regard, the United States more and more resembles the Soviet Union. As this trend has progressed, the United States has urged Japan to take up the slack and has talked about a division of labor with Japan. But the end result is that Japan is becoming the world's kind uncle while the United States is its policeman. People tend to like kind rich uncles and to dislike cops. Does the United States really want to give up the flexibility provided by economic power in its diplomacy?

## A Vision of the Future

In the nearly two years since the original publication of this book, I have lectured and spoken all over the country. I am often asked what the United States can or should do about Japan. Of course, there are many specific proposals I could make, but the key is a change of attitudes. Although the FSX and super-301 actions indicate some change in U.S. thinking, it remains generally true that our policies toward Japan spring from assumptions that have little to do with reality. Thus, all new initiatives and reorganizations will prove inadequate until we grasp reality.

Ultimately, however, I have come to the strong belief that the issue is neither Japan nor the U.S.-Japan relationship. Rather, it is the United States. In the words of Pogo, we have met the enemy and he is us. Our problems with Japan are only symptomatic of a larger flight from reality. In the final analysis, our trade deficit and inability to compete with

Japan spring from the same willful disregard of reality and self-delusion as the decay of our central cities, the permeation of our society with drugs, and the decline of our educational system.

I believe that Americans today face a question they have faced only twice before in history, once in 1776 and again in 1860: What kind of a society, what kind of a people are we and do we want to be? The question is not being posed in the same dramatic terms today as on those previous occasions—but that only makes it all the more pressing, for we can only deal with it after we have recognized it.

The uniqueness of Japan is constantly repeated. And, of course, it is unique. By definition, all countries are unique. But the most unique country is not Japan. It is the United States. From its founding this country has been a special place with a magnetic attraction to people around the globe. The United States has always been an offerer of haven and hope and opportunity. And the question facing America today is whether it will continue to be that in the twenty-first century or whether it will become just another country.

In seminars and sophisticated gatherings, I am often asked, somewhat condescendingly, why America has to be number one or whether America can be number one in everything. The question is usually asked with a certain smugness by one who wishes to demonstrate his or her cosmopolitanism by implying a disregard for crass nationalism. It is, of course, a trick question, for if I answer in the affirmative, I immediately brand myself a xenophobe or chauvinist in the eyes of the questioner and the cosmopolites in the audience. I am always sorry to hear the question because in my view, rather then demonstrating worldliness, it reveals ennui, aimlessness, and self-doubt among those who purport to be our élite and our leaders.

The answer is simple. I usually give it in terms of the experience that most of us have with our children. When my children bring their report cards home, sometimes the grades are not as good as I think they should be. I ask, "Why did you get that C in physics." There are two possible answers. One is: "Gee, Dad, I did the best I could. Stayed up late every night studying and didn't go out on Saturday so I could study for the test. But you know that physics is not my best subject. Besides, the teacher is really tough, and all the other kids in the class are National Merit finalists." If I believe him, that is an acceptable answer. He did his best. I can't ask for more than that. But the other possible answer is: "Well, Dad, you know I got that new guitar, and I was on the basketball team, and all that with my new girl friend, I just didn't have time to study." That is not an acceptable answer. It is not acceptable to me, and it shouldn't be to him. Because fundamentally there is something dishonest about a person, or a society, that doesn't do its best. So does America have to be number one? Can it be number one in everything? Of course not. But it has to try. For not to try is to deny one's own value.

And what are the consequences of that? Well, today every major city of the United States is living off its capital. Drive into Manhattan from LaGuardia Airport. Much of the landscape looks like Bangladesh. The unfunded maintenance bill of New York City is in the billions of dollars. And just multiply that by Detroit, Chicago, Los Angeles, St. Louis, and hundreds of other cities. The unfunded maintenance bill of the United States is in the trillions of dollars. Take Washington, D.C. Half—that's right, half—the children in our nation's capital will not graduate from high school. We are the only major nation that has had a decline in literacy in the past twenty years. At a national level we are effectively taking a quarter of our kids and throwing them on the scrapheap of history. The Japanese don't do that. The Germans don't do that, and neither do the Koreans or the Taiwanese or any other of our competitors. Ultimately, whether the United States can compete will be determined in the ghetto.

Or let's look at Washington, D.C., again. At night at least half the city is in the control of drug kings. Eight blocks from the White House, in the capital of the most powerful nation the world has ever known, the President has no writ.

Or let's turn to the southwest of our country. Here we are experiencing tremendous immigration. So much so that by the year 2000 over half the population of California will be minorities. In much of this part of the country, the language of choice is not English, but Spanish, or Vietnamese, or some other tongue. But will the United States be able to absorb these immigrants, and offer them opportunity, and integrate them into the mainstream of its society as it did their predecessors?

What are the consequences of not trying? As a stumbling, declining society that has lost faith in its own values, we will not be able to rebuild the crumbling infrastructure, or educate the kids in the central cities, or eradicate the drug kings, or offer the old haven and hope and opportunity.

The interesting thing is that average Americans know this. Audiences all over America tell me that despite the incantations of political leaders that America is back, standing tall, they know something is wrong when all the TV sets and radios, and telephones, and watches, and cameras, and VCRS, and many other products are made by non-U.S. companies. They express concern that they will be the first generation of Americans to pass on less than they received. And they ask what they can do.

There are really only two cures. One is a dramatic crisis such as a war or depression, and the other is leadership—leadership that is guided by more than the daily public opinion polls. The conventional wisdom in political circles today is that you can't ask the American people for sacrifice. To the marrow of my bones, I believe that is wrong. Jack Kennedy became one of our most popular presidents by urging that we ask not what the country can do for us, but rather what we can do for the country. Throughout the books and papers of the Founding Fathers, the word "posterity" is repeated again and again. You hardly see it today, but the founders of our nation were leaders who had faith in their own values and who were trying to make the country be the best it could be for posterity.

If a president or candidates for president would stand up and tell the American people that they do not propose to be leaders of a nation in decline. That they will make the achievement of industrial and technological leadership their top priority, more important than Gorbachev or Star Wars or China, because everything else rests upon such leadership. And that they need Americans' help, and, yes, their sacrifice for the sake of posterity, they would get a tremendous response.

But to get it they must have a vision of the future that is more than politics as usual.

# PART I

## *The Sleeping Giant*

# 1

# THE END OF THE
# AMERICAN CENTURY

---

It is much harder to nullify the results of an economic conquest than those of a military conquest.
                    —KOREKIYO TAKAHASHI, 1936

ON 2 September 1945, the Second World War was concluded ceremoniously aboard the battleship *USS Missouri* as the ships of its escorting Third Fleet crammed Tokyo Bay. The flag at the masthead was the same one that had flown over the Capitol in Washington, D.C., on 7 December 1941 when Japan had attacked Pearl Harbor. The flag spread over the ship's rear turret was the one Commodore Matthew C. Perry had flown ninety years before when he had been the first to succeed in forcing Japan to abandon nearly three hundred years of self-imposed isolation and to open itself to world trade. The day was overcast with gray clouds, but as the last signature was affixed to the surrender document, the sun broke through. Then came the event that all who were there remembered most vividly—the flyover. As General Douglas MacArthur announced the proceedings closed, four hundred B-29s, which had left

Guam and Saipan hours before to arrive over Tokyo Bay at this precise moment, appeared across the horizon to be greeted by one thousand five hundred fleet aircraft that had lifted off from the flattops below.[1]

This was American power at its zenith, and it was fitting that it should be demonstrated by the size of the fleet and the hundreds of aircraft darkening the sky. For Japan had not been defeated because her soldiers lacked valor. On the contrary, the Americans who fought the Japanese had come to have an immense respect for their courage and spirit in battle. No, the United States had won because of the technology and productivity of its incomparable industrial base. Japan's great admiral Isoroku Yamamoto had warned, before the war began, that it would be madness for his nation to attack the United States, whose economy dwarfed that of Japan at the time. And Yamamoto had been proven correct. From the early 1900s, the United States had been a power on the rise. Even during the Depression, our industry had grown stronger relative to that of other nations; and with the outbreak of war, we had gone on an investment and production binge that not only brought victory but also established the United States as the world's dominant power. In 1945, as MacArthur established the headquarters for his Occupation officials in the squat, brick building of Japan's Ministry of Finance, people began to speak of the twentieth as the American century, and few could imagine a time when the United States would not dominate the world economy.

On Monday, 19 October 1987, that optimism was dashed. The New York Stock Exchange opened for trading as usual at 9:20 A.M. Just the previous week the Department of Commerce had released the U.S. foreign trade statistics for August, which had shown that despite nearly three years of a depreciating dollar, U.S. imports—and especially those from Japan—were continuing to exceed exports by record amounts. From the opening bell, the market was inundated with sell orders. Neither computers nor brokers could keep up as the ticker fell hours behind. When it was all over, the market had lost nearly a quarter of its value as the Dow Jones industrial average fell by 508 points, dwarfing the 31-point, 13-percent plunge of Black Friday in 1929 that signaled the onset of the Depression. In just one day investors had lost half a trillion dollars which, when added to earlier losses, brought the total since August 1987 to a cool $1 trillion. Nor was the panic limited to Wall Street. In Tokyo, Hong Kong, and London, the story was the same.

In the aftermath of Bloody Monday, experts from the President on down tried to explain what had happened and why and what to do about it. In an eerie echo of Herbert Hoover, President Reagan said that he could not understand what all the fuss was about because all the economic indicators were up (except of course the stock market) and the U.S. economy was fundamentally sound. Other leaders and commentators were less sanguine, with many predicting an economic recession and some even fearing a worldwide depression. It was generally agreed by them that the main sources of the problem were the U.S. budget deficit, an overvalued dollar, and sluggish economic growth in Europe and Japan. If the United States would just let the dollar fall, raise taxes, and cut spending while Germany and Japan stimulated their economies, said the experts, all would again be well with the world. Few recognized the event for what it was—the end, twelve years before its time, of the American century.

With luck and fancy financial footwork, the market might recover as it had in 1929–30. But the crash threw a bright light on a situation that until now many had preferred to ignore. It was summarized by the former British defense minister Dennis Healey: "The type of world role the United States has carried since the war may no longer be possible."[2] The French political strategist François Froment-Meurice was even more emphatic: "The whole basis of the postwar world could be turned upside down."[3]

The crash elicited these comments because it was the culmination of other events.

- The United States had effectively lost its consumer electronics industry by the mid-1970s and had also been forced to protect its textile and steel industries. In 1981, it begged Japan to restrain auto exports.
- In 1984, the President's Defense Science Board warned that the nation was falling behind in high technology.
- On 5 November 1985, members of the President's cabinet met at the White House to consider the crisis in the semiconductor industry. The heart of the high technology underpinning both the nation's prosperity and its defense, this key industry was being devastated by Japanese competition. Nevertheless, most present opposed taking any action, believing—as one of the President's top advisers remarked—that "If our guys can't hack it, we ought to let them go."
- In June 1986, Robert Noyce, a founder of two major semiconductor companies and co-inventor of the integrated circuit, the foundation of the modern electronics industry, testified before the Defense Science Board. Noyce is one of our guys and if anyone can hack it he can, but he warned that the semiconductor industry was doomed without a change in U.S. government policies.
- On 24 October 1986, Japan's leading computer manufacturer, the Fujitsu Corporation, made an offer to buy the Fairchild Semiconductor Company, but withdrew it after opposition was voiced by Secretary of Commerce Malcolm Baldrige and Secretary of Defense Caspar Weinberger on the grounds that the United States was becoming too dependent on Japan for critical technology.
- On 27 March 1987, President Reagan, for the first time ever, announced retaliatory measures against Japan for unfair trade of semiconductors. The very next day, the stock market suffered one of its largest single-day declines up to that point and interest rates rose as investors, especially Japanese investors, abandoned the market for fear of a trade war.
- Over the summer of 1987, as the United States became the world's largest debtor, interest rates continued to rise as foreign investors, primarily Japanese, demanded a higher return for investing in an increasingly risky U.S. market. One French leader noted that the United States now had two central banks, the Federal Reserve system and the Japanese insurance companies.[4]
- Also in the summer of 1987, it was revealed that the U.S. navy's submarine hunters in the North Atlantic had suddenly become the hunted through the advent of dramatically quieter

submarines. The Soviets had been helped by the Toshiba Machine Company, which had sold them sophisticated equipment for milling quieter propellers. The sale had occurred in 1983, at approximately the same time that the President had rejected a U.S. industry petition against Toshiba Machine and other Japanese companies for their unfair trade activity in the machine tool industry—a rejection that had resulted in Japanese domination of critical segments of the U.S. machine tool market.

- In late 1987, as U.S. international debt surpassed that of Mexico and Brazil combined, U.S. payments to foreign investors exceeded U.S. income from holdings abroad for the first time in fifty years; meanwhile Japan became the world's largest creditor and passed the United States in per-capita GNP.

The truth is that the bell that sounded the end of the trading session on Bloody Monday 1987 signaled as clearly as any bugle call the most serious defeat the United States has ever suffered. It was somehow appropriate that it should have occurred on a trading floor and been triggered by what normally would be considered mundane trade statistics. For the defeat was a most unusual one. There were no military weapons and no armed troops. There were casualties but no blood; tears, but no one missing in action. It was an economic rather than a military defeat, partially self-inflicted, and partially at the hands of friends and allies among which Japan was foremost. That this was difficult to understand only meant, as Korekiyo Takahashi, Japan's prewar finance minister had understood so well in 1936, that the defeat would be more difficult to overcome.

For me personally, these developments were the culmination of an epic tale of reversal with which I have been involved for most of my life. I first went to Japan in 1965 as a graduate student to study the Japanese language at Keio University and at the Tokyo Tower Language School. Although Japan's vitality was then already apparent, only a few observers anticipated its later extent. I was not one of these. When I returned to Japan in the mid-1970s, however, the shape of the future was clearer. As a consultant to and director of several companies in Japan, I could see both how

the unusual cohesion of Japanese society resulted in a cooperation between business, labor, government, academia, and
the press that justified the label "Japan Inc."; and that—
combined with the dynamism of Japan's companies, the
ready availability of U.S. technology, and prevailing international circumstances—created an irresistible economic force.

In 1981, as this force increasingly clashed with U.S. industry, I was invited to join the U.S. Department of Commerce where as counselor to the secretary I became one of
the leaders in a series of key negotiations dealing with semiconductors, machine tools, telecommunications, and other
industries and revolving around issues that this book exam-
ines in detail. Although I had hoped to contribute to a relaxation of the tensions that had for some time been growing
between the United States and Japan, miscommunication,
misperception, and ignorance on both sides seemed only to
make the situation worse.

I resigned from the government in mid-1986. As I observed developments over the following year, I realized I
had witnessed a truly historic turn of events. During the past
six years the United States had spent nearly $2 trillion on
defense to maintain primacy as the world's military and political leader. It had photographed nearly every inch of the
Soviet Union and spent billions of dollars to listen to every
turn of the screws of Soviet ships. Yet far from being more
secure or more powerful, this country was less so. Despite
all the hoopla about standing tall, it was not morning in
America. If anything, it was dusk. In 1981, the secretaries of
commerce and defense would not have noticed—let alone
objected to—Fujitsu's bid for Fairchild. Now they did. In
1981, the United States, although less dominant than previously, was still the world leader in industry, technology,
and finance as well as in military power. In 1987, it was the
leader only in military power, and even there was facing the
necessity of reducing commitments. In other areas, the
United States, which had played the role first of occupier

and then of protector and mentor, had traded places with its former protégé—Japan.

## The Opening of Japan

There was both poetic justice and historical irony in this development. When Commodore Perry arrived in Tokyo Bay in 1853, he confronted a country still in a feudal stage of development, a country that had so rigorously sought to isolate itself from the rest of the world that it even refused to accept the return of its own shipwrecked fishermen who had been rescued at sea by foreign vessels. In the first appearance of what would prove to be a persistent American desire to remake Japan in its own image, Perry issued a demand that would echo over the next 130 years: "Open your market, or suffer the consequences"—presumably blockade by his ships. He then sailed away, promising to return within the year for Japan's reply.

Japan faced a painful choice. The Tokugawa Shogunate, which had ruled and isolated it for over 250 years, was not eager to open the country, but Perry's steam frigates represented a level of technology far beyond Japan's. As a result, even though his squadron consisted of only four ships, Perry was potentially in a position to blockade and starve Tokyo which received its food supply by sea. Throughout their period of isolation, the Japanese had carried on trade with the world through Dutch merchants stationed at Nagasaki and confined to an island in the harbor called Deshima. As a result of this window and of other reports, the Japanese, in a pattern that would repeat itself, knew much more of the outside world than it knew of Japan. They had already seen the shattering impact of Western technology and culture on

China, their long-time model and tutor. They now saw that, as a result of Western technology, all the barriers they had so carefully built against foreign contamination might be breached by superior technology, and realized they faced the same fate as China.

Japan's response to Perry became classic. For the Japanese, a proud people with a warrior tradition, there was never any question but that the nation would resist intrusion by outsiders. But they understood that it would be foolish to fight without equal or superior technology, and so determined on a strategy to obtain it while maneuvering to minimize foreign penetration in the meantime. When Perry returned, he was told that the answer was yes, Japan would open its market. But of course it couldn't be done all at once. There were to be two places where foreigners could trade: the small port of Shimoda on the Izu peninsula about 150 miles from Tokyo, and the small fishing port of Hakodate in the far north of Japan. This was the first of what would become known in later years as "market-opening packages." While thus attempting to limit the extent of foreign intrusion, Japan immediately launched an intensive and historic effort to catch up with the industry and technology of the West.

Missions were dispatched to Europe and America and foreign experts hired to come to Japan to transfer the technology and skills that had put it at such an uncomfortable disadvantage. Cameras were not much in use in those days, but the assiduity of the notetakers gave the first evidence of a thoroughness and an attention to detail that the world would later come to know well. While Japan had been forced to accede to unequal trade treaties, it had negotiated them so as to prevent foreigners from doing business in the interior of the country. It also avoided any foreign investment, having seen how disastrous that had been for Turkey and Egypt. Japan wanted the technology of the West not in order to become westernized but to maintain its autonomy and purity as a society.

All of the efforts to develop industry and the economy were at the behest and under the guidance of the government authorities. This mission was too important to be left to those known as "entrepreneurs" in the West. Results came with amazing speed. By 1900, Japan's capital industries had reached a level of technology, if not yet a scale, comparable to that of the West. The efficacy of Japan's effort was dramatically demonstrated in 1905 when, with all the world watching, the Japanese trapped and sank the pride of the Russian navy in the straits of Tsushima, thereby avenging to some extent the humiliation inflicted by Perry.

In the rubble of postwar Japan, the West somehow came to regard Japan as a developing country—an attitude that ignored the fact that by 1938 it was already one of the world's leading industrial and military powers. In the 1930s, Japan dominated Asia's textile markets and was making such large inroads elsewhere that it was being condemned for unfair competition by Western countries that only eighty years before had demanded it enter into trade with them. At this time, its steel production was greater than that of France and Italy and nearly the same as that of Great Britain; and its industrial growth was faster than that of the United States. With the outbreak of war in 1941, U.S. airmen quickly learned that the long-belittled Japanese made the best fighter planes in the world, the famed Zeroes.

Japan's postwar economic miracle is by now a familiar tale. It once more began to scour the world for technology and rededicated its formidable energy to making up for lost ground. While again maneuvering to minimize foreign incursion, it quickly reconquered the textile and shipbuilding industries and from there moved on to steel and consumer electronics. For years, the United States watched these developments with unconcern and with the pride of the teacher in a star pupil. Americans were confident that they would always be ahead.

# Cracks in the Hegemony of the United States

## THE HIGH-TECH CRISIS

Against this background, Fujitsu's offer to buy Fairchild
Semiconductor had great symbolic significance. Fairchild
Semiconductor was Robert Noyce's first company. Founded
in 1957 when the investment banker Arthur Rock put the
Fairchild Corporation together with Noyce and seven other
young engineers, it was the first commercial semiconductor
company in the valley at the south end of San Francisco Bay.
It was literally and figuratively the mother of Silicon Valley.
Its establishment led to an explosion of start-ups and venture
capital that transformed a valley of apricot orchards into
today's Mecca of high technology. In the thirty years after its
founding, engineers who originally worked at Fairchild
Semiconductor started over twenty-five companies that created not only a new industry but a new culture. There were
no coats and ties in these new companies, and no chains of
command. Management was by consensus, and, as in Japan,
the company inculcated its values into the employees. The
culture of Silicon Valley seemed to many observers to symbolize America's future.

By the late 1970s, the well-known problems of the mature
industries of "smokestack" America seemed intractable. But
as these old industries of the East and the Midwest crumpled
and fell in the face of Japanese and other Asian competition,
the companies of Silicon Valley and its clones became the
stars upon which businessmen, politicians, and economists
fixed their hopes. As they had lost out to the Japanese in
industry after industry, Americans had consoled themselves
with the thought that these were, after all, old, dirty indus-

tries plagued by troglodyte management and neanderthal unions, no longer suitable for Americans whose future lay in high technology. Mayors and governors in the Rust Belt of northern industrial states now in decline vied to offer incentives that would spark development of their own Silicon Valleys. Even François Mitterand, the president of France, flew to San Francisco in 1984 and met with Steve Jobs, the twenty-seven-year-old co-founder of Apple Computer, and other entrepreneurs to try to learn how to reinvigorate the French economy.

But the most intent watchers of all were the Japanese. In the year Fairchild was founded, they began to organize to take the lead in electronics, as they had already planned to do in steel and other industries. During the next thirty years, the competition between the American and Japanese semiconductor industries became bitter and intense. The newspaper reports of the offer for Fairchild indicated that the Japanese were winning.

The story was much bigger than Fairchild, however, or even than semiconductors. It encompassed virtually all the high-technology industries. Whether in disk drives, robots, printers, optical fiber electronics, satellite ground stations, or advanced industrial ceramics, the Japanese have come to dominate. New consumer products such as digital audio tape recorders appear first in Japan; and while their longtime drive to overtake the United States in computers has not yet succeeded, many products associated with U.S. companies, such as the IBM and Apple personal computers, are largely composed of parts made in Japan or elsewhere in Asia. Even the U.S. lead in such areas as aircraft and biotechnology is rapidly being whittled away. In a process known as "hollowing," more and more U.S. manufacturers have moved their plants to Asia in order to be able to compete with the Japanese. As a result, U.S. workers in these industries have gradually lost critical skills—even as Japan has pushed its work force to refine its skills. Even more im-

portant, the United States is losing basic leadership in technologies. In a report in 1987, the National Academy of Engineering reviewed the competitive situation in thirty-four
critical areas such as artificial intelligence, optoelectronics,
and systems engineering and control, and concluded Japan
to be superior to the United States in twenty-five of the technologies.[5]

## CRISIS IN WALL STREET

Nor is the problem limited to the manufacturing industries. In the early 1980s, popular myth had it that the United
States was leading the world into the "postindustrial age";
and that, in the future, American competitive strength
would be based on service industries. It was not clear exactly
what this would mean. It was difficult to envision U.S. hair-
dressers giving perms to French ladies, and anyone who has
ever taken a Washington cab or tried to hail an American
waiter must surely have wondered how the United States
thought it was going to be competitive in services. In fact,
the discussion at the time mostly boiled down to financial
services. U.S. financial institutions were deemed to be innovative, aggressive, and internationally minded. The idea was
to unleash their full power and watch the money pile up
without the bother and mess of having to manufacture
something.

The service-industry idyll was blasted in November 1986
when Nomura Securities announced that it had handled, entirely on its own, the placement of a major bond issue for
General Electric Credit Corporation. Nomura was the first
foreign company to do such a thing in the United States.

The report of Nomura's action—buried in the back pages
of the *New York Times*[6]—was just one of several early tremors
indicating a major shift in the tectonic plates of the power
structure of world finance:

- In 1980, a ranking of the world's ten largest banks had included two U.S. banks and one Japanese.[7] In 1986, it included seven for Japan and one for the United States.[8]
- The Sumitomo Bank's purchase of a 15-percent interest in the Wall Street firm of Goldman, Sachs caused a stir of press comment in the summer of 1986. Few people knew, however, that Japanese banks had accumulated over 20 percent of the banking assets in California by acquiring four of its top ten banks.[9] In the following year, a succession of Wall Street houses would announce partial sales of themselves to Japanese financial interests.
- In January 1986, for the first time Japan passed the United States in the share of international banking business held. It was predicted that "the Japanese now are on their way to becoming the world's banker."[10]
- In 1986, Japan's four largest investment banks accounted for virtually none of the trading on the New York Stock Exchange. By the end of 1987, they did nearly 10 percent of the trading, and the volume of Nomura Securities alone was approaching that of the giant Merrill Lynch, the largest U.S. trader.[11]
- In August 1987, four decades after it became the first U.S. bank to provide financing to rebuild Japan's war-torn economy, the ailing Bank of America was rescued by nine Japanese banks, which agreed to rescue it with a $130-million capital infusion. Observers called the agreement a "powerful symbol of Japan's pre-eminence in world financial markets."[12]

The process echoed what had already happened in the manufacturing industries. Just as in those cases, the Japanese had lower capital and personnel costs. While virtually locking foreign interests out of their home market (all the foreign financial institutions in Japan put together did less than 3 percent of the business in 1986 despite having been there for from ten to twenty years),[13] they drove aggressively into foreign markets, making whatever bids were necessary to get the business without regard to short-term profit. It looked like Silicon Valley or Detroit had come to Wall Street. It was music to the ears of the battered American semiconductor and auto executives to hear the investment bankers, who had scorned them for years as incompetent protectionists, talking about a "level playing field."

The picture was the same in the other service industries. For example, by 1987 Japanese construction and engineering companies had gone from nearly zero three years before to close to $2 billion in contracts in the United States, while foreign firms were barred from bidding on Japanese projects.[14]

As Japan came to dominate one industry after another, many commentators blamed American executives, urging them to adopt Japanese management techniques. Quality circles and "just in time" delivery became the watchwords of the day. Of course, these concepts are important, and there is plenty of room for improvement, but poor management is an insufficient explanation. Not only was I in Europe in the early 1970s when American business expanded vigorously there, but I have also managed companies in Japan and have seen Japanese executives up close. While some are excellent, the percentage of outstanding Japanese managers is no greater than what I observed in France, Belgium, or Italy, and certainly not than in the United States.

Management, good or bad, is not an isolated phenomenon but operates in the context of a particular nation. Few, if any, American companies can compete with the Japanese in the areas the latter deem important. The social and industrial structure of Japan have made it an extremely difficult market to penetrate; furthermore, the Japanese government views industrial performance as akin to national security and pours enormous energy into ensuring that its industry is the world leader. By comparison, the United States has been relatively easy to penetrate. Its open society makes for an open market that has welcomed foreign goods and foreign businessmen. Most important, however, the United States does not view industry as a matter of national security as Japan does.

The crux of the situation is that the United States and Japan have fundamentally different understandings of the purposes and workings of a national economy. While the United States embraces Adam Smith, the seventeenth-century prophet of free trade, and has concentrated on consumption as the main economic engine, Japan has focused on production and dominance of key industries that will enhance its strategic position. While the United States has encouraged and written into law adversarial relationships between business and government and labor and management, Japan has striven to achieve cooperation. No doubt there is much that management can and should do, but these conflicting points of view are integral to the history of the United States and Japan, respectively; and it is they—and not the quality of management—that account for the radical shift in the relations between the two countries.

In my view, the easy assumptions and tranquilizing bromides underpinning much American economic and strategic thinking are faulty and have contributed immeasurably to the U.S. decline. Even more important, however, is the issue of fundamental American values. Deeply rooted in the American spirit is the concept of individuality—a concept most completely embodied in the myth of the lone cowboy standing tall, who succeeds without help against long odds by dint of ingenuity, zeal, and determination. It has long been a seductive picture for Americans, but can all too easily develop into an ethic of every man for himself, as in the "me generation" of the 1980s.

During the past forty years, the U.S. businessman has been the cowboy of the world marketplace, rolling back the frontier, laying the trails, marking the water holes, and moving on. The Japanese have been more like our early settlers. As portrayed by the popular media, settlers are seldom glamorous. They dress like hicks, worry a lot, and are never fast on the draw. But in the hundreds they come, and they stick together. Hampered by children and oxen and grandma, they don't travel fast, but they do move inexorably west. By working together. By fixing wagon wheels—together. By raising barns—together. By starting towns—together. Under attack they circle the wagons together and take on all comers. And win.

When Japan conquered mature industries such as textiles,

steel, and autos in the past, the United States told itself they were expendable and, cowboy-like, moved on to a future in high technology and services. But now the Japanese appear to be conquering that future too. The situation faces the United States with questions as crucial as any in its history: if the new, enlightened entrepreneurial culture of Silicon Valley, along with the service industries, cannot compete with Japan and its imitators in the Far East, then what in America can? And if America cannot compete, what is its future economically and geopolitically? And if the future of the United States is in doubt, what of the world that looks to it for leadership? Can or will Japan, or some other nation or nations, assume America's role? Or will the world become a more dangerous place as U.S. power dwindles? Can it be that the notion of individualism, so sacred to the United States, is also its fatal flaw—the basic strength that works against itself to reduce strength? Can the United States somehow regain the ethic of the settlers and revitalize itself? And can it do so without the crisis of war or depression?

## THE CRISIS INTENSIFIES

These questions have been posed in Japan for some time. Among the first to weigh the United States and find it wanting was Naohiro Amaya, the chief Japanese negotiator of the 1981 agreement to limit Japanese automobile exports to the U.S. market. A small, slim man with a pleasant manner, Amaya's disarmingly boyish smile hides a mind that operates with computer speed and has the toughness of carbon fiber. He entered the Ministry of International Trade and Industry (MITI) in the early 1950s and became an architect of Japan's dramatic industrial development. An individualist in a Japanese bureaucracy noted for conformity, he was interested in history and poetry, but his specialty was the future. It was as a negotiator for Japan's surging textile industry in the 1960s that he realized that the United States could not compete with Japan in that industry, and foresaw that the United States would be similarly outpaced in most other areas in the years to come. It was to avoid such a fate for Japan in its competition with Korea, Taiwan, and other developing countries that Amaya became a champion of Japan's thrust into high-technology industries.

By 1980, before the advent of the huge U.S. budget deficits and the overvalued dollar which economists usually pointed to as the cause of U.S. problems, the deteriorating U.S. situation was the subject of formal comment. In its *Vision of MITI Policies in the 1980s*, MITI wrote, "Although the U.S. remains the pre-eminent world power, its relative status is declining."[15] And in the fall of 1981, a report by the Nikko Research Center detected a "growing crisis" in the United States and predicted intensification of tensions between the two countries.[16] When I joined the Department of Commerce that same fall, however, I discovered that what was clear in Tokyo was less so in Washington. The first task was to convince anyone there might be a problem.

Lionel Olmer was the undersecretary of commerce for international trade when I joined the department. Tall and graying, Olmer had the slim wiryness of the marathoner he is, and his T-shirt was often hung to dry in an office window after his morning jog to work. Olmer had spent most of his career in the navy as an intelligence officer, eventually coming into the circles of William Casey, President Reagan's director of the CIA. Upon retirement from the navy, Olmer had joined the Motorola Corporation where with customary indefatigability he undertook the task of attempting to crack Japan's hitherto tightly closed telecommunications market. His Herculean efforts succeeded in making Motorola the first foreign company to sell a significant piece of telecommunications equipment, a pocket pager, to Nippon Telegraph and Telephone (NTT).

In the course of this experience, he had become gravely concerned about the future of the United States and its relationship with Japan. He knew that U.S. national security strategy rested on the assumption of technological superiority, and realized that that advantage was fast disappearing. Thus when Casey asked whether he was interested in joining the Reagan administration, Olmer had volunteered for duty at the Commerce Department in hopes of alerting the nation to the challenge posed by Japan and its imitators. Along with two department economists, William Finan and Frank Vargo, Olmer and I now set out to place the issue high among the administration's priorities.

A bearded old pro, Vargo had been looking at the trade figures with Japan with growing concern for a long time. He knew that Japanese exports to the United States were now twice those of the United States to Japan. Just to hold the trade deficit where it was, then about $10 billion, would require U.S. exports to grow twice as fast as Japanese exports. Nothing in recent history suggested that that was remotely possible. Indeed, the trend was in the other direction. Thus, in 1981, Vargo forecast a $50-billion trade deficit with Japan by 1990.[17] Olmer and I cited Vargo's forecast in several speeches and invited comment from other observers. The reaction was uniform disbelief. Vargo's report was scorned as an alarmist and unsophisticated straight-line projection. Economists at the Council of Economic Advisers said the dollar would weaken against the yen and bring trade into better balance long before the numbers ever got that big.

As part of a study requested by the Cabinet Council on Commerce and Trade, Finan, who is both an electrical engineer and an economist, wrote an extensive economic analysis in 1982 showing that the ability of U.S. high-technology industries to compete had declined across the board and would continue to do so regardless of management performance unless U.S. policy was changed.[18] In November 1982, to dramatize the issue and to learn as much as possible, Olmer, Finan, and I traveled to Japan and visited many of its high-technology companies.

We started at the central laboratories of Nippon Electric Company (NEC) where the director, a former employee of

Bell Laboratories, gave us the tour. His intense pride in his facilities and people was evident and clearly well justified. During lunch he accidentally gave us an insight into a key element in Japan's success when he casually mentioned that he is on the phone three or four times a week with officials of the Japanese government. This statement raised our eyebrows because the head of Bell Laboratories does not call the Commerce Department three or four times a week—and, in fact, rarely calls there. It was obvious to us, however, that this NEC director could not operate without calling officials as a matter of course.

We visited the Yamazaki Machine Tool Company in Nagoya, where the night shift required only one supervisor as robots whiled away the hours assembling other robots. Despite being the object at that time of an unfair trade complaint by U.S. machine tool manufacturers, Teruyuki Yamazaki was a gracious host. His family-run company has grown in his lifetime from humble origins to become a major player in the world market for flexible manufacturing systems. His boardroom, looking like something from Star Trek, provided a modern contrast to our luncheon surroundings, which was a replica of a rustic Japanese farmhouse that had been constructed adjacent to the plant.* We were impressed with Yamazaki and his company. He was a tough, capable entrepreneur, and his people were first rate. They probably would have been successful anywhere, but the company had certainly prospered in part because of a series of government actions aimed at promoting Japan's machine tool industry.

We went on to the Kyocera Corporation, whose story matched any of Silicon Valley's. Begun on a shoestring by Kazuo Inamori, a young entrepreneur with a vision of a new industrial ceramics industry, the company struggled through difficult early circumstances and now dominates the world market for ceramic packaging for semiconductors. The object of our attention was the car with the all-ceramic engine that

---

*One of the nicest things about Yamazaki was his cars. They were all Rolls Royces. No problem with a "buy Japan" mentality there.

Kyocera had built as a test model. First conceived by a British scientist, the ceramic engine could revolutionize the automobile industry by doing away with the need for cooling. Kyocera had developed the car with the aid of a government grant and was now offering test drives. In truth it did not drive very well, but it did demonstrate feasibility. We learned other interesting things while at Kyocera. For example, we were told that during the oil crisis of 1979, Kyocera's company union had actually suggested a wage freeze to management in order to preserve competitive capability. We also learned that most of the women on the production line were so-called part-timers who worked thirty-eight hours per week. "Part-time" simply meant they did not receive company benefits or lifetime employment considerations.

Olmer, Finan, and I left Japan even more impressed with its high technology and more concerned for the future of American industry than when we had arrived. The dynamism of Japanese management, the cooperative and flexible attitude of labor, and the supportive role of the government all appeared to be formidable aspects of Japan's success.

In presenting our views to President Reagan and the cabinet in December 1982, Olmer stressed that the military, political, and economic power that gave the United States its unique leadership position depended on its pre-eminence in advanced technology. He emphasized that high-technology industries contribute disproportionately to economic well-being because of their rapid growth and contributions to increases in productivity. He explained that by every measure the United States was losing ground and was likely to continue to do so unless new policies were developed. Reviewing Japan's success and noting particularly the important role played by the Japanese government in targeting development of certain industries, he urged that the U.S. government review its trade and economic policies with a view toward halting the erosion of the leadership position of its high-technology industries.

After Olmer concluded, there were at first only a few questions of a desultory nature. Many cabinet members seemed not to have read their briefing papers in preparation for the meeting. Then David Stockman, director of the Office of Management and Budget (OMB), presented the arguments against Olmer's suggestions. He said that the loss of relative position was only to be expected as other countries developed. One of his pet projects had been to try to close the Export-Import Bank, which finances important American exports, including its largest export item—commercial airliners. A subsidy to big business, he called the bank. He now rejected any suggestion of reacting to foreign industrial policies or of taking any measures to support our own industries.

While Secretary of Commerce Baldrige attempted a rebuttal, the economists present agreed with Stockman. But the argument didn't really matter. For a glance at the President revealed that he was not very interested: at times he appeared to doze off as the discussion droned on. The meeting broke up inconclusively, as did similar subsequent gatherings.

As time passed, the Commerce Department predictions all came true. Indeed, it became clear that we had erred only in being too cautious. Spurred by the folly of huge budget deficits combined with the lowest rate of savings in U.S. history and a soaring dollar, the already chronic and rising trade deficit with Japan hit $50 billion in 1985, five years ahead of schedule. In 1982, Baldrige had pleaded with the cabinet to prevent the dollar from soaring too high. Then he had been rebuked as Undersecretary of the Treasury Beryl Sprinkel asked rhetorically, "Who says the dollar is too high?" and Secretary of the Treasury Donald Regan boasted that the dollar would be strong to the end of the decade because it reflected the strength of the U.S. economy.

By September 1985, however, both the overall trade deficit and that with Japan had become so large that the Treasury was forced to reverse itself: it took steps to drive the dollar down in an attempt to staunch the flood of imports by making them more expensive while stimulating exports by reducing their prices in foreign currencies.

Economists were virtually unanimous in predicting that the trade deficit would begin to shrink if the United States could just get the dollar down from around 245 yen to the dollar to 200 to the dollar. But the flaws in the assumptions behind these predictions were soon demonstrated by events. Within a year the dollar was at 200 yen, but the deficit only continued to grow, while economists opined that 180 was really the most desirable level. By December 1987, the dollar at 133 yen had lost nearly 50 percent of its value, but the trade deficit was higher than ever and continued to grow.

By now foreign penetration of U.S. markets was so extensive that the United States just did not make a lot of products any more, so the price was not very important. If, for example, one wanted to buy a VCR, it had to be an import regardless of price. Moreover, to offset the strong yen, Japanese exporters actually cut their overall export prices by 20 percent.[19] In desperation, economists who had predicted that a 200-yen dollar would solve the trade problem were now calling for yet more devaluation, to 120 yen or even to 100 yen. But there lay a subtle trap. If the dollar fell faster than the amount of imports, the trade deficit would continue to rise even as the physical amount of imports declined. Moreover, it was assumed that a cheaper dollar would spur U.S. exports. It did to some extent. But hardly at all to Japan, the nation with which we had the biggest deficit. Finally, by December 1987, some economists began to question whether devaluation could save us. It had not in the past worked either for us or for others such as Great Britain, they noted.[20] In effect, it seemed that we were impoverishing ourselves to achieve what Perry thought he had accomplished over a century ago—the opening of Japan.

While the weak dollar did not significantly increase U.S. exports to Japan, it did lead to sales of assets. America was now cheap, and foreign investment poured into real estate as well as into high-tech and financial companies from Bos ton to Houston to Los Angeles. While this investment was generally welcomed as a source of new jobs and new capital for the U.S. economy, there was evidence that some foreign companies were already using the threat of takeovers to muscle U.S. high-tech companies into unwanted joint ventures and transfer of technology. To some observers the trade and investment patterns of the United States were beginning to look like those of an underdeveloped country.

As time passed, Americans became poorer. Despite all of the hoopla about the great American job machine, statistics on real family income showed that living standards in the United States were not rising. Real wages in 1986 were at the same level as in 1973, having dropped from the high point of 1977. Family income had stayed about the same, but only by dint of more family members going to work. The job machine seemed to be substituting labor for capital in the classic pattern of underdevelopment. By comparison, Japan was doing the opposite, investing nearly twice as much per capita as the United States. In April 1987, *Business Week* carried a special twenty-two-page report on America's economic dilemma. Stating that the standard of living in the United States had "hit the wall," the report asked the inevitable question: "Is the American dream about to end?"[21] In its issue of 16 November 1987, a month after the crash, the magazine answered its own question. In an article entitled "Say Hello to the Lean Years," it noted that U.S. living standards might drop by as much as 7 percent before the end of the century.[22]

But rapidly accumulating debt was an even more sobering phenomenon. By 1987, the proud U.S. Treasury was totally dependent on Japan. Huge budget deficits had to be funded by selling more government bonds. And because of their high rate of savings and enormous trade surpluses, the people with the money to buy were the Japanese. One question was whispered nervously in the halls of the Treasury Department before each bond auction: "Are the Japanese still in the market?" For if they were not, either interest rates or inflation would soar with unknown consequences for the world economy. This phenomenon was noted by Richard Koo, a senior economist with Nomura Securities. Pointing out in September 1987 that U.S. interest rates were up significantly as the result of Japanese reluctance to continue buying, he said, "Think of that jump as tuition for America. Now you have learned how dependent you are on foreign capital."[23] And the growing dependency compounded the problem of the trade deficit. *Business Week* estimated that U.S. foreign debt could reach $1 trillion in the early 1990s, and the interest payments on that could more than offset any export increase or import decrease arising from a devalued dollar.[24]

Finally, there was the matter of national security. The opposition to the sale of Fairchild Semiconductor to Fujitsu was the result of a growing disquiet over the loss of U.S. technological pre-eminence predicted by Finan and Olmer five years before. By 1984, various studies had concluded that the Pentagon was becoming dependent on foreign suppliers in a way that made it increasingly vulnerable not only to supply interruptions, but, more basically, to a withering of technological capability in the United States.

This fear became reality in 1984–85 for the Cray Research corporation, the developer and largest manufacturer of supercomputers, which are used in a variety of essential national security areas, ranging from code breaking by the National Security Agency to aircraft and missile design by the defense industry. Cray accounts for a large percentage of all supercomputer installations, but depends on Japanese suppliers for critical semiconductor components. These suppliers have recently also become Cray's biggest competitors as a result of a decision by the Japanese government and manufacturers to focus on development of supercomputers. In one instance, a major Japanese supplier delayed delivery to Cray of certain new kinds of components that Cray had actually designed, thus giving its own computer group a one-year lead time in designing them into its own machines.

In response, Cray began a special project with Fairchild Semiconductor in an attempt to develop a domestic supplier. Fujitsu's proposed acquisition of Fairchild was thus an unpleasant surprise to Cray. Aside from the problem of technology dependence, however, is the simple fact that the declining U.S. economy can no longer support a huge military machine and at the same time compete with Japan, while the latter bears few of the burdens of world leadership.

## The Real Challenge to American Power

In 1857, when the competition between Japan and the United States began, the shogun's adviser, Masayoshi Hotta, observed:

> I am therefore convinced that our policy should be to stake everything on the present opportunity, to conclude friendly alliances, to send ships to foreign countries everywhere and conduct trade, to copy the foreigners where they are at their best and so repair our own shortcomings, to foster our national strength and complete our armaments, and so gradually subject the foreigners to our influence until in the end all the countries of the world know the blessings of perfect tranquillity and our hegemony is acknowledged throughout the globe.[25]

Hegemony. Power. These are what ultimately concern nations and determine the circumstances of the lives of their citizens—as the United States recognizes when it commits vast amounts of money and energy to maintain its power in the face of the Soviet challenge. But the United States has seemed to understand power and hegemony only in military and political terms, and has failed to note—as Hotta did over a century ago—that they can have economic dimensions as well.

Today the real challenge to American power is not the sin-

ister one from the Eastern bloc, but the friendly one from the
Far East. U.S. industry is not withering in the face of Soviet
competition and the Soviets are not sending shivers through
our financial markets. Of course, the Soviets cannot be ignored—and we have not ignored them. We have developed
technology and industry and strategies to counter them. Far
from misperceiving the nature of the Soviet Union, we deal
with it in many ways and at many levels, sometimes successfully and sometimes not, but always with a view to how
our interaction will affect our power and our ability to continue to lead the free world.

To the friendly challenge from the East, however, our response has been quite different. We have gone to great
lengths—sometimes even hurt our industry's competitive
strength—to prevent the Soviets from obtaining even outdated semiconductor or machine tool or other technology.
But when these U.S. industries have faltered in the face of
Japanese competition fostered by Japanese government policies aimed at achieving industrial leadership, our government leaders have agonized over what to do. They have
hesitated to enforce U.S. trade laws even in cases of clear
violation. Ultimately, as in the case of the objection to Fujitsu's bid for Fairchild Semiconductor, the United States has
sometimes acted to preserve what it perceived as a critical
capability. Often, however, the actions have appeared irrational because they have been taken without a broad plan, and
have thus exacerbated many situations, because the United
States has appeared vindictive to no effective purpose.

The problem is not confined to any one administration. An
unwillingness to take effective action has characterized all
the postwar administrations. Each has been unable or unwilling to recognize the contradiction between their assumptions about both economics and the nature of Japan, on the
one hand, and the demands of world power, on the other.
Power demands capabilities in certain industries and certain
key technologies. But the formulators of economic equations
in this country have assumed that the only purpose of the

economy is to satisfy consumer needs, and that the best way to do that is to minimize government intervention in the free market. Thus, we respond to the Soviets because defending against a military threat is seen as a legitimate government role, but have difficulty responding to Japan's challenge because the steps required to do so appear to conflict with the requirements of an efficient economy. In dealing with Japan, the U.S. government has always seemed to fear that we would diminish our overall economic power if we intervened in a strategic component of it. The difficulties are only compounded by our obliviousness to the very different assumptions that guide Japan.

As accelerating decline has worsened the dilemma of the conflicting demands of its economic doctrine and its role as world leader, the United States has sought to negotiate for change within Japan. But lacking strategic economic goals, the United States has insisted on a general opening of all Japanese markets, without concern for any particular market or any specific result. This demand has led to a series of uncoordinated and endlessly multiplying negotiations over a grab bag of complaints about Japan. For example, the Japanese considered American baseball bats unsafe, and each one had to be physically inspected before entering Japan. The new Osaka airport authority effectively banned bidding by American engineering firms. Japan strictly limited the sale of American tobacco and even banned the importation of bull semen. Some of these issues were important and some were not. But in all cases the United States was fighting practices, attitudes, and policies that are deeply embedded in the fabric of Japanese life. Negotiations over them have inevitably resulted in bitter haggling which increasingly poisons what Mike Mansfield, ambassador to Japan since 1977, never tires of calling "America's most important bilateral relationship bar none."

The Japanese have become particularly frustrated because they know, even if U.S. businessmen and government officials do not, that the issues raised by the latter are not at the heart of the matter. Thus, the Japanese have grown ever more resentful at being harassed on secondary issues by those whom they likely see as very stupid U.S. negotiators. As resentment in Japan has intensified, so has frustration in the United States, making for a vicious circle in which U.S. demands lead to Japanese resentment, further frustrating the United States, and, hence, further angering the Japanese.

The American attitude is based on a fiction that grows out of a critical misunderstanding about the nature of Japanese society and economic thinking. In dealing with Japan, U.S. policy assumes that the Japanese economy responds more or less in the same way and to the same stimuli as the U.S. economy. We assume also that Japan's economic policy has the same consumer-oriented objectives as that of the United States—an assumption we have a large stake in. Japan was the protégé of the United States, our showcase success story. To doubt that Japan is like the United States is to suggest that the policies of the past forty years have been inadequate.

In addition, U.S. policy makers have not understood the concept of industrial structure strategy. American national security strategy is narrowly and militarily oriented, focused on how many carriers, planes, and missiles we have. The U.S. government has not attempted to change the structure of a whole industry to achieve the strategic power that domination in that industry would confer. While we are prepared to use the economy as a tool of power by imposing trade sanctions on the Soviet Union or South Africa to respond to specific undesirable policies, we would consider it inefficient and improper government intervention consciously to build the economy to sustain or extend U.S. power. The Japanese did not and do not share the American view. To them, promotion of key industries is not economically harmful but is, on the contrary, necessary to ensure the future prosperity of the nation, which they see as inextricably linked to its power.

Thus, as a result of policies based on false assumptions and ignorance, the power of the United States and the quality of American life is diminishing rapidly in every respect. It is these false assumptions and the policies arising from them that are the real challenge to America; and it is they that I set out to examine in this book. I begin with the vital semiconductor industry which the United States has, while asleep, nearly allowed the Japanese to spirit away quietly in the night (see chapter 2). Since it is far from my intention, however, to "bash" Japan, I turn, in part II, to the elements in their culture, history, and traditions that drive the Japanese to resist foreign penetration of their own market, while relentlessly pursuing markets abroad, as the natural course in their scheme of things: natural in respect to their governmental bureaucracy, to their industrial policies, and to the way companies operate in Japan. After observing what makes Japan run, I return in part III to the United States in an effort to show how our most basic ideal—the individual —is, while the source of great strengths, also the source of the winding down of this country as a world power. Because of our lack of cohesion, the nature of business and its relation to government is very different in the United States; and even our best companies find it very difficult to compete with Japan, as exemplified by the experience of the Motorola company (see chapter 7). Further, we misunderstand the relationship between economic and national security, as exemplified by the fate of the crucial machine tool industry (see chapter 8). Of immense importance in the conduct of trade and negotiations with other nations are the U.S. Congress and the various organs of government, with their various interests, that contribute to our policy. After discussing these, I trace, in part III, a series of negotiations in which I played a part between 1981 and 1987, to show how, despite endless discussion, tensions between the two countries have worsened as, increasingly and inevitably, the United States and Japan are caught within the vision each has of the other as well of its own role in the world and toward its own people.

The future is upon us. And this future is very different from, and much less secure and prosperous than, anything envisioned in our fond and long-held expectations, both for ourselves and others. It calls into question, for example, our ability not only to lead the free world but also to play our historic role as haven for the world's weary and huddled masses yearning to breathe free. If we are to change the situation, halt our decline, and preserve the hope of the American dream for our children and, indeed, for the world, we must re-examine our assumptions and our priorities. This is a necessity not only for ourselves but for the victorious Japanese: they, too, need to open their eyes to drawbacks to themselves and others of their own system, so that they as well as we can be full and equal partners in a new and better world. This, then, is the thrust of part IV and my conclusion to the book.

When I visited Japan in the fall of 1986 and again in the summer of 1987, I found an increasingly resentful public and worried leaders. Among the Japanese I talked with were three important contributors to Japan's postwar success: Naohiro Amaya, of whom I have spoken; Akio Morita, chairman of the Sony Corporation, who is well-known in the West; and Keichi Konaga, a former vice minister of the Ministry of International Trade and Industry, one of the most powerful positions in Japan, and also a former assistant to and ghost writer for Kakuei Tanaka, Japan's most powerful postwar prime minister. All three men expressed pride in Japan's accomplishments, and appeared also to be proud of their own contributions, although they were too polite to say so. They were, at the same time, subdued and worried. Their goals had been to strengthen Japan, not to weaken the United States, for which they had respect and affection. Yet it seemed that the more Japan succeeded, the more the United States failed. They did not apologize for trying to make Japan rich and strong: that was their duty, and expected of the leaders of any country. They clearly saw the contradictions and failures of American policies, and they could not understand why the United States allowed itself to continue to decline. They shared my concern that, as U.S. power continued to diminish, the relationship between the two countries would become even more strained.

These Japanese leaders quite openly said that Japan could not and did not want to replace the United States as leader of the free world. Indeed, Amaya emphasized that there is no alternative to a strong United States, and talked about ways Japan could reinvigorate the United States. Morita wondered whether the United States knew that it was throwing away its industry, and whether it understood the consequences of that carelessness. It was a question of Konaga's, however, that struck me the most forcefully, a question he addressed to the United States: "Why don't you wake up?"

# 2

# LOSING THE CHIPS: THE SEMICONDUCTOR INDUSTRY

Leadership in commercial volume production is being lost by the U.S. semiconductor industry. U.S. defense will soon depend on foreign sources for state of the art technology in semiconductors. This is an unacceptable situation.
—NORMAN AUGUSTINE, 11 February 1987

VARIOUSLY called the rice of the electronic age and the crude oil of the twenty-first century, semiconductors are the fundamental building blocks of modern electronics. These small, rectangular "chips" of the element silicon—each one the size of a fingernail and crammed with microscopic circuits capable of storing and processing enormous amounts of information—operate products ranging from digital watches and videocassette recorders to supercomputers and the telephone network, and recently have even become essential parts of children's toys and washing machines. In addition, they are essential to advanced weapons systems. On the list of strategic industries, the semiconductor industry is near the top.

Shortly after the Fujitsu bid for Fairchild Semiconductor, Norman Augustine, chairman of both the semiconductor task force of the Defense Science Board and the Martin Marietta Corporation, reported to Secretary of Defense Caspar Weinberger and confirmed what the bid had seemed to symbolize.[1] Augustine stated bluntly the central dilemma facing the United States: The U.S. semiconductor industry was rapidly going the way of the television and automobile industries as it staggered under relentless pressure from Japan (see figure 2.1). Under present circumstances, this industry cannot compete with the Japanese in commercial markets.

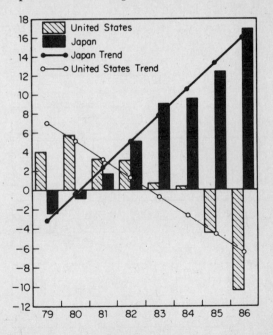

FIGURE 2.1
*Cumulative Change in World Semiconductor Market Share
Since 1978
(Percentage points)*
SOURCE: Semiconductor Industry Association

This situation has enormous national security implications: twenty-one absolutely critical U.S. military systems contain chips available only from foreign, mainly Japanese, sources. More important, development momentum is also with the Japanese. Of twenty-five key semiconductor technologies, the Japanese lead in twelve, are equal with the United States in eight, and are closing the gap in five.

Moreover, the Japanese are displacing not only the U.S. semiconductor industry but also the critically important equipment and materials manufacturers who supply it. Because advances in semiconductor technology are closely linked to equipment and materials capabilities, the decline of these suppliers means that the United States is not only suffering production losses (see figure 2.2); it is actually losing the ability to stay at the leading edge and is becoming de-

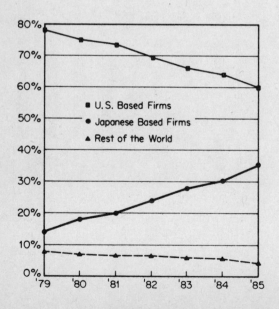

FIGURE 2.2
*Semiconductor Manufacturing Equipment World Market Share*
*(Percentage of world shipments)*
SOURCE: Semiconductor Industry Association

pendent on Japan for the technology critical for its entire defense strategy.

The story of how the semiconductor industry, invented in the United States and symbol of its dynamism, passed from being the epitome of the country's future to an industry in distress is both a paradigm of the rise of Japan and the decline of the United States and one of the great dramas of the latter half of the twentieth century. What follows is a behind-the-scenes look at that drama which unfolded largely unnoticed for nearly forty years until Augustine's report.

## Early Days of the Semiconductor Industry

### THE INVENTION OF THE TRANSISTOR

The story began in 1948, when three American scientists at AT&T's Bell Laboratories—John Bardeen, Walter Brattain, and William Shockley—invented the transistor. Until then vacuum tubes that amplified and switched electronic signals had been the backbone of the telephone system as well as of radios and other electronic equipment. The first computer, the ENIAC (electronic numerical integrator and computer) which was completed in 1946 at the University of Pennsylvania, ran on 18,800 vacuum tubes; and when it was running, room temperatures reached 120 degrees. The size of a house, the ENIAC spent more time under repair than in operation. The vacuum tube was bulky and burned out rather quickly. As the telephone network expanded and the world entered the age of computing, the size and unreliability of the tubes became a limiting factor. It was to overcome this problem that Bell Labs had put together the team that produced the transistor, the first semiconductor device.

A hundred times smaller and requiring only a fraction of

the power needed by a tube, the transistor initiated the electronic revolution, facilitating expansion of the telephone network and manufacture of products heretofore impossible—such as portable hearing aids and small portable radios. Of particular importance in spreading the revolution was the licensing policy of AT&T which, as a regulated monopoly under U.S. antitrust law, made its inventions available to all comers, foreign as well as domestic.* Among the first licensees was Japan's Sony Corporation. It could hardly believe that AT&T would make this seminal technology available to a foreign company. Certainly Japan's NTT would not have done so at the time. Indeed, this policy was unique among nations, and led to rapid dissemination of AT&T's transistor technology which became the basis for development of both the U.S. and the Japanese semiconductor industries. The competition between the two may be said to have begun in 1956 when the technology began to move out of the laboratory, and commercial semiconductor industries were founded on both sides of the Pacific.

## THE INDUSTRY IN THE UNITED STATES

In 1956, after receiving the Nobel Prize for Physics along with his two colleagues, Shockley returned to his boyhood home of Palo Alto, California, and established the Shockley Semiconductor Laboratory, not far from where the original three-element vacuum tube had been invented by Lee de Forest in 1906. Determined to build the world's leading semiconductor company, he recruited the brightest young physicists, chemists, and engineers he could find—among them, Robert Noyce.

The son of a Congregational minister, Noyce had grown up in Grinnell, Iowa, where he had imbibed the spirit of its

---

*Had deregulation been in effect at the time, AT&T would probably not have licensed this technology and would probably be the world's dominant semiconductor producer today, as well as perhaps the leading computer manufacturer.

founder, Josiah Grinnell. It was to Grinnell, a young Congregational clergyman who had been dismissed by his southern congregation for antislavery views, that, in 1854, Horace Greeley gave the immortal advice: "Go west, young man, go west." Grinnell did go west, bought five thousand acres of land in Iowa, and set about creating the ideal Congregational community. While the strictures of this new town were rigorous—only those who agreed to abstain from alcohol in perpetuity could buy lots—the fact that all saw themselves as engaged in the Lord's work gave rise to an austere but warm egalitarianism that eschewed concern with rank and status.

Noyce had majored in physics at Grinnell College where he had had the luck to study under Grant Gale. In the summer of 1948, upon learning that his former college roommate, John Bardeen, and two other men had invented the transistor, Gale immediately wrote to his friend and quickly received two of the earliest transistors, which enabled him to offer the first course in solid state physics in the world during Noyce's senior year.

After receiving a doctorate at MIT and spending an unhappy year working on semiconductors at the Philco Company in Philadelphia, Noyce, too, went west—to Palo Alto and Shockley's laboratory. Characteristically, his first step upon arriving in the San Francisco Bay area was to buy a house, after which he went to discuss his new job with Shockley. The new company was exciting, but disagreement soon arose over the direction of research; and in 1957, seven of Shockley's young charges, not including Noyce, took a step that would become familiar in the valley in the years to come. They met with an investment banker to discuss starting their own company. It was this group that Arthur Rock introduced to the Fairchild Camera and Instrument Company, and that became the founding nucleus of the Fairchild Semiconductor Company after prevailing upon Noyce to join as a kind of coordinator because of his natural leadership qualities.

Thus began Silicon Valley. With Noyce as the moving spirit, Fairchild not only pioneered semiconductor development but also gave definition to a new business culture, whose essence was an austere, egalitarian individualism. Informality characterized the new approach as the titles and status symbols of conventional business were de-emphasized in favor of consensus management and decision making based on expertise instead of rank. An effort was made to give everyone a stake in the business, and individual workers were expected to take responsibility without waiting for direction. The engineers attracted to this style were a new breed. They worked like demons, first for others, later for themselves. Within the first few years, several found venture money and left Fairchild to found their own firms, always taking the new culture with them. There was no stigma attached to such moves; indeed, they were applauded. These were heady times: the rewards went to the aggressive, the entrepreneurs, those latter-day cowboys who were marking new trails to the future.

The action was not limited to Silicon Valley. In Chicago, Motorola's founder and his son—Paul and Robert Galvin— risked the company's future by investing heavily in a new semiconductor facility in Phoenix; and in Texas, a small company called Texas Instruments was already on the trail of major breakthroughs. Large corporations such as General Electric, RCA, and IBM were also active, with the result that by 1960 over one hundred companies were plunging into the new market which had a total value of only a few million dollars. There were no guarantees as these companies took huge risks based on the hope of a long-term reward. Many expected the giants to dominate, but their elaborate investment analyses and corporate caution often led to hesitation that opened opportunities for the small and the swift.

The entrepreneurs focused on new and increasingly sophisticated technology. In 1959, Noyce and Jack Kilby of Texas Instruments invented the integrated circuit almost simultaneously, by combining several discrete components into a complete circuit on a single wafer. This introduced the second electronic revolution, which led to a host of new products, such as the hand-held calculator, and a host of new companies to make them. NASA chose Noyce's chips for the Apollo moon rocket, and total industry sales grew rapidly to over $100 million by 1969. Noyce himself left Fairchild in 1968 to found the Intel Corporation. With no chain of command and with regular corporate culture sessions, at which attendance was mandatory, even for Noyce, the company based its phenomenal success on another revolutionary device: the dynamic random access memory known as DRAM or D-RAM, or often simply as RAM, the term I shall use here. This keystone product—capable of storing about 1,000 bits (1K) of information accessible from the outside, much as a single telephone in a network can be reached by dialing—became the memory bank for all electronic products and established fundamental technological directions for the next two decades, dramatically increasing computing power and reducing costs.

Then, in 1971, Intel's Ted Hoff invented another revolutionary device: the microprocessor, or computer on a chip, which put all the power of a room-sized machine on a sliver of silicon the size of a postage stamp. This was followed in 1973 by Intel's new generation 4K RAM (RAM capacity always increases in multiples of four) which could store 4,000 bits of information in a space about the same size as that of the older 1K device. Then in 1975 the 4K chip gave way to the 16K RAM as the Mostek Corporation took the lead, to be quickly followed by Intel, Motorola, Texas Instruments, and other companies.

During this time, the Americans virtually had the field to themselves. The Europeans maintained a small presence; and the Japanese, who were way behind, moved to protect their markets from the superior and less expensive U.S. products. Few in the United States seemed to care. After all, the United States was by far the biggest market, and its companies were dominant by virtue of their incredible innovativeness, which produced a never ending stream of revolutionary products. It seemed that no foreign competitor could touch them, and their culture and management style were hailed as the wave of the future.

The role of the U.S. government was important but not central. It had nothing to do with any of the inventions and did not participate in the creation of any of the companies. During the 1960s, it did fund the NASA moonshot and the Minuteman missile programs, both of which created important markets for the new chips and spurred research and development and expansion of an already expanding industry. However, the U.S. government did not concern itself with the structure of the industry, with who did or did not get venture money, with who could or could not expand production, or with any special tax or financial measures aimed at especially promoting this industry. Moreover, it did not protect U.S. companies from foreign competition. And when the government's major projects began to wind down, so did the level of its procurement and funding and its interest in the industry's capabilities.

No one in Silicon Valley would have considered consulting the government about strategic business questions; and, if asked, U.S. government officials would have been flabbergasted and unable to respond. Neither side saw that kind of advice giving as the proper role of government in a free-market economy.

THE INDUSTRY IN JAPAN

While Noyce and his partners were laboring in an open room to etch the first circuits in silicon of their new venture, a different kind of entrepreneur was busy on the other side of the Pacific. In Tokyo the rooms were also open and without dividers, but there the similarity ended. Japan's Ministry of International Trade and Industry (MITI) officials were trained in law, not engineering; and their tools were pens rather than micrometers as they worked to enact the Extraordinary Measures Law for Promotion of the Electronics Industry.

In 1957, Japan's electronics industry was growing, but it was weak compared with that in the United States—a discrepancy MITI had decided to change. The new law signaled to the nation that the electronics industry was to be the object of a major national effort to catch up to the United States. Under the law, MITI, in consultation with industry, was directed to select products and projects in research and development for special promotion, to set production, quantity, and cost targets, and to ensure adequate funding of the programs both by providing subsidies and by directing bank lending activities—everything, in short, that U.S. companies did on their own. The law also authorized the creation of cartels in cases deemed useful by MITI and established, under the control of MITI, an Electronics Industry Deliberation Council consisting of representatives of industry, academia, and the press, to develop plans and provide coordination.[2]

The development of the electronics industry in Japan was not to be simply a matter of private enterprises seeking profitable new fields. That element existed too, but the Japanese government had decided that the electronics industry was too important to be left only to businessmen. The Extraordinary Measures Law made development a community effort with MITI leading the Japanese wagon train to settle a new industrial territory.

# The Competition between the United States and Japan

## THE JAPANESE TAKE ON IBM

Initially, computers received more attention than semiconductors. In 1959, as Noyce and Kilby drew their first integrated circuits, IBM introduced its second-generation 1401 computer, and it became painfully obvious to the Japanese that IBM was far ahead of their own computer makers. Obsessed by the fear of foreign domination, the new Deliberation Council declared that Japan's top priority must be to build a world-class domestic computer industry, and IBM became the target.

The council's decision was momentous. In 1959, Japan's electronics products were less advanced, of poorer quality, and more expensive than their American counterparts. According to Western economic theories, Japan should have imported these products while producing others that were more competitive. Thus, in targeting IBM, Japan was implicitly rejecting Western theories. Japan was saying that the short-term benefits to consumers of buying better, less expensive American computers were outweighed by the long-term national interest of having a strong domestic industry. Further, it was betting it could come from behind and create a competitive advantage despite having few of the resources considered necessary. This policy was later called "picking winners and losers" by U.S. experts who said it could not be done effectively. The Japanese explained, however, that the market had already picked the winning industries; they just wanted to be sure that Japan rode with the winners.

Behind this thinking lay Japan's strong desire to maintain its autonomy and homogeneity. It believed it could not survive as a nation if foreign companies took large shares of its markets. The decision to target IBM was thus seen as a matter of national security. The result was an effort that can be compared in many ways to the U.S. Apollo program. Like it, the Japanese project centered on a few large companies chosen by the government, and led to development of the same broad consensus in support of the effort and the same sense of national purpose. Americans later complained of a "Buy Japanese" mentality, but just as we would not have used Russian rockets to go to the moon, so the Japanese wanted to use their own computers and parts. Indeed, in 1987, when U.S. rockets and space shuttles were grounded by mishaps, the U.S. government moved to prevent U.S. companies from using Russian rockets to launch their satellites. This was not very different from Japan's actions regarding semiconductors and computers.

MITI's first step against IBM was to raise computer tariffs. When IBM tried to get around them in 1960 by manufacturing in Japan, MITI refused to permit such production until IBM agreed to license its basic patents to fifteen Japanese companies. In addition, because Shigeru Sahashi, then head of MITI's Heavy Industry Bureau and one of the key architects of Japan's postwar industrial policies, said he would appreciate it if the IBM "elephant" would avoid trampling the Japanese "mosquitoes,"[3] IBM had to agree to follow MITI's guidelines on both the type and the number of machines it could produce in Japan and to obtain MITI's approval each time it wished to introduce a new model. A high IBM–Japan official indicated to me recently that this agreement continued in effect at least until 1979, allowing MITI to control to some extent IBM's market share. IBM had no choice if it wished to do business in Japan.

Texas Instruments got the same treatment in the early 1960s when, as the world's largest semiconductor manufacturer, it applied for permission to begin production in Japan. Negotiations stalled until TI discovered that several Japanese companies were infringing on its patents, and threatened a suit to bar their goods from the U.S. market. In return for licensing its patents, the company was then permitted to manufacture in Japan, but with the proviso that it would take no more than 10 percent of the Japanese market.[4] Other companies such as Motorola that did not have the strong patent position of Texas Instruments continued to be excluded.

While handcuffing the foreigners, the Japanese government, which controlled bank lending, allocated Japan's then-scarce capital to the companies it had chosen as its champions in the computer race—Hitachi, Toshiba, Fujitsu, Nippon Electric Company, Mitsubishi Electric, and Oki Electric. It also provided various tax incentives for them and established the Japan Electronic Computer Corporation as a government-backed leasing company which, by buying computers as soon as they were produced, provided fast cash while at the same time preventing price wars. Finally, the government pressured users to "buy Japanese." One currently high-ranking MITI official was well known in those days for throwing import license applications into the wastebasket. Another official acknowledges that computer importers were always asked, "Why do you have to use a foreign computer?"[5]

That these efforts worked was affirmed in an interview in September 1982 with Taiyu Kobayashi, the chairman of Fujitsu, in the respected Japanese magazine *Bungei Shunju*. Agreeing that the Japanese computer industry could not have succeeded without government help, he explained, "Before we even knew whether they'd run or not, MITI was there helping us out by getting after the automakers and steel companies to start using domestic computers."[6]

## THE RACE FOR THE 64K RAM

In the early 1970s, two events turned the computer war into a semiconductor war. IBM introduced its third-generation 370 computer. Based on the new RAM memory chips, it shocked the Japanese who were still trying to catch up with IBM's second-generation machines. Then during negotiations for the reversion of Okinawa,* Japan agreed, in 1972, to begin removing the formal restrictions on foreign access to its electronics markets. Although these had been in violation of the rules of the General Agreement of Tariffs and Trade (GATT, the treaty and organization that governs most free world trade), the United States—confident of its over-

---

*Having wrested this island of the homeland from the Japanese at great cost in 1945, the United States had continued to occupy and administer it even after the end of the Occupation of the rest of Japan.

whelming economic strength—had not protested. Now the United States was facing mounting trade deficits with Japan and pressed it to open its markets in return for Okinawa.

The Japanese reaction to these events revealed the chasm that separates their thinking from U.S. economic views. There was no talk about the benefits to consumers of free trade. On the contrary, the Japanese press likened the prospective influx of foreign goods and investment to the arrival of Commodore Perry. Motorola's announcement of its desire to put a plant in Japan was seen as the cause of "mounting tension,"[7] and Texas Instruments was said to pose a "major threat" to local industry.[8] Most Japanese saw opening the market as a major concession, a sacrifice that Japan would have to endure for the sake of getting Okinawa back and keeping their U.S. protectors happy.

Under pressure from its industry which demanded continued protection, MITI managed to stretch the market opening out over three years until the end of 1975, and used this time to organize what it called countermeasures to the liberalization. Now the target became the U.S. semiconductor industry. Realizing that the new RAM chips in IBM's latest machines were the key to computer superiority, MITI moved to strengthen its semiconductor industry which at this time lagged far behind the U.S. firms. Along with the government-owned telephone monopoly Nippon Telegraph and Telephone (NTT), MITI organized the major computer companies in early 1975 into consortia to do joint research aimed at leapfrogging the U.S. lead. The current generation of memory chip was then the 4K RAM. The third-generation 16K RAM was expected momentarily. The Japanese aimed to beat the Americans to the 64K RAM by 1980.

These measures were another expression of Japan's determination and of its rejection of Western economics. To challenge the lead of the innovative, low-cost U.S. producers was a daunting task which Western trade doctrine said would be counterproductive. Nevertheless, the Japanese had reason to believe they could be successful. It was true the

Americans were innovative and dominated many world markets by being first with new products. But the Japanese had already found in the cases of radio, stereo, and television that in the long run those advantages really did not matter. The American technology could be obtained rather easily. Its transfer could be made a condition for access to the Japanese market. U.S. universities welcomed foreign students. U.S. professional and industry associations were open to foreign membership; and U.S. companies, prevented by U.S. antitrust law from coordinating licensing activities among themselves, could be played off against one another to extract technology licenses. Moreover, they were often quick to license what they called old technology, supremely confident that they could always stay ahead. As a last resort, U.S. products could also be copied. Once they had the technology, the Japanese were confident that their great skill in refining would enable them to take any U.S. product and make it cheaper and better than the Americans could.

Of course they needed time. MITI thus let it be known that there was a limit to how much it would open Japan's market. On the eve of full liberalization, the MITI minister Toshio Komoto stated, "The government is resolved to keep a careful watch on the trends in the computer market, with the aim of preventing any adverse effect on domestic firms which might lead to confusion in the computer market."[9] ("Confusion in the market" is a favorite Japanese term for undesired outcome.) Komoto added that the future of Japan's industry hinged on its ability to obtain a sufficient share of the domestic market, and that MITI would carefully monitor trends to ensure a desirable outcome.

On top of being a rejection of Western economics, these actions appeared to be at variance with Japan's obligations under the GATT, which required that it not attempt to nullify any concessions made in negotiation. There is no record, however, that the U.S. government protested or that its embassy in Tokyo even reported on these developments—a critical oversight. During the period of formal restriction, the U.S. share of Japan's semiconductor market had varied at around 10 percent.[10] In view of the U.S. industry's superiority, its share was expected to expand in the wake of liberalization, but in fact there was little change. This surprised even the Japanese, who attributed it to lack of effort by U.S. management. It is clear in retrospect, however, that the Japanese countermeasures had the intended effect.

A Nippon Electric company executive best expressed the real significance of the Japanese efforts when he said: "Private capital cannot undertake investment if there is too much risk. MITI gave us the confidence."[11] While Western analysts would later debate over how much of a subsidy was given to the Japanese industry, subsidies were only incidental. The real key was creation of a favorable environment. The Japanese government had a serious problem. Contrary to later perception, its businessmen were not long-term risk takers like those in Silicon Valley. Yet it wanted to get the results of Silicon Valley. The only way was for the government to reduce the risk.

As it did so, the great engineering, manufacturing and financial strengths of the Japanese corporations came into play with impressive results. The first Japanese 16K RAMs came into the world market in 1978–79 and quickly took a 40-percent share. Five factors lay behind the success of the Japanese producers despite their late arrival in the market: First, in view of the drive to create a domestic industry, it was certain that they would capture their own market. Second, market demand surged in 1979, and U.S. producers had difficulty in satisfying it. The Japanese came into the open U.S. market and filled the gap, unhindered, of course, by any countermeasures against imports or requirements for technology transfer to the United States. Third, the Japanese showed how to use quality as a marketing tool. In 1979, Hewlett Packard, a major scientific instrument and computer manufacturer, announced that the failure rate of Japanese

chips was one fifth that of U.S.-made chips. It was not that
U.S. quality was poor—it met the specifications of the
buyers; but the Japanese had surpassed the specs. Fourth
was the practice of "second sourcing." Uneasy with relying
on only one supplier for critical components, customers
often demanded that a supplier license another producer to
make the supplier's chips as a second source. Japanese customers, of course, always preferred a Japanese second
source. Moreover, in one of the great ironies of all time, U.S.
producers often purposely chose to license the Japanese as
second sources because they were viewed as less dangerous
competitors than other U.S. companies.

The final factor was dumping, the practice of selling below
cost or below the price at home in foreign markets. The
American market was the largest, and it was essential that
the Japanese obtain a large share of it to have sufficient production volume to become cost-competitive (costs fall as production increases). Because they were latecomers, Japanese
production costs were higher than those of the Americans,
as was reflected by the high prices in the Japanese market.
Nevertheless, the Japanese came into the U.S. market with
prices well below those prevailing in either country. The
strategy made good business sense. Customers usually like
bargains; and by offering them, the Japanese could generate
the volume necessary to get their costs down. The only
problem was that dumping is illegal both under U.S. trade
law and under the international rules of the GATT. The reason is that dumping may be an attempt to use market power
to export unemployment or an effort to gain market position
through predatory actions similar to those outlawed by U.S.
antitrust laws. Indeed, these laws were precipitated around
the turn of the century by the price-discrimination tactics,
similar to dumping, of companies like Standard Oil, which,
having gained a monopoly position in one market, would
raise prices and use the profits thus generated to slash prices
in new markets in an attempt to drive competitors out of
business.

Here was one of the classic problems in trade between the United States and Japan. U.S. law frowns on price discrimination between customer or markets; but in Japan, where there is no tradition of antitrust, it is the rule. Thus, while the U.S. producers accused the Japanese of acting illegally, the Japanese thought they were just being good businessmen. They needed customers, and the easiest way to get them was to cut prices. That did not seem to them unfair. However, when U.S. producers threatened law suits for dumping in 1980, the Japanese eventually reduced prices at home, while raising them a bit in the United States to achieve parity in the two markets. By that time, however, they had achieved the volume required to be competitive.

Also in 1980, the Japanese achieved the goal they had set five years before and sent out the first commercial samples of the new 64K RAM. They were not actually first with the product because IBM had earlier begun to use the new chip in its computers. But IBM, along with AT&T, is considered a captive producer, manufacturing only for its own use. It was with merchant firms like Intel, Motorola, and Texas Instruments, who sell in the market, that the Japanese were competing. These companies had all been working on the 64K chip, and all had striven in typical American fashion for sophisticated, innovative designs. By concentrating on refining the older, standard design, the Japanese beat them to the market by from six months to a year. Then late in 1980, NTT announced it had made the world's first prototype 256K RAM. This was truly a first and showed that Japan had overtaken the American lead in the most critical area of semiconductor technology. Combining their new edge in memory technology with the aggressive pricing tactics of the past, the Japanese began a sweep of the world RAM market.

The October issue of *Scientific American* has become a kind of bulletin board for Japan's electronics industry, which each year places an advertisement in the form of a long article explaining the thinking of Japan's electronics establishment.

The ad in the issue of October 1981 was one of the most powerful published statements ever made by any industry group. Placed by seventeen Japanese companies—including Toshiba, Fujitsu, Matsushita, Sony, Hitachi, and Mitsubishi —it quite simply declared victory.

Noting Japan's rapid advance in semiconductors, the ad emphasized that any lingering doubts that Japan had surpassed the United States had been put to rest at the world semiconductor conference in San Francisco in 1980, when NTT and NEC had showed detailed descriptions of their 256K devices, while the Americans were still struggling to get their 64K chips out of the lab. It explained at length that Japan had triumphed owing to its superior industrial system, and cited the leadership role of government, and particularly the wisdom of not leaving everything to the dictates of the free market. It also pointed to the peculiar financial structure of Japanese industry based on large corporate groups (heirs of the prewar *zaibatsu* [see pages 000–00]), the cooperative relations between management and labor, the high quality of the Japanese educational system, and Japanese management techniques. The article closed by emphasizing that the focal point of innovation was shifting to Japan, which would be the new "epicenter" of the world electronics industry.[12]

That was how the world looked from Tokyo in the fall of 1981.

## THE STORY BEHIND THE STATISTICS

At the time, however, only a very few in the United States were aware that the battle might be over. It certainly did not look that way if you believed the statistics. At the end of 1981, U.S. producers enjoyed a 57-percent share of the world market for all types of semiconductor, while their Japanese competitors had only 33 percent.[13] The Japanese had the lead in RAMs, but the Americans had strong leads in most other major products, including microprocessors and logic devices. Semiconductors looked like one of the few industries, along with computers and airplanes, that U.S. companies still dominated. The question, therefore, is what did the Japanese know in 1981 that we discovered only in 1987 when Norman Augustine made his report to the secretary of defense?

To begin with, they understood the concept of the key item, or "technology driver." They knew that the RAM is the linchpin of the semiconductor industry because, as the best-selling device, it generates not only revenue but also the long production runs plant managers use to test, stabilize, and refine their production and quality-control processes. Compared with many other chips, it is a relatively simple product, which makes it a more attractive vehicle for developing new techniques. The latest technology has always been incorporated first in RAMs, which have always been the first product to appear as a new generation. Once RAMs are refined, new generations of other products follow. Thus the 64K RAM was followed by the 64K EPROM (electrical, programmable read only memory), the 64K SRAM (static RAM), and so forth. The Japanese knew that if they could capture the lead in RAMs, they would be well on the way to overall semiconductor superiority.

The Japanese also knew the power of the experience curve. Observation of hundreds of industries over the past fifty years has shown that doubling production and sales of any product—be it semiconductors, limestone, or chickens —cuts the total cost of bringing it to market by 20 percent to 30 percent. This phenomenon is particularly powerful in fast-growing industries characterized by frequent introductions of new products (see figure 2.3).

For example, assume that company B's market share is 50 percent, that company A's share is 10 percent, and that the market is growing at 30 percent annually. Further, assume that A is growing at 40 percent annually; and B, at 20 percent. Company B may be the low-cost producer today, but it is facing bankruptcy down the road, even though its 20-per-

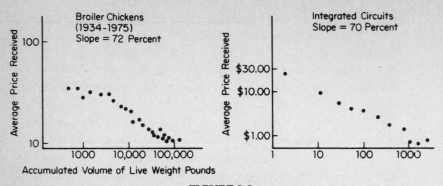

FIGURE 2.3
*Examples of Experience Curves*
SOURCE: Braxton Associates

cent growth rate may be very pleasing to shareholders, who compare it with that of the overall economy or of other slower growing industries. The reason is that A is growing twice as fast as B. Even though A's share of the market is lower at the moment, it is increasing, and A's costs are falling faster than B's. At some point, A will have the larger share and will be the low-cost producer. As that happens, B's profits will be squeezed, making investment in new plants and equipment unattractive. The cutback in investment will result in outdated plants and laboratories, and B will fall further behind. The shareholders may pressure B's management to diversify into oil or something else it knows nothing about. A good example is RCA, which moved into carpets and rental cars as the Japanese ate into its electronics businesses. Today RCA is an also-ran in the industries it pioneered and has ceased to exist as an independent corporation. And it all happens so quietly. B is dead but does not know it, as it announces record profits and dividends to the oh-so-happy shareholders in the early days of the competition. Even later, B may not know what happened, rationalizing that the market has become a commodity market with no product differentiation, not attractive to an innovative company (see figures 2.4 and 2.5).

Thus, the Japanese knew that if they could grow faster

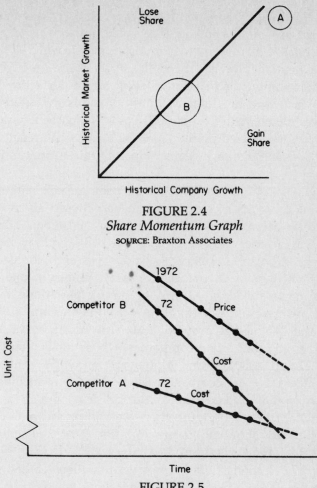

FIGURE 2.4
*Share Momentum Graph*
SOURCE: Braxton Associates

FIGURE 2.5
*The Margin Paradox*
SOURCE: Braxton Associates

than the Americans in the RAM segment of the market, they could become the low-cost producer of RAMs. And if they controlled RAMs, they would have taken a long step toward dominance in other semiconductors. And if they had semiconductors, semiconductor equipment, materials, and everything that semiconductors went into, such as computers, would be next.

If the Japanese understood the dynamics, they were masters at the structure, knowing that stable, low-cost, and patient capital is necessary to support rapid growth. *Nihon Keizai* commented on this necessity in an article on 6 May 1980: "Semiconductor makers in Japan are in a position of being able to procure huge amounts of funds for research and investment over a long period. There is a possibility that such strength enjoyed by the Japanese makers will result in raising the tone of attack against Japan by the American industry."[14]

Growth of 30 percent and 40 percent a year requires increasing amounts of money. Japan had chosen six major diversified companies—Fujitsu, Hitachi, Toshiba, NEC, Mitsubishi Electric, and Oki Electric—to be its primary standard bearers in the industry. Not only was each company large in its own right, but each was a member of one of Japan's major industrial groups, or *keiretsu* (economic linkages known as *zaibatsu* before the war), such as the Sumitomo and Mitsubishi groups, and each could count on support from other group companies, whose total resources might exceed $300 billion. Moreover, since the primary shareholders of these companies were other group members and banks that backed semiconductor development as a strategic move for the group, there was no pressure on the companies to show short-term profits. Nor in Japan's lifetime-employment system (see pages 290–92) was there danger of defections of key employees suddenly bitten by the entrepreneurial bug and bent on taking what they had learned and starting their own competitive companies.

Behind this stable, solid structure stood the government of Japan, which would do all in its power to ensure the industry's success. Its policies reduced risk and lowered the cost of capital (a key cost for a capital-intensive industry like semiconductors) in Japan to a third of that in the United States. The Japanese could thus operate from a strategic point of view, investing heavily even when markets were depressed, so that they would have the capacity to gain a greater share in the next market upswing. And when entering a new market, they could afford to price at whatever level was required to get the business. As a top NEC executive said to me, "When the market is growing and you are trying to establish your position is no time to worry about profit."

Finally, the Japanese knew where they would generate the sales that would allow them to keep expanding production and reducing costs. By now they had had much experience in selling in the United States. With no restrictions to stop them, they had been building large organizations there for years. They knew that the United States is a porous society and therefore an easy market to enter, and that U.S. regulations and procedures are open, transparent, and not strictly enforced. Moreover, in the event of problems, Japanese operations in the United States would be accorded the same rights and protection as any domestic corporation. Thus, the Japanese were virtually assured of making large inroads in the U.S. market.

They also knew that they would dominate their own market. The U.S. companies had been prevented from establishing organizations when they had had clear superiority; and even if they made a major effort now, it would take time to become established. Furthermore, the Japanese chip producers were also the biggest users, and would naturally tend to reject foreign chips in favor of their own. Also, the Japanese knew that their affiliated companies and group members would tend to buy from them. Most of all, they knew that, as they became the low-cost producers and dominant suppliers as a result of strong positions in both markets, there would be no reason for Japanese companies even to consider a foreign supplier. The best would be in Japan, and who could blame them for wanting to buy the best-quality goods at the best price? There would no longer be any need for "Buy Japanese" policies because the very structure of the market would prevent penetration by foreigners.

Finally, the Japanese knew the opposition. The U.S. companies were all relatively small and more dependent on semiconductor sales than were any of the Japanese chip producers. None of the U.S. companies, including even IBM and AT&T, had the financial resources and government backing the Japanese had. While they were very innovative, the U.S. companies were also very vulnerable. Their shareholders demanded profits. Their best people often left to start companies of their own which were sometimes willing to trade technology to Japanese companies for much-needed cash. And both their culture and their law prevented them from working together. None of them could slug it out toe to toe with the Japanese juggernaut.

### VICTORY REALIZED

The prediction of the Japanese advertisers in the *Scientific American* of October 1981 was soon confirmed. Between July 1981 and August 1982, Japanese capacity for production of 64K RAMs increased from nine million devices per year to sixty-six million;[15] and while the Americans struggled to redesign their chips after the simpler Japanese mode, the Japanese took 65 percent of the world market (see figure 2.6). Between 1981 and 1985, the U.S. firms invested the equivalent of 22 percent of their sales volume in new plants and equipment—more than double the U.S. industrial average; but in Japan, where there are few constraints on the availability of capital and no need to obtain high returns, the figure was nearly 40 percent. As a result, Japan passed the United States in total absolute investment in semiconductors after 1983.[16] The picture was similar in R&D spending. The U.S. semiconductor companies consistently spent about 8 percent of sales on research and development, compared with the U.S. average of 4 percent. But the Japanese spent about 12 percent.[17] The result was that, despite the best efforts of the U.S. companies, the Japanese continued to set

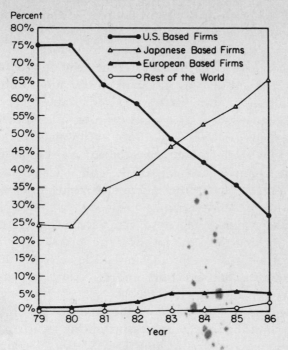

FIGURE 2.6
*Memory Products: World Market Share*
*(Percentage of world shipments)*
SOURCE: Dataquest

the pace in quality while surging into the lead in productivity.

Semiconductor production takes place in four basic stages. First is the growing of cylindrical crystals of silicon that are then cut into wafers. Wafer fabrication consists of etching the circuitry for several chips onto a large wafer, which is then cut into individual die that eventually become separate devices. The die are tested, assembled into packaged devices, and tested again before being shipped to customers. Assembly is relatively labor intensive; and to offset the lower labor costs of the Japanese which for a long time were about a third those of the Americans, the U.S. producers moved this part of their operations to Southeast Asia. For a time this gave the U.S. companies an overall cost advantage, but the real key to low costs is yield, the percentage of good chips that survive the process to be shipped to customers. Because even a speck of dust or smoke can ruin a chip in production, the key to yield is a clean environment and automated, stable processes controlled by a skilled, stable labor force. With no engineers leaving to start ventures of their own, the Japanese had a stable work force. With their enormous spending on research and development and capital equipment, the Japanese were able to install ultra-clean rooms and automated equipment that increased yields dramatically. While the best U.S. companies obtained yields of 50 percent to 60 percent; the best Japanese were getting 70 percent to 80 percent, making them the low-cost producers. This did not mean that all Japanese producers had lower costs than all U.S. producers. But some did, and this, coupled with their high quality, made them formidable.

The aggressive investment of the Japanese was matched by a repeat of the equally aggressive pricing tactics that had first been used with the 16K RAMS. Prices sank as if weighted with lead. A high-placed NEC executive predicted that "no one will be profitable" and that the "latecomers will be shaken out."[18] The latecomers were the Americans, who were indeed being shaken out. Where there had been fourteen U.S. producers of the 1K chip, fifteen of the 4K, and twelve of the 16K, eventually only two merchant firms remained in the 64K market.[19] Among the Japanese, there were no dropouts. The power of the financial strength of the Japanese producers and of their industry structure was now making itself felt. The game was becoming one of capital investment and price cutting rather than primarily of innovation, and the Japanese excelled.

The imbalance in the relative openness of the two markets also became critical. The battle was always taking place on American soil. The Japanese could make a mistake and try again, but there were no second chances for the Americans.

As they began to lose out to the Japanese, the innovative, risk-taking Americans had reluctantly to look to the U.S. government as the only entity with the power to rebalance the competitive equation.

# Negotiations between the United States and Japan

## THE DUMPING PROBLEM

Negotiations between the U.S. and Japanese governments were almost continuous after 1981. The U.S. semiconductor companies complained of unfair trade and argued that they were competing not only with Japanese companies but also with the Japanese government. The Japanese resented being called unfair. They had no malicious intent, but hoped only to build a more prosperous and powerful country in ways natural to them. It seemed to them that the Americans were illogically urging them not to do their best in order to preserve a position the Americans were no longer capable of maintaining on their own.

Nothing in U.S. law or tradition, however, anticipated the possibility of industry and trade being organized as part of an effort to achieve specific national goals rather than on the individualistic Western model. The United States understood military competition and competition in space, but not national industrial competition. The result was a series of negotiations that never focused on the main issues and that dealt with symptoms instead of causes.

The first of these was the dumping problem. From the start, the U.S. industry's prices had declined by 20 percent to 30 percent annually as they followed costs down the experience curve. With the Japanese introduction of the 64K RAM in 1981, the curve began to look like Niagara Falls, with prices dropping 80 percent in one year.[20] Even the Japanese could not reduce costs that quickly. That no one was making money was bluntly confirmed by *Nihon Keizai* in an article on 15 September 1981: "The current market... price does not necessarily reflect the true situation."[21] A few months later, on 14 December, *Business Week* reported, "Industry analysts question whether any of today's players, including the Japanese, can be turning a profit."[22]

It was at this juncture in the fall of 1981 that representatives of the U. S. semiconductor industry began making regular trips to Washington. Among them were Noyce, Charles Sporck, and Jerry Sanders. As a young mechanical engineer out of Cornell, Sporck had joined Fairchild Semiconductor in the early days and worked his way up to be head of manufacturing. It was his genius for low-cost production that led the then-struggling National Semiconductor Corporation to invite him to come in as president and try to rescue it in 1967. By 1980, he had built it from a nearly bankrupt company with $7 million in sales into the third largest U.S. semiconductor company with sales of over $1 billion dollars annually.

Sanders had grown up poor, the oldest of a family of twelve children in Chicago, and had earned a degree in electrical engineering on a scholarship at the University of Illinois given by an entrepreneur of an earlier era, George Pullman, inventor of the Pullman railroad car. After rising to be head of marketing at Fairchild Semiconductor, Sanders was fired in a corporate shake-up in 1969. Not one to despair, he rented a Malibu beachhouse with $600 of his last $1,000 of severance pay and sat down to consider the future. The future was Advanced Micro Devices (AMD), the company he founded in 1969 with several other engineers and the help of friendly venture capitalists. Listed in a high-tech magazine at the time as the semiconductor company least likely to succeed, AMD had beaten all the odds and become a major force in the industry. It was particularly known for its Japanese-style emphasis on quality and its "no lay-off" policy.

Appealing to Washington was not easy for these men and the others like them in the industry who embodied the ideals of the American dream. Coming from modest, even poor, backgrounds, they had succeeded through initiative, inspiration, and perspiration, in founding an industry widely seen as the key to the twenty-first century. They had done it on their own as lone riders without government help—indeed, sometimes in the face of government harassment. Their traditional view had been that the best thing the government could do for them was to get out of the way.

All internationalists, they saw their industry in global terms and had factories in Europe, Latin America, and Southeast Asia. They lived by free trade and had nothing but disdain for the executives of the steel, automobile, and textile industries who had earlier trooped to Washington to ask for protection. To the denizens of Silicon Valley, asking the government for help was an admission of weakness or incompetence or both; and they were doing it only because, in their view, an individual company could not face the combined might of Japan's government and industry without assistance from the U.S. government.

These representatives of the semiconductor industry visited the departments of Commerce, State, and Treasury as well as the U.S. Trade Representative and members of Congress. They asked not for protection but for an end to the Japanese dumping, for the same opportunity to sell in Japan as the Japanese had in the United States, and for an end to Japanese copying of new chip designs.* They got a reception as cool as the autumn weather in Washington. The lawyers, academic economists, and career bureaucrats who filled

---

*One example of copying occurred in August 1982 when Peter Stoll of Intel, in examining a chip under a microscope, saw that, in one case, two transistors were disconnected. He immediately recognized the defect as a repair he had made on Intel's 8086 microprocessor which had corrected a logic flaw and helped make the chip a great success. What surprised Stoll now was that the chip before him was not Intel's but an NEC product.[23]

many key government positions shared a suspicion of business as protectionist and opposed to consumer interests. To them, the semiconductor industry seemed healthy: while it might have problems in one or two areas, over all it was 50 percent bigger than the Japanese industry and remained profitable, while growing much faster than most U.S. industries. Few officials understood the experience curve and that an industry could be dying even while growing rapidly if in the process it was losing market share to even faster growing competitors who were eroding its technological advantage. Indeed, many officials echoed the Japanese. American management, they said, was just plain lazy and needed to work harder. Thus were the workaholics of Silicon Valley, who often had risked everything they had and who for years had neglected home and families while putting in eighteen-hour days to form a whole new industry, chastised by people who by Silicon Valley standards didn't even know what effort was.

Lionel Olmer and I, who represented the Commerce Department in these meetings with industry, disagreed, however, with the majority of other officials. Unique in the group in having had industry experience, we knew that the U.S. firms faced unequal competition and were in serious trouble. Believing that the industry's demise would not be good for the country, we took steps to prevent it by trying to stop the dumping. Because the industry had not filed a formal complaint and the administration had no policy on the matter, we were on our own. (The industry declined to file suit because legal proceedings are often too costly and too lengthy to be meaningful; in rapidly changing markets, a product's life cycle may be ended by the time a decision is rendered.) Our only tools were bluff and persuasion. Olmer, who was responsible for administering the antidumping laws, warned MITI officials in Washington that the Commerce Department might begin to monitor Japanese chip prices. Our ability to do so was in fact limited, but we hoped to make the Japanese more cautious by suggesting the possibility.

It worked for a while. The prices of 64K RAMs began to stabilize, as MITI warned Japanese companies. Then, the Justice Department struck with righteous fury and, on the basis of what proved to be false press reports that the Japanese were colluding to restrain supplies and thereby drive up prices in the U.S. market, launched an investigation of possible antitrust violations by the Japanese companies. On the morning of 22 July 1982 (at 1:00 A.M. in Tokyo), a MITI official called to tell me how perplexed and embarrassed his ministry was at having Japanese companies investigated for responding to warnings the Commerce Department had urged MITI to give. So much for bluffing.

As the situation of the semiconductor industry worsened, so did the anger of Congress over the rising trade deficit and what it saw as Japan's unfair tactics. Threats of retaliation against Japan multiplied almost daily. The assistant U.S. trade representative Richard Heimlich, known both as a champion of U.S. interests and as a skilled bureaucratic maneuverer, saw opportunity in this adversity. The United States, he believed, needed a mechanism to exert pressure on Japan, but he knew the administration as a whole did not agree and would not provide one. The Japanese needed a way to soothe Congress and to hold the United States at bay while their industry consolidated its position. Heimlich knew that the normal Japanese tactic in such situations is to engage in lengthy talks that freeze the United States into inactivity while Japan's industry creates a fait accompli. Hoping, nevertheless, that some maneuverers on the U.S. side might turn such talks to their advantage, he suggested to the Japanese that they suggest talks. It was not an ideal solution, but it was the only possible way to obtain any U.S. government involvement in the fate of the U.S. industry. The Japanese responded by proposing creation of a High Technology Working Group to resolve high-tech trade problems. The United States agreed to the proposal, and an assistant U.S. trade representative, James Murphy, and I became co-chairmen of the U.S. delegation.

EARLY AGREEMENTS

It was a critical time. The Japanese had the upper hand in this strategic industry and had declared victory, but it was not too late. The U.S. industry was still present in all product areas and had not abandoned R&D efforts on RAMs. If the United States had at this point simply limited the Japanese share of the U.S. market to that obtained by the U.S. companies in Japan, the superiority of the U.S. industry could probably have been maintained. Without the sales volume generated in the U.S. market, Japanese costs would have risen and become uncompetitive. But such a policy might have meant temporarily higher prices for consumers and was unthinkable under U.S. free-trade doctrine. Thus, to preserve a healthy U.S. industry, Murphy and I had to be able to bring enough pressure to bear to create a more equal competitive environment in which price was related to cost and real sales opportunities were equal in both countries. It was possible; but the longer talks continued without results, the more difficult the U.S. situation would become. We therefore aimed for quick results and had two major objectives: to prevent dumping in the U.S. market and to increase U.S. sales to a significant share of the Japanese market.

The latter objective was critical and particularly difficult. The U.S. companies had well over half the market outside Japan, but only about 10 percent within it. The problem was much more subtle than tariffs and other formal trade barriers, which had largely been removed. It arose from several factors: the tight ties between Japan's manufacturers and their suppliers and distributors, which entail social obligations that go far beyond contractual dealings; the interlocking relations between major companies which enable them to ignore Western-style financial discipline; and the fact that, having long been encouraged by its government to displace foreign products, Japanese industry now did so as a kind of reflex action. In a word, the problem was structural. The whole industry was structured so as to reject, more or less automatically, penetration by outsiders or newcomers.

Clearly, standard measures such as lower tariffs and simpler import procedures would not change this situation. In the spring of 1982, however, in response to congressional threats of legislation to close U.S. markets, Prime Minister Zenko Suzuki had promised to open the Japanese market and had gone on television to ask that his countrymen buy more foreign goods. Murphy and I hoped to use his promise to persuade MITI actively to promote imports of semiconductors. In effect, like disadvantaged U.S. minorities, we wanted an affirmative-action program that would offset the effects of past discrimination by actively working to increase imported chips. We also hoped to stop dumping by establishing a system to monitor both semiconductor shipments and prices. In addition, we wanted MITI to curb its industry's tendency to invest regardless of profitability which arose in response to MITI's inducements and led inevitably to production far in excess of demand and consequent severe price cutting.

That was what Murphy and I wanted, but these talks were not a top White House priority. A few concerned officials had maneuvered an unconcerned administration into them. Most of the key administration figures were not engaged. Although some of us thought otherwise, in the eyes of most of the cabinet this was a long way from arms control and Star Wars. Thus, there was no mandate to achieve anything specific. As a result, we had to operate within the bounds of a consensus obtained from the various agencies on the U.S. negotiating team that included members from the Office of the U.S. Trade Representative, the Council of Economic Advisers, the National Security Council, the Office of Management and Budget, and the departments of State, Labor, Treasury, Commerce, and Defense.

The consensus was that, while it was appropriate to request better market access, asking for a specific market share or sales volume would violate free-trade doctrine and hence be unacceptable. Similarly, with regard to dumping, collecting data on the volume of shipments was acceptable—but not on prices, because in the view of the Justice Department that might violate antitrust laws on price fixing. Any attempt to get MITI to restrain semiconductor investment was rejected as being anti–free market. Thus, before talking to the Japanese, we limited ourselves to asking simply for a more open market, whose meaning we did not define, and a system of gathering statistics on semiconductor shipments. Moreover, the consensus, strongly influenced by the State Department and the National Security Council, would not allow—even as a tactic—the suggestion of any retaliation if Japan did not respond favorably for fear that the overall relationship between the two countries might be harmed.

With our interdepartmental negotiation out of the way, Murphy and I led a U.S. delegation, which included virtually every department in the government, to meet with the Japanese in June 1982. As we debated, I noted that Kengo Ishii, a deputy director general at MITI, led a team composed almost entirely of MITI officials with the exception of a man from the Foreign Ministry, and seemed to find it easy to reach a consensus on his side. The first question posed by the Japanese revealed their real concern. The U.S. Justice Department had just dropped its ten-year-old antitrust suit charging IBM with monopolizing the computer market. Projecting onto us their own conceptual framework, the Japanese wanted to know if that indicated that the U.S. government was thinking of using IBM to counter Japan's thrust into high-tech industries. I assured him that was not the case. He wouldn't have understood the truth: that no one on the U.S. side was even capable of thinking in those terms, because the United States did not conceive of industrial competition as a matter of national concern.

Although it took an enormous amount of time and energy,

the First Semiconductor Agreement of November 1982 was more a monument to clever drafting than anything else.[24] The only concrete result was the system for collecting statistics on chip shipments. We still hoped to inhibit dumping through monthly monitoring of shipments; but since collection of the critical price data was barred by the Justice Department, the system was of marginal value. On market access, the Japanese would agree only to "seek to ensure" opportunities equivalent to those afforded Japanese companies in the United States—a stand that was not only disappointing, but raised critical questions. Why couldn't Japan ensure equal opportunity? The prime minister had promised to open the market, not to "seek" to open it. What did the prime minister mean by "open"? Did his bureaucracy agree with him? And if it did not, could he control it?

The agreement was greeted enthusiastically in Washington (agreements with Japan always are by all administrations), and Murphy and I were praised for a successful negotiation that had helped to bank the angry fires in Congress. In fact, we had been handled. While we were debating whether to "ensure" or to "seek to ensure," Japan's industry continued its economic conquest. Nothing had changed; and within three months, further threats of congressional action along with the possibility of private unfair-trade suits drove the U.S. delegation to a second round of negotiations, one focusing entirely on market access. Once again the invocation of free-trade doctrine by most of the U.S. government agencies made it impossible to negotiate for concrete results. Yet all agreed that the surest evidence of greater access would be greater sales. Thus, our task was to get measurable increases in sales without asking for them.

This time Murphy and I tried to cast our requests in terms the Japanese understood. We reasoned that if MITI could give "guidance" to its companies to restrain exports, as it did in the case of automobiles, maybe it could also give guidance to increase imports of chips or to restrain the Japanese investment binge that was leading to vast overcapacity and

chronic dumping. As a concrete objective other than a specific sales figure or market share, we introduced the "long-
term relationship." We knew that Japanese suppliers had
such relationships with their customers. In fact, these ties
are a key part of what we called the structural problem. A
long-term relationship means that a supplier is informed in
advance of the customer's development plans and that he
knows he will get future orders. The Japanese had always
treated U.S. producers as swing suppliers, buying only on a
spot basis or when there was no Japanese company making
the product. U.S. companies wanted to become part of the
Japanese structure, so we pressed for MITI to agree to guide
its companies to develop long-term relationships with U.S.
suppliers—an outcome that, we reasoned, would automatically yield more sales while being sufficiently nonspecific to
be acceptable to both MITI and our colleagues in the U.S.
government.

MITI's new negotiator Yukiharu Kodama was a rising star
in the ministry. Cosmopolitan and a shrewd negotiator, Kodama gave nothing away, but I believe he sincerely wanted
to resolve the trade problem because he saw an enfeebled
United States as not necessarily in Japan's interest. The key
part of the Second Semiconductor Agreement, concluded in
November 1983, was the confidential chairman's note from
Kodama to Murphy and me, in which Kodama said that
MITI would "encourage" (a euphemism for "give guidance
to") the major Japanese chip users to buy more U.S. chips
and to develop long-term relationships with U.S. suppliers.[25]

## THE BOTTOM FALLS OUT

For a while in 1984, the agreement seemed to work. The
demand for chips worldwide suddenly skyrocketed, and
producers in both Japan and the United States put their customers on allocation. The U.S. share of the Japanese market

actually increased by a couple of percentage points in early 1984. Murphy and I should have quit while we were ahead. It all collapsed at the end of that year. Demand slackened just as the full impact of Japan's massive investment drive began to be felt, and a flood of new chips hit the market. While demand in the Japanese market fell by 11 percent, U.S. sales there fell by 30 percent. The new "long-term relationships" had lasted less than a year.

The new chips were the next generation of 256K RAMs which the Japanese introduced well ahead of the U.S. companies, including even IBM and AT&T, the first U.S. companies to develop the product. Buoyed by rosy forecasts of a quick market upswing and unconstrained by any real financial discipline, the Japanese companies continued to pour on new plant and equipment even as the Americans scaled back capital expenditures in the face of mounting losses. When the upswing failed to materialize, the Japanese did not scale back production as the Americans did. Rather, they continued to run at maximum capacity in an attempt to cover the high fixed costs resulting from their high debt levels and lifetime-employment practices. Excess production meant that prices fell faster than ever, and the Japanese quickly took over 90 percent of the worldwide RAM business as all the American merchant companies abandoned it, except Texas Instruments and tiny Micron Devices.[26] IBM and AT&T continued to produce for themselves, but even they began to buy so many Japanese RAMs that senior executives worried about being overly dependent on Japan.

As they abandoned RAMs, the U.S. producers concentrated on more sophisticated products such as logic chips and EPROMs (electrical programmable read only memories), where they said innovation and creativity would really count. In 1985, the Japanese slashed EPROM prices. Hitachi's U.S. subsidiary told its salesmen to concentrate on Intel and AMD (Advanced Micro Devices, Inc.) customers and to cut prices in increments of 10 percent until they got the business, while guaranteeing distributors a 25-percent profit.[27] By 1986, the Japanese had nearly half the market for many of the more sophisticated products. The only refuges were small, specialty markets, as the total Japanese semiconductor market became bigger than the U.S. market (see figure 2.7).[28] The United States had long ago lost its consumer electronics industry to the Japanese, and products such as VCRs (which are known as "semiconductor hogs" because of the great quantities of chips they contain) were entirely made in Japan. In the past, it had been necessary for the Japanese to penetrate the huge U.S. market to become competitive. Now the U.S. industry had to sell to Japan as a matter of survival. Yet it remained unable to do so.

In fact, the U.S. semiconductor industry was staring death in the face. It reported losses of nearly $2 billion for 1985 and 1986, while twenty-five thousand people lost their jobs.[29] The Japanese companies lost twice as much money as the

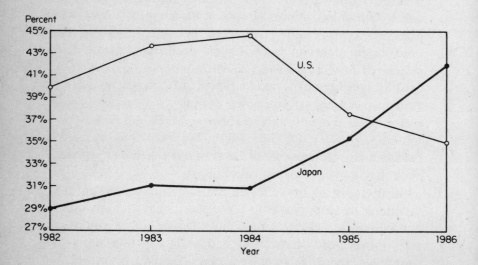

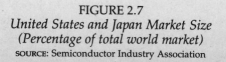

FIGURE 2.7
*United States and Japan Market Size*
*(Percentage of total world market)*
SOURCE: Semiconductor Industry Association

Americans in semiconductors, but, as they had foreseen, in a contest of deep pockets theirs were deeper. Maybe they were not so innovative, but their structure had staying power. As the U.S. companies abandoned ever more segments of the industry, the Japanese expanded their market share.

## THE LEGAL WAR

With survival at stake in the spring and summer of 1985, executives of the U.S. companies and their industry association descended on Washington. They filed a dumping action on EPROMs and a blanket unfair trade petition, under section 301 of the U.S. Trade Act of 1974, charging the Japanese with illegally nullifying negotiated tariff and quota concessions by consciously taking countermeasures to protect their domestic industry.[30] The petition further claimed that the Japanese had reneged on the two recently negotiated high-tech agreements. Section 301 gives the president power to take any step necessary to prevent or retaliate against the unfair trade practices of foreign countries which harm U.S. commerce. The industry did not ask for retaliation or protection. Rather it once more asked President Reagan to negotiate for a commitment from Japan to encourage its companies to buy significantly more U.S. chips and to observe the U.S. and international dumping laws.

As the petition was filed, the Defense Science Board and the C.I.A. began to express concern about the rapidly increasing dependency of the Defense Department on foreign suppliers. Nevertheless, the petition had a mixed reception in Washington. While Commerce and the Trade Representative's office were sympathetic, other departments such as State, Treasury, the National Security Council, and even Defense argued that Japan had opened its market by removing formal tariffs and quotas in 1975. They dismissed the countermeasures to the liberalization as merely a matter of Japanese government exhortation to its industry with no concrete significance and again blamed the problems of the U.S. industry on poor management which had not taken the long-term view and had not really tried to get into the Japanese market.

The 301 procedure calls for the president to make a formal finding based on evidence that a foreign country is engaging in unfair acts, and then to negotiate an end to them or to retaliate against them until they cease. Because Japan is both friend and ally, and because the problem with Japan arose from a set of interrelated policies carried out over many years rather than from a specific trade action, there was great reluctance in Washington, particularly at the Department of State and the National Security Council, to brand Japan an unfair trader. Here was a major flaw in U.S. law. A trade problem could not be addressed except in moralistic terms inappropriate for dealing with an ally. The U.S. Trade Representative was therefore directed to undertake negotiation without a finding. The U.S. objectives were once again greater market access and a halt to dumping. It was thought that the potential of a future finding would encourage the Japanese to negotiate seriously. But the latter knew that they could count on the State Department and the NSC to stop any actions against them. Talks began in August, but got nowhere.

Then a fluke occurred. On 19 September 1985, as the U.S. trade deficit approached $150 billion, and Congress again threatened stringent trade legislation, the President tried to fend it off by giving a tough speech in which he announced that he had created a strike force to deal firmly with unfair trade activities. At the time, the strike force was only a speech writer's rhetorical flourish; but after the speech the White House hurriedly put Secretary of Commerce Malcolm Baldrige, who had a reputation for being tough on trade issues, in charge. It was a wholly political move. There had been no prior planning, no one knew what this strike force should do, and most officials really didn't want it. But when a president established a strike force with much public fanfare, it must strike at least once. The questions thus became where and when. Baldrige asked me to respond.

All that summer, *Nihon Keizai* had published many articles bemoaning the low semiconductor prices and the fact that the Japanese producers were losing money. On 10 July 1985, the newspaper quoted a senior executive of a Japanese company as saying, "If I said we made a profit, I would be lying. There is no longer any point in making 64K RAMS."[31] This statement was made at a time when evidence of massive dumping of both 64K and 256K RAMs, coming into the hands of the Commerce Department from sources in both the U.S. and Japanese industries, indicated that Japanese companies were selling at prices that barely covered their costs for materials. 256K RAMS, which cost a minimum of $3.00 to produce, were being sold for well under $2.00.[32] In view of the tremendous overcapacity resulting from Japan's investment binge to gain market share, such pricing practices were not surprising but they were illegal.

With the life of the U.S. semiconductor industry ebbing away, the talks under the 301 petition were grinding forward slowly and uncertainly. The relaxed Japanese were handling them with their usual skill and aplomb. With every passing day, the U.S. industry was in worse shape. Since shock treatment was needed in order to get some negotiating leverage, I recommended that the U.S. government do what it had the legal authority to do but never had done before: start its own dumping case on 256K RAM chips without waiting for private industry to file a suit, and thus move the government from the position of intermediary to one of advocate. Moreover, because the Japanese industry stood to lose billions of dollars, Japan would have a real incentive to negotiate. Although we were often described as hardliners, neither Baldrige nor I had any animus toward Japan. Both of us had lived there, had had business experience there, and considered ourselves friends of Japan. We did not want to hurt Japan, but we did want to save a critical U.S. industry. Baldrige accepted the recommendation and directed that we proceed to obtain cabinet approval.

It was obvious to all informed observers that for the U.S. semiconductor industry to remain healthy without protection of U.S. markets, two things had to happen: in order to have the volume to be cost-competitive, the industry had to get a significant share of the Japanese market and have an environment that did not make winning or losing strictly a matter of who could afford to lose the most money—as, clearly, the Japanese could. Until now none of our negotiations had ever really addressed the fundamental issues. Not realizing that the logic and structure of the Japanese market was against it, the United States kept asking for a market access defined in terms of the nature of the U.S. market, and kept feeling cheated when successive agreements yielded no results. The same situation held true with regard to dumping: U.S. demands that it be halted did not allow for the fact that Japan's industrial structure and competitive dynamics made dumping inevitable. To avoid repeating the mistakes of the past, a whole new approach was needed. Recognizing the wholly different nature of the two markets and the needs of both industries for survival, I hoped to use the threat of the dumping case to stimulate broad negotiations on all the aspects of the problem and to obtain a package deal that would create new ground rules for competition between the two industries. It was a very ambitious goal.

Before getting cabinet and presidential approval, we had to clear another obstacle from an unexpected source: parts of the U.S. electronics industry. While most of these companies were concerned about their growing dependence on their major overseas competitors, many were already wholly dependent on the Japanese for RAMs and other important chips. Three years before, they had not been dependent and there would not have been any objection to our proposed action. Now their dependence led them to oppose enforcing

U.S. law and to lobby against the interests of their fellow entrepreneurs in the semiconductor industry.

The industry opposition almost stopped the action cold before it got started. Bruce Smart, the new undersecretary of commerce who had just replaced Olmer, began to wonder if we should even submit our proposal to the cabinet. To better ascertain the industry position, he and I placed telephone calls to several key computer and electronics executives. By dint of supplying themselves, the captive producers, AT&T and IBM, are, as I have previously noted, among the largest chip producers. Most economists and trade experts had come to believe that as long as these two giants remained in the business, the demise of the merchant suppliers was of no importance. This view had even been encouraged in the past by IBM and AT&T, which prided themselves on being able to compete with Japan. At one meeting, an IBM executive had told me the Silicon Valley producers were nothing but crybabies. Now, however, our phone calls revealed an entirely different view. Virtually all of the top executives we called said they were concerned about the rapid decline of the U.S. semiconductor manufacturers. But the key comment came from a top IBM executive: "Not only should you act, you must act for the good of the nation." He explained that IBM and AT&T could not keep all the equipment and materials suppliers, who are the key to technological advances, in business by themselves. As these companies declined along with their U.S. customers, the giants were forced both to divert more of their own resources to semiconductor development and to become more dependent on their Japanese competitors. So even mighty IBM and AT&T were at last feeling the impact of the Japanese encroachment strategy. Our earlier doubts were overridden, and we decided to move ahead.

On 24 October 1985, the cabinet-level strike force met under Baldrige to consider whether to initiate the dumping case. Baldrige presented the evidence we had gathered, and

asked those present to approve a recommendation that the
President direct him to enforce U.S. law. The following are
the key themes as voiced by various members of the agencies
in the subsequent discussion:

> U.S. TRADE REPRESENTATIVE'S OFFICE: Things are really popping be-
> hind the scenes in our discussions with the Japanese. We're
> getting all kinds of calls and we ought to handle them care-
> fully. Let's see what emerges before we launch any missiles.
> [An element of turf was involved here. No one knew of any
> new developments. The official feared Baldrige might take
> some of the negotiating responsibility away from the U.S.
> Trade Representative's office.]
>
> BALDRIGE: This would give you more negotiating leverage.
>
> USTR OFFICE: It might not. It could foul up behind the scenes ne-
> gotiations.
>
> NATIONAL SECURITY COUNCIL: We have to keep in mind SDI [the
> Strategic Defense Initiative, better known as "Star Wars"]. We
> think Japan will endorse SDI and we don't want to do any-
> thing that would undermine that. Besides, we are more cre-
> ative than the Japanese. IBM is way ahead of them. [Of course,
> IBM had just told us it was not.]
>
> STATE DEPARTMENT: Isn't it mostly the fault of our companies? I
> heard that they just took the wrong track in product develop-
> ment. If we do this, are we moving toward an industrial pol-
> icy?
>
> TREASURY DEPARTMENT: Exactly. Dumping benefits the society re-
> ceiving it. If we decide we want this industry, no matter what,
> we are making industrial policy.
>
> TREASURY DEPARTMENT II: Secretary Baldrige is right. We know
> Japan is predatory. The argument that we are more creative
> sounds like what the United Kingdom says about itself. Look,
> Japan doesn't have any defense burden. We do. Japan has to
> be dealt with.
>
> COMMERCE DEPARTMENT: We have to think of national security in
> the broadest sense, in terms of the survival of our industrial
> base. We have to show we mean business. Otherwise, the
> president's statement on cracking down on unfair trade will be
> a joke.

Eventually, when Baldrige asked if anyone was opposed to
enforcing U.S. anti-dumping law, no one was willing to say
yes openly. Thus Baldrige's decision memo urging that the

U.S. government initiate an action to prevent dumping of RAM chips was forwarded from the strike force. A month of complex jockeying ensued. The trade representative still believed that he could negotiate a deal behind the scenes. He arranged with the NSC and White House staffs, which had disliked the Commerce recommendation, to sit on it while he tried one more time. In an effort to halt initiation of the dumping case, the Japanese now made an offer. MITI said that it would establish an export floor price and would also arrange for a 25-percent increase in U.S. sales in Japan in 1986. Although it was presented as a device to save the U.S. industry, the floor price was very important to the Japanese. The popular myth, fostered by the Japanese, was that all Japanese producers had lower costs than all U.S. producers. In fact, some Japanese companies had quite high costs. The antidumping law requires each producer to sell at his full cost. If they had to do so, some Japanese would be driven out of the business. Thus, MITI pushed the floor price. Another reason was that it united the Japanese side whereas, if each company had to sell at its own cost rather than the market price, the Japanese interests would be splintered.

Initially, the Trade Representative's office presented this as an attractive offer, but when it was pointed out that a floor price is anticompetitive because it does not relate price to cost, and that the 25-percent sales increase was not meaningful, because that was the expected overall market growth, the offer was rejected and Baldrige's memo went to the President who, on 6 December, signed the order to proceed.

That seemed final. But the Japanese had retained, as their lobbyists in this case, William Walker, an influential Republican and former deputy U.S. trade representative, and Stanton Anderson, a former State Department official and a Republican party fund raiser. In the next two days, these men got to key National Security Council and White House staffers. It was easy for them to do so because some of the staffers in question owed their positions to the political influence of men close to Walker and Anderson. They persuaded the staffers that the Commerce Department was exceeding the President's instructions on the dumping case. In its notice to the *Federal Register*, Commerce had defined the subject goods as 256K·RAMs and all succeeding generations. It had added succeeding generations because there was no sense in halting the dumping of 256K chips only to have it repeated in the next generation. From the Japanese point of view, however, if the case could be limited only to 256K RAMs, it would have only limited impact precisely because of the rapid succession of generations in the technology.

In arguing that because discussion in the cabinet had centered on 256K RAMs, the President meant for action to be limited to them, Walker and Anderson implied that they knew both the content of the cabinet discussion and the President's order. No one asked at the time how they might have such knowledge because it was common for such lobbyists to know instantly what occurred in closed cabinet meetings. Instead, a White House staffer, a former financial editor whose earlier nine-month stint as an assistant secretary of Commerce had made him the resident trade expert at the White House, ordered Commerce to withdraw the notice of its action from the *Federal Register*. It took a weekend of phone calls from Baldrige, who was then in Moscow, to the White House chief of staff, Donald Regan, to calm the situation. Protests also came from the U.S. embassy in Tokyo, which sent cables saying it regretted the action; and the deputy chief of mission in Tokyo told me that he personally was very upset because he felt that the U.S. government was being too harsh with Japan.

Despite the protests, by January 1986 the U.S. government was pursuing a dumping case of its own on 256K RAMs, one dumping petition from private industry on 64K RAMs and one on EPROMs, and a 301 unfair-trade case against the Japanese on semiconductors. This was the most powerful leverage the United States had had for a long time in its trade negotiations with Japan. If properly used, I thought that it might be possible to achieve a modus vivendi with the Japanese industry that would give the U.S. industry a chance to regain its health. Of course, for that outcome to occur, more than a mere trade agreement would be necessary, but it could not occur without one. The bleeding of the U.S. industry had to stop before the other steps necessary to return it to health could be taken.

## THE AGREEMENT OF 1986

The U.S. objectives remained what they always had been: greater access to the Japanese market (meaning more sales) and an end to dumping. Although superficially simple, these objectives implied other, more complex arrangements. For example, we wanted a halt to sales of chips at below-cost prices in the U.S. markets in order to raise prices to make it possible for efficient producers to make a profit. But the industry is international, and any agreement that raised chip prices only in the United States would tend to drive the chip users to search for cheaper products overseas—the reverse of our aim. Thus, effectively to halt dumping in the United States, it would be necessary to stop sales at below-cost prices in all markets, including that of Japan. In other words, we would have to persuade the Japanese government to force up prices in its home market as well as in third-country markets (that is, markets in countries other than the United States and Japan). This amounted to getting the Japanese government to force its companies to make a profit and even to impose controls to avoid excess production—in short, a government-led cartel.

For the free-traders of the United States to be asking Japan to cartelize its industry was the supreme irony. Yet it was logical. By systematically reducing risk for its industry, Japan had created a juggernaut that did not respond to Western market and financial disciplines. There were three possible responses. The United States could allow its industry to disappear; or it could restructure it in the Japanese mold by disavowing its own antitrust laws and its abhorrence of government-directed industrial policy; or it could get the Japanese government to substitute its discipline for that of the market. Being unwilling to accept the consequences of the first response or to execute the second, the U.S. government chose the third. It was subsequently criticized for doing so, but it had little choice. Even if it had not initiated its own dumping case, those of private industry would have resulted in imposition of dumping duties, making the United States an island of high prices and driving U.S. chip users overseas in search of cheaper components. The original Japanese intervention in the market had given rise to market distortion that could be corrected only by further intervention. There was no alternative to a comprehensive agreement.

The situation regarding market access was similar. As long as their home market was not protected, the U.S. firms could not survive over the long term unless they could sell in the Japanese market. That they held over 50 percent of the world market outside Japan while holding less than 10 percent of Japan's seemed to indicate some barriers in Japan (see figure 2.8). Yet experience told us that larger sales in Japan were unlikely as a result of agreements to remove barriers. Again, the Japanese market did not respond along Western lines, and we needed a comprehensive agreement including affirmative action by Japan to achieve some specific market share or sales target.

I thought these ambitious objectives might be achieved through pressure and skillful negotiation. MITI needed something this time, too. The dumping duties that would be levied on Japanese companies were potentially enormous. The popular myth was that all Japanese producers are extremely efficient. The truth is that while some are efficient, others are actually fairly high-cost producers. Our duties might drive some of these latter out of business. Moreover, although Kazuo Wakasugi, then MITI's vice minister for international affairs, was one of the ablest negotiators I have

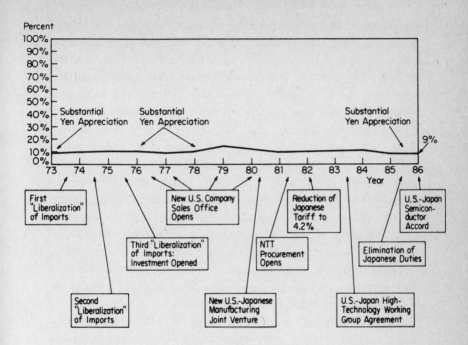

FIGURE 2.8
*U.S. Share of Japanese Semiconductor Market*
SOURCE: Semiconductor Industry Association

ever known, he had a concern for the health of the U.S. industry. He and others, like Kodama and Konaga, preferred the United States to be strong rather than enfeebled. They knew they had a problem in the tendency of Japanese industry to overinvest and then to get rid of excess production by going on export binges. They felt some responsibility for the problem, and U.S. negotiators could wisely appeal to that sense of responsibility.

The talks stretched out over many months, but again it was the negotiations among the Americans that proved decisive. As the U.S. trade deficit with Japan headed toward $50 billion despite continuous dollar devaluation, Congress demanded concrete action and began yet again to consider

tough trade legislation aimed at Japan. In response to this
pressure, Michael Smith, the deputy U.S. trade representative who was now leading negotiations with Japan, was allowed to suggest to the Japanese that a reasonable market
share for the U.S. producers might be 20 percent to 30 percent. This figure was based on a study by the economist William F. Finan indicating that the U.S. industry would have
obtained this share had Japan not pursued its industry-targeting policies.[33] But the abhorrence of managed trade on the
part of the departments of State, Treasury, the National Security Council, and other key agencies prevented us from
actually negotiating for specific amounts. Over all, we were
in a hypocritical position: we kept saying we only wanted
market access and not managed trade; yet at the same time,
we said that as a result of access we expected the cash regis-
ters to ring—and when the Japanese asked how loudly, we
said it had to be a solid ring.

Negotiations with Japan are always drawn out as the Japanese wait for divisions or personnel changes on the U.S. side
to weaken its position. In this case, the legal procedures of
the dumping cases fixed 31 July 1986 as a de facto deadline
for an agreement, if there was to be one. It was a foregone
conclusion that the talks would go to the wire. The Japanese
never make an offer except at the last possible moment and
under the severest pressure. No exception, these talks became a classic example of Japanese negotiating tactics. For
example, they made a great effort to divide and conquer. The
deputy U.S. trade representative Mike Smith was considered
a hard-liner by the Japanese; while his boss, the U.S. trade
representative Clayton Yeutter, was seen as more concilia-
tory. At one point the Japanese went over Smith's head to
Yeutter by having one of their lobbyists call Yeutter at home
at ten o'clock in the evening to request an immediate meeting. That it was highly unusual for a lower-ranking foreign
official to request a meeting with a cabinet officer at all, let
alone at that hour and at his home, did not deter the Japanese. In this case it did not work, but sometimes it did.

On 17 and 19 March 1986, the Commerce Department and the U.S. International Trade Commission made formal preliminary findings of massive dumping with some prices at only half the cost of production.[34] This meant that without an agreement the Japanese companies would probably be subject to huge fines. On 21 May, the House of Representatives voted 408 to 5 to urge the President to retaliate against Japan if no satisfactory agreement was reached soon.[35] Then in late June, Smith informed the Japanese that the cabinet was prepared to make a finding of unfair trade if Japan did not soon conclude a satisfactory agreement.

This was a truly dramatic moment. For the entire postwar period, the United States had ignored Japanese trade practices in the larger interest of maintaining a friendly overall relationship. Now for the first time after years of crying wolf, the government of the United States actually raised the possibility that it might be prepared to brand Japan an unfair trader. The critical change had been at the State Department, which for years had acted to protect Japan from its critics. Now the lack of American market penetration, after repeated liberalizations and the clear evidence of dumping, along with a statement in January by MITI's vice minister for international affairs that the U.S. might have to nationalize the supercomputer maker Cray Research to protect it from Japanese competition, had finally led State to believe that something other than free trade was taking place. In fact, no one will ever know whether the cabinet would actually have voted against the Japanese. To some extent Smith's move was a ploy to scare them. But it was close. The Japanese feared the unfair label because they knew that if it stuck in this case it might stick in hundreds of others. They could not afford to take a chance, and so a deal was struck at the last moment on 30 July 1986.

Signed formally on 2 September 1986, this third agreement on semiconductors had two main points.[36] The first dealt with market access and said the government of Japan would provide sales assistance to help U.S. companies sell in Japan and would encourage long-term relationships between Japanese users and U.S. suppliers. It also said that both governments anticipated improved opportunities for foreign sales in Japan. In the second part, Japan undertook to monitor costs and prices of products exported to the United States and to third markets to prevent dumping in accord with international rules of the General Agreement of Tariffs and Trade. Thus, the United States achieved a monitoring system in 1986 that its Justice Department had prevented it from requesting in 1982. In return for all this, the United States agreed to suspend the dumping cases and the unfair-trade case.

Such was the content of the public documents. But there was a confidential side letter. A favorite device of the Japanese bureaucracy, the side letter allows them to appear to concede to U.S. officials while maintaining publicly that there has been no concession. As U.S. officials change, the matter may be forgotten or reinterpreted with the result that there is no concession. It is an ambiguous device for retaining bureaucratic power which inevitably leads to later problems. In this side letter, the Japanese said that they understood, welcomed, and would make efforts to assist the U.S. companies in reaching their goal of a 20-percent market share within five years. The U.S. negotiators said that this commitment meant there would be a guaranteed increase in the U.S. share of the Japanese market.

Hailed by U.S. officials as a major step forward, this agreement was seen as outrageous by the press, economists, and many companies dependent on Japanese chips. The press and the economists condemned the agreement as a cartel and a blatant abrogation of free trade. The companies said that their ability to compete would be harmed if they had to pay higher prices for Japanese chips. There was no sense of identification with the American producers who only ten years before had been idolized as the new wave of American management. Unlike the Japanese, no one in the United States spoke of "our" industry and of the need to cooperate to help it. After all, industrialists were cowboys and if they couldn't hack it, they ought to move on and make way for the settlers from Japan who knew how to stick together better than anyone else in the world.

## THE UNITED STATES IMPOSES SANCTIONS

The initial result of the agreement was minimal. By the end of January 1987, sales below cost were still occurring in third-country markets. More important, despite a 40-percent fall in the value of the dollar, U.S. sales in Japan had hardly budged. In November 1986, MITI had promised the United States that the American market share would rise from 8.5 percent to 10 percent by March. Now MITI said that it was having difficulty obtaining the cooperation of its industry.

For the U.S. negotiators this was the last straw. After six years of agreements that produced no results, even the most reluctant agencies of the U.S. government had concluded that the Japanese market was effectively closed. Japan now seemed to be backing out of yet another agreement. MITI's comments also came at a particularly bad time, as Congress, with the total U.S. trade deficit at $150 billion, was once again threatening to pass what the White House called bad, protectionist trade legislation. If the agreement with Japan was not honored, the administration would not be able to stop Congress. Thus on 27 January 1987, the United States gave Japan sixty days in which to show it was fully in compliance with the agreement, and also began to prepare retaliatory measures.

Discussions continued until the end of March. MITI argued it had committed only to encourage Japanese companies to buy from U.S. producers, not to guarantee that they would. It said that it was keeping its part of the bargain and accused the U.S. negotiators of claiming a commitment where none existed. Here was the mischief of the side letter. The Americans truly thought they had been promised a material gain in sales in Japan. Was there a true misunderstanding among the negotiators, or was it a clever ploy by the Japanese to avoid a secret commitment by disclaiming it publicly? The Japanese claimed the former; the Americans, the latter. In any case, the sixty days produced no changes.

On 27 March, despite frantic Japanese lobbying and with a weather eye on Congress, the President announced sanctions in the form of tariffs of 300 percent on various Japanese products ranging from laptop computers to home power tools.[37] The irony was striking. While, in 1982, Murphy and I had been prevented from negotiating for a market share or for the data necessary to prevent dumping, now after five years in which the U.S. industry had been severely weakened, the President was saying the Japanese were unfair because they had not produced the results we had not been allowed to request. In response, MITI imposed strict production and export controls, and the dumping stopped while U.S. sales climbed a bit. A high MITI official told me MITI had made a mistake by not taking the United States seriously sooner.

The President's action appeared to be a firm defense of U.S. interests. In some respects it was, as it forced MITI finally to take firm measures that eventually did halt Japanese dumping and provide respite to a badly battered U.S. industry. On the other hand, a few months after imposition of the sanctions, the U.S. share of the Japanese market had actually dropped, and a highly placed MITI official told me that the sanctions actually demonstrated U.S. weakness. In explaining why, he noted that the list of products against which the sanctions had been imposed had been difficult to choose and included no items of significance and, most particularly, not semiconductors. The trick had been to impose tariffs in such a way as to punish Japanese producers but not hurt American consumers. In attempting to find products of importance to Japanese companies for which there were many alternative suppliers to the U.S. market, the President's trade experts had discovered that there are all too few:

indeed, the United States is so dependent on Japan that it was difficult even to draw up a meaningful list.

Moreover, once prepared, it had been necessary to present the list to public hearings. At these hearings, many U.S. consumers protested any action against Japanese products; and in letters to the U.S. trade representative on the subject, many members of Congress, while supporting the sanctions in principle, opposed any specific ones that hit their constituents. It became suddenly apparent how far Japan had penetrated the United States. Police chiefs from Montana, executives of major corporations, and obscure small businessmen all came forward to say their only source of supply was in Japan. And even the firmness of the President was soon called into question. Within two months, he had announced a partial lifting of the sanctions as a gift to his friend Prime Minister Yasuhiro Nakasone at the Venice summit meeting in June 1987. U.S. sales had not moved at all, but there was less dumping; and when Nakasone asked for a reward for showing progress, he received it. No one in Washington wanted to mistreat a friend and ally.

The report issued by Norman Augustine's Defense Science Board task force, released just before the announcement of sanctions, confirmed MITI's view of American weakness, and proposed that the Defense Department invest $600 million over six years to back a collective comeback effort by the U.S. industry. Called Sematech, the project was to be a joint business-government effort with thirteen U.S. companies—including, most significantly, IBM—contributing half the cost of developing prototype production lines that would enable the U.S. industry to catch up with Japan in the manufacturing of semiconductors. In the thirty years from 1957 to 1987, the U.S. and Japanese industries had traded places. Augustine's committee was now proposing for the United States a variant of what MITI had long ago established in Japan. The inevitable question was: Will it work?

By the summer of 1987, even mighty* AT&T had stopped producing RAMs, as well as all other memory products. It was now totally dependent on the Japanese for these devices as were most other major U.S. computer and electronics companies except IBM. This last, undefeated American giant was now very clearly feeling the effects of the Japanese concerted thirty-year drive to surpass it. IBM knew it was the ultimate target and that the dependence of the rest of the U.S. electronics industry would tend to neutralize it politically while turning it into a distribution pipeline for Japanese goods. Its surprisingly strong support for the Sematech project was evidence of its concern. Even more telling was the fact that, in mid-1987, IBM approached the Digital Equipment Corporation (DEC), its most dangerous domestic rival, and offered to transfer certain key technology. At first DEC suspected a trick. Then it realized the objective was to prevent DEC from falling even further into Japanese hands.

But despite this activity, MITI is now the arbiter of the world semiconductor industry. By controlling Japanese production, it determines world prices and the availability of critical devices. This became crystal clear in the summer of 1987 when I was asked by a major American semiconductor manufacturer to use my contacts at MITI to help arrange an increase in its supply of a key chip. That one of the pioneers of the U.S. semiconductor industry and one of the main forces behind the complaints that forced the agreement was now reduced to begging MITI for chips was a measure both of MITI's power and of how far the Americans had fallen.

The position of the U.S. government is also weak and ironic. Although it has long tried to persuade MITI to abandon its industrial policies, it is now asking MITI to intervene in the market in precisely the ways that were earlier described as objectionable. In doing so, it is enhancing the very MITI power it wishes to see decline. The United States is acting this way partly because of its own ideological reluctance and legal inability to intervene; but mostly it is doing so because it has no choice. The United States is now so dependent on Japan that it cannot move unilaterally to take the steps necessary to strengthen its industry even if it wants to, which is still far from clear. For example, a sharp drop in the value of the dollar would certainly help the industry. But the U.S. government cannot afford to let that happen because of the danger that it might lead to a cutoff of the flow of foreign capital on which it depends. At the same time, many in Congress were skeptical of funding Sematech. Why, they asked, should the government take risks private industry is unprepared to bear? They still did not understand, as the Japanese did, that reduction of risk by the government was the key to the whole game.

When I met with the heads of Japan's semiconductor manufacturers in the summer of 1987, they were confident and relaxed. None of them was dependent on any U.S. supplier and I was told that U.S. companies would be prevented from increasing their market share in Japan by the structure of the industry and the market there. And certainly no one in Japan was willing to change that structure, which was seen as a part of the nation's culture. Despite $4 billion[38] in losses over the past few years, no one there was thinking of abandoning the semiconductor industry. Their stock prices had not dropped; in some cases they had actually climbed, and even if they had dropped there would not have been any particular problem. There are no "green knights" or "white knights"* in Japan, and no one was going to take them over. The Japanese said the semiconductor industry is a strategic one in which they intend to remain, regardless of profits or losses. They had little regard for their U.S. competitors who, they claimed, are now behind in technology as well as in financial staying power. While the agreement was helping the U.S. companies, it was also helping the Japanese. Now that they had largely driven the U.S. firms out of the RAM business, the U.S. government was asking them to take the classic action of a monopolist and raise prices. Not a bad deal

---

*Green knights are unfriendly companies who engage in "greenmail": that is, the practice of making a hostile bid for a company's shares in order to force management to buy them back or sell to another at an inflated price. White knights are friendly companies that may come to the rescue of those under attack.

at all, the Japanese CEOs said, as they predicted that their next investment race would be in application-specific chips, a sophisticated field still controlled by the U.S. producers and not covered by the agreement. They were confident they could win in this area too, because, as they said, they had long focused on the strategy of building superior industrial structures, thinking of it not only as a means for obtaining wealth, but also as a tool for enhancing national power. And the structure they had built was more robust than that of the Americans.

Shortly after, in Silicon Valley, I met with Noyce, Sanders, and other U.S. industry leaders, who echoed the Japanese. The old entrepreneurs were working to get the Sematech effort off the ground, and they continued with the innovation that had always been their hallmark. You had to admire them. They never gave up. But they acknowledged that the days of the lone rider were over, and that the future depended on the U.S. government and the country at large. Operating by themselves, they said, the only possible strategy was to abandon any market the Japanese entered in force, which meant that the U.S. producers would always be confined to relatively small markets. So, can Sematech work? Can the U.S. industry recover? Of course it can. But only if it understands that the Japanese society, market, government, and companies do not operate according to the rules and assumptions of Western logic.

# PART II

## *What Makes Japan Run*

# 3

## PERCEPTION GAP: "UNFAIR" TRADE AND "OPEN" MARKETS

What the United States is asking is impossible.
—TOKUYUKI ONO, August 1987

IT was late in February 1982, and Masumi Esaki, a leader of Japan's ruling Liberal Democratic Party (LDP), looked like the kindly grandfather he is as he faced Secretary of Commerce Malcolm Baldrige across the long conference table in the latter's office. (Esaki was seated, as were all Japanese visitors, on the inside against the wall, because that is the traditional place of honor in Japan.) The Commerce Department had just announced the 1981 trade figures, which showed a sharp rise of the deficit with Japan to $16 billion.

President Nixon had called it unacceptable at $2 billion in 1972, and the Carter administration had warned the Japanese of a possible congressional explosion when it hit $11 billion in 1978. It was now 50 percent larger and headed higher—much higher. Just a year earlier it had seemed that the agreement by the Japanese to limit their exports of autos to the United States had relieved the growing tension between the two countries. But now the situation was worse than ever. As more and more people in the United States complained that Japan was always prepared to sell but rarely to buy, the administration urged Japan to open its market. Baldrige was one of the severest critics of Japan in this regard, and Esaki was here to explain a new set of Japanese market-opening measures and thereby to pour oil on troubled waters. If he could soften Baldrige's attitude, he could call the mission a success.

Physically and in personality, the men formed a contrast. Baldrige was tall, lean, and laconic. At the age of fifty-nine he was still a ranking roper in the National Rodeo Association and roped steers nearly every weekend. Asked once by a journalist to explain the difference between a cowboy and a politician, he replied, "A cowboy generally doesn't speak unless he has something to say." He had come to Washington after a career as a business executive. Esaki is short and plump and has a politician's ready smile and volubility. His career had been made as a mediator and consensus builder in the Japanese Diet (legislature) and the Liberal Democratic Party.

Despite the contrast, the two men had much in common and summarized in their personal experiences some of the most important elements in the history of relations between the two countries. At the time of Pearl Harbor, Baldrige had been eighteen and had enlisted in the army. During much of the war, he had fought in the Pacific and had been part of the Occupation in the Aizu–Wakamatsu area. He once described that experience to me:

> Our division had been fighting the Japanese for a long time, most recently on Okinawa. I had some concerns about how my troops would react to occupation duty. On arrival, we saw mostly older people, women, and kids without enough to eat. They were scared half to death of the long-nosed mustached GIs who, according to Japanese propaganda posters, would rob, rape, and

pillage. But pretty soon candy was passing from GIs to kids. Hell, those people in that town were no enemy. We did the best we could to help them out.

He had gone on to become chief executive of Scoville Industries, building it from a small brass manufacturer into a large, diversified maker of products ranging from tire valves to home appliances. Among other things, the company had built a profitable operation in Japan.

Esaki had missed the fighting because of poor health, but he had not escaped the devastation that befell Japan. He had entered politics immediately after the war and was first elected to the Diet as a young man of thirty-one in 1946. As a budding politician, he had closely observed the nature of the Occupation and of the Americans who administered it. Like all Japanese, at first he had not known what to expect and had shared the fears of his countrymen. But he soon recognized a generosity and goodwill among the Americans that gave him hope for the future. That future took Esaki to the top of Japanese politics as a government minister and key party operative, and all along the way he had been a friend of the United States.

Now these two men, who had become adults on opposite sides in a war, and had come to respect and have affection for their former opponents, were sitting across from each other trying to find a way to prevent any further conflict between their two countries.

## The Problem of "Unfair" Trade

The trade problem with Japan has always been defined in terms of the ballooning trade deficit and explained in terms of overall economic factors such as exchange and interest rates. In the minds of most commentators and of the public at large, the size of the deficit became a measure of the seriousness of the problem. This was particularly true among the Japanese, who were convinced that the main difficulty was with the numbers. In a sense, this was true, and it was also true that part of the reason for the bad numbers were the basic economic factors. But the United States had large trade deficits with other countries such as Canada which did not engender the same feeling as the deficit with Japan. In fact, the unusual emotion and potential for conflict that surrounded the issue in the case of Japan was linked to something much deeper than mere statistics. It was the American sense of fair play.

This concern for fairness was signaled most strongly by Senator John Danforth of Missouri. In February 1982, upon returning from a trip to Tokyo, he had promptly introduced reciprocity legislation aimed at denying Japan access to the U.S. market until it granted similar access to its own market. He explained that his reason for doing so was that he had seen no change of attitudes and no genuine opening of the Japanese market over the past several years despite commitments to the contrary.

That was the nub of the problem. It is undeniable that the Americans would have preferred smaller deficits. But the strong emotions engendered by the unequal balance of trade with Japan stemmed from a feeling that Japan wasn't playing fairly, that it kept its markets closed to others, while its exports penetrated foreign markets ever more deeply. Japan's imports of manufactured goods as a percentage of gross national product had been 1.5 percent in 1960. In 1986, they were 1.6 percent despite several rounds of liberalizing trade negotiations in which Japan had made what appeared to be significant concessions. Over the same period, the U.S. numbers had gone from under 1 percent to 4.4 percent, and those for the European Economic Community (excluding intra-European trade) from 1.1 percent to 4.5 percent.[1] Thus the amount of imports had quadrupled in the United States and European economies in response to liberalization, while remaining virtually unchanged in Japan. Moreover, there was the pattern of Japan's trade: whenever a product was manufactured in Japan, imports of it were nearly nil. For example, while the largest export and import items for France and Germany were automobiles, Japan's huge auto exports were unmatched by more than token imports. The United States was both an importer and exporter of electronic equipment. Japan exported, but imported very little.

Beyond the statistics, stories and complaints about unfair trade flooded Washington. It seemed that nearly everyone who had done business in Japan had one. American soda ash, used for glass and steel making, was 20 percent less expensive than Japanese ash, but could not find a significant market in Japan. While Japanese stock brokers bought seats on the New York Stock Exchange, U.S. brokers were barred from the Tokyo exchange. Although 70 percent of the blood plasma used in Japan came from the United States, U.S. companies could not be the importers or handle shipments in Japan; and U.S. tire valves, which had a 60 percent share of the world market, could not find buyers in Japan after years of road tests. Although a major buyer of U.S. logs, Japan exported more plywood to the United States than it imported.

These cases, coupled with the rapidly mounting trade deficit, were what led Congress in 1981 to call for action and to threaten retaliation if Japan did not open its markets. As a staunch supporter of free trade, the Reagan administration rejected congressional demands in favor of negotiation—a position taken by all postwar administrations. That further negotiations were necessary was, of course, due to the failure of the earlier efforts, and that failure gave rise to a cumulative sense of frustration as Baldrige and U.S. Trade Representative William Brock saw their own market-opening efforts with Japan bog down in 1981. They found it more and more difficult to explain in their frequent testimony before Congress why there was nothing to show for all the hours of talks with Japan except more horror stories. Consequently, they, like the Congress, became increasingly stern in their public comments on Japan.

Japan's early-warning network, consisting of its diplomats in Washington and New York along with the ex–U.S. government officials they retain as consultants, had been monitoring the situation with growing alarm, sending danger signals to Tokyo throughout the summer and fall. Just as in Washington, so in Tokyo frustration mounted. Many in Japan's cabinet and ruling Liberal Democratic Party thought that the Americans could never be satisfied. The Japanese were tired of being criticized for unfair trade each time they took a trip abroad, particularly because they thought the criticism unjustified. Japan, they reasoned, had worked hard for its success and was now being made a scapegoat for the laziness and incompetence of the Americans. How could these people expect to export to Japan when they could not even defend their own domestic markets? To the Japanese, the problem was not barriers in Japan, of which they believed there were few, but simply that the Americans did not try hard enough—a feeling particularly strong among younger members of the party, whose memory of the war, the Occupation, and the U.S. role in Japan's recovery was vague if not nonexistent.

The recurrent pattern in the relationship between the United States and Japan had by now become a kind of ritual. First, the United States would demand that Japan open its markets. After prolonged and tedious haggling, Japan would offer some apparent relaxation of restrictions and the United States would thank the Japanese profusely and hail the measures as great progress. Shortly, however, those sent to execute the new agreements would find that things did not work as anticipated. They would then complain of unfairness and of new barriers and renew the demand for opening.

The history of this pattern goes back to Perry's arrival in Tokyo Bay. After demanding that Japan open itself to trade, he had sailed away, promising to return within a year for the

Japanese answer. When in 1855 the answer was yes, Perry returned home a hero. Among other things, he thought he had obtained agreement to the exchange of consular representatives. However, when Townsend Harris arrived in August 1856 and announced himself as the new U.S. consul general, he was surprised to find that the Japanese were not expecting him. They said they had agreed to the exchange only if both sides thought it desirable, and they definitely did not. Poor Harris's first task was literally to negotiate his way off the ship into the country he had been told Perry had opened for trade.

Moreover, once off the ship, Harris found himself controlled at every turn. He was not allowed to buy goods or even groceries directly from merchants, but had to turn over his money to the authorities who then made purchases for him. Guards were assigned to "protect" him, but when he asked that they be removed, it became clear that their real task was to control his movements. Everything that Perry thought had been agreed had to be renegotiated, not "in principle," but in terms of the precise manner in which it would be executed.

By the fall of 1981, the pattern was being repeated increasingly often, and many of the Japanese were becoming as disgruntled as the Americans. Esaki, however, argued that the United States had helped Japan back onto its feet when it was down; and that if America had run into trouble now, it was Japan's turn to help. When the Japanese cabinet became convinced in the fall of 1981 that Japan should offer yet another batch of market-opening measures, it had naturally turned to Esaki to take charge of the development of what came to be known as the "Esaki package of new market-opening measures."

Now in the winter of 1982, he had come to Washington to present his program and to seek the blessing of Secretary Baldrige upon it. As Esaki explained it to us, the package dealt with ninety-nine issues that had been the object of foreign complaint. Of these, the Japanese said that fifteen were the result of misunderstanding, eight were problems on which Japan deemed its policies to be right and necessary, and nine required further study. For the remaining sixty-seven, action would be taken to eliminate the complaints. A major innovation was also announced. In 1980, the independent Advisory Council on U.S.-Japan Relations, better known as the "wise men's group," had proposed that Japan create an Office of Trade Ombudsman (OTO). Esaki now said that such an office would be established and would be available to listen to foreign complaints about trade and re-solve them by overcoming misunderstandings and bureau-cratic bottlenecks.

There were two problems. One was the package itself. Of the sixty-seven items, action on nineteen had been an-nounced previously, five were counted more than once, and five were supposed to have been solved in a previous agree-ment.[2] Thus, it was clear that the economic impact of the package would be minimal. The ombudsman proposal was interesting, but as presented it appeared the office would be little more than a mailbox for foreign complaints, with no independent authority to effect change.

Aside from this, however, was the more fundamental problem of the basis of the package, which reflected the view of the Japanese that their market was basically as open as any other. They did not see many barriers. Foreign com-plaints were viewed as relatively minor problems, usually due to misunderstanding of the culturally very different Jap-anese, and easily resolved through technical, bureaucratic measures. Since the Japanese did not recognize the broader, systemic barriers of which Americans spoke, they could not respond to them.

It was clear that the secretary was not going to bless these measures. The only important question with regard to our ultimate attitude was Esaki's sincerity. Did he really believe that these measures were going to solve the problems, or was he just engaging in maneuvering and delaying tactics?

I had been skeptical at first, because I wondered how anyone could possibly think that action on these ninety-nine or sixty-seven measures would remove the poison from the trade relationship between the U.S. and Japan. Some in the United States were already calling the package an insult. But as I listened to Esaki and heard the tone of hope in his voice as he described the office of the ombudsman, I felt he was sincere. He had had to develop the package rapidly and thereby inevitably had become to some extent the captive of the Japanese bureaucracy from which his staff had been drawn. He was also subject to the vested interests in the Liberal Democratic Party that made it very difficult for Japan's leaders to deliver on their commitments. He knew the ninety-nine measures were not going to make a difference, but he was hoping the ombudsman would. I was pleased by this, but also a bit sad. Baldrige was also sincere and wanted to solve this problem just as much as Esaki did. But I knew Esaki's explanation was not going to sound convincing to Baldrige or anyone else on the U.S. side.

The Japanese had told the secretary that they wanted his "frank" opinion, and Baldrige took them at their word. In just slightly more polite language, he told them that the package was not worth considering. He said that unless Japan took some dramatic action to open its markets soon, the reciprocity bills of Danforth and others in Congress would pass and lead to restrictions on Japan's exports to the United States. Baldrige managed to give the impression that that course might not entirely displease him.

As I looked around the table, the shock of the Japanese was palpable. They had asked the secretary to be frank, but they had not meant this frank. In Japan the omission of effusive praise is like a slap in the face; in New Mexico, where the secretary had his ranch, they tell it like it is. The two styles mixed with difficulty.

Esaki asked the secretary what specific measures, in addition to those already announced, he wanted the Japanese to take. But Baldrige was not interested in lists. He responded by saying he wanted U.S. businessmen to have the same opportunities to sell, produce, and invest in Japan that Japanese businessmen had in the United States.

Esaki looked puzzled. "But what specifically did the Americans want?" asked one of his aides. At this point, time ran out and the meeting ended. As Esaki left, I could tell he was frustrated. I knew that the secretary was as close to angry as he ever got, and I was saddened by the realization that two men of goodwill had talked but had not communicated. In that instant, I realized what the problem was: they were not speaking the same language. It was not a matter of translating English into Japanese, or vice versa, but something much more profound.

The point was reinforced when Esaki returned to Japan. In addition to Baldrige, nearly everyone else he had met in the states had received his package coldly—a result that elicited anger in Tokyo, where Baldrige was portrayed by the press as unreasonable. The prime minister criticized the U.S. demands as abstract and without specific details. Undersecretary Olmer responded that Japan was trying to create a smokescreen by concentrating on specific issues rather than dealing with larger, underlying problems.

But misperception was rife on both sides. After the war, Japan had molded itself along the lines of the capitalist, democratic model. It had a strong urge to be accepted as a full member of the club of industrial democracies and thus presented its system to Americans as being more or less like their own. Since the form was similar, Americans tended to accept that substantively it also worked about the same way. When U.S. officials asked Japan to *open* its markets, they did not think of defining that simple term because they assumed the Japanese understood it. But the Japanese had no conception of what the Americans meant by *open*.

Prime Minister Suzuki's frustrated plea for specifics was not a smokescreen. It was a cri de coeur. He thought Japan's market was already open. Although there were some important exceptions, its tariff rates were among the world's lowest, and it had fewer quotas on imports than many other nations. On top of that, his government had just offered a package of unilateral concessions on problems about which the Americans had been complaining for years. Reading between the lines, I could almost hear him saying to himself: "It is true that none of those concessions is likely to have much effect on the trade figures, but when we finally got them out of the clouds of generality about being open, that is what they said they wanted. What more can we do?"

The misperceptions involved were best captured in a remark made to me by Henry Marini, an old Japan hand who was president of Revlon–Japan at the time. Describing the difference between Japan and the United States, he said that in the United States, everything is allowed unless specifically prohibited, while in Japan, everything is prohibited unless specifically allowed. The problem was the meaning of *open*.

In the United States, *open* is rich with implicit, rarely articulated meanings. Openness implies law-making procedures where any citizen can walk into a hearing room and watch as bills are prepared and debated for passage into law. It implies the ability of one solitary citizen to obtain an injunction that can stop the whole U.S. government dead in its tracks. It implies a judicial system that provides reasonably speedy justice, the concept of affirmative action to overcome the effects of past injustice, a multitude of checks and balances to prevent agglomerations of both economic and political power, and a system of buying that operates on the basis of the best offer rather than the relationship of buyer to seller. Little as Baldrige and other Americans thought about these things consciously when they used the term *open*, that is what they meant.

The meaning has grown out of the nature of the United States. Nations set themselves tasks, sometimes consciously, sometimes unconsciously. The great task of the United States for over two hundred years has been to take people of all creeds, races, nationalities, and walks of life and integrate them into one society, in a way that establishes a coherent nation while allowing citizens the freedom to maintain their differences. The Latin motto of the United States—*E Pluribus Unum* ("out of many, one")—describes this process best.

Americans often tease themselves about having too many lawyers, which is probably true. But in a society of immigrants, one cannot assume automatic understanding or trust. Thus the rule-making and enforcing procedures become vitally important. Transparent and open procedures, the right of appeal, protection of the rights of the minority from the tyranny of the majority, due process, habeas corpus—these concepts and others are crucial to making that kind of society successful. They also make it "open."

Suzuki and Esaki and their countrymen, albeit living in a form of capitalist democracy, do not breathe that kind of air. Their society is very different, however similar some of the forms.

## The Japanese Sense of Difference

The study of what makes the Japanese different has filled many volumes. It is a subject that particularly fascinates the Japanese: at last count, there were close to a thousand *Nihonjin-ron*, books mostly by Japanese, about what makes them different from everyone else. Some of the more bizarre explanations include the idea that the Japanese have about thirty more feet of intestines than other people, and that the Japanese brain performs its functions in different areas than the brains of other nationalities.[3]

The fascinating aspect of this phenomenon is not the particular explanations but the near obsession of the Japanese with their uniqueness. Indeed, the concept even extends beyond people to things. One of the recent trade issues involved the contention that Japanese soil is different from that of other countries. This sense the Japanese have of their own uniqueness, which has struck all observers of Japan as one of the keys to the nature of its society, gives rise to a certain tribal pride. In the fall of 1986, Prime Minister Nakasone made a speech in which he said that Japan's homogeneity enabled the attainment of higher educational levels in Japan than was possible in the United States with its large minority groups. This statement led to such an uproar in the United States that Nakasone partially retracted it. But those familiar with Japanese thinking were not surprised.[4] On the day Nakasone made his remarks, I had a meeting with a senior official of MITI in the course of which we talked about the factors behind Japan's great economic success. He listed three: the system of lifetime employment, mutually supportive business-government relations, and harmonious labor-management relations. Then he added a fourth—homogeneity. Although he was aware of the makeup of my family, he said it without any thought that I, who have a wife of Chinese ancestry, an adopted Japanese son, and an adopted Filipino son, might find the statement odd or offensive. To him it was an obvious, objective fact.

## THE IMPORTANCE OF THE GROUP

One of the aspects of Japan that surely is unique, at least among major societies, is the extreme emphasis on the group, rather than the individual, as the key social entity. All societies organize into groups for the purpose of accomplishing various tasks that someone working alone cannot perform. But in Japan there is virtually no life outside groups, which define a person's existence. When asked what kind of work he does, a Japanese man will respond with the name of the organization that employs him. He usually won't say that he is a salesman or an engineer unless pressed for a further explanation, because the key to his identity is not the specific kind of work, but the organization to which he belongs.

Those who have studied Japan have noted this phenomenon and have given various explanations for it. One of the first Western commentators was Lafcadio Hearn, an Englishman who lived in and wrote extensively on Japan at the turn of the century. In acquiring a house, he found that he had gotten not only a house but also gardeners and other workers who, having serviced it before, continued as in the past, despite the change of ownership. They belonged to the organization of that house. Hearn thought that this group mentality arose from the religious obligations of the community to care for the spirits of the dead.[5] Other observers have attributed it to the cooperative efforts required in rice cultivation, while still others have argued that it has to do with the fact that in Japan success is measured more in terms of power and influence, which can be exercised only in groups, than in those of accumulation of wealth, which is more an individual undertaking. Whether these are origins or just further manifestations of the group mentality is probably an unanswerable question. But anyone who has watched Japanese tourists flock around the leader holding the group's flag realizes something of the importance of the group in Japan.

The model for groups is the *ie* (household). In fact, one might think of Japan in terms of concentric circles of groups, such as school class, clubs, company, and ultimately, nation, all attempting to imitate the household group that is at their core. Membership in a group entails forming personal relationships with deep social and emotional meaning. Each group functions as a surrogate household, and people have the same obligations to and derive the same support from other group members as from family members.

A great deal of the time and energy of most Japanese is absorbed in building these intensely personal relationships and nurturing them in order to maintain group morale and one's status as a group member in good standing. The long hours of the Japanese businessman are legendary. Many of those hours are spent not working but socializing with fellow employees or members of some other group. This activity is an important part of maintaining the close personal ties that provide the group's spiritual sustenance in the same way family ties do. The very language reflects the Japanese view of the company as a family. One businessman in conversation with another will refer to his own company as *uchi*, the diminutive form of "my house," and to the other's company as *otaku*, the honorific form of "your house."

The importance of the group identity in Japan might be compared to that of sects like the Amish of southeastern Pennsylvania. They, too, have identified themselves as a people apart, following beliefs and customs very different from those around them. To maintain this apartness requires constant nurturing of the ethic or creed and of the ties between the group members. This nurturing in turn engenders emotional dependence on the group which makes separation painful. Among the Amish, the ultimate punishment is the practice of shunning, whereby a member is effectively banished. In Japan, *mura hachi bu* (separation from the village) is thought of as akin to death.

The emotional dependence of the Japanese on the group was brought home to me when I worked as general manager of the Japanese subsidiary of an American medical equipment company. Our office was in downtown Tokyo, which made for a two-hour commute for most of our salesmen. Rather than have them come to the office before beginning sales calls every day, I instructed them to go to their appointments directly from home and to come to the office only for a weekly sales meeting. Although this is a common way for a U.S. sales force to operate, it was a disaster in Japan. Sales fell, as did morale. I quickly changed the policy and had everyone come to the office every day. Sales immediately climbed as the salesmen reinforced their group identity.

## THE CONCERN WITH HARMONY

For the Japanese, the foremost value is harmony within the group—an idea unfamiliar to Americans imbued with the concept of the importance of justice for the individual. I learned it the hard way, while consulting for a U.S. manufacturer in Japan. The company's Japanese distributor had copied its product and had begun to sell it in competition with the original. At the same time, the distributor kept a large inventory of the original American product and continued to offer that to customers while it tested the new Japanese product. I urged the Japanese manager of the U.S. company to get a court injunction against the distributor for selling the product without authorization. It was not fair, I argued. But he responded that such an action would be seen as disruptive and could mortally wound our reputation, thus doing us more harm than good in the long run. As it turned out, the business we lost was almost a mortal wound, but the reasoning of that manager impressed upon me the importance the Japanese attach to harmony, as opposed to the Western emphasis on justice.

Achieving and maintaining harmony among human beings is not easy. In the West, the emphasis is on means internal to the individual, such as brotherly love and conscience. In the group-oriented society of Japan, however, the stress is on external pressure, such as conformity, group ethics, and close human ties.[6]


## THE CONCERN WITH CONFORMITY

The emphasis on conformity is best illustrated by a topic currently of great concern in Japan: that is, *ijime*, which roughly translates as "bullying" or "picking on someone." Many incidents are reported of groups of children—sometimes even led by a teacher—harassing, at times even brutally, those who seem different for one reason or another. This is a particular problem for Japanese children who have lived overseas for a time and then must return to school in Japan. They are often ostracized for being different and un-

Japanese. The problem is great enough that some schools, such as the International Christian University, have organized special sections and courses of study just for returnees.

Japanese observers acknowledge that the main instrument for imbuing the code of conformity is the school system, which is rigidly centralized, with standard texts and courses established by the Ministry of Education. The system emphasizes rote memorization of such materials, which are imparted in a prescribed manner by a teacher who is an authority figure. Graduates of the system report that from the first grade, teachers stress both the uniqueness of the Japanese and rigid conformity to group norms. Questions and individual activity are discouraged. The Japanese government is now studying ways to introduce more emphasis on individuality. It will be interesting to see the results.

## GROUP ETHICS AND WATCHING

Conformity requires both group ethics and constant watching. Nothing wrecks the harmony of a group more quickly than the individual with a sudden attack of conscience. The Japanese ethic is nearly captured in the proverb *Minna watareba kowakunai* (If everyone crosses, there can be no trouble). To understand this, envision a group of people at a traffic crossing with the "Do Not Walk" sign flashing. If only one person in the group crosses against the sign, he or she may feel slightly guilty or even be subject to a fine for jaywalking. But if all cross, there is no guilt or shame and probably no fine, since the police are not going to arrest everyone. In this situation, the person who insists on remaining until the light changes is the one who makes people uneasy and thus shatters the harmony of the group.

A fascinating example of this ethic at work was the reaction in Japan to the Hitachi–IBM spy incident in 1982. Because of its strategy of making IBM-compatible computers, it has been important for Hitachi to keep itself informed about the development of new IBM products. To do this it employed consultants from the United States, some of whom were former IBM employees. At one point, one of these consultants, William Palyn, thought that what Hitachi was requesting him to do was illegal, and informed the FBI. The bureau, which had been running a sting* operation in Silicon Valley for some time in an effort to prevent theft and the transfer of technology to the Soviet bloc, now caught both Hitachi and Mitsubishi obtaining proprietary IBM documents in questionable ways.

Most Americans who were aware of the incident thought the culprits deserved to be caught and punished, since theft is wrong and illegal. The Japanese reaction was quite the opposite. Sting operations are considered distasteful in Japan, and are used only in narcotics cases. The reason is not hard to comprehend. A society in which acceptable behavior is determined by following strictly what others do is vulnerable to stings, which involve the police in deliberately encouraging unacceptable behavior. The feeling in Japan is that if some members of the group are doing something, the others really cannot be expected to refrain from doing it also. Thus, the operators of the sting rather than its victims are to be condemned for consciously leading the group astray.

As for the concept of watching, harmony requires sensitivity to the needs of others. To be sure that one's behavior is acceptable, one needs to watch what others are doing. Mutual watching has a long tradition in Japan. In the Tokugawa era (1600–1867), the shoguns (military dictators) employed what was known as the *go-nin gumi* system, where groups of five households were held responsible for the actions of individual members for such things as tax and loan payments and infractions of sumptuary laws. During the Second World War, *tonari gumi* (neighborhood associations) were used to

---

*A "sting" operation is one in which police may pose as accomplices to an illegal activity in order to catch those breaking the law.

enforce a rigid control of society. Today Western officials are often amazed by the strong reaction of their Japanese counterparts to newspaper stories and leaks: the reason is that Japanese officials watch the press intently in order to divine in what direction the group is likely to go.[7]

### THE IMPORTANCE OF PERSONAL RELATIONSHIPS

*Ningen kankei* (human relations) is the glue of all Japanese groups. Establishing good personal relations with colleagues and others of possible influence is an overriding priority with the Japanese. In the West, contracts or professional obligations often are expected to take precedence over friendship or even family ties. In Japan, personal ties and family relationships are far more important. A small but telling example of this is the practice Japanese officials and business executives have, when moving from one post to another, of carefully informing all acquaintances. I still receive such notifications from men with whom I have had no dealings for years.

The Hitachi–IBM case is another example. From the American point of view, in reporting his suspicions, Palyn was acting ethically. He had profited from his long association with Hitachi and would have made more money if the association continued. Since he stood to lose by upholding principle, the fact that he upheld it nevertheless was thought admirable by Americans. The Japanese, on the other hand, felt his conduct to be despicable and dishonorable. In their eyes, this man had betrayed those who had taken him into their trust. He had committed the gravest sin: he had broken a human bond and proven unreliable. Rather than condemning Hitachi, as the Americans did, the Japanese rallied to its side; the attitudes of IBM–Japan employees toward their own company were uncertain enough to compel top IBM executives to rush to Japan in an effort to maintain loyalty and morale. In Japan it was Hitachi, not IBM, that was

seen as the aggrieved party. Indeed, most Japanese saw the
FBI's involvement as proof that the U.S. government was
carrying out an industrial policy aimed at preventing Japanese industry from surpassing IBM.

## THE CONCEPT OF HIERARCHY

Families are traditionally authoritarian, hierarchical organizations, and so are Japan's groups. The concept of hierarchy is so deeply ingrained that it is literally impossible to
speak Japanese without first establishing a hierarchy. In
many respects, Japanese is a simple language, with no
plurals, no gender, and only vague grammatical rules. But it
is the richest language in the world in hierarchical forms.
The polite *vous* and informal *tu* of French suggests the guiding principle, but in Japanese this concept is taken to an extreme degree. Verbs, adjective endings, and entire forms of
expression change depending on whether the person addressed is higher, equal, or lower in the hierarchy than the
speaker.

For example, the head of a division in a Japanese corporation will address a subordinate named Suzuki as *Suzuki-kun*.
*Kun* is an informal diminutive form of the well-known Japanese *san*. In English, this would be like using "Bobbie" to
address someone named Bob. A subordinate, on the other
hand, will address a department head as *Shimizu bu-cho*, or
simply as *bu-cho san* (division head Shimizu or honorable division head). This hierarchy of language is one of the reasons
for the Japanese custom of exchanging business cards. What
many in the West see as an example of Japanese efficiency is,
in fact, an essential step to establish the tone and form of the
conversation to follow.

This concern with hierarchy, deeply rooted in Japanese
history, permeates every aspect of Japanese life. The Tokugawa shogunate, while not creating the hierarchical concept,
did enforce it rigidly for 250 years and engrained it deeply in

the national psyche. Japan long ago ceased to be a feudal society, although the *bu-cho* (department chief), *ka-cho* (section chief), *sha-in* (employee) structure of all Japanese organizations corresponds to the rankings in the ancient clan armies and the authority of the superior coupled with the total dedication expected of the subordinate in Japanese organizations still strikes Westerners as being slightly feudal.

I witnessed an example of this respect for position recently at Dulles Airport in Washington, D.C. As I was entering the airport, I noticed the arrival of a former vice minister (the highest career rank in the Japanese civil service) of Japan's Ministry of Posts and Telecommunications. As I walked over to greet him, I saw a throng of Japanese—representatives of the embassy and of Japanese companies with Washington offices—lined up in a corner of the baggage claim area to shake his hand. His baggage was taken care of, and a limousine was on hand to whisk him to his hotel. Shortly thereafter, during a flight to Washington, I noted that my seatmates included a former secretary of defense and a former national security adviser. When we landed, no one was there to greet them, and they probably had to explain to a non-English-speaking cabdriver where they were going, just like everyone else.

## THE SENSE OF EXCLUSIVENESS

While all societies recognize a difference between members and strangers or foreigners, Japan emphasizes the distinction. Exclusionism comes naturally to groups that are tightly bound by a self-conscious sense of uniqueness, in which deep personal relationships are intensely nurtured in the context of hierarchical structures that stress the importance of an assigned place for everyone. New entrants disturb the intricate web of relationships. Because the only position open to newcomers in an established hierarchy is at the bottom, there is no room for an outsider for whom a

higher rank may be more appropriate. Such a person
threatens harmony, the ultimate value of the group, and
therefore tends to be rejected.

All foreign residents of Japan have their favorite stories
illustrating the results of this attitude. Mine came from my
experience in adopting a Japanese baby as my son. An
unwed Japanese mother decided to make her baby available
for adoption. My wife and I saw the boy the day after he was
born and agreed to adopt him. After caring for the child for a
year and going through the procedures of the Japanese family court, we were made the legal parents. We had then to
move the child's birth registration from the town in which he
was born to the one in which we resided. When we went to
our local ward office to accomplish this, I was informed that
even though my wife and I were the legal parents, our signature wasn't sufficient. We were told that we would have to
find the natural mother (whom we did not know and who
wasn't particularly eager to be found) and obtain her signature. After an extensive search, we located the woman and
got the required signature. But our troubles were not over.
To leave Japan, we needed a Japanese passport for the boy.
Although we were the legal parents, the passport had to be
issued in the name of the natural mother. As a result, my
son was brought to the United States on a passport bearing a
name that was not his. It was very difficult for the Japanese
to understand that one of them could also be one of us.

The boat people and refugees of Indochina are another example. Since the fall of Saigon in 1974, over 413,000 of these
people have settled in the United States. One young woman,
Jean Nguyen, was hailed by President Reagan during his
1985 State of the Union message for her graduation from the
United States Military Academy. Another, Hoang Tran, grad-
uated at the head of his Air Force Academy class in 1987.
Japan took in fewer than 3,000 boat people and did so only
under the pressure of world public opinion.[8] It is inconceivable that the children of any of those people, let alone a
woman, could enter Japan's élite services.

Indeed, the perfect contrast to the example of the U.S. Military Academy graduate was provided in 1986 by Tokyo University, the training ground of Japan's élite. Traditionally, entrance to the university has been possible only by passing a difficult examination for which preparation in Japanese secondary schools is practically a prerequisite. Since this practice had the effect of excluding foreign students and even Japanese who had spent long periods abroad, it was proposed to establish a special track for these students in the entrance examination system. This plan was opposed by many who thought it would be unfair to provide easier access to some just because they happened to be foreigners or from Japanese families living abroad. Despite the opposition, the university decided to go ahead. But the apparently progressive nature of the decision was belied by the explanation of it. A Tokyo University education, said the school, should be aimed only at those who pass the entrance exam and who in principle are Japanese. On the other hand, since Japan has emerged at the center of the international stage, it might be a good experience for these students to meet foreigners while at the university and also to come in contact with Japanese who behave differently from other Japanese by dint of having lived overseas. For that reason, stressed the university, it would not introduce any special curriculum for these new students because it did not want to Japanize them to the extent that the experiment in international education would be undermined. As the Tokyo University professor Shumpei Kumon later said, it was as if the foreigners were to be exhibits in a museum or guinea pigs in a laboratory experiment.[9] Yet these attitudes do not mean the Japanese are unsympathetic or unwilling to help. Japan's expenditures on foreign aid, for example, place it in the ranks of the largest donors. But it is difficult to help if help means absorbing something new into its society, because the group tends to expel intruders.

The identification by the university of Japanese living abroad as akin to foreigners points to another important phenomenon: the difficulty the Japanese themselves sometimes have fitting back into their own society after living abroad. At a recent going-away party for a Japanese diplomat in Washington, I remarked to his wife that she must be glad to be going home after so many years. Her immediate and emphatic reply, "Not at all," wasn't what I had expected. She explained that in the United States she had great freedom. "Here I'm alive," she said. "I accompany my husband to parties and am included in the life of the embassy and of the city. In Tokyo I'm excluded." She went on to explain that she was also concerned for her children. She was looking into one of the special programs that some of the schools offer for returnees. Even so, she thought the children would have some difficulty being accepted by their classmates.

Later the same evening, I spoke with her husband. Knowing he had a great deal of accumulated vacation time, I asked if he was going to stop over in Hawaii and take some of it before starting on his new assignment. He said he might stop for a day, and then, somewhat self-consciously, added, "You understand." I did understand. He had obtained a degree from a prestigious U.S. graduate school and was an accomplished and cosmopolitan person. He wanted a vacation, but knew that to take one would make his re-entry more difficult, because it would raise the suspicion that he had become too Americanized. It might be interpreted as a kind of disloyalty to the group he was about to rejoin.

Agnes Niyekawa, a University of Hawaii professor, has studied the problems of Japanese returnees for some time. In an interview with the *Wall Street Journal* on 6 May 1986, she noted, "Japan is so homogenous and intolerant of deviation that even after ten years back in Japan, returnees may be criticized because their way of thinking is too direct." In the same article, Seinosuke Kashima, an official with a Japanese trading company who had returned to Japan after several years in the United States, remarked, "Japanese tend to form groups naturally. And every returnee is viewed as a newcomer, even if he has been in the group before. It took me some time to fit back in."[10]

Much of what we associate with Japan derives from the dynamics of Japan's hierarchical groups. For instance, lifetime employment has not always been the standard for all workers in Japan. But there has never been much turnover among employees of Japanese companies for the simple reason that to leave one company and join another means to be a newcomer in a new group. No matter what the formal position might be, in actuality it means starting at the bottom and attempting to climb all over again. For a company to hire an executive from outside for a key management position, as is done in the United States, is close to impossible. The new man would not fit and would not know how to manage the intricate web of relationships carefully nurtured over the years. The scarcity of entrepreneurs in Japan is also easy to understand. Both the emphasis on conformity and the fact that an entrepreneur cannot, by definition, be in a group, at least not at the beginning of his undertaking, limit any such efforts.

While Americans observing Japan usually note with envy that it appears to have few lawyers and little litigation, in fact virtually all of Japan's bureaucrats and many of its businessmen are trained in law and perform many of the functions in Japanese society that lawyers perform in American society; and while it is true that there is little litigation, that does not mean that there are no disputes in Japan. It means only that they are handled informally through negotiation and the play of personal relationships. Even in the United States, members of a family do not normally haul each other into court. While this has the advantage of preserving harmony, it does not necessarily provide for due process or fairness in the American sense. In disputes between important persons and unimportant persons, the unimportant person is at more of a disadvantage in Japan than in the United States because his rights derive only from his position in the group, not from the belief that individuals have rights.

While the intervention of the government into the smallest

nooks and crannies of Japanese life and the apparent expectation of the Japanese that it should do so often strikes
Americans as strange, it is quite natural for members of a
hierarchical group to look to the élite levels of the group to
act in a paternal fashion. Indeed, since the group members
are essentially trading loyalty for security, the élite derives its
legitimacy only to the extent it can maintain harmony and
security. Hence the tremendous emphasis Japanese leaders,
both business and government, put on stability and smooth
transitions. A shock suggests that the élite is not properly
performing its function for the group.

The Japanese tend to negotiate forever and to haggle over
the smallest concessions. Anything new that might impinge
on the harmony of the group has to be carefully studied and
considered before being absorbed. Beyond that, the primacy
of the maintenance of ties between group members and the
necessity to demonstrate total loyalty to personal duty
means that concessions to those outside the group can be
made only after it has been demonstrated that there is absolutely no alternative.


THE HIERARCHY OF GEOGRAPHY

Doing business in such a society is not at all like doing
business in the United States and in other societies that place
more emphasis on the rights and roles of the individual than
on those of groups—a fact that was vividly brought home to
me in a conversation I had with one of Japan's exceptional
entrepreneurs.

Kazuo Inamori, the founder of Kyocera, was born in 1936
in Kagoshima at the southern tip of Japan. Tokyo is to Japan
as Paris is to France, only much more so. The hierarchy of
Japan is expressed in geography as well as in personal relationships. A traveler in Japan heading for Tokyo takes the
*nobori-sen* (the upward or ascending line) and one who is
leaving takes the *kudari-sen* (descending line). That Kago-

shima is as far from Tokyo as it is possible to get in Japan is some indication of its place on the Japanese ladder of importance. In a country where graduation from Tokyo University is practically a guarantee of success, Inamori went to Kagoshima University, which guarantees nothing. After graduating, he went not to Tokyo, where most important companies have their headquarters, but to Kyoto, where there are hardly any such companies. He was intensely interested in the properties of industrial ceramics, such as artificial diamonds. Since ceramic materials do not corrode or conduct electricity, are excellent insulators, and can be made extremely hard, he foresaw expanded usage in the electronics, medical, and other industries. After a short time he found that his employer was not prepared to accept his ideas—or at least not as rapidly as he desired. He then resigned and with the initial backing of a few thousand dollars from friends, set up shop on his own in 1961.

He described those early days to me. It was difficult to find employees, because working for a small start-up company is not the preferred route for most risk-averse, status-conscious Japanese. It was even more difficult to obtain financing. Inamori's name was not famous in Japan. He was not connected to any established group. Few banks were interested in him. Suppliers were also a problem: his lack of connections made them cautious and some demanded C.O.D. payment. Most difficult of all, however, were potential customers, who were extremely reluctant to buy from an unknown, unconnected start-up company headed by an entrepreneur in his twenties. Orders came slowly.

Then, in 1965, Inamori decided to make a trip to the United States. In future years the lack of success of American businessmen in Japan would be attributed to their lack of ability to speak Japanese. In the United States, however, the fact that Inamori spoke little English did not matter. Among his stops was Texas Instruments in Dallas, at that time the largest independent semiconductor manufacturer in the world. It did not know Inamori's firm very well, but it was interested in some of the new ceramic components he presented. Without checking on his financial backing or his corporate connections or insisting that he maintain large inventories or even a plant in the United States, it gave him a trial order. This test shipment was quickly followed by other larger orders, and Inamori's business grew rapidly. His company developed a ceramic package for semiconductors that was quickly ordered not only by Texas Instruments but by other U.S. semiconductor companies as well.

As the relationship with Texas Instruments progressed, a fascinating development occurred. Japanese companies, noting the growing business Inamori's Kyoto Ceramics was doing with U.S. manufacturers, decided that the company was acceptable and began placing larger orders. The business expanded further, and Kyocera, as it was later known, came to dominate 90 percent of the world market for ceramic semiconductor packages. It also entered a number of other markets and even developed the automobile powered by a ceramic engine that Olmer and I had seen in Kagoshima. Inamori confided that selling in the U.S. market had been easier for him than selling in Japan. It was, he said, one of the most important factors in the success of his company.

Some time later, at a conference with Akio Morita, the chairman of Sony, I mentioned my conversation with Inamori, and Morita immediately responded that he had had the same experience. Sony, he said, had developed as rapidly as it had by being able to sell in the United States, which he said had been an easier market to penetrate than Japan. Others have had the same experience. Honda, for instance, has a larger share of the U.S. auto market than it does of the Japanese market.

THE DRIVE FOR SELF-SUFFICIENCY

Precisely because they believe that no one else can really understand them or empathize with them, the Japanese feel insecure in relying on others who are not Japanese. A non-Japanese, they believe, cannot know the intricate web of responsibility, obligation, and loyalty in all its aspects. In a crisis, one may not know how or want to perform as expected; and if one does not, disaster could ensue. Thus, the Japanese lay great stress on self-sufficiency—and do so all the more precisely because Japan knows it cannot be self-sufficient. Most Japanese reiterate the theme that their country is a small island nation with no natural resources in order to rationalize and justify its efforts to be dependent on nothing beyond natural resources simply not available in Japan. For example, during a hiking vacation in the mountains of Japan, I came across a government-run farm which provided grazing for cattle trucked in by farmers for the summer months. During the rest of the year, the cattle remained indoors or cooped up in small spaces. With its lack of open space, Japan is far from a paradise for cattle raising. Nevertheless, as a result of the efforts of the Ministry of Agriculture, Japan is supplying 70 percent of its own beef.[11]

Another time, several years ago, I was negotiating on behalf of a chemical manufacturer who wished to enter the Japanese market. Eventually every discussion came down to the point of whether my client was willing to maintain a one-year inventory in Japan. Nearly all foreign businessmen who attempted to sell to Japan feel the effect of that concern as they are pressured in every discussion to transfer their technology, to do *kokusan* (domestic manufacturing) in Japan. In one case, a client was actually urged by his Japanese partner to install a second factory essentially as a spare, "in case of an earthquake." Where domestic production is not possible, the Japanese insist on large inventories.

Thus, the very people who expect Americans and others to be content to depend on a flow of goods from a Japanese supplier ten thousand miles away, insist on domestic production and the maintenance of large local inventories. The Japanese see nothing strange in this dichotomy; they know

Japanese can be relied upon, but they are not sure of foreigners.


## A Closed Market


The self-perception of uniqueness, the group orientation, a
suspicion of foreigners, and the drive for self-sufficiency—
these factors combined make the Japanese market very difficult to enter. Many Americans, particularly those in
academia and the press, tend to blame poor management
and inadequate effort for the lack of American success in
selling to Japan. They argue that U.S. businessmen do not
speak Japanese, or reside for long periods of time in Japan,
or attempt to understand Japanese culture, or adapt their
products for the Japanese market, or provide the quality and
service the Japanese require.

Some of this is valid; and, in some cases, all of it is. There
is no doubt that the performance of U.S. business in Japan is
often less than sterling. But if the problem is merely poor
management, it should be limited to Americans, and it is
not. In December 1984, Governor Edward Youde of Hong
Kong, lamenting the fact that Japan exported ten times to
Hong Kong what it imported, called on Japanese authorities
to take steps to increase Japan's imports. In the same month,
the deputy prime minister of Thailand urged Japan to take
concrete measures for opening its market.[12]

In the spring of 1984, the European Economic Community
presented Japan with a fifteen-page list of requests for market-opening measures, and followed it up with further demands in 1985 and 1986.[13] In January 1985, the *Singapore
Monitor* charged Tokyo with "protectionism";[14] and the Ma-
laysian prime minister, Mahathir Mohammad, castigated
Japan for its "colonialistic" foreign policy.[15] Korea, too, com-

plained that Japan restricted transfer of critical technology; and Taiwan arbitrarily raised tariffs on fifteen hundred Japanese items in an effort to force Japanese markets to become more open.

It seems that everyone, including the world's greatest trading nations, has difficulty with Japan. The reality is that, even if one studies the culture for a long time and speaks the language, it is still difficult to be accepted into the group. One can be an honored guest (for which there is a place in the structure), but to become an insider is, in effect, impossible—a situation that inevitably leads to charges of unfairness.

It does not seem fair to Indonesia that Japan can buy its logs but not its plywood. Singapore does not understand why its gasoline is good enough for cars in Europe and Southeast Asia but not for those in Japan. Taiwan cannot understand why the electronic equipment built there by the subsidiaries of Japanese companies can be exported to the United States but not to Japan. But is Japan being unfair, or is Japan just being Japan?

I pondered this question when I heard a story from Marini about the hair dye Revlon had developed in 1984 especially for the Japanese market. As an American businessman, Marini cannot be faulted in any of the ways I previously listed. A resident of Japan for nearly thirty years, he speaks Japanese so fluently that on the phone he is often mistaken for a Japanese. He knew that the Ministry of Health and Welfare had a list of approved ingredients for such things as hair dyes. As recently as three years ago, this list had been secret; a manufacturer had to guess what was on it, submit his product to the ministry for approval, and hope it would not be rejected because he had guessed wrong. As a result of U.S. pressure for "market opening," the list had been made public.

Marini instructed his labs in New York to make the product using only the stipulated ingredients. In the United States, if a company uses officially approved ingredients, it simply lists them on its package and puts the product on the market. The Food and Drug Administration does not interfere, unless there is some complaint. But in Japan the product has to be submitted for approval, even if it is made only from the approved ingredients. So samples of the new Revlon product were sent from New York for submission to the ministry.

Nothing happened for several months. Marini visited the ministry and met with the *ka cho* (midlevel bureaucrat) in charge. Yes, the man agreed, all of the ingredients were on the approved list, but one of them had never actually been used before. It would take some time to evaluate the product. Several months went by, and still nothing happened. Marini, who had people monitoring the progress, or lack thereof, at the ministry, made another visit. Sales representatives had been hired. Advertising was ready to be placed, and promotional material to be sent out to stores. Marini had also found that the offending ingredient had been used on at least one previous occasion. Still the official was reluctant. It had not been used enough, he explained. Would Revlon reformulate and resubmit? Marini was deep in the red on the product by this time. Redevelopment would be expensive. He called a friend in the U.S. government. Could the government assist in any way? As it turned out, it could and did. The product was eventually approved and is now selling well. But not without a struggle.

Was this unfair? A Japanese company would not have faced such an arduous road in the United States. Many at Revlon–USA thought it was unfair. On the other hand, Marini was quick to admit that Japanese companies ran the same gauntlet at the Ministry of Health and Welfare as he had. They could maneuver a little better because they all employed former officials specifically for the purpose of maintaining good relations with the ministry. But the essential situation was not different for them. From the Japanese perspective, there was nothing unfair. Everyone had essentially been treated the same way. It was just that the Japanese way was not that of an open society.

Another classic example of the difficulties encountered when dealing with the Japanese is the case of the aluminum baseball bats. Aluminum requires so much electricity in its production that it has been called "congealed electricity." Japan, with its high energy costs, has high electric rates. The United States has low rates, which helps to make American aluminum baseball bats less expensive than Japanese bats.

The biggest market for bats is the Japan Soft Baseball League, a Japanese Little League that consists of 80,000 teams and 1,600,000 players and plays a Japanese variant of the game that uses a rubberized ball instead of a hardball.

Like much else in carefully structured Japan, the league is organized by the government—in this case, the Ministry of Education, which would be akin to having the Little League in the United States run by the Department of Education. To sell to it, the league required a producer to have an official league seal imprinted on the bat. Until the spring of 1980, the league had declined to make such seals available for U.S. bats. But as a result of the latest round of international trade negotiations, such seals and stamps of approval were now supposedly to be made available to foreign manufacturers on the same basis as to domestic producers. Thus it was that Rawlings and Easton, two U.S. bat producers, asked Herbert Cochran, the veteran Japanese-speaking commercial officer at the U.S. consulate in Osaka, to help them obtain the seals.

A three-year saga ensued. When Cochran asked baseball league officials for information on obtaining the seals, he was politely told that it would be impossible for a foreign firm to be approved, because rubberized baseball was a "unique" Japanese variant of baseball requiring Japanese bats. Foreign firms could not expect to produce only for export to Japan. Moreover, there were already ten other Japanese firms waiting for approval, and there would be too much competition if all the firms that could technically meet the requirements were approved.

This was contrary to all the commitments to open the Japanese market, and Cochran could have made the matter a major issue immediately. As an old Japan hand, however, he knew the Japanese prefer to settle things through quiet talks to preserve harmony, and therefore attempted to enlist the help of some of the companies involved in distributing bats to the league. In a meeting with a representative of the Sporting Goods Retailers Association, he pointed out that Japan is a signatory to the international code that calls for the seals to be available to all. The response was at least frank if somewhat undiplomatic: "Those international trade agreements are one thing, and doing business in Japan is another." Representatives of the wholesalers association were even more blunt. Admitting that U.S. bats were actually of higher quality than Japanese bats, they said, "That business about seals is just an excuse. The fact is if we let U.S. bats in, there will be too much competition." Moreover, they noted that if they accepted the bats, they might also have to accept volleyballs, and the market would be flooded by cheap goods from Taiwan. Finally, they emphasized that even if the seals were given, it was they, the distributors, who determined what was sold, and they were not at all sure that anyone would want to sell U.S. bats.

Undeterred, Cochran enlisted the aid of the U.S.-educated son of the president of one of Japan's major sporting goods companies, a big exporter to the United States. After a year-long effort without success, he explained to Cochran that there was a strong feeling that because rubberized baseball was indigenous to Japan, foreign companies could not supply products for it. He was embarrassed to admit that sometimes Japanese have a different idea of fair play. "Sometimes," he apologized, "they want to keep out foreign products."[16]

At this point in the fall of 1981, after more than a year of useless quiet talks, Cochran sent a cable to Washington describing how he had struck out. This cable lighted a fire. Even the U.S. ambassador to Japan, Mike Mansfield, who usually did not bother with commercial matters, became engaged; and the U.S. government made a formal demarche to the Japanese government in October. In response, league officials announced that as of February, any bat meeting its standards, which it said were similar to the government safety-law requirements, could be recommended for the famous seal. This became one of the items listed as acted upon in the Esaki package.

That seemed to solve the problem, and all concerned heaved a sigh of relief. But the details of the new standards were not published until February 1982. When they were finally passed to U.S. officials on stationery with no letterhead, it became apparent that they required use of an aluminum alloy not generally used in the United States and of a base plug not found in U.S. bats. The matter was back at square one, and the U.S. government filed a formal complaint against Japan at the GATT in Geneva. Japan quickly brought the new league standards into line with those required to obtain the government S-mark assuring safety. Thus at the end of May, the solution to the problem was hailed for the second time. But, again, relief was premature. In June, the Easton Aluminum Company applied to have its factory inspected and registered in accord with MITI's requirements for using the S-mark. It was told that foreign factories could not be registered because there was no travel budget to send inspectors abroad; and even if there had been, they would not be sent because Japanese regulations could not be enforced in the United States. Moreover, despite the fact that the U.S. government commonly accepts certifications in such matters from third parties in Japan, Japan said it could not accept a third-party inspection from the United States. Instead, each lot of bats shipped to Japan would have to be opened and inspected individually before receiving the S-mark.

The whole debate began again. Although the Japanese proposal was clearly discriminatory and contrary to the international agreements on standards, the U.S. embassy in Tokyo and the departments of State and Treasury urged its acceptance as a good compromise. Commerce and the deputy U.S. Trade representative David MacDonald, however, continued to insist on equal treatment. NHK, Japan's major broadcasting company, did a television series on the issue in which the commentator concluded that, while the Japanese system was not constructed to exclude imports, it nevertheless tends to do so. The problem was a matter of culture and tradition, he said, which meant that the U.S.–Japan trade friction was not just a matter of minor misunderstanding, but rather was something deeply rooted, complex, and wide ranging. Ultimately, Japan relaxed the formal restrictions by completely rewriting its laws on safety standards and changing them for a whole range of products. Four years later, however, the Americans still had less than 1 percent of the Japanese market. The distributors had the last laugh.

The accumulation of such negotiations with Japan embittered its relationship with the United States. The Americans perceived a persistent pattern of rejection. Consistent with their view of Japan as an open economy, however, Japanese officials always responded to these cases as isolated incidents. The method of handling was always that of the bat case: problems were attributed as a matter of course to "misunderstandings," a characterization followed by long, tedious haggling over arcane bureaucratic regulations, each of which the Japanese contended was integral to Japanese culture. Ultimately, regulations would be altered in some way, only to produce no concrete results in terms of sales. Such situations served to confirm the original convictions of both sides: that of the Japanese that the Americans were not making enough effort; and that of the Americans that they were being discriminated against.

The key to it all was my insight into Masumi Esaki in Malcolm Baldrige's office that day in the spring of 1982. The Japanese cannot "open" in the American sense. They think of openness as removal of restrictions case by case, as the bureaucratic giving of permission, and have not the generic Western concept of an absence of the need for permission. With their strong perception of themselves as unique, to be

Japanese is by definition to be different and to belong to an exclusive group of like people. Thus, to ask the Japanese to "open" is to ask them to become less exclusive and thus less Japanese. Some Japanese recognize the cultural nature of the question. Amaya, for example, says that Japan must change its closed nature in order for its society to catch up with its economic success. But whether that can be done is not clear. As Tokuyuki Ono, a Japanese banker in New York, remarked to me in August 1987, "What the United States is asking is impossible."

# 4

# THE MANDARINS: JAPAN'S POWERFUL MINISTRIES

---

Prime ministers come and go, but we [ministry officials] are forever.
—An official in the Ministry of Posts and
Telecommunications, Spring 1985

AT the top of Japan's close-knit, homogeneous hierarchy are the great ministries of its government and the officials who run them. By cultural heritage, education, attitudes, status, and influence, these men are spiritual heirs of the old Chinese mandarins. They are of key importance in the Japanese government, as was recognized by the Japanese official who made the remark above during trade negotiations in the spring of 1985, when the U.S. team had referred to a market-opening promise by Prime Minister Nakasone.

The point was expanded later in the year when I met with Sony's chairman Akio Morita, who was also serving that year as chairman of the Electronic Industries Association of

Japan, to discuss the semiconductor trade problem, then in its most intense period. We discussed how the problem could be resolved without continued resort to legal measures, which were costly for both sides. While commenting on how to curb the excess production that had led to dumping in the U.S. market, Morita slapped his knee and said, "MITI must give them strong guidance." What he meant was that Japan's government should direct its manufacturers to reduce production of semiconductors and raise prices. I was taken aback. Here was one of the world's great entrepreneurs talking as if government direction of industrial activity were quite normal. MITI had certainly had that kind of power in the past, but Japanese officials as well as learned U.S. commentators all emphasized now that those days were gone. "But would the companies listen?" I asked. "Yes, if the guidance is firm," said Morita.

The frequent visitor to Tokyo finds that the Japanese government—not only in its role but in its nature—is very different from that of the United States. Morita's comment on "guidance" went to the heart of the matter. Its meaning was illustrated in the conversations I had in September 1986 during a trip to Japan. My first meeting was at the Ministry of Posts and Telecommunications with its new vice minister, Shigeo Sawada. In his early fifties, Sawada had, like all Japanese officials, spent his entire career at the ministry where he had now reached the top rung. He and I were old negotiating opponents who had developed a respect and liking for each other in 1985–86 while conducting talks on telecommunications issues, some of the most difficult trade negotiations the United States and Japan had ever had. Physically, Sawada has the square-jawed appearance of one who would be a good ally in a fight. In negotiation I had found him to be a tough but fair opponent. Now we talked about a new paging service to be offered in Tokyo. A consortium including the Motorola Corporation had been an early applicant, but other candidates were now coming forward, and Sawada confirmed a newspaper story to the effect that his ministry was trying to persuade all the applicants to form one joint company to compete with the existing service of Nippon Telegraph and Telephone.

I was astonished. He and I had negotiated long and hard to achieve a rough parity between the United States and Japan in terms of the openness of their respective telecommunications markets. But it was inconceivable that the Federal Communications Commission or the Commerce Department or any other U.S. agency would hold up processing applications while it tried to play investment banker to a merger. Because the ministry had long resisted foreign entry into Japan's telecommunications markets, many suspected that the real objective of the joint company was to make the market unattractive to Motorola. In response to my questions, Sawada explained that his ministry was just trying to give guidance so that the new company would be the healthiest possible competitor for NTT. That this guidance would have the effect of reducing Motorola's share of the business was coincidental, he said, as he went on to discuss the progress of other entrants into other communications transmission business. One of these, Daini Denden, was a private company in which Morita and Inamori of Kyocera were major shareholders. The other two, Telecom Japan and Teleway Japan, were commonly acknowledged to be under the guidance of the ministries of Construction and Transport. We finished our talk with a discussion of the *modus vivendi* that his ministry was working out in its bitter dispute with MITI concerning which ministry would control the development of Japan's information industries as computers and communication became more intimately linked.

From the Ministry of Posts and Telecommunications, I walked across the street to its great opponent in Japan's bruising bureaucratic battles, the Ministry of International Trade and Industry, to meet with Yukiharu Kodama, the new director general of the Machinery and Information Industries Bureau. Again, Kodama and I had spent many a long hour together at the negotiating table. A well-traveled man who had been assigned by MITI to London for several years, he speaks English well and, unlike many Japanese, has an appreciation of Western humor. That he was a pleasure to be with became in itself a negotiating weapon. I had found him to be a subtle bargainer who won points without seeming to. Over the years I came to know his family and to think of him as a friend. When I asked about his new position, he reported that he was very pleased with it. He had been working on the minister's staff and said he now felt like a ship's captain stepping onto the bridge of a new command with the salt air blowing in his face. I was struck by his obvious sense of having a hand on the destiny of his nation. There were people in the departments of Defense and State and on the National Security Council who had that sense in the U.S. government, but not in the Commerce Department or any other U.S. trade or economic agency.

I asked about his objectives. The great task, he responded, is to ensure the sufficient health of research and development for the future and smooth, steady movement to an information-based society. He noted MITI's technopolis programs, under which twenty-one cities are being developed around the country on the model of Silicon Valley for the purpose of utilizing and developing technology. We also discussed how MITI had brokered a joint venture between Boeing and Japanese aircraft companies for the development of a new airliner. He then added that restructuring the mature industries, such as shipbuilding and coal mining, was the second great task. "We have to take care of the bow and stern of the ship now," he said. "Everything in between is in pretty good shape." Although he did not say so, it was clear that if it were not, MITI would intervene to do something about it.

I suggested that MITI, in its perception of its own role and its relationship to the nation, was akin to the U.S. Defense Department. Kodama agreed that in some ways that observation was true, and noted that MITI had particularly understood Defense's talk of the "industrial base" in some of our earlier negotiations. MITI, he said, sees industrial and trade issues as closely related to the nation's overall security. We discussed guidance. I asked why Japanese companies, which saw no need to inform the U.S. government, commonly told MITI of their investment plans in the United States. Although I was unaware of it, even as we spoke, Fujitsu was in the process of informing MITI of its plans to acquire Fairchild. I also asked why people like Morita thought companies would listen to MITI's advice. Kodama explained that the companies valued MITI's advice because of its superior information and its analytical ability. He also credited tradition. But when I pressured him, he was honest enough to agree that MITI also had some powers of persuasion not available to U.S. officials.

That power was my topic of discussion that evening when I had dinner with an executive who had been involved in negotiating a recently announced joint venture in Value Added Networks between NTT and IBM. The announcement of the joint venture caused a major shock in many quarters in Tokyo. As one of my friends at NTT explained, IBM had long been thought of as the enemy, while most Japanese, and especially employees of NTT, saw NTT as a champion in Japan's drive to equal IBM. That NTT was now joining hands with its great rival bordered on sacrilege in the eyes of many. Without a manufacturing capability of its own, NTT had traditionally been supplied by a few favored companies known as the NTT family. The heads of these major companies certainly now felt betrayed and pressured the government to reverse the deal. I asked my friend how NTT had managed to close the deal and, more difficult, to get it approved. He said NTT had known that the Ministry of Posts and Telecommunications would probably oppose it. If both MITI and MPT opposed it, the deal could not be made. So NTT and IBM representatives had met quietly with friends at MITI who advised that, as long as the deal was made to appear relatively small, they would be able to keep their ministry from opposing it.

But, I objected, IBM and NTT are private companies. I could understand their consulting Japan's Fair Trade Commission over antitrust concerns, but how could MPT or MITI stop them? Certainly in the United States, IBM would not consider consulting the Department of Commerce about its joint venture negotiations. "They have many pressure points," he responded, "and neither NTT or IBM wants to antagonize them."

Those pressure points were a topic later that night when I had a discussion with a friend at MITI about the famous Lion Petroleum case. Lion is a small Japanese company that in 1984 tried to import gasoline from Singapore for sale in its gas stations in the Tokyo area. MITI has long nurtured the Japanese refining industry. Japan's refineries, based on naphtha, operate at relatively high cost. To keep its industries competitive, MITI keeps fuel oil prices low and allows the refineries to make money through high gasoline prices to consumers. Lion saw a chance to undercut this situation by importing inexpensive gasoline from Singapore. While Lion's actions were not illegal, they could, had they succeeded, have threatened MITI's established price structure.

The importation of gasoline was officially allowed, and the market looked like an open market. Yet this became one of those familiar cases where there was no tariff, no quota— and also no imports. The reason was that to effect the importation, Lion had to notify MITI. MITI refused to accept the notification. While never issuing a direct order, MITI pressured Lion and its backers not to import the gasoline. Lion has not tried again; and, to ensure that it does not, the Japanese government's representatives in Singapore and the Philippines have warned those governments against allowing sales to other such operators in the future.[1] Of perhaps greatest interest was Lion's response—or, more precisely, its lack of response. Had Lion been a U.S. company and had the U.S. government tried a similar tactic, the company would have hired a lawyer and gotten an injunction against the government. Very likely Lion would have wound up getting rich and the government would have been chastised. But in Japan, nothing of the sort occurred. As my friend said, the Japanese government usually does not lose in court.

"Guidance" is another word for power. The great contrast between U.S. and Japanese officials lies in their power. Morita would never have considered suggesting that the U.S. Department of Commerce issue guidance to the U.S. semiconductor industry to hold down production. Neither the Federal Communications Commission (FCC) nor the Commerce Department would have considered orchestrating a paging service consortium. Certainly no one in any economic agency in the United States talked about its plans for restructuring either new or old U.S. industries. Sometimes they have stepped in with a Chrysler or a Lockheed bailout in response to an exceptional, political- or defense-related, crisis, but there is no systematic thinking about the structure of U.S. industry. That, it is thought, is best left to private businessmen.

The contrast between the U.S. and the Japanese governments was sharply and unwittingly drawn by the Senate minority leader, Robert Dole, in an article in the *Los Angeles Times* of 31 March 1985.[2] Speaking of the difficulty of effecting change in bureaucratic practices in Japan, Dole said he did not accept the excuse that the career bureaucrats in Tokyo just listen politely and ignore the instructions of their political superiors. He added that it was difficult to imagine a political system where elected officials could not get something done if it was sufficiently important. But from the prime minister on down, the officials of Japan live and work in just such a system.

In order to understand the differences in power and motivation separating U.S. and Japanese officials we must go back to 1853 when Perry and his four ships steamed into Tokyo Bay.

## Early Industrialization

The memory of those ships—known as the "black ships" because of both their color and their impact—is forever etched into Japan's psyche. The trauma for Japan was twofold. First, there was the opening itself; second, the realization that, despite its presumed unique and superior status, Japan was behind the West, at least in technology. This first of what the Japanese came to call "shocks"* ranks—along with Agincourt, the Mongol invasions, and the defeat of the Spanish Armada—as a turning point in world history. Within thirteen years of Perry's arrival, the Tokugawa shogunate crumbled, as the forced opening to Western intrusion sapped its credibility and stirred rebellion by those who resented foreign influence. For over two hundred years, Japan's emperors had lived in quiet seclusion in Kyoto while the shoguns ruled Japan. Now dissident samurai (analogous to medieval knights), mostly from Japan's outer provinces, sought to gain power by returning authority to the emperor. Under the slogan "Restore the emperor and expel the barbarians [Westerners]," these men turned power back to the Emperor Meiji and established a new regime and new era which was called the Meiji Restoration.

The character of this new regime and the forces that motivated it were to be critical for the future of Japan. Those who seized power called their coup a restoration, not a revolu-

---

*Any significant change is called a shock—*Shokku* in Japanese. The "Nixon shock" occurred when President Nixon visited China in 1972 without informing Japan until the last moment. The oil crises of the 1970s are called "shocks" in Japan.

tion; and this restoration was carried out by one group of ruling-class samurai against another. Power changed hands, but not classes. There was no assertion of citizen rights; and, while the class structure did eventually change, that was not in itself the purpose of the coup makers. They seized power not to destroy the system but to preserve it.

To do that and to expel the barbarians, the men of Meiji knew they would need modern military forces and the industries that made them possible. The first step in this process was their own transformation from feudal samurai to modern bureaucrats. In effect, they turned in their swords for the *hanko*, the stamp by which the Japanese bureaucrat, even today, signifies approval. As Professor Chalmers Johnson, the leading expert on Japan's bureaucracy, has noted, the first entities created by the new Meiji government were the ministries that were to guide Japan's forced industrialization. They preceded political parties, a constitution, or a parliament. Their first efforts were focused on building what would later be called "targeted" industries.[3]

One of the most perceptive observers of Japan was E. H. Norman, who was Canadian born and raised in Japan by missionary parents and who wrote about it in the 1940s. In discussing the modernization of Japan, he described how its "keenest minds were concerned with such questions as the creation of trade and industry, not for their own sake, but rather to establish those industries which one might conveniently call *strategic* as the *sine qua non* of a modern army and navy, the creation of which was the central problem of the day."[4] These industries included shipbuilding, iron, machinery and machine tools, railroads, coal mining, and telegraphy. Norman pointed out that in Japan, as a result of the concern with "strategic" industries, the normal order of the stages of capitalist development had been reversed. Classically, the starting point in the nonadministered economies of the West had been light industries that produced consumer goods, but in Japan, heavy industry had received the first emphasis.[5]

A fascinating aspect of Japan's early industrialization was the source of its capital. At a time when U.S. industry was being built on a foundation of foreign, especially British, capital, Japan never contemplated using foreign financing. Yet there was hardly any effective means of capital accumulation in Japan at the time, and it desperately needed investment to move ahead rapidly with its plans for building a modern industry and armed forces. But in its aversion to any semblance of foreign control or intrusion, it rejected most foreign investment. Japan's industrialization was to be a bootstrap operation, with capital derived from reducing Japanese consumption. Thus the "save and export" ethics were planted early in the soil of modern Japan.

Lacking capital, Japan also, of course, lacked capitalists. To overcome this problem, the men of Meiji made the government the investment banker. Government ministries established or backed the establishment of shipyards and foundries. Special loans and subsidies were made available; and in many instances, the ministries actually created industries and then sold them off at "fire sale" prices. The pattern was for the government to nurture an industry in its early stages and then search for or create private companies that could be enticed into taking over the operations.[6]

## The Rise of the Ministries

As explained by Johnson, Japan's ministries were the central organizations in governing the country and founding its industrial economy. They viewed economics and industrial development as vital matters of national security. Their primary concern was the advancement of the wealth and power of Japan as a nation rather than the promotion of an environment in which particular interests would flourish. The ministries could take this approach because they were run by autocrats whose writ was law and whose only rivals for real power in the society were each other.[7] Neither political parties, nor commercial interests, nor other social groups had the material or intellectual strength to challenge them. There was no effective parliament or concept of individual rights; and by long tradition, the emperor reigned but did not rule. In effect, the government was the ministries which were supreme in the sectors of society under their authority.

Once established, these patterns continued. Kodama's Ministry of International Trade and Industry and Sawada's Ministry of Posts and Telecommunications, and their traditions, attitudes, and rivalries, run in a direct line back to these founding agencies. MITI first came into being in 1881 as part of the Ministry of Agriculture and Commerce (MAC). In 1885, today's MPT was established as the Ministry of Communications with the combining of the postal and telegraph services. It has always been in the nature of these agencies to try to expand their power, often at the expense of each other. The Ministry of Communications, for example, started with the mails, the telegraph system, maritime shipping, and the lighthouses. In the early 1900s, it added telephones and electric-power generation, and later took charge of developing railroads and hydroelectric power. Later still, it took over postal life insurance and, early in 1925, added civil aviation and the aircraft industry, which might more naturally have gone to MAC.[8]

In the early years of the twentieth century, Japan's industrial structure resembled that of the West perhaps more than at any other time in its history. The autocrats had succeeded in creating a capitalist society; and with success, the role of the ministries diminished as that of the zaibatsu and other private interests grew. In a sense, Kodama's comments about "everything in between being okay" were appropriate to the situation then. Because all was well, there was less need for intervention. Recession, depression, and war enhanced the ministries' roles. The immediate predecessor to today's MITI was the Ministry of Commerce and Industry (MCI), which was separated from MAC during the severe recession of 1925. In its first and characteristic act, MCI identified a root cause of the recession as "excessive competition" and authorized the establishment of cartels to curb it. Such actions would later become a staple of MITI policies.

In 1927, as a financial panic swept Japan, MCI established the Commerce and Industry Deliberation Council as a joint public-private group under its authority to develop recommendations on what government and industry should do to avoid disaster. This forerunner of today's Industrial Structure Council introduced the concept of "industrial rationalization," which has become the backbone of Japanese industrial policy. In essence, industrial rationalization theory asserts that since absolutely free competition tends to result in economic crises, a comprehensive industrial plan with some governmental control is needed to replace excessive competition with cooperation among firms.

Throughout the 1930s, a series of laws were written by MCI and passed by the Diet. These laws elaborated this doctrine in concrete terms, gradually enhancing MCI's ability to influence the economy as a whole. Laws were passed allowing MCI to form cartels and to approve investment as well as encourage curtailment of production. These legislative actions provided the foundation for later administrative guidance. The practice of passing laws to govern specific industries was also begun during the 1930s. One law of particular interest in light of subsequent developments was the 1936 Automobile Manufacturing Law.[9] The inability of Detroit to sell cars in Japan is usually blamed on the laziness and incompetence of the automobile company executives. Many commentators have called Japanese industrial policy a failure because MITI's attempt to force Japan's makers into three large entities was successfully resisted by companies such as Honda and Mitsubishi. Such critics and apologists would do well to remedy their ignorance of the 1936 Automobile Manufacturing Law, which required auto producers to be licensed by the government. The government put up half the capital for those firms lucky enough to obtain licenses and eliminated taxes and import duties for five years. Two companies, Toyota and Nissan, were licensed. Ford and General Motors, which until then had had a large share of the Japanese market, were eventually put out of business. They would not be permitted to return for nearly four decades.[10]

During the Second World War, MCI temporarily became the Ministry of Munitions. It took authority for electric power and aviation away from the Ministry of Communications and assumed control of much of the wartime economy. Just before the U.S. Occupation began in August 1945, however, there was much bureaucratic scurrying around as the Ministry of Munitions was transformed back into MCI by one of the last imperial ordinances of the wartime period. The result was that after the war the economy was largely run by the same bureaucracy that had run it before the war.[11]

The position of the postwar Japanese government mandarins was worse than that of their forefathers after the arrival of Perry. They were still behind in technology. The industrial base they had labored hard to construct was in ruins, and the Japanese people were close to starvation. Worst of all, the barbarians were not just knocking on the door; they were already in the door. The resolve and the drive of the heirs of the men of Meiji did not waver. They set about at once to rebuild the industrial base, to regain sovereignty, and to catch up with the West. In this they were greatly aided by a fact upon which Shigeru Yoshida, the great postwar prime minister, commented in his diary: "The Occupation, with all the power and authority behind its operation, was hampered by its lack of knowledge of the people it had come to govern, and even more so, perhaps, by its generally happy ignorance of the amount of requisite knowledge it lacked."[12]

There was no purge in Japan as there was in Germany, and the Occupation was indirect. For its administration it relied on the existing Japanese bureaucracy—that is, the same people who had been running the country both before and during the war. The tradition of *Menju Fukihai* (appearing to accept an order on the surface but reversing it in the belly) is old and honored in Japan. With the Americans knowing little of what they were doing, political parties just coming into existence, and business institutions in a weakened state, the bureaucrats had more or less complete power, just as their Meiji forebears had had nearly a century earlier.

MCI became today's MITI in 1949. The Foreign Exchange and Foreign Trade Control Law, passed in that same year, was meant to be a temporary measure at a time of great economic distress in Japan. It required any citizen who acquired foreign exchange through trade to turn it over to a government account. With the end of the Occupation, MITI was given responsibility for administering this law, which stayed on the books for thirty years and is still there, though in greatly modified and weakened form. Along with MITI's existing authority over imports, technology flow, joint ventures, and investment, the law became the foundation of MITI's great postwar power. Johnson calls it "the single most important instrument of industrial guidance and control that MITI ever possessed."[13] By controlling foreign exchange, MITI was able to allocate capital in the Japanese economy; and, with this added authority, MITI was more powerful than any of its earlier incarnations, including the Ministry of Munitions.

At the same time, the Ministry of Finance rigidly controlled Japan's financial structure. The Ministry of Posts and Telecommunications, although shorn of much of its old responsibility because it had been a hotbed of nationalism before and during the war, still controlled the postal savings system, which became the largest bank in the world. Nippon Telegraph and Telephone, which had been split off from MPT to become an independent government monopoly, used its monopoly revenues and laboratories to continue the

tradition of government promotion of industrial development which had been started by its old ministry.[14]

With these institutions in place, the new mandarins were
prepared to repeat and even improve on the accomplishments of the old. The story of the Japanese "economic miracle" is oft told. As before, it ran counter to all Western
expectations. Indeed it is almost axiomatic that the experts
are always wrong about Japan. As knowledgeable an observer as Edwin Reischauer, a professor and former ambassador to Japan, wondered if Japan would ever have a
satisfactory standard of living.[15] In the opinion of most experts, Japan should have emphasized labor-intensive industry, taking advantage of its abundant and cheap labor
supply. Desperately needing capital, it should also have
opened itself to foreign investment.

The Japanese never contemplated this advice for a minute.
"We did the opposite of what they said," Amaya told me. As
it had one hundred years before, Japan strictly limited foreign investment and concentrated on rebuilding the "strategic" or "targeted" industries. Again the ministries took the
lead. Special legislation for the promotion of the shipbuilding, steel, electronics, and machinery industries was passed.
Funds were funneled from the postal savings system into the
Japan Development Bank and other governmental agencies,
which lent at below-market rates to targeted industries and
companies. The commercial banks were encouraged to loan
beyond the limits of their own capital with the understanding that the government-controlled Bank of Japan would
stand behind the loans. On the basis of this policy, industry
borrowed up to 90 percent of its capital, secure in the knowledge that the government was underwriting the risk.

Other ingenious tools were also used. Under the "link system," for example, the shipbuilding industry was given the
license to import sugar. Since the Japanese market was
heavily protected, the domestic price was well above the
world price. The shipbuilders bought sugar on the world
market, then imported and sold it at the Japanese price. The

profit subsidized the export of ships. Sometimes the Export–Import Bank of Japan also joined in by providing low-cost financing for sale of a ship to a foreign broker who would immediately resell it to the originally intended Japanese customer.[16] This practice enabled the domestic customer to obtain the low-cost financing supposed to be available only to support exports. The classic case of these early targeting efforts was the reconstruction of Japan's steel industry. MITI led the effort, making available low-cost financing, government-guaranteed loans, and government financing of such elements of the infrastructure as ports and roads. MITI also actively directed the merger of the Yawata and Fuji steel companies to form the giant Nippon Steel.

Kodama, Sawada, and their colleagues were heirs to a tradition in which government influence over microeconomic decisions was seen not only as legitimate but necessary. They were also the heirs, and worthy ones, of a tradition of great men.

## The Japanese Bureaucracy

### THE MAKING OF A BUREAUCRAT

The original officials of modern Japan were samurai who had long been members of the governing class. They had a burning mission to gain what they saw as Japan's rightful place at the top of the hierarchy of nations by developing its industrial might. In 1877, to ensure that the mission would be carried out in the future, they founded Tokyo University for the purpose of training worthy successors, and in this, as in much else, they achieved their objectives.

The civil service in Japan has always been the élite of élites. Whereas in the United States parents tend to hope

their sons and daughters will become doctors or million-
aires, in Japan the most wished-for position is civil servant,
especially in the first tier of ministries such as MITI or the
Ministry of Finance. The reason is that the Japanese view
success as a matter of status and power. In Japan's group-
oriented society, the civil servants are the keepers of the
flame for the ultimate group, the nation. In the hierarchy,
they are at the top.

Entry into this ultimate in-group is difficult and requires
rigorous preparation. Graduation from Tokyo University's
faculty of law is not a formal requirement, but more than 90
percent of all top civil servants are graduates of that school.
Only a few of the nation's best students are able to enter
Tokyo University. To get there, they endure a study regimen
and examination system whose difficulty and intensity is un-
equaled anywhere in the world. For them high school is a
constant grind, broken only by extra study in special
preparatory schools at night and on weekends. Of those few
who enter Tokyo University, only a few graduate from the
faculty of law. Of these only a few pass the civil service ex-
aminations. Each ministry chooses between twenty and
thirty newcomers as its entering class each year. These men
(and they are men almost without exception) are the cream
of the crop, and they know it. Entering the ministries is the
culmination of an arduous climb, and they have the pride
and satisfaction of all climbers in having reached the pinnacle. While they sometimes display an intellectual snobbery
often associated with graduates of élite schools, they let it be
tempered by a sense of duty.

Once in the appropriate ministry, the course of the careers
of these men is fairly well charted, and the group associations that will control their destinies become established.
One of the exclusive groups is that of graduates of the Tokyo
University law faculty. Another is the ministry they have entered. And within the ministry there will be a special bond
between members of a particular class, so that members of

one class may maneuver against members of another for supremacy in the ministry. Rising slowly, grade by grade, the civil servant will be assigned to each part of the ministry, so that by the end of his career, each one knows its workings thoroughly. At some point, one may be sent abroad to study at an American or a British university. Not only are officials of the Foreign Ministry stationed abroad, but so are many officials of other ministries, such as MITI and MPT. At first all are promoted together, but eventually the pyramid narrows, and by age forty-five or so a few will begin to be promoted over the others.

At about age fifty-five, the final cut is made. The lucky few become vice ministers, who essentially run their ministries under the broad guidance of a politically appointed minister. It can be argued that these men are the most powerful in the country. A measure of their importance—and, indeed, of that of all civil servants—is the fact that their promotions are closely followed in the press. Each year *Nihon Keizai* (Japan's *Wall Street Journal*) features a complete list of the personnel changes in the ministries, with a picture and short biography of each man. In the days preceding these announcements, speculation on who will be moved where is prominent in the press. It is as if the *Wall Street Journal* were to devote large parts of its best space to the career progress of civil servants from the rank of deputy assistant secretary through undersecretary in each U.S. government department. In fact, the only comparable coverage in the United States is of cabinet members and prominent congressional committee members.

Those who do not make it to the pinnacle in Japan are nevertheless well rewarded. They perform what is known as *amakudari* (literally, "descent from heaven"). In this case, heaven is the bureaucracy, and the descent is into a posh position in a large bank or corporation, or possibly as head of another public body or a think tank. The descent is arranged by the ministry, which has the responsibility to see to it that its graduates are well cared for in their postbureaucratic life.

This system of outplacement is also a source of power for the ministry, which gains eyes and ears and even a mouth in the organization to which its "old boys" graduate.

These men are imbued with a sense of mission and duty that is found in the United States only in the officer corps of the military services, and even there, it is not as broadly defined. Where a U.S. military officer has a mission to accomplish a defense-related objective, an official in Japan's civil service has a mission to make Japan the best in whatever area of endeavor he is engaged, a goal that derives from the view the bureaucrats hold that they function "not as public servants but as public mentors."[17] This view was impressed upon me again in September 1986 during a breakfast in Tokyo with an acquaintance who had just returned to Japan to work in MITI's aircraft and ordinance division after several years at the Japanese embassy in Washington. In describing his new work, he mentioned that part of his task was to persuade Japan's aircraft industry to shoot for higher targets in order to improve its overall capability—a statement he made just as naturally as Ivan Lendl might say his job is to win tennis matches, but inconceivable in any U.S. official. A Department of Defense official might aim at improving U.S. performance for some defense-related purpose, but not for industrial performance as an end in itself.

The style of operation of these men is also an interesting commentary on their motivations and purposes. They live under great pressure to demonstrate dedication, loyalty, and sincerity. Like the form of their organizations and their spirit, this pressure, too, has what we might think of as a slightly military flavor, occasionally including a tendency toward a sycophancy sometimes associated with the armed forces. Rank in Japan is very important, and the honoring of it sometimes results in formalities that seem unnecessary to Americans. A Japanese government official in Washington once expressed his amazement to me after delivering a message to then U.S. trade representative William Brock at his home on a Saturday. Brock had answered the doorbell himself. That, said the official, could never happen in Japan, where the doorbell of a minister would be answered only by a servant or aide. The official also explained the difficulty he had had with the men in charge of a meeting in Florida between Brock and the MITI minister. Some officials at the Japanese consulate had insisted on arranging a motorcade of limousines to meet the minister at the airport and carry him to the hotel—a procedure they thought only proper in view of his position. My friend thought a motorcade might be out of place and even an embarrassing ostentatious display, because he guessed that Brock would probably just catch a cab. To cancel the limos, however, took an appeal to the minister himself.

Along with this concern for rank, however, is a total dedication to accomplishing established objectives. If I wanted to speak with a Japanese official at any hour of the day or night, he was available. It was common to receive phone calls from MITI, Foreign Ministry, or MPT officials at what were, for them, the wee hours. They were available to work on Saturdays and Sundays. I recall walking into MPT at a time when it was attempting to pass new legislation. Officials, from the highest to the lowest ranks, were sleeping on mats in their offices rather than going home for the night.

During negotiations on semiconductor trade issues in Washington in 1986, I visited the head of the Japanese delegation at his hotel at about 11 P.M. His team had established what was essentially a command post. The whole staff was gathered, and they had evidently eaten their dinner together in the room. The negotiating head was alternately on the phone to Tokyo or barking orders to his team. The pervasive sense of camaraderie in common purpose was all but palpable—a phenomenon I frequently noticed. Japan's officials, often schooled in the United States, are carefully trained and rotated so that they become knowledgeable about many industries and about international trade. They work together as a team for many years, which results in a certain esprit as well as a smooth-running operation. They enjoy the highest status within their society, and their clearly defined objectives are backed by the nation. While one can like or dislike particular Japanese officials, they are among the most capable in the world, both individually and as a class.


BUREAUCRATIC POWER

Some U.S observers of Japan attempt to downplay the power of today's bureaucrats. It is argued, for example, that while the Ministry of International Trade and Industry formerly was powerful when it controlled foreign exchange and allocated capital through the overloaned Japanese banking system, its role is now minor because it has lost those powers. Such arguments are misleading because of the tendency to equate diminution of power with loss of power. In particular, there is an obtuse tendency to interpret Japan in terms of the United States and to assume that if there is not an overt legal basis for power, it does not exist. To accept this fallacy is vastly to overemphasize the actual loss of power and to ignore the subtle, nonlegalistic nature of Japanese society.

It is true that the Japanese ministries do not have quite the stranglehold on the nation that they had in the immediate post-Occupation period. However, a hypothetical U.S. version of MITI would include the departments of Commerce and Energy, the Office of the U.S. Trade Representative, the Export-Import Bank, the Small Business Administration, the National Science Foundation, the Overseas Private Investment Corporation, the Environmental Protection Agency, and parts of the departments of Defense and Justice.

Even that description does not fully convey the scope of the ministry's authority. For instance, not only does MITI include the equivalent of the U.S. Department of Energy, but it has authority over electric power rates and other energy prices in Japan. It issues licenses for nuclear power installations. No plant, supermarket, or department store is built anywhere in Japan without notification to and authorization by MITI. MITI establishes industrial standards. The Japan Development Bank invests at MITI's direction. MITI has the power to suspend the antitrust laws and to declare cartels, either for the purpose of aiding industries in recession or of developing particular target industries. Important military procurement decisions are not made without its consent, and it must approve most licensing of Japanese technology.

A look at the Ministry of Posts and Telecommunications is also instructive. After the war, the old superministry was broken up into Japan National Railways, Japan Air Lines, Nippon Telegraph and Telephone, the independent electric power companies, and MITI's energy agency. Nevertheless, one should not grieve too much for poor old MPT. Most of Japan's recent prime ministers and key politicians have managed to serve as its minister at some point in their careers. The reason is that it influences a lot of votes and at the same time controls the world's largest financial institution.

Of Japan's 23,000 post offices, nearly 18,000 are franchises that are paid a commission on the stamps sold and on money collected for the postal savings system. The desire of the franchisees to maintain the established national system makes them a potent political force. It has been estimated that each postmaster controls some 80,000 votes.[18] The postal savings system has assets of nearly $1 trillion, making it several times the size of First National City Bank, the largest in the United States. These holdings are augmented each month by regular deposits collected by the 50,000 postal workers who visit households in their districts.[19] Thus is the Oriental saving ethic assiduously encouraged. The money enters the government coffers, where it is used to fund such bodies as the Japan Development Bank.

In addition to regulating and structuring the entire telecommunications industry, MPT illustrates another aspect of the power of Japan's ministries. Of the members of the Diet, several are former officials of MPT. The career route in Japan that includes being bureaucrat, Diet member, and high-ranking politician is well trod. Of the first 17 postwar prime ministers, 15 were formerly senior bureaucrats.[20] Today over a quarter of the 727 members of both houses of the Diet are ex-bureaucrats, and they make up about half the members of the Liberal Democratic Party.[21] A MITI acquaintance recently complained to me that the ministry was falling behind in placing its former officials in the Diet and would have to work on this aspect of its program. Since Japan has been ruled only by the LDP since the war, the relationship between party and ministries is incestuous. The bureaucrats can use their connections to the party to become candidates. The MITI official's comment was not facetious. Japan's ministries count their former officials as an important source of power and influence. As in so much of Japanese life, the group mentality is extremely important. As already noted, a civil servant in one of the élite ministries is a member of several exclusive clubs in the world's clubbiest nation. He does not lose membership when he leaves his ministry, and no new group he joins will be as exclusive or have the same call on his loyalty as the old ones.

Amaya, when asked once what he would do after retiring as vice minister of MITI, replied that he did not know and was not even thinking about it because MITI would take care of it. He was right. High officials in the ministries take much time in placing their former colleagues in good positions. They are sprinkled throughout the large companies and banks. Trade and industry associations are another favorite destination for outplacements, particularly because most such organizations must be chartered by one of the ministries. Sometimes former ministry officials are even placed on the boards of the Japanese subsidiaries of foreign companies, which may think they are obtaining a window on the ministry. While they may be, what is certain is that the ministry is obtaining a window on them. This network is one of the key ingredients in the glue of Japan, Inc., and one of the subtle levers of the power of the ministries.

The role of the Diet and the relationship of the ministries to it is much misunderstood in the United States. A U.S. politician recently asked me if Japanese companies employ lobbyists to lobby the Diet as U.S. companies do to lobby Congress. The answer, of course, is no. The similarity between the Diet and the U.S. Congress is one of form only. Although it consists of an upper and a lower house, the Diet is a parliament, not a congress. It does not initiate or really debate laws or policies; it only ratifies them. Lobbying efforts are directed at the ministries, as well as at key operatives in the Liberal Democratic Party structure who can influence the ministries. Rather than employing lobbyists for this task, companies take *amakudari* officials into their organizations to carry it out.

In addition, part of the job of every Japanese executive is to keep abreast of what the ministries affecting his organization are doing. The reason is that laws, their implementing ordinances, and other policy initiatives originate in the ministries. The pages of *Nihon Keizai* indicate the scope of MITI's activities:

> 12 August 1983: MITI proposes a bill to stabilize the position of the biotechnology industry.
> 28 February 1984: MITI will extend and revise the law to help modernize small textile firms.
> 7 June 1984: MITI is drawing up legislation to foster start-up ventures.
> 6 May 1985: MITI proposes promoting high technology industries, alleviating crowding in large cities, and spurring economic growth outside major urban areas.

This is a sample of what just one ministry is doing. The handling of these proposals is as important as their scope. In the United States, departments of government also propose bills, but these are then submitted to Congress, where they are debated in open session. Or, if it is a matter of adminis-

trative rule making, hearings are held and appeals procedures are available. The bills and rules may or may not pass,
depending on the debate, which is generally open to the
public.

In Japan, the procedure is much different. Proposals such
as the preceding ones are developed by MITI with the advice
of the Industrial Structure Council, which consists of experts
from business, academia, labor, consumer groups, and the
press. The council reviews MITI proposals or may make ones
of its own, which are discussed in sessions closed to the
public. Eventually legislation is drafted within MITI and then
submitted to the cabinet. If approved there, it is submitted to
the Diet, where it is generally rubber-stamped without significant debate. Thus, when one reads a newspaper report of
a MITI proposal in Japan, one can reasonably expect it to
become law.

There are various reasons for the lack of debate. The fact
that the Liberal Democratic Party has been in power for all
but six months of the postwar period makes Diet debate a bit
superfluous. Diet members have small staffs, as do Diet
committees. They do not have the resources to develop their
own sources of information. Moreover, they are often graduates of less prestigious schools than the bureaucrats and
stand somewhat in awe of them. On top of all that, as I have
noted, the bureaucrats have infiltrated the Diet with former
ministry officials.

The result is a somewhat paternalistic insider system that
gives great power to the bureaucratic mandarins. Because
the party has been in power for many years, some key Liberal Democratic Party figures have also developed expertise
and accumulated power. This has been enhanced recently by
jurisdictional disputes, which the ministries have been
forced to ask party leaders to adjudicate. For most of the
postwar period, however, it is accurate to say of Japan that
the politicians reigned while the bureaucrats ruled. That this
is no longer entirely true does not mean, as some would
have it, that the mandarins have withdrawn from the field.

PROCEDURES AS POWER

A key source of the bureaucrats' power has been and continues to be the issuing of ordinances and administrative guidance. The bills that go to the Diet are broadly written. After passage, they return for elaboration to the ministry that wrote them. Critical details such as definitions, standards, and procedures are spelled out in ministerial ordinances and directives. Thus, for practical purposes, much of a given law may be written after its actual enactment, and the writing will be done out of public view by those who will be responsible for administering it. The power of the ordinances is enhanced by a lack, first, of independent appeals procedures and, second, of a strong judiciary. The result is that ministries write the laws, then write the interpretive ordinances, administer the laws, and handle most complaints arising from them.

This power is frequently evident during trade negotiations. Renewal of the law for depressed industries (a measure to allow for the rescue of failing industries through the creation of production and price cartels) in 1983 critically affected the ability of some U.S. petrochemical companies to do business in Japan by compelling them to cut production. As we will see, the proposal by the Ministry of International Trade and Industry in 1984 to change Japan's copyright laws on computer software was ultimately stopped, but it could easily have undermined the competitive ability of the U.S. computer industry (see pages 468–69).

A dramatic example of the power of the ministries emerged during the preparation of a study in 1985 on Japanese trade barriers by the Tokyo Trade Study Group, a committee of business and government officials from the United States and Japan established to resolve trade problems. Monsanto was assigned responsibility for writing the chapter dealing with agricultural chemicals. Its draft, which contained some mild criticism of the Ministry of Agriculture, Forests, and Fisheries, was passed to MAFF by one of the Japanese members of the group without Monsanto's consent. The result was a phone call from a MAFF official to a senior Japanese executive at Monsanto. If Monsanto hoped for favorable treatment from the ministry on its agricultural chemical registrations, said the caller, it would be wise not to proceed with the draft.

The power of ordinances came clearly into focus during negotiations on telecommunications in which I led the U.S. team in 1984–86. A change in the basic law governing the Japanese telecommunications industry had produced the potential for severe restriction on U.S. access to Japan's market in areas where the United States had a clear advantage. Arduous negotiations resulted in removal of the formal restriction from the law. However, there remained a seemingly innocuous notification requirement: to enter certain kinds of network business, companies would have to notify the ministry by letter before proceeding; in some cases, they would have to submit a more detailed registration form.

While, to the unskilled eye, this small requirement appeared innocent enough, just a matter of good record-keeping, in fact it was rich with bureaucratic possibilities. Sources at MITI, MPT's long-time rival, pointed out that in cases in which they opposed the plans of certain companies, Japanese bureaucrats have been known to refuse to accept delivery of a letter or to lose it, thereby preventing formal notification from taking place and halting the project. MPT pointed out that MITI could expound on this technique because it had so often utilized it. The important point for us was that, if the ordinance did not specifically require the ministry to act within a specified period, an unwanted notification or registration might languish for a very long time. We pressed for and obtained such provisions in another round of negotiations, but in the end I wondered how much difference it made. In Japan, if a company has to inform a ministry of its plans, the very knowledge puts the officials in a position to exert subtle pressures. Given the power of the ministries, only a foolhardy company would ignore them.

The system of bureaucratic power contributes greatly to a perception by the Americans that Japan is unfair and deceptive on trade issues. Time and again, Japanese prime ministers have visited the United States and made commitments to opening the market. But when the actual negotiations have come, there have always been difficulties. The truth is that the prime minister's power is limited. The fact that he cannot deliver on commitments his officials do not accept, contributes to the United States's perception of deception. The relatively closed nature of Japanese procedures also leads to a perception of unfairness. In the United States, representatives of the Japanese government and Japanese industry participate in public hearings. For example, Keidanren (the Federation of Economic Organizations, the main big business lobbying body in Japan) regularly sends missions to lobby Congress and even state legislatures. They attend the markup sessions and committee meetings in which U.S. laws are written, and often influence them. Yet when I and other U.S. negotiators asked to see drafts of bills or ordinances in Japan, we were told that the drafts are secret.

This secretiveness led us to press constantly for transparent procedures in Japan. The Japanese had advance knowledge, and helped shape the development, of trade policy in the United States. In an attempt to achieve similar participation on the part of the United States in Japan, we made various proposals in 1983–84. One was for the inclusion of Japanese executives of foreign companies in Japan on such bodies as MITI's Industrial Structure Council. Our hope was to enable foreign companies, who employed thousands of Japanese citizens, to have the same window on the system that Japanese companies have.

The hostility of the reception accorded the proposal was itself evidence of the power the ministries derive from the system. One high official was quoted as saying our proposal

was akin to Japan demanding seats on the U.S. National Security Council. It was repeatedly said that we wanted to put
foreigners who could not speak Japanese on the council. In
fact, our proposal concerned only the possibility that Japanese citizens working in the Japanese subsidiaries of foreign
companies have the same rights as other Japanese. Ultimately, we made some progress; and some Japanese executives of foreign companies in Japan were put on some
advisory councils. Nevertheless, these and most other negotiations were always difficult. At a time of intense trade friction, when Japan's diplomats and politicians were constantly
proclaiming their support for open markets, its officials
stoutly resisted relaxation of bureaucratic procedures, the
reason being that the power of the mandarins, their ability to
administer guidance, was dependent on the very things we
were trying to dismantle. They had gone through the hell of
the Japanese examination system to get to the top of Japanese society. They had put in the long hours expected of
Japanese civil servants. Writing regulations, administering
them, and guiding the entities under their jurisdiction was
what being at the top was all about. In effect, we were asking them to throw it away, and they were not about to.

MITI's advice to us on MPT's registration scheme was the
evidence of another continuing theme in Japan. Not only is
power the name of the game, but the competition for it now
is, as it was in the nineteenth century, primarily among the
ministries. In the case of the ministries of International Trade
and Industry and of Posts and Telecommunications, the battle was over control of the information industries. MPT
hoped to expand its administrative guidance authority from
its telecommunications base into computers and other information areas traditionally MITI's domain. Conversely, MITI
hoped to extend into telecommunications. Already certain
towns in Japan have been designated as test areas for advanced information concepts. Those under MPT authority
are called Teletopias, while those under MITI are called New
Media Towns. To a U.S. audience, this may seem much ado

about nothing. But a broad consensus has been created in Japan on the necessity of creating what is called the "informationized society." The battle is for the power to lead Japan into the twenty-first century.

For outsiders, however, the question is whether the policies of these mandarins, interested in controlling what happens in Japan's highly structured society, can accord with an open-market, free-trading system.

# 5

# MANDARIN STRATEGIES: JAPAN'S INDUSTRIAL POLICY

---

We violated all the traditional economic concepts....
The realization of the myth that if you entrust things
to the market mechanism, the invisible God's hand
will bring about a rational result is quite limited.
—NAOHIRO AMAYA

ON 23 July 1983, a delegation from Nippon Telegraph and Telephone arrived at Hughes Aerospace Corporation in El Segundo, California. Its mission was to buy software. In 1979, NTT had unwillingly agreed to open its annual procurement of about $6 billion to foreign bidders. Prior to conclusion of the agreement, NTT's chairman had said the only thing NTT could buy from foreign companies would be buckets, mops, and telephone poles.[1] However, under great pressure from the United States as a result of the increasing trade imbalance and frictions, NTT had acceded. Although initially hailed in the United States as a major step toward opening Japan's market, by 1983 the agreement itself had become a source of friction because NTT had bought only about $30 million of U.S. goods, mostly in the bucket and mop category. As a result, NTT was again being pressed to buy something significant from a U.S. manufacturer, and NTT's new chairman, Hisashi Shinto, had dispatched this team to look into American software, for which he had great admiration.

The Japanese and U.S. accounts of this meeting differ as night and day. That evening I received an irate telephone call from a Hughes executive. Did I know, he asked, that this group, which the U.S. government had encouraged him to receive, was trying to obtain the plans and technology for constructing their own telecommunications satellite in Japan? No, I responded, I understood they were looking for software. "Well," said the executive, "they described the software they're interested in, and it essentially involves teaching them how to build a satellite. We told them that building satellites is what we do, that we're very good at it, and that we'd be glad to sell them a satellite if they're interested, but we won't give them the plans and blueprints for making one of their own." Then came the clincher. "Furthermore," said the executive, "we know they're in the market for a satellite, and when we asked if we could bid, they told us that they couldn't buy an American satellite, because it's Japanese government policy to develop a Japanese satellite."

The story as told by NTT is quite different. Its representatives maintain that they were interested only in software that would make their satellites work better. They say that they did not indicate interest in plans or drawings for building a satellite, and expressed surprise at Hughes's reaction.

Whatever the truth of the actual situation, the subsequent facts are not in doubt. News of the meeting sent a shock wave through Washington. The U.S. government immediately asked the Japanese government to explain its policy on building satellites, a request that was important for two reasons. First, in the area of telecommunications satellites, all informed observers acknowledge that the U.S. industry is superior to Japan's. Not only does the former build bigger and more sophisticated satellites, but it builds them less expensively. If, in fact, NTT could not buy such a satellite, suspicions that NTT remained closed to the idea of buying from outside Japan would be confirmed, and all the praise the U.S. administration had heaped on Japan for opening its telecommunications market would be shown to have been misplaced. Second, as a result of difficulties in the telecommunications, semiconductor, and machine tool industries, many Americans were emphasizing that Japan's markets are closed because the industrial policies of its mandarins specifically target development of certain industries. In response, the President had directed that talks be held with Japan to ascertain the trade effects of its industrial policies, and preparation for these discussions had just begun. Thus this development concerning satellites took on great significance as a test case.

For several months, the Japanese response to the U.S. inquiry was crashing silence. Finally, in October 1983, Foreign Minister Shintaro Abe stated in a formal letter to U.S. Trade Representative Brock that, indeed, Japan's policy was to ensure autonomy in the development of satellites, as stated in a 1982 government white paper entitled *Long Term Vision for Space Development*, which called for both development of a Japanese capability and eventual export of satellites. This was precisely the kind of policy that had already led to the serious trade problems I have noted. Japan's response to Brock thus triggered a long series of negotiations in which the U.S. government pressured NTT and the Japanese government to allow Hughes and other U.S. producers to bid on NTT's satellite purchases. The negotiations were a classic chapter in the annals of trade talks between the two countries. Ultimately, Japan agreed to buy two satellites, but the most interesting aspect of the talks was that, despite the obvious contradiction between free-trade doctrine and a policy of autonomy in satellites, Japan did not compromise easily and never compromised fully. Ultimately, it agreed that private companies could buy foreign satellites. This was a kind of sleight of hand. NTT was then being transformed from a government monopoly into a private company. By saying private companies could buy satellites, Japan was making it possible for NTT to buy a U.S. satellite and thereby relieve trade pressure. At the same time, by reserving the government market, which was by far the largest, Japan maintained its self-development policy. This was made clearer by the fact that Japan continued to require NTT to consider the national interest in its satellite procurement, even though in principle it was free to buy abroad.

Shortly before the NTT visit to El Segundo, another important event had taken place in Japan. In June 1983, the law for restructuring specified depressed industries had been renewed. Despite the image of the Japanese as manufacturing and business supermen, some industries in Japan—such as aluminum, paper, petroleum refining and petrochemicals, and basic chemicals—have been in distress for a long time. Plagued by excess capacity, plants that are too small, and high-cost energy, these industries depend on government support for their existence. The law gave MITI the power to declare industries officially distressed and to establish cartels for the purposes of temporarily restricting production and reducing capacity in order to stabilize prices. It also allowed depressed companies to engage in collusive activity, such as joint buying, marketing, and stockpiling.

These events highlighted the two key elements in the industrial strategies of Japan's mandarins: promotion of a Japanese capability in high-technology industries and intervention to revitalize declining industries, both aimed at achieving the maximum degree of autonomy.

## The Purpose of Industrial Policy

The purpose of Japan's industrial policies was explained by Ministry of International Trade and Industry officials to U.S.

trade negotiators in 1983 and 1984 in the series of talks on the effect of such policies on trade. These talks, called "The Industrial Policy Dialogue," were held pursuant to complaints of unfair trade by the U.S. machine tool industry. Said the Japanese, "When the technology concerned is critical to the security of a nation's economy, the government of that country will be forced to take the necessary measures to develop the industry concerned so that its firms can become competitive and assure the security of the country's economy."[2] This approach was consistent with MITI's statement in its *Vision of MITI Policies in the 1980s* (the white paper of MITI's blueprint for the decade) that the focus of its efforts would henceforth be on developing indigenous technologies aimed at enhancing Japan's "autonomy and bargaining power."[3]

In Japan's view, economic power and security go hand in hand. Industrial policies, which include those of ministries other than MITI, are also national security policies, and because Japan tends to define security in terms of remaining apart from the world, such policies are an expression of its age-old drive to guarantee to the maximum extent possible its autarkic position among the world's nations.

## The Theory of Industrial Policy

There has been much discussion in the United States about the reasons for Japan's success. Many American experts argue that, at best, the effect of Japanese industrial policy has been minimal. Given its high savings rate, well-educated labor force, and relatively large population, they say, Japan would have achieved the same results with or without an industrial strategy or policy aimed at promoting key industries. The secret was nothing more than sound economic policies, a free market, and free trade. In effect, goes the somewhat condescending argument, the Japanese succeeded by doing well what we told them to do. That this view is very wide of the mark is evident from the fact that no Japanese hold it. The misperception is based on the assumption that everything begins with macroeconomic policy and that high savings and investment rates and educational levels arise from cultural bases. Industrial policy is seen as at best a bauble added to these basic conditions. But in fact, in Japan, industrial policy is the starting point. As the economist Hiroya Ueno has noted, the Japanese government has always intervened "to attain a specific economic order or economic structure viewed favorable to the national or public interest."[4]

Japan's first critical decision—made in 1867 and repeated in 1952—was to have a certain type of industrial structure. From that determination, everything followed. If a nation decides on rapid industrialization, it obviously needs capital. If it decides that the capital will not come from abroad (as Japan decided in order to preserve its treasured autonomy), it must generate the savings to provide its own. In the 1930s, Japanese savings rates were not exceptional. Today's rate of about 18 percent did not occur by accident[5] but was encouraged by tax-free postal savings accounts, no interest-payment deductions (even for mortgages), no consumer credit, bonus-based salary systems, and other measures. As for education, while it is true that the Confucian tradition which Japan inherited from China emphasizes education, it is also true that technology never loomed large in Confucian education. A modern industrial state needs well-trained people, especially engineers. The thousands of engineers pouring out of Japanese universities today are the result of policies that deliberately encourage students to pursue engineering studies, as is evident from the fact that Japan graduates relatively few chemists and physicists.[6]

Looked at in this way, one can almost characterize macroeconomic and even social policy in Japan as tools of indus-

*1982 First Degrees*

|                    | U.S.    | Japan  |
|--------------------|---------|--------|
| Sciences and Math  | 102,000 | 12,000 |
| Engineering        | 68,000  | 74,000 |

SOURCE: Science Indicators 1986, National Science Board, Washington, D.C.

trial policy. For instance, Japan maintains low interest rates, which benefit its heavily leveraged (carrying high debt) capital-intensive industries. At the same time, consumer loans, if available at all, usually carry high interest charges. Most unions are enterprise unions which Japan's labor laws encourage and which are today more malleable than industry-wide unions. Japan sets energy prices relatively high for consumers but keeps them low for industry. In short, everything in the environment is structured with one objective in mind: to achieve industrial strength. This is the opposite of the U.S. approach where the consumer is king; in Japan, the consumer comes last.

American misperception is rooted in Western economic doctrine which understands greater consumption to be the purpose of economic activity and which, based on the writings of Adam Smith and David Ricardo, holds that what nations produce is based on their resource endowment. The unseen hand of the free market allocates these resources most efficiently to those users and industries that reflect the demands of consumers. Internationally, the doctrine asserts that nations specialize in what they produce best—called a "comparative advantage"—and trade for the rest. If, for example, a nation like the United States is dominant in making aircraft, the assumption is that it has a resource endowment particularly suited to making aircraft. Instead of competing with the United States, other countries should make other products to trade for aircraft. If a nation has a large unskilled labor force, then theoretically it should concentrate on making textiles or other labor-intensive goods, while trading for things like airplanes.

It is on this old and hallowed thinking that the international trade system rests. Implicit in this thinking is the notion that all industries have roughly the same economic and strategic value. Because advantages are linked to resource endowment, it is also assumed that nations cannot, and therefore will not, try to change the areas of their advantage.

The Japanese have two difficulties with this theory: it is static and implies a certain permanency about the economic activity of nations; and the Japanese believe that some industries are more important than others. Airplanes, for instance, tend to be expensive and to justify high wage levels, while serving as the object for technological development in other industries. Airplanes also contribute to a nation's power as textiles do not. For a technologically less advanced nation, therefore, acceptance of Western economic doctrine implies a permanent lag and a kind of colonial relationship that is clearly unacceptable to the Japanese.

An alternative view of capitalist economic dynamics was offered by Joseph Schumpeter, an Austrian economist who has generally been ignored in the West. Writing in the early 1940s, he viewed capitalism as an evolutionary process in which competition takes place around innovations by dominant firms.[7] In his theory, what matters is not price competition or resource endowment but the competition arising from new technology, new sources of supply, and new types of organization. Such dynamic competition can reverse a decisive cost or quality advantage by striking not at the margins of profits but at the foundations of the existing system. An example of what Schumpeter meant is the Toyota production system. Toyota did not concentrate just on squeezing a few percentage points of improvement from its production lines. Rather, its "just in time" inventory system led to a doubling and even tripling of productivity. For this kind of development, Schumpeter argued, perfectly free markets with their emphasis on price competition are not always the best model.[8] Research and development is necessary in order to develop new systems, and vicious price competition which erodes profit margins may retard R&D investment.

Schumpeter's concept of dynamic competition based on factors other than price suggests the possibility of catching up and the legitimacy of government intervention in order to do so. Although at odds with much of the accepted Western doctrine, this theory accords well with the samurai instinct of the Japanese who cannot accept that Japan remain behind in anything. As Amaya indicated to me in September 1986, "We did the opposite of what American economists said. We violated all the normal concepts." In his writings, Amaya has noted that the "American view of economics may help business to increase current production or to lower current costs, but that research and development is necessary for the future and it is a gamble. Businessmen are risk averse. They hesitate to take the gamble on research and development. Therefore, if the invisible hand cannot drive the enterprise to research and development, the visible hand must."[9] Amaya was saying that the nation cannot rely entirely upon the free market and industries based only on current resource endowment. A key objective in any economy, he said, is to create an industry that produces technologically sophisticated products with high income elasticity (that is, the higher a person's income, the more one buys of those products) and a rapid growth rate (for example, VCRs). That objective, according to Amaya and most other Japanese observers, cannot be achieved without government intervention.

Among American observers, the policy of government intervention has often been described as one of picking winners and losers. Usually this comment is made in a pejorative sense, because in the United States it is firmly believed that government should not be concerned with the nature of the nation's industry and that in any case, bureaucrats can never do anything except pick losers. The Japanese view is very different. According to Miyohei Shinohara, a professor at Tokei University and a longtime member of Japan's Industrial Structure Council, the objective of Japanese industrial policy has been to attain as much industrial autonomy as possible. Thus, the council reviews all industries with any potential and attempts to develop domestic capabilities in them. At particular times, special attention is given to particular industries to establish the base for advancing to the next stage in the drive toward the overall goal of national autonomy.

Shinohara explains that, in choosing which industries to emphasize at a particular time, the objective is, first, always to move toward industries with high elasticity of demand and high-technology content, in which costs decline rapidly with increases in production. Second, it is important to promote industries that have "ripple" effects on other sectors of the economy. Because semiconductors, for example, are used in many products, being a low-cost producer of semiconductors helps a country to be a low-cost producer of computers. Finally, industries that lead to further increases in knowledge are favored.[10] These criteria seem simple and straightforward to the Japanese, who do not feel that they rely on a mystical laying on of hands by bureaucrats and do not claim any special clairvoyance. In fact, they say, their policy is not to pick winners but, rather, to identify and back the winners the market has already picked, to ensure that Japan rides with the winners.

## The Tools of Industrial Policy

### THE VISIONS OF INDUSTRIAL POLICY

Like the theory behind it, the process of industrial policy making in Japan is much misunderstood in the United

States. When Americans look at Japanese industrial policy, they tend to focus on specific quantifiable items, such as subsidies, tariffs, and overt directives. But in practice the policy is much more varied, sophisticated, and subtle than these devices suggest. The key bodies in developing industrial policy in Japan are the Industrial Structure Council of the Ministry of International Trade and Industry, the Telecommunications Advisory Council of the Ministry of Posts and Telecommunications, and similar groups established to advise other ministries. These councils usually consist of approximately fifty members chosen from among leaders in business, consumer groups, labor unions, academia, government, and the press. Below the councils themselves are a series of subcommittees, which have a similar kind of membership, organized along industry lines. Thus, for example, the aircraft industry is overseen by the Aircraft and Machinery Industries Council. The staff work for this council is done by MITI's aircraft and ordnance division which also receives the council's recommendations.

These councils constantly study the industry under their jurisdiction, as well as the relationships between it and other industries. They issue a steady stream of white papers, often termed "visions," that point the direction for Japanese industry. The procedure is for the ministry bureau concerned to write its plans for an industry and then submit them to the council, which generally blesses them. On the basis of these visions, legislation is developed for promoting specific industries or for restructuring depressed industries. Proposals for research and development are also created based on a council's recommendations. From the visions and subsequent legislation flow what are known as "elevation plans," which are detailed plans that MITI officials are directed to develop for specific industries. These plans specify such things as production amounts for exports, as well as spending on research and development for particular projects. These detailed plans, which look much like the two- or three-year plans of major corporations, are drawn up in conjunction with representatives of the industry.

Many U.S. observers have dismissed these efforts as mere exhortation. MITI, in an effort to make its policies palatable to the Americans, has told them that the various visions and plans are not binding; and the legalistic Americans have concluded that this means that they are not effective. In fact, however, the dedicated men who run Japan's government do not go through these exercises to entertain the public. In Japan's group-oriented hierarchy, these procedures create a powerful consensus and an atmosphere conducive to achieving the objectives the mandarins desire. Noteworthy in this regard is the practice of co-opting the press by putting its members on the councils.

The violent Japanese reaction to U.S. proposals in 1984 for placing Japanese representatives of foreign companies on the councils provides the strongest evidence of their importance (see pages 245–46). Many in the United States viewed as hyperbole the Japanese comparison of the Industrial Structure Council to the National Security Council. In fact, it was apt.

## THE PROMOTION OF NEW INDUSTRIES

At the policy-execution stage, the Japanese ministries have many tools at their disposal. Special depreciation rates, tax incentives, and government-supported research and development are standard devices. Beyond these are more imaginative measures, such as the creation of the Japan Electronic Computer Corporation, the government-backed leasing company. The control that the Ministry of International Trade and Industry exercises over the establishment of industrial standards constitutes another industrial policy tool. When a Japanese industry establishes standards differing from those of other nations, it is automatically protected from invasion by foreign producers without the necessity for a tariff or a quota. Guidance to banking and financial institutions on preferred areas of loan activity can strongly influence industrial development, as can such things as delay in granting patents.

Again, the American focus on specific subsidy amounts and specific government intervention causes misperception. For example, the government-controlled Japan Development Bank makes low-interest loans to specified projects. Because the interest rate is usually only just below the market rate and the amount loaned is often not substantial in terms of the total project, Western economists tend to dismiss these loans as insignificant. What they do not realize is that, by long tradition, Japan Development Bank and other government institution loans are a signal to the financial community at large that it should give preference in its own lending to these targeted projects. For example, in its 1981 annual report, Japan's Long Term Credit Bank says it must "serve as a pipeline through which the government can channel funds to the private sector by purchasing bank debentures."[11]

Beyond favorable finance there exist such devices as legal cooperative agreements between companies on the types of goods to be produced. Such an agreement provided overall direction to the machine tool industry, where for most of the past thirty years manufacturers agreed on who would produce what kinds of product. These devices have one thing in common: they induce investment and sometimes disinvestment by reducing risk. This point is extremely important. While Japan is a conservative, conformist, risk-averse, non-entrepreneurial society, it nevertheless produces businessmen who are lauded the world over for their long-term strategic thinking and "risk taking." The solution to the paradox is that because of the policies of the Japanese government, there really is no risk. In such circumstances, it is easy to be a long-term thinker.

*Losing the Advantage: The Optical Fibers Industry*   Although industrial policy in Japan is associated with the Ministry of

International Trade and Industry, Nippon Telegraph and Telephone has used similar tools to promote particular Japanese capabilities. One example among many is that of the optical fibers industry. In the late 1960s, the optical fiber was invented in the United States by Corning Glass Works, as the result of privately funded research and development. Corning filed for patents, which were issued in the United States in the mid-1970s. In Japan, however, many of the key patents were not issued for more than ten years, leaving Corning's technology unprotected in this major market.

In the 1970s, Corning and AT&T, which was licensed by Corning, dominated the world market, giving the United States a "comparative advantage" in optical fiber production. When Corning attempted to sell its fiber and cable in Japan, however, NTT, the monopoly buyer, told the company that Japan would develop its own technology. NTT also suggested to Corning that it might consider a joint venture with one of the Japanese companies. At the same time, NTT launched a joint-development optical fiber project with three Japanese companies: Furukawa, Sumitomo, and Fujikura. Each company contributed to the cost of development. NTT agreed to buy the product from them when it was eventually developed. Furthermore, this buying was to be done not on the basis of bids but, rather, in proportion to each company's share of the development cost—a procedure similar in many respects to defense contracting in the United States. The factors at work—long delay in patent issuance; a protected domestic market; research and development that was government-backed although not directly funded;* and an assured end market at a profitable price—reduced risk at every step of the way.

In discussing possible joint ventures with Japanese companies, Corning invited many representatives to its plants and laboratories and provided useful data and information. After

---

*Although statistics always show Japanese government funding of research and development as much lower than in the United States, much funding is hidden in government procurement which guarantees producers of inflated prices.

long negotiations, Corning was informed by a company with which it had been negotiating that a joint venture was impossible because NTT would not buy from a foreign joint-venture operation. With Corning thus locked out, the Japanese developed a process so similar to Corning's that the U.S. International Trade Commission (the body that hears and rules on complaints under U.S. trade law), Canadian courts, and finally U.S. courts found that it infringed Corning's patents. NTT eventually announced plans to switch its main transmission lines to optical fiber, and its three development partners received all of the business at very high prices. But the story does not end there.

In 1979, NTT signed the agreement to open its procurement to foreign bidders, in order better to balance its offer in the government procurement code negotiations of the Tokyo Round.[12] Representatives of the joint-venture Siecor (Siemens and Corning), which produces optical fiber cable from Corning's fibers, visited Japan to propose its new loose-tube-design optical fiber cable for sale to NTT. Siecor's product was selling for about a third the price NTT was paying. Siecor's cable was of a different design than that supplied by the Japanese manufacturers, and its low price resulted from this more modern, sophisticated design which also gave better performance. To outside observers it seemed that Corning and Siecor were good candidates to be among the first significant foreign suppliers to NTT. To submit a formal bid, Siecor needed a copy of NTT's specifications for optical fiber cable so as to be sure to conform with all technical requirements. It was only after months of haggling and the exertion of pressure by the U.S. government that NTT provided the specifications. And meanwhile, procurement from the Japanese manufacturers was expanding rapidly.

Having made specifications available, NTT insisted that Siecor not only meet them but also provide the same cable design as the Japanese manufacturers. On its face, this seemed a reasonable request; and as in many of these cases, Siecor was criticized for not trying hard enough and—when it insisted on offering its own design—for not adapting to the requirements of the Japanese market. Here was a classic case of the U.S. company saying the market was closed, while the Japanese said the company simply was not making a proper effort. It was sometimes difficult to know where the fault lay. When Siecor asked the U.S. government to help, I advised that the company needed to make a stronger effort itself. On the other hand, even some NTT executives told me that the real problem was simply that NTT believed it had to support its own industry.

The fact was that Siecor's cable performed better than the Japanese cable for one third the cost. By international agreement, the technical specifications were supposed to be written in terms of performance, not of design.* However, the Japanese knew that Siecor's cost advantage was related to its design; and that to conform to the existing Japanese design, Siecor would have to install a completely new plant, a very expensive undertaking. Nevertheless, Siecor said it would do so if it were guaranteed a share of the market, as its Japanese competitors had been. Such a guarantee was denied, however, as not being in accord with free trade; and Siecor was effectively denied any business. It then tried selling optical fiber to Japanese cablers, but they were tied to Japanese fiber producers and declined the offer. Thus, as risks were reduced for the Japanese suppliers, they were raised for the foreign suppliers.

While this was going on, the designation in Japan of the optical fibers industry as an industry of the future attracted the desired investment. Japanese manufacturers built enough capacity to fill their own market three times over. Inevitably the search for export markets began; and the biggest export market was, as always, the United States. By 1983, Sumitomo and the other Japanese manufacturers were selling optical fiber in the United States at prices well below

---

*Under the terms of the procurement code, specifications for international bids are to be based on performance rather than design or appearance to prevent the use of specifications as nontariff barriers.

the market. Corning brought suit in Canada and the United States on grounds of patent infringement. In Canada, the suit was upheld, and imports were halted. In the United States, the finding of patent infringement was also upheld, but the International Trade Commission ruled that the infringement was not causing significant loss of sales or profits to Corning and declined to penalize Sumitomo in any way.[13]* Corning then took the case to the federal district courts which found willful infringement on 13 October 1987. By then, however, the patents had only a short term of validity left.

This was promotion policy at work. Siecor had started with a comparative advantage as a result of its innovation. But the Japanese system had systematically reduced the risk of entering the business for its own industry. By denying Siecor the fruits of its innovation and subsidizing investment in direct and indirect ways, industrial policy induced an eventual overcapacity for production which led to very aggressive pricing policies by Japanese companies in the United States and consequently to more trade friction.

On the other side of the equation, while the Japanese government was reducing risk and seeking a comparative advantage, the U.S. government ignored its industry. It assumed that the free play of the market would allow the best man to win. Although the Japanese market remained effectively closed while the U.S. market was open, the U.S. government took no action, and U.S. law even handicapped American industry by hampering its ability to stop patent infringement. The result was that Japan became a powerful competitor, and various U.S. observers congratulated it for its diligence and foresight, while criticizing the corpocracy of American business.

Stories such as this receive attention in the United States

---

*This ruling points to a curious aspect of U.S. law that favors foreign manufacturers. In a domestic case, infringement is alleged per se and, if found, must be halted with the infringer paying damages. If the infringer is a foreign company, however, no action is taken unless the domestic complainant can show that it is actually losing money and laying off workers as a result of the infringement.

only sporadically and are often treated as isolated cases. In fact, they are not. Virtually every industry has had the same experience. Indeed, the Japan expert Henry Rosovsky of Harvard emphasizes that Japanese policy since 1952 has been systematically to deny foreigners the profits of innovation. And while many experts portray the Japanese policies as relics of the past, every high-technology industry, from biotechnology to industrial ceramics to superconductivity, is currently the object of similar efforts. The examples of supercomputers and aircraft are indicative.

*Supercomputers and Aircraft*  Supercomputers flared into the headlines in the spring of 1987, when a secret cable from the U.S. embassy in Tokyo to the State Department reporting on trade talks during the week of 27 January 1987 was leaked to the press.[14] Supercomputers are the heavyweights of serious scientific number crunching and are used for such tasks, among others, as cracking codes, nuclear weapons design, oil field exploration, and weather forecasting. These machines were pioneered by the Control Data Corporation and Cray Research Inc., which currently control about 80 percent of the world market, with Cray alone holding about 65 percent.[15]

Cray's is a quintessentially American story. Its founder, Seymour Cray, is a true genius. One of the founders of Control Data in 1958, he has had a career interest in building the biggest, fastest computers possible. Racing drivers get their kicks from fast cars. Cray gets his from fast computers. Pursuing his vision of ever-greater speed, he struck out on his own in 1972 and founded Cray Research. His new machines quickly became absolutely essential to U.S. national security as users such as the National Security Agency came to rely on them. Indeed, the President's daily intelligence briefing cannot be done without them. As a result, the company quickly enjoyed huge success.

Cray shaped his company to reflect his own personality. Its headquarters is in Minneapolis, Minnesota, where the management of the company is in the hands of professional

managers. Cray himself lives in splendid isolation in Chip-
pewa Falls, Wisconsin, and concentrates on expanding the
limits of technology at a design center next to his home. He
is the true American hero, conquering and bettering the
world through his own genius and rugged character: a real
cowboy.

The secret U.S. embassy cable that had been leaked to the
press in the spring of 1987, reported a top MITI official as
saying that Japan would not change its policies regarding
supercomputers, and that if the United States wanted to
save Cray from losing its market to Japanese producers it
might have to consider nationalization. The cable concluded
in a shocked tone that Japan is intent upon dominating the
world market for supercomputers. The MITI official was Makoto Kuroda, vice minister of International Affairs. Not the
most diplomatic of diplomats, Kuroda is blunt even by
American standards. In terms of sheer brain power, he has
few equals; and his subordinates at MITI joke that no one
can write a report for him because he already knows the
report is wrong. He does not suffer fools gladly—which may
account for the discomfort he caused many U.S. officials
since he seemed to consider most of them to be fools. Nonetheless, I found that, in addition to his obvious intelligence,
he had one very attractive quality. If you wanted to know
what Japan was really thinking beneath all the layers of po-
liteness, you listened to Kuroda. You might not like what he
said or the way he said it, but if you listened, you heard the
real Japan talking.

In this case, U.S. officials should not have been shocked.
Kuroda was only telling them what had been obvious for
some time. Cray had first entered Japan in the 1970s and had
sold two machines in 1980. In 1981, however, MITI announced a supercomputer-development program; and, at
about the same time, several Japanese computer makers announced their own projects. From that time, Cray's prospective customers in Japan seemed to disappear. A major part of
the market for these machines is government research insti-

tutions. Some of these told Cray it was a waste of time even to send salesmen to visit them because the ministries that controlled their budgets would not allocate funds for procurement of foreign supercomputers.

The apparently closed nature of the Japanese market became a trade issue in 1982, during the time I co-chaired the High Technology Working Group. With no Japanese supercomputers on the market, the Americans indisputably had the best and least expensive machines. Many suspected that the various government-run institutes in Japan were declining to buy from the Americans in order to preserve the market for the Japanese makers when their machines were ready. The feeling of unfairness this reluctance engendered was only exacerbated by the knowledge that the Japanese computer companies were receiving advice from U.S. government laboratories, such as Lawrence Livermore, in designing their machines. In response to U.S. inquiries, however, the Japanese government explained that because its research institutes were small, they had little use for such large machines. Two years later, however, when the Japanese supercomputers were finally introduced, many of the small institutes placed orders. Today, sales in Japan are booming. As a result of enormous U.S. government pressure, as well as its own efforts, Cray has sold a few machines in Japan, including two to NTT, but its share of the Japanese market remains relatively small. The furor unleashed by the leaked cable led the Japanese government to promise more open bidding procedures for supercomputers in July 1987. Time will tell whether this will effectively open the market. Meanwhile, the Japanese computer makers have already begun an export drive, based on extremely low prices, into the U.S. market. In November 1987, the Massachusetts Institute of Technology canceled plans to buy a supercomputer from the Nippon Electric Company at about one-third of the normal price only after being warned of a possible antidumping investigation by the Commerce Department.

The drive for autonomy evident in the cases of satellites, fiber optics, and supercomputers is also evident in the field of aviation. Throughout the summer and fall of 1987, the question of who would produce Japan's next generation jet fighter, the FSX, became a major trade issue. In the past, Japan's fighters had been versions of U.S. aircraft. Initially, most of the planes had been produced in the United States, which was cost-effective because of the long production runs in the United States and the avoidance of duplication of development and engineering costs. Gradually, however, the Japanese had insisted on building more and more of the planes in Japan under license from the U.S. producers. Now strong forces in Japan were urging that it build the FSX entirely on its own, despite the fact that to do so would cost three times more than building under license or buying from the United States.

U.S. officials were dismayed. The desire for interoperability of forces had been the reason for licensing Japan to produce U.S. planes. Now Japan was proposing a wholly different aircraft. Moreover, aircraft is the one area in which the United States has a clear advantage over Japan. In view of the enormous and growing trade deficit and the great imbalances in respective military burdens, how could Japan even consider building an entirely domestic airplane at much greater cost? Enormous pressure was put on Japan to choose an advanced U.S. plane for continued production under license; and in the end it agreed in principle, ironically as a kind of favor to the United States, to engage in co-development of a modified version of the F–16 built by General Dynamics. But the fact that Japan chose to fight this battle at a time of bitter trade disputes is a measure of its dedication to self-development and autonomy. Moreover, the meaning of "in principle" was very broad (see pages 186–87).

The United States should not have been surprised. The Japanese policy was the culmination of long effort. As early as the 1960s, the Ministry of International Trade and Industry had sponsored development of a commercial airliner.

Although it was not successful commercially, the effort to develop the industry continued. In February 1984, Japan's updated space-development policy was published. It called for establishing autonomy in this area, saying that Japan must have its own capability so that it "can perform in a steady and broad manner."[16] About a year later, the Aircraft and Machinery Industries Council published its recommendations, saying that Japan had to have a modern aircraft industry in order to be a technologically advanced nation.[17] During this same time, MITI was acting to achieve the goal by promising to provide $1 billion to $2 billion for development of the Boeing Commercial Airplane Company's new generation 7J7 jet liner, so as to enable a consortium of Japanese companies to become 25-percent equity partners in the project. Concurrently, MITI announced plans to promote development of aviation subsystems such as avionics, flight control, engines, and fuel systems.

MILITARY COPRODUCTION

The emphasis on aircraft and particularly on the FSX highlights another extremely important industrial policy tool—military coproduction. Under a coproduction program, the United States enters into agreements that provide for foreign companies to be licensed to produce U.S. military equipment. The United States enters into these agreements to improve the military readiness of its allies and to promote standardization of equipment and systems. Such agreements are approved by the secretaries of defense and state. The secretaries of commerce and labor and the U.S. trade representative are not involved in any significant way.

The picture is just the opposite in Japan. In order to understand why, it is first necessary to understand that Japan does not defend itself. The postwar constitution, written largely by U.S. Occupation officials, barred Japan from possession of more than a small self-defense force. As a result,

Japan's total expenditures on defense are only about 1 percent of its gross national product (the United States spends 6 percent–7 percent), and Japan does little defense-related research and development. The United States carries the bulk of the burden of Japan's defense. In a study published in March 1982, the Government Accounting Office reported that the key objectives of Japan in entering coproduction programs are to enhance its high-technology employment base, to develop future export industries, and to increase military self-sufficiency. For example, MITI sets policy for both military and civil aircraft production and assigns its personnel to the Japan Defense Agency's Equipment Bureau. This prime example of the concept of economic security at work enables integration of military and commercial development activities to attain an overall industrial goal.[18]

Coproduction with Japan began in the 1950s, when some of its companies were licensed to build the F–86 fighter. Since then there has been a stream of other products, including the F–100 in the 1960s, the P–3C in the 1970s, and currently the F–15. These programs have made significant contributions to both Japan's technology base and its strategy for developing a world-class aircraft industry. It was by working with U.S. manufacturers and gradually taking over more and more of the production responsibility that Japan developed the capabilities that allowed it to propose building the FSX plane. A measure of the importance Japan attaches to obtaining the technology is the cost it bears as a result of coproduction. Because of relatively short production runs, it costs Japan two to three times as much as the United States to produce military aircraft. In view of Japan's limited defense budget, it seemed advisable to many in the United States that Japan get more defense for its money by buying American. But Japan has a different definition of defense: it insisted on coproduction and eventually even on sole production. For the Japanese, defense and acquiring technology are the same thing.

In separate studies, the General Accounting Office and the

*Washington Post* found that U.S. efforts to limit the technology loss have been useless.[19] After concluding the coproduction agreement on the F–15, Air Force specialists at the Pentagon drew up a detailed list of technologies considered too sensitive to be transferred to Japan because of the danger of their falling into Soviet hands. The list was obtained almost immediately by Japanese officials through the U.S. Defense Security Assistance Agency. They confronted U.S. defense officials with it and indignantly demanded that the technologies be released on the grounds that otherwise it would be difficult for them to make repairs. To soothe their ruffled feelings, Defense reviewed the list and released much of the technology.[20]

It was at this same time in the late 1970s that U.S. defense officials put special emphasis on standardization of equipment between the United States and its allies. They strongly promoted coproduction and transfer of U.S. technology. As a result, the traditional ceiling on the percentage of the plane that could be built by Japanese companies was omitted, clearing the way for massive flows of technology to Japan. Virtually every U.S. defense contractor was permitted to license design and manufacturing processes to Japanese companies. The result of such generosity is seen in the case of the speed brake of the F–15, which is made of carbon composites. Japan was adamant about obtaining this technology. The Air Force strongly opposed any transfer but was overridden by the secretary of defense; by 1981, Japan had the technology. Japanese executives later acknowledged that it had been valuable to several commercial projects.

I saw a concrete example of this technology transfer when I visited the Mitsubishi F–15 production line in Nagoya in 1982. There, on a line next to the F–15 line, Mitsubishi was producing a corporate jet, all models of which had to be exported to the United States because such jets are not allowed in Japan.

The Japanese approach to coproduction has been particularly distressing to U.S. officials who have tried to negotiate agreements for the transfer of dual-use (military or commercial) technology from Japan to the United States. Years of negotiation finally produced, in November 1983, an agreement in principle that Japan would permit such transfers. To date, however, virtually no technology has been transferred. Japan's attitude was best revealed in the negotiations that led to its decision in 1987 to participate in SDI (Star Wars) research. Although the United States practically begged Japan to join, there was hesitation in Tokyo, because many believed that Japan's technology is more advanced than U.S. technology and that Japan had little to gain. It did eventually agree to participate, but the discussion showed the essential difference between the two countries. While the United States has sought security by giving away technology, Japan has sought it by hoarding technology, even from the United States, its primary source. This has been the strange denouement of the concept of economic security. In a sense, the United States, the defender of Japan, has become its target, not in any sinister sense or even by plan: it was a result inherent in the logical dynamic of this concept.

## RESTRUCTURING MATURE INDUSTRIES: CARTELS

Once new industries are successfully established in Japan, the need for specific policy intervention is reduced. As industries begin to decline, however, the other major component of industrial policy—restructuring—comes into play. As Kodama said, it is the bow and stern of the ship that need attention.

The combination of Japan's industry promotion policies and the peculiar nature of its companies, which I will examine in chapter 6, tends ultimately to create the problem of excess production capacity, which in turn leads to what the Japanese call "excessive competition" involving severe price cutting and financial losses. As noted earlier, this concept has a pedigree dating back to the financial panic of 1925.

Although in the United States it is seen as a boon for consumers, Japan dislikes excessive competition because, if left unrestrained, it can damage organizations that may be critical for long-term efficiency. Japan does not believe that productivity is enhanced by the merger and acquisition activity so popular in the United States. The Ministry of International Trade and Industry, sensitive to the charge that over-capacity results from its own promotion policies, reverses the argument. Excessive competition, MITI says, arises from the nature of certain industries and requires measures to control it.

While the Occupation gave Japan its Fair Trade Commission, neither this agency nor Japan's antitrust laws have taken root. To restrain excessive competition, Japan has developed an elaborate set of tools, providing for the establishment of legal cartels under which companies may engage in such collaborative activity as joint restrictions on production and joint reductions in capacity. Administration of these measures involves extremely close cooperation between industry and government and gives officials even greater power than does industry promotion. The object, as stated in the 1983 law for depressed industries, is to restore the industries to a healthy status. If that cannot be achieved, then the secondary objective is the establishment of the industries overseas under Japanese control.

Industries qualify for these measures when they meet certain criteria concerning financial losses. Perhaps the best example of how this policy works is Japan's steel industry, which for years has been the object of various cartels, joint-buying arrangements, and restructuring. In 1977, fifty-two electric-furnace steel producers, which were suffering from over-capacity and low prices, were directed by MITI to form a capacity-reduction cartel. Some of the healthier companies resisted. MITI directed the resisters to cut production by 35 percent and threatened them with a fine if they did not comply.[21] They complied. In 1979, when imports threatened to take 3 percent of the domestic market, MITI moved to protect the market by suspending the preferential tariff treat-ment it had been extending to certain developing countries on steel (at the time Japanese producers held about 6 percent of the U.S. market).[22] In mid-1982, MITI issued a "guideline" to reduce production while prices were raised, thereby re-storing a measure of profitability.[23] Thus at different times various measures were employed; but throughout this pe-riod, the constant policy was to maintain the health of the industry. Japan's Fair Trade Commission investigated from time to time but took no action.

The "guideline" is indicative of the close cooperation be-tween government and business in these matters. An article in *Nihon Keizai* on 7 Janaury 1981 described the process from close up.[24] It noted that, every Monday at noon in the Ni-honbashi section of Tokyo, black limousines swarm around the Iron and Steel Building. From them emerge men from Japan's eight major steel companies; they go to room 704, where a sign on the door reads, "Regular Monday Club Meeting." The men take their places at a large, rectangular table, at whose head is the chief of MITI's Iron and Steel section of the Basic Industries Bureau. First organized in 1958, the group has met every Monday since then to iron out a consensus on the MITI "guideline" for appropriate levels of investment and production.

Other examples are provided by the paper, petroleum, and aluminum industries. Paper, in trouble for many years, has been in and out of cartel status. In September 1981, the four largest producers announced they would engage in joint purchasing and possibly in joint research and develop-ment and distribution under a plan coordinated by MITI.[25] The Petrochemical Industry Plan for the 1980s found the in-dustry at a crossroads and called for a restructuring. It sug-gested joint investment, procurement, and marketing in order to maintain the industry's present size and to keep imports at the cheaper end of the scale.[26] MITI's role in such matters was recently underlined for me by an official who stated that the government would probably have to buy into some of Japan's petrochemical plants in the Middle East to save them from bankruptcy. Even though they belong to companies that are part of the biggest industrial combines in the world, MITI felt compelled to offer help.

One of the most interesting examples is that of aluminum smelting. With the highest energy costs in the industrial world, Japan's smelting industry languished after the successive oil crises of the 1970s. It, too, went in and out of cartel status as world prices fell far below production costs. MITI gave it preferential electric rates, special loans, and other aids. In 1982, when the world price was half that in Japan, the industry and MITI, concluding that it could not be revived, set in motion a plan to move it to overseas locations in Indonesia and Brazil. This plan gave Japanese smelters a tariff-free import quota, while other importers had to pay a tariff. By importing duty-free and reselling, they made a profit that was applied to closing old plants and building new ones abroad.[27] Of particular significance was the long-range plan for importation. The Japanese government could have allowed its users to contract with foreign producers for their entire needs. Instead, it consciously set out to ensure that a large part of the necessary supply would come specifically from Japanese overseas installations.

For Americans, the issue again is the effect of these policy tools on trade. Japan has insisted in international forums that it is winding down these industries to make room for imports. Not surprisingly, in view of the emphasis put by the programs on keeping Japanese industry alive, the effect has tended to be the reverse; and even if imports rise, they tend to be under Japanese control. In a major study conducted in 1981, Frank Upham, an economist at New York University, found that, of fourteen officially designated depressed industries in Japan, only two saw increases in imports, while several actually had decreases.[28] From several experiences with these industries, I could understand why.

In the summer of 1984, I made a trip to Japan during which I visited with representatives of several depressed industries. The meeting with the petrochemical industry association was particularly interesting. Association representatives told me that they planned to reduce capacity for polyethylene production from around 6 million tons to about 4 million tons. When I asked the association members how they had arrived at their figures for reduced capacity, they responded that, since the optimum operating rate for their factories was about 90 percent of capacity, and Japanese demand is about 90 percent of the 4-million-ton level they were attempting to reach, the choice had been easy. They planned to supply the entire domestic market by producing at their optimum rate. I asked about imports. It was well known that the Japanese industry had relatively high costs. Here was a great opportunity for Japan to reduce its trade surplus and for foreigners to enter the Japanese market. The response was that imports would fill whatever demand was left over after the Japanese factories had sold their production. But, I persisted, how could they be so sure? How could they control it? The answer that it would be taken care of highlighted a key aspect of the policies for depressed industries: control of imports by producers. Sometimes this was done informally through ties to trading companies. Sometimes it was done formally: for example, Japan liberalized imports of refined petroleum products in 1985–86. However, only refiners could be importers.

Later I met with representatives of the Japan Pulp and Paper Importers Association, which had recently been chartered by the Ministry of International Trade and Industry, as most such associations are. Its representatives said a possible surge of imports into Japan was causing "confusion" in the market, and that their purpose was to avoid such confusion. When I asked if this meant reducing the level of imports, one of the representatives said yes. Perhaps this was one reason that American paper makers, whose costs were lower than those of the Japanese because of their favorable energy and raw material situation, nevertheless had only a small share of the Japanese market. In fact, there was an interesting contrast here. U.S. producers of the linerboard used for cardboard boxes had about the same cost advantage over their Japanese competitors that Japanese auto makers had over U.S. auto makers. But while Japan had about 20 percent of the U.S. auto market, the United States had less than 10 percent of the Japanese linerboard market.

An important characteristic of the various cartels is that reductions of production or capacity tend to be made in relation to market share, rather than on the basis of who has the most efficient plants. This practice exacerbates the already existing tendency of Japanese industry toward overcapacity. In effect, the measures tend to create the situation they are designed to remedy. The effect of the promotion measures in the early stages of an industry's development is to induce more than normal investment levels. As the industry grows, companies investing in it must anticipate its eventual maturity. Because capacity is reduced in proportion to market share, the law virtually guarantees market dominance in perpetuity to those who dominate at the point of maturity. There is thus a continuing tendency to overinvest in an attempt to gain dominance. The risk is low even for the eventual losers, because they know every effort will be made to keep them alive.

There is a certain ineluctable logic in these measures from the free-market point of view. A government that takes measures to revitalize and strengthen a declining high-cost industry cannot welcome sharp influxes of imports. The whole point of a cartel is to raise prices, and influxes of inexpensive imports can destroy the basis of the cartel. It is not surprising, therefore, that despite their depressed status, foreign penetration in most of these industries is relatively small.

## OTHER TOOLS: PRESS, MINISTRIES, GOVERNMENT OFFICIALS

All of Japan's industrial policy activities require consensus building. Among the most powerful of the industrial policy tools in this area is the use of the press. Each ministry has reporters assigned to it who form a press club that becomes known as the MITI Press Club, the MPT Press Club, or the press club of another ministry. The press club becomes another in-group that identifies with its ministry. By feeding leaks and giving preferred treatment to club members, the ministries tend to co-opt their assigned reporters. Until recently, foreign reporters were barred from the clubs; and even today, they have only observer status. They are not allowed to ask questions at some press conferences and are not included in informal gatherings with key officials. This means not only that Japanese reporters get the news from their assigned ministry before the representatives of the foreign press, but also that there are few to ask discordant questions.

A striking aspect of the Japanese press is its hesitancy to ask questions. When they hold press conferences in Japan, U.S. officials are always surprised to find that the questions are mostly from foreign reporters. With some exceptions (such as the Asahi newspaper's great reporter Yoichi Funabashi), the Japanese press is not noted for investigative reporting, and the ministries are often able to use the press as a way of molding public consensus. The importance attached to this potential became evident to me in the winter of 1984. After one negotiating session, I suggested a joint press conference. The Ministry of International Trade and Industry said it would be impossible because the reporters did not speak English. Although I pointed out that we had been using interpreters all day, MITI demurred, obviously fearing that a joint press conference might hinder its ability to control public perception of events. On another occasion, I was having dinner at the home of a high official when a reporter appeared at his door at about midnight, uninvited and unannounced, for a nightcap before going home. My friend excused himself, indicating to me that this was a relationship that had to be cultivated.

The reason for this elaborate care and feeding is that the

Japanese press is even more influential than the U.S. press. For one thing, the Japanese press is essentially national while the U.S. press is regional. The five or six largest dailies in Japan have three or four times the circulation of the largest U.S. papers. Hence, any statement made to the Japanese media is known instantly nationwide. A second factor in the great influence of the press is, as I discussed in chapter 3, the intense watching of what other members of the group are doing. When the group is the nation, the watching takes place via the press. He who commands the headlines commands the Japanese consensus—as Japan's mandarins know well. Thus, members of the press are included on the Industrial Structure Council and other advisory councils. Their job is to create the national consensus for the measures the various ministries propose.

## How Japan Explains its Policies

The result of these policies and programs has been the strongest sustained economic performance of all time— along with a rising tide of resentment among Japan's trading partners who have increasingly complained of unfairness. The Japanese have not been able to understand this. In their own eyes, they are only trying to save, work hard, and educate their children. They do not understand complaints that their markets are closed, and emphasize that their average tariff level is lower than that of the United States and that they have few formal quotas. They see the Americans and others as being jealous of Japan's success while remaining unwilling to work hard enough to equal it.

The problem is that Japan's prosperity rests on the U.S.-sponsored free-trade system; and, to the American mind, there appears to be a logical contradiction between Japan's avowed adherence to free-trade doctrine and its policies aimed at achieving specific industrial outcomes. In this context, formal tariffs and quotas are not important because Japan's policies operate at many levels and focus on creating attitudes conducive to achieving certain results. Americans wonder whether Japan can really be for free trade in satellites while striving to create an industry of its own, or whether Japan can welcome import surges in industries operating under depression cartel rules. It is this apparent contradiction between free trade and industrial policy that leads to charges of unfairness, which in turn threaten to end the U.S. free-trade policies on which Japan's welfare depends. A major task of Japan's mandarins is therefore to explain industrial policy in a way that reconciles the apparent contradictions.

Such explanations are typically difficult: having rejected the economic theories of the West, Japan nevertheless tries to show that its policies are not at variance with them. In attempting to do so, Japan always insists that Americans misperceive its policies and that its measures do not restrict imports and are in accord with the guidelines of the Organization for Economic Co-operation and Development (OECD), the main multinational organization that collects and analyzes trade data.[29] It also insists that its officials are powerless and unable to influence trade flow—an explanation contradicted, however, by actions such as a 1981 letter from the director of MITI's iron and steel products division asking Japan's steelmakers to use domestic ferro chrome, and by the restricted buying of foreign satellites and supercomputers.

Yoshizo Ikeda, the former president of Mitsui Bussan (one of Japan's giant trading companies), addressed this contradiction directly in an article in the New York Times on 23 October 1983. Nobody, he asserted, believes the Japanese officials when they say they have no power and that industrial policy has no effect—because it is not true. Instead of equivocating, Ikeda advised, Japan should acknowledge its policies of intervention and make any adjustments necessary to bring them into accord with free-trade precepts.[30] Ikeda's candor was refreshing, but his prescription indicated that even he did not fully comprehend what troubled the United States. He, too, thought the problem could be solved through better explanations and perhaps a few minor adjustments here and there.

That the issue goes much deeper was made evident by the aforementioned U.S.–Japan industrial policy dialogue. At the key session in September 1983, Keiichi Konaga, then director general of MITI's industrial policy division, led a MITI team that attempted to explain Japan's views to somewhat skeptical U.S. officials. Lying at the heart of the ministry's mission, the industrial policy division develops the "visions" by which MITI attempts to define Japan's future and writes important legislation to implement those visions.

As was to be expected from one of Japan's best, Konaga made a masterful presentation. Japan, he explained, is not unique in pursuing industrial policies: indeed, every government is responsible for developing its economy and promoting the economic well-being of its people. Because industrial activity provides the basis for national economic development, it is only natural that governments should be concerned with, and should conduct, policies related to such activities. Konaga went on to make a point often missed in the United States: industrial policies are not a substitute for macroeconomic policies but are, rather, a complement to them. On the other hand, macroeconomic policies set the conditions for applying industrial policies, which in turn support macroeconomic policy through, for example, the stable expansion of tax revenues.

Others on the MITI team modestly explained that their power to coerce private industry to move in desired directions is limited. MITI, they said, is only able to use "soft-handed guidance." It simply studies industries carefully, writes reports, and makes forecasts. These forecasts were likened to the *U.S. Industrial Outlook*, an annual forecast of U.S.

business activity published by the U.S. Department of Commerce. The fact that industries sometimes listened to them stemmed from MITI's superior information and analytical ability. As for subsidies and financial incentives, the MITI representatives acknowledged that they provide some, but pointed out that comparisons with other countries show Japan's government-supported research expenditures and special tax incentives to be smaller than most. The Japanese government supports only about 30 percent of Japan's total research and development, while in the United States, they noted, government support accounts for over 50 percent of the total expense. While technically correct, they neglected to mention that the reason for the large U.S. figure is a defense burden that Japan does not bear.

With regard to U.S. industrial policies, the MITI team stressed its belief that huge U.S. defense expenditures stimulate U.S. technological development and enhance the competitive power of major companies such as IBM and Texas Instruments. They were careful not to criticize this situation. On the contrary, they praised it, saying they "highly evaluate" U.S. efforts to develop technology. They acknowledged that these programs are aimed at military, not commercial, development, but said that did not matter because they result in "spin-offs." In this way, U.S. defense policy acts as its industrial policy. It was in this context that they said governments must take all measures necessary to develop tecnologies that are critical for assuring a nation's economic security.

What was most interesting was that the remarks were obviously made without any thought that they might be controversial. Throughout the discussion, MITI had been careful to downplay things like administrative guidance and subsidies, which it knew concerned the Americans. It was clear the Japanese took it for granted that there could be no question of disagreement with these assertions of the necessity for government intervention to assure economic leadership.

Yet these were the most significant remarks in the whole year-long series of discussions. The term *security* implies the existence of a threat. The threat MITI saw was an economic one that could arise from not having superior industrial capability in the hands of domestic companies in certain critical but undefined technologies. To avoid that, MITI insisted on the necessity of governmental action.

Although such action was taken as a given by the Japanese, the Americans were surprised. National security in a military sense was clearly understood by them, as was the possible need for government action to ensure certain capabilities critical to the military. But Japan seemed to be saying that a threat to the nation also arose if foreign companies were ahead of its own in commercial areas. Moreover, it was clear that in these terms an American company manufacturing in Japan was considered foreign. In addition, since the areas were undefined, the implication was that a lag in any industry could be seen as a threat that would justify intervention to overcome it.

The Japanese statements led the U.S. delegation to these talks to conclude that Japan's industrial policies are at odds with the doctrine of free markets and free trade. The whole point of free trade is to enable an entrepreneur or a firm with a particular capability to exploit it worldwide. Free-trade doctrine says that this is a benefit, not a threat, because it allows consumers everywhere to enjoy the fruits of discovery. The VCR is a good example: American consumers enjoy Japanese sets, and no one feels threatened although Japanese firms dominate the market. Japan seemed to be saying Americans should feel threatened.

Even more troublesome was a second implication. The view of defense spending as an engine of technological progress was particularly important. The United States is the only country with any significant technological advantage over Japan. Japan seemed to be saying that its companies had to be the equal of those of the U.S. in all key areas. But to the extent the U.S. lead derived from defense spending, this meant the Japanese government felt the necessity to intervene to offset the effect of U.S. defense programs. Thus, the supreme irony: the United States was spending, at least in part, to defend Japan; while Japan felt compelled to spend to help its industry overcome the results of the U.S. defense effort.

Disturbing as it was in many respects, the Japanese view has a certain logic. Since the time of Perry, they have seen foreign economic intrusion in colonialistic terms. Their dependence now on the United States for defense makes them more anxious than ever to avoid economic domination. But American technological superiority, spurred by defense spending, holds the potential for such domination unless the Japanese government acts to offset it. The insistence of the Americans on open markets in such areas as satellites seems colonialistic to the Japanese, appearing to be a clever use of free-trade propaganda that will deprive Japan of the chance to acquire innovative technologies and lock it forever into a second-place status.

Here the abjuration of a significant military role by Japan has a strange and troublesome effect. Japan is correct to some extent. The U.S. military and NASA budgets are a kind of distortion of the theoretical free market. They have contributed to U.S. superiority in some industries, particularly aircraft. Without a significant defense industry or armed forces of its own, Japan can see itself becoming increasingly dependent on the United States. Moreover, it can see this happening not as a result of the action of the unseen hand of the free market, but, rather, because of intervention in the market by the United States, even as the United States preaches non-intervention.

No nation can rely completely on another. In lieu of a significant military establishment or policy, industrial policy aimed at achieving "economic security" has become Japan's national security strategy and its only assurance of some degree of independence of action on the international stage. As a result, Japan's industrial policies encompass broader concerns than merely those of economics. Japan's economic and strategic thinking is integrated. Economic policies are formulated with an eye not only to their contribution to Japan's material welfare, but also to their effect on Japan's power— not military, but of an overall political sort. Such policies are not conceived with short-term consumer welfare as the major objective, and cannot and will not always be in accord with the principles of free trade, which are based only on economic considerations. Moreover, this situation will endure for at least as long as the defense programs of the United States continue, because to some extent it is technological advances sparked by U.S. defense programs that engender Japan's industrial policies as a response.

Since the latter in turn engender charges of unfair trade from the United States, it seems likely that confrontation between the two countries will continue—especially because Japan's commercially oriented intervention is a much more effective way to develop civilian technology than the spin-off approach of the United States. Thus, the competitive ability of Japanese companies will become more formidable as they move to ensure the nation's economic security.

Japan's industrial policy response is essentially an expression of its age-old drive to preserve its exclusivity. It does violence to American economic thinking, but it is not necessarily wrong. It is difficult, after all, to criticize Japan's economic performance, and the policy is only wrong if one accepts Western economic theory, which Japan does not.

# 6

## *KAISHA:*
## DOING BUSINESS
## IN JAPAN

---

Survival of the fittest.

—CHARLES DARWIN

### A Japanese Company

The historical drive of Japan's government for a strong industrial base and the cohesive nature of its society has created an extraordinarily supportive environment for its businessmen. They in turn have poured enormous talent and energy into creating the great *Kaisha* or companies that have come to be the champions of the nation and the expression of its vitality. Every industry is different, and each company has its own history. Nevertheless, there are a few that typify the experience of all. Nippon Electric Company (NEC) is one of these.

I first met NEC's chairman, Koji Kobayashi, in the summer of 1982 during a luncheon at Keidanren, the citadel of Japanese big business, similar to but much more powerful than the U.S. Chamber of Commerce. I was with Lionel Olmer on one of our innumerable market-opening trips to Japan. We had requested a meeting with Japan's business leaders to discuss frankly and informally the worsening trade situation. The lunchtime discussion was enlightening with regard to the attitude of Japan's businessmen. The chairman of Nippon Steel, who is sometimes referred to in Japan as Mr. Cartel, expounded the virtues of free trade. Others complained that the strong dollar made it difficult to import American products. Still others urged Olmer to prevent Congress from passing protectionist legislation. As lunch ended, Kobayashi took the microphone. Over eighty years old, he is a short, solidly built man with a weathered face and a keen mind. As the large display downstairs blinked the latest yen-dollar exchange rate, he introduced one of his favorite themes: the lack of effort on the part of U.S. firms, and their short-term thinking. In so doing, he recounted the history of his own company.

It was founded in July 1899, as a joint venture between Western Electric and two Japanese businessmen to produce telephone equipment for the Japanese communications ministry. In 1925, a U.S. antitrust ruling forced Western Electric to divest all of its overseas holdings, and it sold its shares in NEC to what came to be known as International Telephone and Telegraph. From that time, the company prospered and grew until the end of the Second World War, when the situation became very difficult. Kobayashi did not say so, but I knew that in those days he and other managers told their people to make whatever they could. Some made lunch pails out of aluminum sheet, and others tried to peddle them. By dint of endurance, hard work, and refusal to give up, the company managed to get back on its feet. By the late 1970s, it was doing very well. At that point, Kobayashi explained, Internatonal Telephone and Telegraph decided to sell its shares. Kobayashi felt that the decision displayed apparent lack of long-term interest in the Japanese market, which explained why U.S. businessmen had problems in competing with the Japanese. Their efforts were insufficient and their time horizons too short, he emphasized. He concluded with a strong endorsement of free trade, urging us to encourage U.S. businessmen to try harder.

Kobayashi is a legend in his own time. Born in Yamanashi prefecture, he reflects the character of the people of that area. According to folklore, in ancient times the people of that landlocked province had difficulty obtaining salt and raided their neighbors in the coastal provinces for it. Eventually tiring of the raids, the lords of the neighboring provinces offered to give away the salt, but the proud people of Yamanashi refused the offer and insisted on finding their own. Throughout his career, Kobayashi has displayed that same tough independence.

A graduate of Tokyo University, he had joined NEC in 1929 and gradually worked his way up the ladder. By the end of the war, he was a senior manager. During the immediate postwar period, when the company was in severe circumstances, Kobayashi showed his mettle. He carried the company's cash receipts around with him in a bandana and tells of leaving by back exits and unknown roads in order to get money to employees before creditors seized it. The toughness of Kobayashi and men of his ilk during those desperate times saved the company and built it into a major force. NEC became the only major computer manufacturer in Japan to build its own system rather than an IBM-compatible one—a decision, some said, that reflected the influence of Kobayashi's Yamanashi origins.

I admired Kobayashi's independent spirit; and, as he spoke, I was struck by two contrasts: one, between the desperate company he described at the end of the war and the powerhouse he now headed; the other, between the confidence in his tone and the concerns increasingly expressed by U.S. businessmen, who wondered if they could compete with the Japanese. In the past, they had been in favor of free trade, and Kobayashi had supported protection for Japanese industry. Now they were having doubts about free trade, while Kobayashi was strongly in favor of it. What business experiences lay behind these changes?

## Employment Policies: Business or Church

To begin with, Nippon Electric is a Japanese company. It is impossible to understand anything about the Japanese economy without understanding the nature of a Japanese company.

As a director of several companies in Japan in the 1970s, I remember being surprised at how carefully they perused candidates for employment. Some of these enterprises were small and in great need of people. They were not formally lifetime-employment companies, and did not offer large compensation. Nevertheless, they administered long entrance exams and also commissioned background checks by outside private investigators who looked into every aspect of the candidates' private lives. Only after such thorough scrutiny did the companies agree to take a newcomer into their ranks. At first I thought the procedure excessive. Later I realized it was not.

Superficially, the hiring process appears to be similar in U.S. and Japanese companies. In fact, nothing could be more different. The U.S. company is hiring a new employee. The Japanese company is adopting a new member into the family. The first kind of obligation is contractual; the second, intensely personal. In the latter, both the prospective employee and the company are preparing to make a long-term emotional commitment to each other. The employee is preparing to devote time, energy, and talent entirely to the well-being of the company. In return, the company is promising not only to support him or her financially and materially but to provide an identity and strong emotional support. In the United States, there is no comparable kind of commitment, except perhaps as a career officer in the military services, or as a member of the clergy.

The company goes to great pains to create an identification of individual with corporate interests. While most of Japan's employment is not formally on a lifetime basis, the ethic is such that all try to make it so. Advancement and compensation are by seniority. Company unions are the rule. Boards of directors are chosen primarily from people within the company, as are all top executives. The Japanese see as very strange the U.S. practice of hiring people from outside to fill key senior positions. They wonder how such executives can understand the way of thinking of their new families without having grown up in them, without having been a member from the start.

These factors minimize confrontation within the Japanese organization. Lifetime employment does away with the fear of dismissal. Seniority minimizes competition among executives. Company unions create a cooperative rather than an adversarial basis for labor-management relationships. In this kind of system, companies can profitably invest in training their staffs because the cost of such training can be amortized over the entire career of an employee. Employees are not worried about the introduction of new technology. Indeed, they welcome it because, far from threatening their positions, it enhances the capability of their organization to survive and prosper. The compensation system of Japan, based on substantial bi-annual bonuses that amount to three to six months' pay, creates an identity of interest between the company and the employee because companies that do well can afford to pay large bonuses and those that do not cannot.

Identification of interests is also manifest at the level of obligations and responsibilities, which in a Japanese company are felt and handled so differently from the way they are in U.S. companies. In Japan, superiors are expected to support subordinates and to assume responsibility for the entire organization. Thus when a Japan Air Lines 747 crashed in 1985 with a loss of 450 lives, the president of the airline took the responsibility himself and resigned. When Toshiba Machine Company was caught violating export controls, the chairman of the entire Toshiba corporation resigned by way of an apology. This is a stark contrast with what happens in the United States, where both business and political leaders are wont to say they were uninformed of and not responsible for the actions of their subordinates.

Managers in Japan are expected to set the example. A company in severe difficulty would never pay a bonus to its president. In fact, in hard times, the managers reduce their own pay before requesting concessions from the workers. Because the company is a kind of family, it is unlikely to be merged or acquired. One does not sell one's kin, after all. Such actions are made even more unlikely by the fact that nearly all directors are lifetime employees of the company, as well as by the fact that any acquisition or merger must be unanimously approved. There can be no hostile takeovers.

The family character of the company which is the source of its paternalism also results in its having a somewhat authoritarian nature. Families are not democracies, and neither are Japanese companies. An example of the control a company can exert over its employees was given by the general manager of the Sumitomo Bank in New York, in remarks to a group of U.S. money managers in June 1987. All employees of the bank, he said, are forbidden to attend horse races because it is feared bank customers would not want their money handled by gamblers. By the same token, he added, employees are discouraged from buying any common stock except that of the bank itself. To buy the bank's shares is seen as an expression of confidence and loyalty, but any other investing could be seen as speculation. When the shocked Americans who were present asked if the employees really followed these guidelines, the general manager said that, in his experience, very few had ever violated them.

The group-oriented nature of Japan's society facilitates this kind of authority. Without the backing of the company, it is usually very difficult for a Japanese to obtain a home mortgage. Membership in a golf club is beyond the reach of most Japanese without company help, and vacations in the mountains are often tied to the use of company villas. Naturally, the bigger the company, the more of such benefits the employees can expect. In Japan the individual without group backing is insignificant. The company gives the individual leverage in the society. In return it expects obedience.

Japan's companies are structured along the lines of the ancient clan armies and there is a military aura about many of them. In lieu of an army, the military tradition of Japan has been to some extent transferred to businessmen who are the latter-day samurai. Companies encourage the martial arts and send employees to Zen-meditation courses to sharpen their discipline. Total commitment is expected.

The results of this system are remarkable. Workers can be called upon to deliver a level of performance possible only in times of crisis in the West. I still remember one of my plant managers in Japan who drove four hours every Sunday just to check on our plant, which did not operate on weekends. This dedication, along with the tremendous stability the system gives to the work force, clearly pays dividends in terms of quality and efficiency. Meanwhile, management, free of the temptation to fashion "golden parachutes" for protection against being fired as the result of a takeover, is able to concentrate on developing new products, reducing costs, and penetrating new markets.

While these factors relieve the Japanese manager of some of the pressures exerted on U.S. managers, the Japanese system creates its own set of demands, which are in some ways more difficult to meet. Precisely as a result of its social nature, the failure of a Japanese company is extremely painful, because its real purpose is survival. It may have to make money to survive, but its true rationale is the continuation and propagation of the social organization that is the company. To the question "Who owns the Japanese company?" the answer is, "The people who work for it." By law shareholders must receive a dividend which is fixed when shares are issued, but beyond the responsibility to pay it, management has no other obligation to them. The company is not run for the benefit of shareholders. It is run to give purpose to the lives of those whom it employs.

This was the kind of company Kobayashi was running. In American terms, it was more like the Marine Corps or an evangelical church than a company.

## The Power of the Group

Just as individual Japanese do, Japanese companies tend to form groups. And they do so for many of the same reasons. Just as the individual has little standing in Japan, so the small, entrepreneurial company standing alone is extremely vulnerable. The myth of the underdog, or of the gifted amateur who comes out of nowhere to win, is not strong in Japan. From sumo wrestling to business, the Japanese preference is for something big, well-trained, and powerful. The result is an inevitable tendency toward alliance among companies. This led to the formation of the four great *zaibatsu* (large conglomerates of interrelated industrial, financial, and commercial enterprises)—Mitsui, Mitsubishi, Sumitomo, and Yasuda—that controlled much of Japan's economy until 1945, and the introduction of antitrust laws by U.S. Occupation officials has not prevented continuance of the trend in the postwar period. It is a basic response to the fundamental forces of Japanese society.

In 1920, the Nippon Electric Company established its first ties with what was then the Sumotomo *zaibatsu*. In 1943, it became a full member and changed its name to the Sumitomo Communications Company. In 1945, however, the name was changed back to NEC. It was known that the United States held the *zaibatsu* partly responsible for the war, and that it might retaliate against them. There was no need to court trouble. At the same time and despite the name change, the tie was maintained.

## ECONOMIC GROUPS (*KEIRETSU*)

In fact, the Occupation forces did break up the *zaibatsu;* but after the end of the Occupation, in 1952, they were quickly reassembled in a new form. Whereas the *zaibatsu* had been directly controlled through family holding companies, the new groups were based on core banks and trading companies. The new Japanese government abolished the Occupation ban on cross-shareholding and interlocking boards of directors, thus allowing a new structure called a *keiretsu* (economic group) to come into being as the major banks and trading companies formed networks of companies.[1] These alliances were linked by cross-shareholdings, common banking affiliations, and the use of the same trading company to procure raw materials and to distribute products.

The Sumitomo *keiretsu* is one of the six major groups that have evolved out of this restructuring (see figure 6.1). The others are the Mitsui, Mitsubishi, Sanwa, Fuyo, and Dai Ichi Kangyo groups. In addition, several new groups appear to be growing around large companies such as Toyota, Hitachi, and Matsushita. The six major groups account for nearly 17 percent of the sales of all Japanese business and nearly 18 percent of the profits—excluding the results of banking and insurance companies which are major parts of the groups. Each group has companies in each major sector of Japan's economy, such as steel, petrochemicals, banking, and high technology.

Most of Japan's major corporations are linked to one group or another. Toyota, for example, is affiliated with the Mitsui

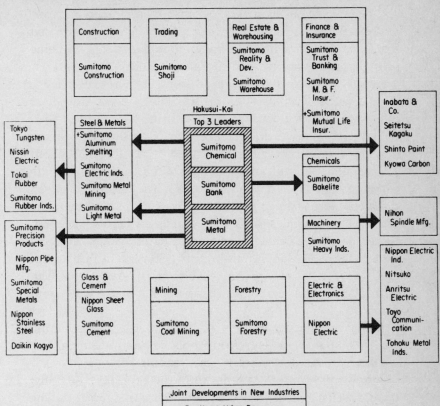

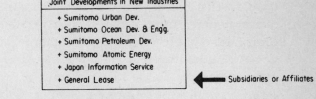

FIGURE 6.1
*Sumitomo Group*

SOURCE: *Industrial Groupings in Japan*, Dodwell Marketing Consultants Revised 1978
Edition, Tokyo, Japan.

Group even though it has assembled a group in its own right. Nissan is affiliated with the Fuyo Group, while Hitachi, which also has its own group, is affiliated with both the Fuyo and the Sanwa groups. Typical is the structure of the Sumitomo group, which has major companies in such fields as banking, insurance, trading, steel, electronics, glass, oil, forestry, and metals; and overall sales of over $200 billion. Similarly, the Mitsubishi Group has total sales of over $300 billion, while the Dai Ichi Kangyo Group has close to $400 billion.[2] By comparison the largest U.S. business organization, General Motors, has sales of only about $103 billion. Ties of affiliation differ depending on the group and on the company, but those of the Nippon Electric Company are indicative. More than 25 percent of its stock is held by other Sumitomo companies, and NEC returns the favor by keeping more than 33 percent of its own shareholdings in other group companies. In addition, about 30 percent of its long- and short-term loans are provided by group institutions. The percentages differ for other companies, but the pattern is similar.[3]

As far as management is concerned, the heads of the major companies of each group hold regular meetings. The chief executives of the twenty-one leading companies of the Sumitomo group, for example, form the *hakusui-kai* (literally, "white-water club"). In addition to this top council, which meets monthly, there is the *hakusen-kai* which includes the counselors of the leading group companies, and the *itsuka-kai* which includes the executive directors. Although the groups are not centrally directed by a chief executive, each has an overall view of its strategic interest in the world, and companies within the group cooperate to promote those interests. There is a tendency toward group autonomy and strong competition between groups. Thus, as the structure of Sumitomo shows (see figure 6.1), each group attempts to have a strong position in each major sector of the economy. As companies in mature industries decline, the group puts resources behind its companies in expanding sectors. This strategy provides the growth that allows flexibility and fulfillment of social obligations. For example, when the Sumitomo Group's aluminum smelting companies became depressed, workers were shifted to other group companies. The strong support the group has given to NEC is based on the club view of NEC as its star entrant within the key high-technology industries.

In their regular meetings, each club discusses its business strategy vis-à-vis the other industrial groups and coordinates the activities of its member companies with regard to political, business, and world affairs. For example, in 1973 the Sumitomo Group made donations of $2 million to the Japan Society in New York and $1 million to Yale University. These matters were discussed in the *hakusui-kai*.[4]

In 1981 the Mitsubishi Group established the Mitsubishi CC Study Committee to plan how the group could move more rapidly into the area of advanced communications including Value Added Networks (VANs) and satellite communications systems. In 1982, the Mitsui Group established the Mitsui Information Systems Council to coordinate members' efforts in new media research. The Sumitomo Group's Society of Space Station Utilization coordinates group activity on commercial uses of space, while the Fuyo Information Center is working on videotex systems.

To grasp fully the significance of these groups, it is useful to imagine something similar in the United States. An American Sumitomo Group might be formed through the arrangement of cross-shareholdings and a network of cooperative arrangements between, for example, the Chase Manhattan Bank, Inland Steel, Pittsburgh Plate Glass, Reynolds Aluminum, IBM, and the DuPont Company. A monthly meeting of the chief executives of these companies to discuss how to deal with political parties, other competitive groups, and foreign governments would be an American *hakusui-kai*. A decision for members to make donations to a Japanese university or to cooperate in developing a worldwide communications network would be similar to Japanese group activity. The

Justice Department would die first, but it is interesting to speculate on whether such a group could compete with Japanese industry.

A good example of how group support can be mobilized behind a member was the rescue of Mazda, which the Sumitomo Group engineered in the early 1970s in order to acquire a foothold in the auto industry. Mazda ran into financial trouble with its rotary engine and was close to bankruptcy until the Sumitomo Group rallied to save it. Sumitomo banks provided additional funds, while other group companies took redundant Mazda workers and bought Mazda products while selling supplies to Mazda on favorable terms. The result was the resurrection of Mazda into today's very healthy company.[5]

Group members do not always buy from each other and often have important relationships outside the group. Sometimes the Japanese point to these examples as evidence that group membership is not really important. But, of course, if it were not important, there would not be any membership. The fact is that group members largely tend to deal with each other. As a high-ranking executive of NEC told me, "We can always count on a customer base among the other Sumitomo Group companies. It does not mean we get 100 percent of the business, but we know we'll get most of it. It lends stability to our planning and reduces risk." Another example of the significance of group ties was given me by a top executive with Nissan who pointed out that they even influence socializing among employees. He explained that while stationed in London for a time, he and his colleagues at Nissan would golf or socialize every weekend especially with the London representatives of Hitachi rather than those of other Japanese companies. Hitachi and Nissan share the same founder and are allied in the same group in Japan, and Hitachi is the principal supplier of electronic goods to Nissan.

This kind of relationship has important consequences for trade, as shown in the case of Cray Research and Nissan.[6] In 1983, Nissan became interested in a supercomputer for use in designing new automobiles. Its technical center evaluated a number of computers, among them those of Hitachi and Cray. At that time, Cray held the dominant position in the industry worldwide, while Hitachi had yet to install a working commercial machine. The technical evaluation demonstrated Cray's superiority, and a recommendation was made to buy Cray. At the executive level, however, Hitachi management called for solidarity; and Nissan appeared to be preparing to buy the Hitachi computer, despite its poorer performance.

At that point, officials in the U.S. government became aware of the situation. Nissan was then selling about $3 billion worth of automobiles in the U.S. market annually and the case became an example of what the Americans called "unfair trade." It also shed light on another aspect of trade negotiations with Japan. Some at Nissan did not want to buy an inferior computer. They leaked information to the U.S. government which put pressure on both the Japanese government and Nissan to buy from Cray. This is known in Japan as *gaiatsu* (foreign pressure) and is often used by the Japanese to force resolution of problems they cannot resolve internally. Eventually Nissan did buy from Cray, but only in order to reduce trade friction and as a kind of favor to the United States. Under normal circumstances, the group tie would have been decisive.

To the Japanese, this practice does not seem unfair. Rather, it respects mutual obligation by providing a cushion against shocks. Today Nissan may buy a Hitachi computer. Tomorrow it may ask Hitachi to take some of its redundant workers. The slightly lesser performance it may get from the Hitachi computer is balanced against the broader considerations. Moreover, because the decision to buy Hitachi would be a favor, it would bind Hitachi closer and guarantee slavish service and future Hitachi loyalty to Nissan products. From this point of view, it is possible to see that maintaining the old tie might make a lot of sense. This attitude of sticking together is what the Japanese mean by the long-term view; it is what enables them to withstand shocks and to survive over the long term. That it causes trade problems is unfortunate but incidental.

Cushioning is also provided by the general trading companies that are at the core of each of the groups. These giants are the suppliers of raw materials to and the sales and export agents for many of the companies in their groups; together they handle over half of Japan's non-oil imports. This enables them to protect companies in their group from unwanted imports. This was shown in February 1983, when the *Oriental Economist* stated, "As a rule, the trading companies refrain from dealings in imports of steel materials because of pressure from blast-furnace steel makers, particularly Nippon Steel Corporation." Despite this pressure, steel imports have climbed significantly since 1985 as the price difference between Japanese and Korean products has become very large. Still, the foreign share of the market is much less than it could be. As the Japanese journal *Technocrat* once observed, "Sogo Sosha [general trading company] is one of the most powerful agents against any unwanted competitors. It functions as the umbrella company for business groups, by guarding their marketing channels, supplying raw materials, and providing necessary financing."[7]

I observed this phenomenon personally in the soda ash case. Manufactured synthetically in Japan through use of expensive, energy-intensive methods, soda ash occurs naturally and is much less expensive in the United States. As a result, American soda ash can be delivered in Japan at a cost well below that of most of the Japanese manufacturers. In 1981, it came to the attention of the U.S. government that, despite this great cost advantage, the U.S. industry was shipping only 60,000 tons per year to a Japanese market that consumed well over 1 million tons annually. Investigation revealed an interesting pattern. The Japanese buyer, Toko Terminal, assigned a separate trading company to deal with each U.S. producer. Each of these sold one shipload of 12,000 tons to its assigned handler.[8] The trading companies delivered the ash to the terminal, the only modern unloading facility for soda ash in Japan at the time. It was then and is today owned jointly by the trading companies and Japan's soda ash manufacturers. Once unloaded, the ash was sold by the domestic producers at the same price as domestic ash, and the profits were split among the terminal owners.

Theoretically, the trading companies had an interest in buying inexpensive soda ash abroad and in profiting by selling at higher prices in Japan. In fact, however, several of the trading companies had ash producers in their group, and most were tied into Toko Terminal and had obligations of loyalty to the domestic companies. Thus they were not at all aggressive about importing the less expensive soda ash.

Several of the U.S. companies had tried to go around the trading companies, but they faced obstacles. Aside from Toko Terminal, most other storage facilities were either inadequate or in the hands of the trading companies. Beyond that, however, when salesmen for the U.S. firms called on potential customers, they were told to see the trading companies. In some cases, they were told that the customers had been warned not to do business with the Americans. In this context, it must be understood that these customers do much business with the trading companies, relying on them for long-term credit, raw materials, and even for sales of their products. Thus, the customers had no desire to make waves.

The U.S. government brought this situation to the attention of the Ministry of International Trade and Industry and asked its help in removing what looked like trade barriers resulting from a cartel. MITI denied that there was a cartel, and maintained instead that cartels are illegal and that the problem was poor quality and the danger of a strike or other interruption of supply in the United States. MITI agreed, however, to arrange for meetings between the U.S. industry and groups of Japanese users. This was a standard move in such circumstances, and it is important to understand what was happening. Japanese ash producers were in deep de-

pression and were being protected. Users had been warned
not to deal with the U.S. producers. Everyone, including
MITI, knew that, but no one could admit it. So a charade
was organized on the false premise that the whole problem
was lack of communication between seller and buyer. It was
clever, because even though the U.S. companies knew it was
a charade, if they didn't play along they could be dismissed
as lazy and uninformed about the Japanese market. The charade was duly played out and produced no results.

The U.S. government then brought the situation to the attention of Japan's Fair Trade Commission, which in August
1982 seized the records of Japan's producers. Eventually the
commission concluded that a cartel had indeed been in operation since about 1974, and issued a cease-and-desist order.[9]
Almost immediately the sales of the U.S. firms climbed to
the 220,000-ton level. They were happy for a while, until
sales stagnated. Analysis indicated that American sales
should have been at least double that amount, but the word
from the market was that the Americans should be satisfied
with their share.

Several incidents showed not only what was happening
but also the sense of solidarity the Japanese often count on in
difficult situations. Sumitomo Trading Company had no ash
manufacturer in its group and had become quite aggressive
in selling American ash at lower prices. A high executive at
Sumitomo later told me that in the summer of 1984 the heads
of three of Japan's ash producers called on Sumitomo and
begged it to hold down the imports. Another distributor said
he had been warned by government officials that it would
"not be good for Japan" if he distributed American ash. A
buyer for a major glass manufacturer said he had been directed to cap the American share of his procurement at 30
percent. The result was that by the winter of 1987, U.S. sales
were still at 220,000 tons. During a reception in Tokyo at that
time, John Andrews, the head of the U.S. ash exporters association, was informed by MITI's international vice minister
that the Japanese industry was operating at only 66 percent

of capacity, and that American sales had gone far enough. Further, he said that while the practices of the Japanese industry in this instance might be unacceptable in the United States, they are quite normal in Japan.[10] Today U.S. sales to Japan remain stagnant despite a nearly 50-percent drop in the value of the dollar. Similar situations have occurred in the past in other industries.

However bluntly spoken, the vice minister's point is important. To Americans nurtured on the pure market concepts of antitrust, Japanese practice seems unfair and protectionist. But in Japan it is part of not breaking your neighbor's rice bowl. There is a sense of mutual obligation and a duty to help those in trouble. In the case of soda ash, the trading companies acted to help other group members, and all banded together in the name of the ultimate group, the nation itself. In Japan, antitrust theories cannot compete with this kind of thinking.

Americans have often wondered at the seeming dichotomy of Japanese businessmen, as simultaneously fierce competitors and organizers of cartels. The answer is in the appeal for mercy: a competitor who acknowledges defeat and asks for help can expect sympathy because the purpose of a company is to exist. No one wants to see it go out of business—particularly if the defeat is at the hands of foreign interests. It is not a mode that accords well with free trade, but it has its admirable aspects. Thus the *keiretsu* system reduces risk for the Nippon Electric Company and the other Japanese companies through the accumulation of relationships that can be counted upon to cushion shock in time of trouble.

## ENTERPRISE GROUPS *(KIGYO KEIRETSU)*

The Sumitomo Group is a financial *keiretsu* held together by cross-shareholding and other financial ties. Within this type of large overarching group are the *kigyo keiretsu* (enterprise groups), which consist of a large manufacturer and its suppliers and distributors. Japanese concepts of personal relations, the lifetime-employment system, and the "just-in-time" manufacturing system underlie this structure.

In Japan, as I have said, business is done on the basis of personal relationships to a much greater extent than in the West. Personal relationships entail friendship, trust, and loyalty. A supplier who sells to two competing companies or a distributor who sells the goods of competitors may be seen to suffer from divided loyalty. Thus there is a tendency for manufacturers to make captives of their suppliers and distributors—relatively easy to do, because of the weakness of the antitrust laws and their enforcement (including the fact that there can be no private antitrust suits and no triple damages). An example of the attitudes involved occurred in 1979, when I was advising a German company that was attempting to sell to Japan's auto companies. At one point, we scheduled calls on executives of several of the major companies on the same day. Our biggest problem was to arrange to drive the proper car to our various appointments. It seemed it was absolutely necessary to drive a Toyota to Toyota, a Nissan to Nissan, and so forth. We spent a great deal of time just changing cars.

The lifetime-employment system creates several syndromes that reinforce the tendency toward loyalty. First, it makes labor a high fixed cost which employers try to minimize by subcontracting to smaller suppliers, who pay lower wages and do not offer lifetime guarantees. If he is very dependent, this supplier becomes another shock absorber in the system since he can be squeezed in time of recession. Thus, large companies tend to prefer dependent suppliers who can be captured. Another factor is the fact that lifetime means until age fifty-five (or sometimes even fifty). Because retirement pay is generally low, retirees are compelled to seek postretirement positions. The social organization that is the company helps by placing them with distributors or suppliers. As a consequence, the tendency is to create networks of virtually exclusive suppliers and distributors that sometimes appear independent but are in fact dominated by a kind of social security system. Sony, for example, has created language schools and trading and retail companies partly in response to these pressures.

Loyalty is further reinforced by the just-in-time manufacturing system, in which large assembly plants hold minimal inventories of parts and order them only a few days or even a few hours in advance. This system not only cuts inventory cost, but also stimulates high quality since there is no replacement for defective parts. However, when the whole production system depends on precisely timed delivery of zero-defect products, it is absolutely critical to have a high degree of confidence in the supplier. Such confidence requires working closely with him and even assisting him in parts design and the manufacturing process. Because a manufacturer does not like to cooperate in this way with a supplier who is selling to the former's competitor, the tendency toward exclusive dealing is enhanced. Subcontractors to the Nippon Electric Company, for example, do not often supply Hitachi. Of course, the larger a supplier, the more independence he has. But the pressure is toward exclusivity, even with very large suppliers.

An example of the effect of this loyalty occurred in 1983, when a U.S. company, Rolm Corporation, was attempting to sell a telecommunications system to Toyota. After long and fruitless negotiations, the Toyota buyer eventually said that he would buy from Fujitsu because it bought more Toyotas than Rolm did. The fact that Rolm's system was superior, and Toyota was then shipping about $5 billion worth of cars to the United States, was irrelevant. It was the relationship of loyalty to Fujitsu that counted.

Another example is automobile distribution. The high quality and low prices of Japanese automobiles have rightly been praised in the United States. However, distribution is critical to sales. Japanese manufacturers were able to build substantial dealer networks in the United States to a large extent by selling through existing GM, Ford, and Chrysler dealers—not because U.S. auto companies welcomed Japanese competition but because American law protected the independence of the dealer. For the same reason, Hyundai of Korea has established a nationwide distribution network in the United States in about two years' time. Hyundai's cars are less expensive than Japanese cars and of good quality. Indeed, the engine and other key parts are imported from Japan. Nevertheless, no Hyundais had been sold in Japan as of January 1988. One reason is that a Toyota or Nissan dealer who even winked at a Hyundai salesman would find himself in serious trouble with his friendly supplier, who has few antitrust concerns.

The same situation holds with other types of distribution network. NEC, for example, sells 90 percent of its semiconductor output through two nominally independent but essentially captive distributors. Thus, newcomers to Japanese markets must create their own distribution networks, a formidable barrier to entry. Professor Kozo Yamamura has estimated that at one time nearly three fourths of all products sold in Japan moved through captive outlets. For example, Matsushita Electric Company alone had 25,000 affiliated retailers.[11]

In areas of direct operation as well as in broader relationships, therefore, Japanese companies build shock-absorbing autonomous networks based on the emotional tie of loyalty. For purposes of long-term survival, the structure is ideal, affording both great flexibility and great control over the environment in which a company operates. In a word, it reduces risk.


## Growth and Finance Policies


The drive for survival also underlies the Japanese obsession with market share because, in a growing world economy with rapidly developing markets, survival demands growth. As consultant and author James Abegglen has pointed out, "Almost all executives, Western and Japanese, claim growth to be one of their principal goals." But there is a huge difference in the emphasis Japanese and American managers put on growth, as demonstrated by the results of a survey taken by Japan's Economic Planning Agency in 1981. On a scale of 0 to 10, Americans ranked return on investment as their primary corporate goal, with a score of 8.1. Market share got 2.4, and introduction of new products 0.7. For the Japanese, the scores were 4.8 for market share, 4.1 for return on investment, and 3.5 for new products.[12]

The results of the drive for growth were again clearly demonstrated by the Nippon Electric Company. Between 1979 and 1986, its sales went from $3.6 billion to $16.7 billion, for an average annual growth rate of 21.2 percent (exchange rate changes make dollar rate appear greater). In these years, its spending on new plants and equipment averaged about 16 percent of sales. Because some of its divisions are in relatively slow growth areas, the record is even more impressive for high-growth divisions. In the early 1980s, NEC was investing between 30 percent and 40 percent of its total semiconductor sales in new plants and equipment. In 1984 alone, it invested $400 million and aimed at an increase in production of nearly 50 percent.[13]

The picture in research and development was similar, with NEC spending between 12 percent and 14 percent of sales on it between 1980 and 1986. In semiconductors, the figure was even higher. The combined figures showed that the company was spending about 25 percent of sales on investment and on research and development, the basic components of growth; and in semiconductors, an astounding 50 percent. The most impressive aspect of these numbers was that, far from being unusual, they were just about average for similar Japanese companies.[14]

On the other hand, in the United States in 1984, the semiconductor industry spent 8.1 percent of sales on research and development, more than any other U.S. industry and about twice the national average of a little less than 4 percent.[15] At the same time, it spent nearly 18 percent of sales on new plants and equipment.[16] Again, this was more than any other U.S. industry and was a multiple of the national average. Yet the totals put the Americans at about half the level of the Japanese in spending for growth.

Critics have chastised U.S. management for not being more aggressive. But the 8.1 percent of sales spent on research and development in 1984 represented more than 50 percent of the pretax profits of the U.S. semiconductor manufacturers. The total of R&D and capital spending far exceeded their profits in 1985-86 and meant that they were borrowing heavily or otherwise obtaining new financing to support their operations.[17] Of even more significance are other financial indicators. While Nippon Electric Company was spending heavily on growth between 1980 and 1987, its profits by U.S. standards were less than spectacular—only 2 percent to 3 percent of sales; and its return on assets was in the area of 5 percent to 7 percent. Indeed, in 1986 this figure plunged to about 1 percent—about average for comparable Japanese companies, but about half the levels of the American companies. Most spectacularly, NEC actually had a negative cash flow for every year from 1982 through 1985; the cumulative amount was minus $1.2 billion.[18] Again, this was not unusual among the Japanese. Indeed, NEC's stock price rose. If the Americans, with their relatively high profitability, were stretched to the limit to maintain their growth spending, how were the Japanese, with half the profits, managing to spend twice as much?

NEC provides the quintessential answer. Of its total capital in 1986, 70 percent was debt, making it a typical Japanese company because that was exactly the average for Japanese industry as a whole. In the United States, the situation was again the opposite, with most companies carrying about 30-percent debt and 70-percent equity. The high debt level in Japan had two powerful effects: it lowered the cost of capital

and enabled NEC and other companies to leverage investment rates to potentially three times the rate of earnings
growth.

The cost of capital was lowered for two reasons. First, interest payments on debt instruments are usually less than
the total returns expected by shareholders on equity because
of the higher risk assumed by them. Second, and most important, interest payments are deductible from taxes as a
business expense while payments to shareholders are not. In
capital-intensive industries such as steel, automobiles, and
semiconductors, the effect of the capital cost differential is
decisive. It obviously affects the ability of the company to
grow, but beyond that it affects quality and productivity as
well. Those who marvel at the Japanese performance in
these respects should remember that it is difficult to produce
good products efficiently with worn-out tools. For the past
twenty years, the cost of capital—that is, the expense of investing—in the United States has been triple that of Japan.
Indeed, at some points during this period, the cost has actually been negative in Japan.[19] There are many reasons for the
success of Japan and the relative failure of the United States,
but if one had to determine the single most important one, it
would be this difference in the cost of capital.

Leverage is obtained from the ability to increase borrowing. For example, with its ratio of debt to equity, each dollar
of new earnings allows NEC to borrow over two extra dollars. Assuming no dividend payout, for every dollar it earns
it can put three dollars into new investment and thereby
grow at three times its rate of retained earnings. If it had no
debt, it could invest only the one dollar of new earnings and
grow only one third as fast. In management circles, there is a
concept known as the "sustainable growth rate": that is, the
theoretical rate of annual growth a company can sustain over
a period of time, given specified levels of earnings, taxation,
debt, and dividend payout. NEC's is about 24 percent. By
comparison, a company like DuPont is happy to attain 15
percent.

That the power of the Japanese system is not understood in the United States was demonstrated by the New York Stock Exchange. When NEC sought to list its shares in the 1970s, the auditors looked at the company's high debt and told Kobayashi his company was nearly bankrupt. The shares were not listed, but NEC went on to grow at a compound annual rate of over 21 percent, just under its theoretical maximum, and to become one of Japan's premier high-technology companies.[20]

Because high debt levels seem to be the answer to a manufacturer's prayer, why doesn't everyone carry them? And why was the New York Stock Exchange so stupid? The answer is risk. Interest on debt is a fixed payment that normally must be made whether business is good or bad. While debt is always attractive in a growing market, it can be disastrous when things turn sour, as many people discovered in the Great Depression. So the real question is how NEC and the other Japanese companies have made it work.

The answer is the cushioned, risk-reducing structure of Japanese industry. For one thing, NEC's assets are understated. Since on its books it carries at cost land and securities purchased years ago, in real terms it has enormous collateral. Although this means its real financial performance in terms of profitability is even worse than stated, lending to it is not risky. More important, NEC's lenders are its shareholders. About one third of its loans are from the Sumitomo Group.[21] These loans are not going to be called, regardless of the circumstances. NEC is the star Sumitomo Group company. It has group support, whose efficacy has already been demonstrated in the case of Mazda. The loans are safe because the group implicitly stands behind them. A few months, or even years, of poor results will not cause reconsideration, because the investments are not primarily for the purpose of making money but are to ensure the group's position and survival in strategic industries in the future.

Finally, behind this structure stands the government of Japan. The high-debt-oriented structure of Japanese industry has long been encouraged by the Japanese government. MITI officials have acknowledged that they well understand how debt lowers capital costs. They also understand that it can be risky. To reduce the risk, the government has always demonstrated that it will help in some way when major companies get into trouble.[22]

Some will argue that this was more true of Japan in the past than at present. It is certainly correct that debt levels have declined somewhat from their historic highs. Some companies like Toyota carry virtually no debt; indeed, the Japanese now call it the Toyota Bank. But that is just the point. Toyota has more money than it knows how to spend. Funding is not a restraint on its growth. The Japanese are not averse to making money; all things being equal, they'd like to make more. But if the choice is between growth and profit, it will be growth every time. While Japanese managers prefer not to be in the clutches of the banks, if the choice is between debt and growth or no debt and no growth, they will always choose to grow because growth means survival.

There is a final point to be made with regard to shareholding and company ownership. Most of NEC's shares are never traded. They are held by the group or friendly companies for the long term. A drop in earnings will not result in a takeover attempt or any of the other financial legerdemain that in the United States is said to be so useful in making business more efficient. Thus, NEC and other Japanese companies give their managers both the time and the resources to achieve objectives deemed necessary for long-term survival. In this regard, a former NEC executive told me that Japanese managers do not worry about capital costs. He claimed he had never, in his years at NEC, seen a discounted cash flow analysis. Once a direction was decided upon, he said, money was essentially not an object. Indeed, he pointed out that most Japanese managers are engineers who have little understanding of financial concepts.

This explains some of the major misunderstandings that

arise between Japanese and U.S. businessmen. Once, while speaking to a top NEC executive, I realized that he truly did not understand the cost-of-capital advantage his company had over its U.S. competitors, and thus that he tended to explain the problems of the Americans solely in terms of short-term thinking, poor quality, lack of effort, and all the other familiar clichés. He did not realize that his own long-term view was a luxury born out of a low-risk environment with essentially unlimited resources and no real financial discipline, a luxury that allows managers to concentrate on improving their operations rather than preparing their golden parachutes.

## Strategic Concerns: Manufacturing, Quality, Technology

The first concern of the Japanese has always been the manufacturing process. And it is here that they have demonstrated an innovativeness not fully recognized by the rest of the world. It was not a breakthrough invention, but by applying the Japanese emphasis on organizations as whole families or organisms and by exploiting their dedication and talent for refinement, the Japanese revolutionized the manufacturing process. The famous "just in time" delivery system was more than just a new method of inventory control. It was a systematic approach to the entire production process which, instead of maximizing each part of the process, focused on the links between the parts to maximize the whole. It all depended on coordination and the close links and loyalty between Japanese suppliers, producers, and distributors. It was as if the whole nation became one productive organism. The results were productivity increases that cut costs dramatically.

Japan's initial resource advantage in the international industrial sweepstakes was inexpensive labor. It used this resource to establish a foothold in international markets by underpricing competitors. As wage levels rose in response to the success of this strategy, it became necessary to substitute capital for labor. In each area of manufacturing, the Japanese concentrated on achieving large-scale production. They knew that scale is critical in capital-intensive industries because the fixed costs of the company, particularly its interest payments on debt, can be amortized over a larger volume of production. Thus, the larger the production volume, the lower the costs and the greater the ability to invest in the newest, most efficient equipment.

An early example of this emphasis was the Japanese steel industry. From 1951 to 1971, it built twelve integrated steelworks.[23] At the time of construction, each was either the largest or the second largest of its kind in the world. The result was increases in productivity that made it the world's most efficient industry. A more recent example has been NEC and the semiconductor industry, which between 1981 and 1987 tripled capacity and poured money into large-scale, automated operations.[24]

Another aspect of Japan's manufacturing strategy has been focus. At first, Japanese companies did not try to duplicate the entire lines of their Western competitors. Rather, they concentrated on particular segments of a market, where volume was large and prices low. Once their superior manufacturing costs had allowed them to dominate the volume part of the market, they tended to move upscale. NEC and the Japanese semiconductor industry are again prime examples. Initially they concentrated on production of the high-volume RAMs. Having achieved dominance in that area, they moved on to more sophisticated products such as EPROMS (electrical programmable read only memories) and microprocessors (entire computers on a chip).

In moving upscale, the Japanese began to emphasize quality rather than price. They had poured effort into education to raise the skill level of their work force. Now they were able to move the basis of competition from the cost of labor to the skill of labor. Their emphasis on quality has become legendary, and its results became evident between 1980 and 1986 when Americans gladly paid premiums for Japanese cars in preference to the shoddy products of Detroit.

The R&D spending of NEC and other companies is indicative of another change now occurring in Japanese industry. The basis of competition is being moved up another notch, from one of labor skill to one of scientific knowledge. Across the board, Japanese companies are forging into the lead in high technology. James Abegglen and George Stalk noted in 1985 that the top Japanese companies have been increasing their spending on research and development over the past ten years at nearly twice the rate of their American counterparts—a trend that has continued.[25] Among the factors supporting it is the effort of the Japanese government. The 1981 *White Paper* of the Science and Technology Agency called 1980 "the first year of the era of Japan's technological independence."[26] This characterization is in line with similar statements in MITI's *The Vision of MITI Policies in the 1980s* and with the constant promotion by the government of the "informationized society." This trend undoubtedly reflects a view voiced to me by several MITI officials that, because there is little left to copy, Japan will have to develop its own technology.

Even more important than the government role, however, is the fundamental drive of the Japanese company for growth and self-sufficiency. It is sometimes said that Japan obtained Western technology inexpensively. Over a period of thirty years, it entered into 42,000 licensing arrangements for a total in fees and royalties of about $17 billion, or about 17 percent of the American R&D budget for one year.[27] Certainly, over all, the technology came cheap. But for individual companies it was often very expensive. It would have been easier in the short term, and perhaps more profitable, simply to import the products from the United States and act as a distributor. But Japan and its companies winched themselves up by their bootstraps so that they could "stand on their own feet," to use a favorite Japanese expression.

*Kudoka*, "hollowing" in Japanese, referred, for a long time, to the tendency of U.S. companies to move their manufacturing plants overseas in response to foreign competition. Now the term refers to a possible necessity for Japanese companies to do the same thing. With the dramatic rise of the yen in the past two years, one cannot read a newspaper in Japan without coming across the word. The Japanese believe that wealth is created by producing things. They also view technology and production as closely intertwined. Because they have struggled to get both, the idea of closing the hard-earned factories, or of moving them offshore and becoming distributors and purveyors of services, is totally abhorrent to them. They speak of the American disease and how to avoid it, just as the Americans in years past condescended to the British about the same syndromes. The social compact of the company cannot be kept if *kudoka* advances very far. The inexorable march of the yen, however, makes it impossible to hold on to many low-technology industries. High technology, therefore, becomes the only avenue to future survival.

The result is an impressive momentum. Patents issued to Japanese companies both in Japan and in the United States have increased dramatically. In 1984, about 40 percent of patents issued in the United States were to foreigners and, of that amount, nearly half were to Japanese.[28] In 1986, Japanese papers presented at an annual Institute of Electrical and Electronic Engineers conference on solid state circuits accounted for over half of the total. Ten years before, they had been less than 10 percent.[29] In February 1984, the Long Term Credit Bank of Japan determined that Japan had taken the lead in such areas as semiconductors, VCRs, optical fibers, semiconductor lasers, carbon fibers, robots, compact discs,

and office automation equipment, such as copiers and facsimile equipment.[30]

In June 1985, a study done for the Commerce Department
concluded that Japan is ahead of the United States in all
aspects of robotics and in most areas of optoelectronics and
microelectronics. While it expected the United States to continue to lead in basic research in biotechnology, the study
foresaw a commercial lead for the Japanese within five years.
In the computer field, it said that the Japanese are equivalent
or better in most hardware. Software continues to be a problem for the Japanese, but the study predicted a closing of the
gap.[31]

The Japanese were not surprised by the findings. NEC and
the other advertisers had predicted it in *Scientific American* in
October 1981 when they explained why Japan was becoming
the epicenter of the world electronics industry.

## Public Support

### THE GOVERNMENT

One of the key explanations of this success is the existence
of close ties between government and industry, nowhere
better illustrated than in the case of Nippon Electric Company. From its founding, it has been closely linked to the
communications bureaucracy. When former NEC president
Takeshi Kajii became the first president of Nippon Telegraph
and Telephone in 1952, this link became even tighter. In the
ten years from 1969 to 1979, three top NEC executives were
transferred to NTT for temporary stints of service. NTT has
always been NEC's largest customer; in 1975, for example, it
accounted for 31 percent of total NEC sales. Although this
number gradually declined to about 13 percent in 1985, NTT

remained the largest single customer. Historically, sales to NTT have not been on a competitive-bid basis, and the profits to NEC have been even greater than the sales volumes might indicate. In addition, NEC's prepaid accounts (advance payments from customers) typically amount to as much as $250 million, and NTT's share ranges from 25 percent to 40 percent.[32]

The support of the government has also been very favorable to NEC's R&D efforts. Its development of central switching and other telecommunications equipment was funded to a great extent by NTT (while it was a government monopoly), as has been its work in semiconductors. NEC has also been a major participant in all of the MITI-sponsored R&D projects, including the fourth-generation computer (very large scale integrated circuits) and software automation projects. At the moment, NEC participates in projects involving optoelectronics, a fifth-generation computer, supercomputers, and next-generation industries such as industrial ceramics and mechatronics.

The role of the government-backed Japan Electronic Computer Corporation in funding the leasing of computers manufactured by Japanese companies has been very important to NEC, which continues to be a major beneficiary of the leasing company's activities. The role of the Japan Development Bank has also been important, with NEC a significant recipient of its loans. Japan also has three long-term credit banks: the Industrial Bank of Japan, the Long Term Credit Bank of Japan, and the Nippon Credit Bank. The Ministry of Finance has traditionally underwritten the debentures issued by these banks. Low-interest loans are then made upon the recommendation of MITI and are guaranteed by it. NEC's long-term debt from these institutions has typically been in the area of $200 million.[33] Finally, NEC has been a prime beneficiary of special depreciation allowances for robots and high-performance computers and systems, and of special reserves allowed for price changes, currency devaluation, and potential overseas losses.

## THE PRESS

Beyond the support of the government, Japanese companies enjoy a very favorable press which essentially acts as a cheerleader for industry, partly as a result of the Japanese cohesiveness and sense of separate identity, and partly because, as Amaya has explained, "in the postwar world, Japan chose the way of the merchant."[34] The strong sense of nationalism that pervades Japan makes it inevitable that the efforts of its citizens will be viewed as an expression of the nation. Since the Japanese chose to make their efforts in the area of industry, it follows that industry and businessmen are seen as the champions of the country—latter-day samurai.

An observer of the Japanese media is immediately struck by the prominence given to business news. Stories that would be buried in the business section in the United States are on page one in Japan. The tone is usually protective or supportive. It is quite common for writers to use the phrase "our country's industry," establishing a subconscious link between the reader and the subject of the article. One 1 August 1978, for instance, an article in Nihon Keizai stated: "MITI's most important single task is to protect and foster domestic industry in the face of fierce international competition."[35]

Business is frequently portrayed in terms of war with foreigners. Thus, in 1984, when IBM moved two hundred families to Japan—in the course of transferring its Far East headquarters from Armonk, New York, to Tokyo—the move was featured prominently in most of the Japanese press. Several articles referred to the "black ships," indicating that this influx of IBM families was akin to Perry's forced opening of Japan. One newspaper compared the move to the postwar Occupation of Japan and referred to George Conrades, the IBM executive in charge, as a new MacArthur.[36]

Emphasis on Japanese quality is a constant theme. Failures

of Japanese products, such as the recall of Toyotas for faulty seat belts or the breakdown of NEC switches in New York State's telephone system, are rarely reported, while instances of poor-quality foreign goods or inadequate adaptation to the Japanese market are extensively reported. While there is much to praise in Japanese industry and much to criticize in U.S. industry, the view presented to the Japanese public is one of unrelieved Japanese excellence and constant foreign bumbling.

Influenced by the press and by its sense that the achievements of Japanese industry are the achievements of the nation, the Japanese consuming public is uncritical and supportive. For years it has been possible to buy Japanese television, cameras, and other goods in Hong Kong and New York for less than the price in Japan. Most Japanese still work on Saturdays. Beef, rice, oranges, many alcoholic beverages, and imported goods from cars to tennis balls, cost three to ten times as much in Japan as elsewhere; yet there is no Japanese consumer movement. Indeed, in April 1985 a group of Japanese housewives marched on the U.S. embassy, protesting imports of inexpensive food. More recently, representatives of the Japanese *Shufuren* (Federation of Housewives) met with the U.S. trade representative to oppose imports of inexpensive U.S. products such as rice.

## Relationships with Foreign Businesses

The first foreign relationships of the Japanese companies in the postwar period were licensing agreements and joint ventures. NEC, for example, signed its first technical-assistance agreement for development of computers with Honeywell in 1962. Under this agreement, Honeywell provided technology and some products for sale in Japan by NEC. The NEAC series 2200 computer, introduced in 1965 by NEC, was its version of Honeywell's H200 computer. This kind of arrangement was typical as the Japanese companies worked closely with their government in these years to prevent foreign companies from entering Japan. Because licensing and joint-venture arrangements were the only way for foreigners to enter Japan's market, negotiation of such arrangements was coordinated by MITI to assure maximum technology transfer at minimum cost. These actions effectively prevented most foreign companies from capitalizing on their technological superiority to establish strong positions in Japan. Japanese businessmen who later loudly proclaimed the virtues of free trade were notably silent during this period.

When Japan finally began to liberalize its markets, the superiority of foreign companies had diminished and joint ventures persisted as the standard relationship between Japanese and Western companies in Japan because of the intricate structure of Japanese industry and society. The typical Western company considering the Japanese market had a new technology, broadly defined, that it wished to introduce. To do so, it needed experienced personnel, which it found hard to recruit because such people were lifetime employees of Japanese companies (a Japanese executive I had recruited once backed out at the last moment, telling me his company's president had pressured his wife and parents to stop him from leaving). It needed office space, which was hard to find because of cost and crowding; distribution, which it could not get because of *keiretsu* control of distributors; suppliers, which were also controlled; banking relationships, which likewise were difficult to obtain because often the banks were investors in the company's Japanese competitors; and ties to the Japanese bureaucracy, which tended to be hostile to it. A joint venture appeared to be the answer to prayer because the Japanese partner would provide all of these infrastructure requirements.

While there were outstanding exceptions, such as Fuji–Xerox, the joint ventures generally did not work. Attitudes in Japan were against them. For example, while making a tour of a Kyocera factory in Kagoshima in 1984, Japan's Crown Prince noticed some American equipment. It was reported that he asked why they were not using Japanese equipment. Even though formal liberalization had taken place long ago, the emphasis on buying Japanese was still very strong. Since the natural movement of Japanese companies and groups is toward autonomy, the Japanese companies tended to continue to see joint ventures as a way to obtain technology independence. In the implicit swap of technology for infrastructure, the Americans learned that the technology was easier to give than infrastructure is to receive. Once the Japanese had the technology, the major motivation for cooperation faded, and a joint venture typically died.

This transfer of technology and its effects cannot be emphasized enough. The major advantage of U.S. firms in their competition with Japan has been their technological lead. The Japanese system has always worked as a kind of siphon for this technology. The Japanese patent system offers little protection. The average time for issuance of a patent is five years and in the case of many important patents has taken over ten years. Patents are opened to the public for objection before issuance, and it is a common tactic for Japanese companies to file numerous objections to the patent applications of competing companies. Each of these must be answered, and the process can take a great deal of time during which the patent can be copied and used.

Theoretically such copying should be inhibited by the threat of damage suits once issuance has occurred, but in fact such threats are virtually meaningless because the Japanese courts are hopelessly behind. It is normal for cases to take over ten years.

It has been in response to this system that many U.S. companies have licensed technology inexpensively or gone into joint ventures. Neither course was what they really wanted to do, but under the circumstances half a loaf looked better than none. Once in a joint venture, however, the U.S. companies often found it was worse than half a loaf. The staff was generally seconded from the Japanese partner and therefore owed loyalty to him. Usually the U.S. partner never even knew what was happening. He often tried to remedy this by sending someone from the home office to oversee the joint venture's operations. But that person, usually speaking no Japanese and knowing little of the Japanese system, soon became a captive of the Japanese partner. In fact, it sometimes happened that Japanese companies entered into joint ventures specifically to neutralize a feared foreign competitor. The relationships with distributors, banks, and—most important—with customers were always those of the Japanese partner. The U.S. partner never got a real chance to build his own infrastructure.

In fairness, it must be said that the Americans did not always help their own cause. Too often they sent unqualified managers to Japan and engaged in frequent, destabilizing policy changes. There was blame on both sides, but the ultimate result was dominance of the home market by the Japanese and transfer to them of foreign technology.

While securing their home base, the Japanese companies mounted the export drives for which they have become famous. When NEC opened its first subsidiary in the United States in 1962, it was already a latecomer behind such competitors as Toshiba and Mitsui. While the U.S. market posed significant difficulties because of its size, diversity, and different language, customs, and legal system, many Japanese could not believe the freedom of action they were accorded. There was no need, as there was in Japan, to inform either federal or state governments of their plans, no restrictions on investment, and few licensing or inspection requirements; and unlike the situation in Japan where foreigners were rigidly excluded, they were actually invited to become members of U.S. trade associations. Most of all, the distributors and mass merchandisers were strong and independent and could readily be persuaded to change to a foreign supplier for a better price. Finally, the United States was full of consumers who were not concerned that the country might be flooded by cheap foreign goods. In fact, they hoped it would be.

The Japanese companies thought they were in heaven. And in truth they were. They had high-quality products at low prices and consumers who wanted to buy them. They also engaged in various business practices that gave an extra push to their advance. Almost every movement of the Japanese into a new market gave rise to charges of unfair collusion and dumping. The Japanese tactics were both successful and the cause of much bitterness. Given the nature of their industrial structure and motivation, however, nothing else could have been expected.

First, the survival instinct drove Japanese businesses in the United States, as in Japan, to go for market share at all costs. The Japanese companies were not greatly interested in making money, because they did not have to. Survival depended upon growth, an axiom that all Japanese companies understood. The Americans, focused on profits, tended to withdraw from the fray when the going got tough, and were only incidental to the real competition—that between the Japanese. In Japan the competition was dichotomous: fierce in one sense but with understanding about its limits, which were based on various ties, loyalties, and duties. The Japanese came to the understanding on limits in the context of their industry associations and their participation in projects sponsored by the Japanese government. They exchanged detailed information about their operations and thought this cooperation quite natural. However, not surprisingly, in the United States they were often seen as being in "collusion."

One of the most powerful weapons in the Japanese arsenal is the *dango* (conference) system. It amounts to sharing the business. The best recent example is the project of building a new airport for the city of Osaka. Although foreign engineering and construction companies have built airports all over the world while their Japanese competitors have built none, there have been no foreign bidders on the $6-billion project.

As Japanese construction contracts in the United States soared in 1986–87, the case became a major issue of trade friction between the United States and Japan. No U.S. construction company had ever gotten a significant project in Japan. Here was a case in which it seemed the U.S. companies had a major experience advantage, yet were not even allowed to bid. Why? Investigation revealed that Japan's construction industry is ruled by the *dango*.

The *Far Eastern Economic Review* described the system in its 11 June 1987 issue.[37] Japanese construction companies do not compete with each other for work, the article explained, but collude in private restaurant rooms where a prime contractor parcels out pieces of a project to general contractors in return for cash and gifts. The general contractors then reserve rooms at lesser restaurants where subcontractors must come up with enough cash to win their piece of the pie. Overseas, big Japanese construction companies have been able to short circuit foreign bid tendering systems and reintroduce the *dango* dinner by financing an entire project, or "buying the job." That this way of doing business is not limited to construction is evident from the activities of the Monday Club of the steel industry described earlier.

In the case of the Osaka airport, there were long and rancorous negotiations. Americans wondered why Prime Minister Nakasone, who constantly reiterated his commitment to free trade and to opening the Japanese market, could not institute an open bidding system. They also wondered why the Japanese officials and business executives who were forever warning of the danger of rising protectionism in the United States did not speak out against the closed *dango* system. But what in the United States is called collusion and objected to is for the Japanese a matter of avoiding confusion. Confusion is the opposite of the harmony the Japanese cherish, and thus is to be avoided at all costs. Were open bidding introduced in Japan's construction industry, it is certain there would be a major shakeout with many tiny operators going bankrupt.[38] From that point of view, the Japanese system is a kind of social-security system. Fundamentally, this is what Japan's *keiretsu* are all about. They are a kind of *dango* on a large scale. They impose a certain order. Everyone knows who is related to whom, who deals with whom; and in return for certain limitations on freedom, one receives security.

Like collusion, dumping is an inevitable result of the Japanese business environment and arises from three causes: the simple strategy of trying to drive a competitor out of business; the combination of Japanese market-share orientation with the availability of enormous resources unrestrained by any real belief in or strong enforcement of antitrust rules; and finally, what is perhaps most important, the overcapacity which is a chronic result of the combination of the investment inducements of industrial policy and the great resources available virtually without restraint to companies that, like NEC, are the stars in their groups.

The classic response to overcapacity is variable cost pricing. Too much supply drives the price below the full cost of production. But cost includes two components: some costs —like taxes, rents, and interest payments—are fixed and must be paid no matter what; others, like materials, are variable, depending on how much is produced. While manufacturers like to cover both sets of costs, sometimes they cannot. If prices are so low that they cannot cover variable costs, management must shut down the factory. But if they can cover variable costs and some of the fixed costs, they are better off to continue operations.

Producers everywhere act according to this logic. In Japan, however, there is a difference. High levels of debt mean large interest payments. Beyond that, lifetime employment means that labor is actually a fixed cost, rather than variable as in the United States. Thus in Japan variable costs are those for materials, which means that when a Japanese manufacturer does variable cost pricing, the price is much lower than when a U.S. company does the same. The result is prices far below cost in the U.S. market and bitter charges of "unfairness." Semiconductors are the classic example. Overinvestment led to variable cost pricing. Despite suffering large losses, the Japanese were able to continue investing because of the large amounts of capital available to them and the social basis of their strategy.

The preceding explanations are not meant to detract from Japanese achievements. There is no denying the quality of their goods or the vigor with which they pursue chosen markets; and these factors, combined with the deepness of their pockets and their cohesion, have made them virtually unstoppable.

Success, however, has brought trade friction in its wake. As trade talks have become more prolonged and more heated, Japanese companies have begun locating some operations in the United States as a way to avoid potential future restrictions. NEC was one of the first to do so. Its acquisition of Electronic Arrays in 1978 would have been very difficult for a foreign company to accomplish in Japan where, as noted earlier, companies are usually not sold. As the drop in the value of the dollar which began in 1985 ratified Japan's success, American assets became very inexpensive and attractive to Japanese buyers. The trickle started by pioneers like NEC became a river of investment, as Japanese companies began to invest in the United States, and to make major acquisitions such as that of CBS records by Sony.

From trying to hold U.S. companies at bay while seeking technology transfer, the Japanese companies had come full circle. Nothing symbolized the situation better than the announcement by Honeywell in the winter of 1987 that it would sell a large part of its computer division to NEC. Under the arrangement, NEC, the former licensee, would supply Honeywell with advanced equipment. In effect, Honeywell became a distributor for NEC. In fact, it was Honeywell that tried to sell the NEC supercomputer to M.I.T. The teacher had become the pupil. They had traded places.

## Weaknesses of Japanese Business Practices

In the face of these successes, one may wonder whether the Japanese have any weaknesses. In fact, there are some, the main one being the resentment that Japan's behavior arouses among its trading partners. The intricate web of personal and institutional relationships that makes the companies strong also makes it extremely difficult for outsiders to deal with them; and these difficulties lead to trade friction and threats of retaliation. It is thought in Japan that this difficulty might be overcome by investing abroad. But an article in the *Wall Street Journal* on 12 April 1984 hinted at possible problems. It noted that when Marubeni, one of Japan's giant trading companies, moved people from New York to Chicago, it used Nippon Express to do the moving. When Bridgestone Tire Company of Yokohama opened a new plant in Tennessee, the workman's compensation insurance was provided by Yasuda Fire and Marine Insurance Company. The article speculated whether this tendency of the Japanese to stick together contained the seeds of future friction.[39]

Of great significance in this regard are the views of Americans employed by the Japanese. An American executive of NEC confided to me his feelings that the Japanese do not consider their American employees part of the team. "They do not trust anyone but other Japanese," he said. He revealed that the Americans are often excluded from key meetings and are kept uninformed by their Japanese superiors. "They do not let any Americans into their club," he complained, "or give them the trust and the communications channels they need to manage, and then criticize them for doing poorly." Another American employee of NEC told me that all decisions are made in Tokyo and that increasingly more Japanese are moving into executive positions in the United States. "They look at us as they would a desk or chair," he said. "They need us to do certain tasks, but we're not part of the company in their eyes. You just can't get past the us–them mentality."

An executive with a Japanese trading company on the West Coast recounted to me how he had gone to the office one Saturday and found the entire Japanese staff there. When asked why he had not been notified, he was told Americans were not expected to work on Saturdays. His Japanese superior could not understand his feeling slighted. As he said, "The most frustrating part of it is that they are totally blind to it. It just does not occur to them that you could be or even would want to be on their team. In fact, it frightens them, because if others are truly on the team it's no longer really Japanese."

Thus some of those closest to the Japanese advance into the United States had serious doubts about its benefits. Some suggested that the inability of the Japanese to assimilate would eventually prove their Achilles' heel. Not everyone felt this way. Some American executives with Panasonic and Sony expressed liking and admiration for their Japanese colleagues and superiors. But there was enough dissatisfaction among those closest to the Japanese to suggest that the inability to assimilate or to deal outside the circle of their own Japanese relationships might prove to be a serious disability.

Finally, as the case of semiconductors showed, there were increasingly real questions about the vaunted Japanese long-term thinking and Japanese investment decisions. In industries ranging from shipbuilding to ball bearings and finally to semiconductors, the Japanese tended to build more production capacity than markets could absorb. Having done so, the exigencies of their society and their industrial structure drove them to produce without regard to profitability. This natural result of the Japanese survival instinct and herd mentality was made possible by the enormous resources the structure put at their disposal. Once in place, the existence of enormous Japanese production capacity tended to pre-empt the world's markets because, while the Japanese could afford to lose a great deal of money for a long time, foreign producers could not. Initially, the Japanese actions appeared to be farsighted and wise; but as industry after industry became distressed as a result of too much capacity, questions arose. Was it really a long-term view or simply the capacity to absorb losses? Was it really good management to run plants flat out when there was no visible demand for the products? Was it really good management to keep investing because the money was available and it was necessary to match whatever others were doing?

Though all interesting questions, these were only small clouds on the horizon at Keidanren that day in 1982, when NEC's chairman, Kobayashi, spoke with well-founded confidence. As he sat behind the microphone, he knew he was backed by immense resources and dynamism. The society from which he sprang and its industrial organization made it difficult for his foreign competitors to attack him on his home ground. His company was a champion of the nation. The resources of his group were behind him, and behind it stood a supportive government. His employees were first-rate, and his management system created an identification between their interests and his. The most important market in the world, the United States, was easy to penetrate and welcomed investment. If problems did arise, some of America's most important people could be retained to help. There really was nothing to stop him. It seemed he could not lose.

# PART III

# What Makes America Wind Down

# 7

# EVERY MAN FOR HIMSELF: DOING BUSINESS IN THE UNITED STATES

---

*I wish someone would tell me manufacturing is not un-American.*
    —DONALD PETERSON, chairman of Ford Motor
                                        Company

I N 1967, a new book by the French author and journalist Jean Jacques Servan-Schreiber raced to the top of the best-seller lists in Europe.[1] Entitled *Le Défi Americain (The American Challenge)*, it warned that the most dynamic force in Europe was the European operations of U.S. companies which altogether constituted a larger economic entity than most European countries. IBM dominated the computer industry, Ford and General Motors held large shares of the European auto market, and other U.S. companies were expanding rapidly. Servan-Schreiber attributed this dynamism to the American management philosophy and techniques taught at such institutions as the Harvard Business School, which emphasized scientific management and a world view of business. The book sparked a flood of European applicants to U.S. business schools as well as a proliferation of clones in Europe.

In fact, there was much truth in what Servan-Schreiber said. But there was also more to the story. The power of U.S. industry had not been particularly evident in the 1930s. At the beginning of 1941, the country was still suffering from the debilitating decade-long Depression. Then, in response to the attack on Pearl Harbor and Hitler's advances in Europe, the United States launched a wartime production policy that not only brought factories to full operating capacity but increased their capacities several times over. While Japan's ministries had been experimenting for years with tools to promote industrial and technological development, in one short burst of five years the U.S. production program resulted in some of the greatest advances in productivity, technology, and investment that had ever been seen.

While the U.S. government ran proportionately bigger deficits than it has since, even larger than those of 1981–87, it enforced the saving necessary to cover them. Rationing reduced consumption while the government promoted war-bond sales, and U.S. savings rates spurted to historically high levels. There were no strikes, as labor and management cooperated toward common objectives. The government poured money into new plants, equipment, and development of technology, while reducing allocations to industries such as retailing and real-estate development. In short, U.S. wartime-production policies put to shame the subsequent industrial policies of Japan. The result was the tremendous surge of production that filled the sky with aircraft and the sea with ships as MacArthur declared the war ended. And the surge continued after the war. Applying to commerce the technology, management techniques, and "can do" spirit developed during the war, U.S. business took America to a new standard of living and powered the resurgence of the world economy.

Nearly twenty years after the appearance of Servan-

Schreiber's book, however, the inability of U.S. industry to compete had become a national issue; and in 1983, President Reagan appointed a blue ribbon commission to make recommendations for improving U.S. business performance. Thornton Bradshaw, then chairman of RCA, defined the issue in speaking of his own company at a Harvard Business School colloquium I attended that winter. RCA, the company that popularized radio and invented television, had, he explained, moved its television manufacturing, as well as design and development work, to Taiwan and Mexico. As for VCRs, although it had done much of the original development work, it had abandoned them while acquiring a carpet business and Hertz Rent-a-Car. Now it sold VCRs manufactured for it in Japan by Hitachi. Bradshaw boasted that RCA's marketing prowess enabled it to sell more VCRs more profitably than Hitachi. But then he said, "As a company, we are doing fine. But I wonder how our country will produce wealth in the future?" Within three years, RCA had ceased to exist as an independent company, and devaluation had reduced the country's wealth.

RCA was not alone. In 1982, Toshiba began to supply Allied Chemical's blood analyzers. In the next few years, Polaroid announced plans to begin purchasing videotape from Fuji Photo Film, while AT&T named Ricoh as its source for facsimile equipment. The trend became so pronounced that *Business Week* magazine devoted most of an issue to discussion of the "hollow corporation," which it described as a U.S. manufacturing company that was transforming itself into a distributor of goods manufactured abroad. Indeed, it noted that many U.S. high technology start-up companies went directly to Asia to begin production, without even bothering to manufacture in the United States.[2]

Some analysts maintained that this practice posed no problem for the United States. They pointed to statistics indicating that manufacturing in the United States was the same percentage of the gross national product it had always been. Any difficulties were those of particular industries, not of industry as a whole.[3] Those who kept a finger on the pulse of U.S. industry, however, wondered about the relevance of statistics that said nothing about the kind of manufacturing they measured or the context in which it occurred. If, for example, there was increased output of weapons that are put in holes in the ground with the hope they will never be used, but a lag in that of autos or machine tools, the statistics might be impressive, but the health of the economy in the long run might be less so. It was also possible that the United States was losing overall market share while increasing absolute levels of production due to rapid market growth. Again, the production statistics could look good while the long-term consequences of loss of market share would be disastrous as others beat the United States down the experience curve.

Lewis H. Young, the former editor in chief of *Business Week*, alluded to this phenomenon in a *New York Times* article on 10 August 1986. Noting that high-technology manufacturing is being shifted to Japan and the Far East, he expressed great concern about the loss of technological skills that this situation is causing for the overall U.S. economy.[4] Young's fear was that, while the statistics seemed to reflect a healthy economy, in fact a loss of skills was resulting in a less productive, less wealthy economy—an extremely important and little noted point. In the summer of 1985, a senior Sony executive told me his company was considering building a plant for production of VCRs in the U.S. but was hesitating because the skills required to produce the necessary components no longer existed in the United States. In the summer of 1987, a top executive of Toshiba told me he did not want to build a semiconductor factory in the United States because of the difficulty of finding people there with the skills Toshiba requires.

As the hollowing trend gained momentum, and particularly as Japanese companies increasingly penetrated service-industry markets, the debate over the reasons for the poor performance of American business intensified. The easiest explanation, the one most often advanced, was poor management. Deputy Secretary of the Treasury Richard Darman was the most prominent advocate of this view in the mid-1980s. Scion of a wealthy family, Darman had spent most of his career at Harvard and other academic oases, interspersed with stints in government. With James Baker (President Reagan's first chief of staff and second treasury secretary) as his mentor, he had been a powerful White House operative before following Baker to the Treasury. Known as perhaps the keenest intellect in the administration, Darman had been a prime mover of the Reagan tax reform which reduced taxes for individuals while raising them for business. Having thus made it more difficult for business to compete, Darman then blamed it for poor performance. Speaking to the Japan Society of New York in November 1986, he labeled U.S. business a "corpocracy" and criticized its executives for being lazy, shortsighted, unimaginative, and greedy. He was joined in his criticism by Secretary of Labor Brock who told Congress, on 15 June 1987, that many American managers are "turkeys."[5]

Management is an obvious target. The examples of top executives who pay themselves enormous bonuses while demanding wage concessions from workers and governmental protection for their industries are glaring and damning. There is no doubt that many foreign goods are of better quality than competing U.S. products. Books like David Halberstam's *The Reckoning* (1986) highlight the arrogance, greed, and narrowness of many American managers;[6] and the picture is not brightened by the spectacle of some of Wall Street's most highly paid investment executives going to jail for insider trading and other abuses.

Nevertheless, pinning all the blame for poor U.S. performance on business management is simplistic at best and demagogic at worst. Halberstam and other critics speak as if business operates in a vacuum, uninfluenced by government or the society in which it operates. Their views might be justified if the problem involved just one or two industries, but the fact is that this phenomenon exists virtually across the board. Can all American managers be inefficient? Can whole industries be unfortunate enough to be run by uniformly incompetent executives? Indeed, European and Canadian companies have had problems with Japan similar to those of the U.S. companies. Are they, too, run by cretins?

Those were the questions posed by Robert Galvin, the chairman of Motorola, when I spoke with him in the spring of 1987. As a major electronics manufacturer, Motorola has long faced formidable Japanese competition as the American counterpart to the Nippon Electric Company, its competitor in most product areas. Galvin often testifies before Congress on trade matters. A thorough gentleman, he nevertheless has a reputation for being a fighter. Just as Kobayashi and NEC typify Japan, so Galvin and Motorola represent much of American industry. Their experience provides at least a partial answer to the questions of what has been happening to U.S. business.

## A U.S. Company: Motorola

### EARLY YEARS (1928–57)

Motorola was established in 1928 as the Galvin Manufacturing Company. Founded, after two prior bankruptcies, by Galvin's father, Paul, it made battery eliminators for early crystal radio sets. Because consumers were already switching to more advanced radio sets, it was clear that the life span of the product would be limited, but it was a start. Once in business, Galvin believed he could find new products to replace the dying eliminators. There had been two keys to the start-up: one, Sears, Roebuck, which, despite the earlier bankruptcies, encouraged Galvin by promising to list his product in its catalogue (the product was aimed at those who already owned crystal sets); the other, the equipment from one of his failed companies. When it was sold at public auction, Galvin had raised about $1,300. At the auction, the bidding moved in increments of $50. Galvin decided on boldness. With the bidding at $500, he raised it by $250. The ploy worked. He got the equipment for $750 and launched the company with the remaining $550 as working capital.

Like Kobayashi, the Galvins learned something about husbanding their money. Young Robert watched his father survive the Great Depression. Time and again, it seemed the company would run out of cash. At one point, on a hunch the elder Galvin withdrew the company's entire bank deposits. Sure enough, the following week the banks closed. Had the funds not been withdrawn, there would have been a third bankruptcy.

In searching for new products in those early days, Paul Galvin discovered a Long Island mechanic who was installing home radios in automobiles. He visited the operation and determined that he could make a standard radio to fit all cars. After much trial and error, his team succeeded in making such a radio, which he installed in a car that he drove to the radio show in Atlantic City. The product caught on. With the car radio as its mainstay, Galvin Manufacturing became Motorola and moved into the emerging electronics and communications industry.

Motorola's success was bolstered by the approach of war. In 1940, the financial editor of the *Chicago Daily News*, a reserve army officer, called Galvin and told him that the National Guard was hampered by a lack of adequate radio communications. As a result of this call and without a contract from the army, Galvin ordered development of a device to improve on the army's backpack radios. The result was the Handie Talkie radio, a two-way portable unit about the size of a cracker box, complete with microphone, head antenna, and self-contained batteries. Production began in July 1941; and eventually the Handie Talkie radio saw action in every theater of the war, as nearly 40,000 units were produced. From it also developed the more portable walkie-talkie, which ultimately proved critical in several battles.

After the war, Motorola decided to enter the budding television field. Since RCA already had the largest share of that market, the Galvins decided that to compete they would have to offer a set for less than $200. Accordingly, the engineering staff was directed to develop such a set, and the marketing staff was told to plan to sell 100,000 units. As Kobayashi had done, they made these decisions without detailed financial analyses.[7] During the same period, an even more important step was taken. Almost immediately after Bell Laboratories invented the transistor in 1948, Motorola jumped into research and development of the new electronics. By the mid-1950s, the work had progressed to the point where it would require substantially increased investment and expenditures on research and development, or the venture would have to be abandoned.

It was a "bet the company" kind of decision. The engineers at Motorola felt strongly that this new technology represented the wave of the future. The elder Galvin, however, knew that financing the expansion and development would be a tremendous drain on the company's earnings for many years. If the project did not succeed, it could take the whole company down with it. Unlike the *kaisha* that were just gathering their strength across the Pacific, Galvin had no group or bank or government standing behind his risks.

Ultimately, the younger Galvin and the research director, Dan Noble, tipped the balance in the decision to go ahead. They anticipated dynamic expansion based on the new technology and believed it imperative that Motorola be in the forefront. Again, there was no discounted cash flow analysis, and the elder Galvin's fears proved well founded. Motorola lost money on semiconductors for seven years. But ultimately perseverance paid off, and Motorola became one of the first companies to sell semiconductors in significant volume.

In 1956, when Bob Galvin succeeded his father as president, the company's sales were $250 million, and it had 6,000 employees. In the years since, it has grown to $6 billion in sales and has 95,000 employees worldwide.[8] Remaining in the forefront of electronics technology, it developed the first solid-state (that is, without vacuum tubes) color television set, was an important developer of the cellular system for car telephones, and is a leader in semiconductors and telecommunications.

The spirit of public service that had inspired the Handie Talkie radio remained alive at Motorola under the younger Galvin. He has served on numerous presidential advisory committees and devotes much time and energy to public issues. Motorola is also a major charitable giver, and people say it is a good place to work. The last serious attempt at union organization, in 1950, was overwhelmingly rebuffed. There is no rule of lifetime employment, but Bob Galvin still, from time to time, has lunch with the switchboard operators and payroll clerks, who remember him as a gawky young man. And they still tell the story of Bob Galvin applying for a job in 1942. Recognizing him as the owner's son, the employment manager waved him to the front of the line, but Galvin insisted on waiting his turn like everyone else.

Whether Motorola is the best of American companies can be debated, but it is no corpocracy. It was built by a strong entrepreneur who was not afraid of risk, and developed and carried on by an equally strong son. The company believes that it is more than a collection of assets, and many employees speak of the Motorola family. It is an organization capable of both turning a profit and contributing to the welfare of the nation. It is not a church, like Nippon Electric Company, against which it is destined to compete, but it is a good American company. And, as Robert Galvin said to me, both he and the company want to stay in the United States.

## TRADING WITH JAPAN: FIRST EXPERIENCE

Motorola's first contacts with Japan, in the mid-1950s, stemmed from the U.S. postwar policy of aiding Japanese economic development. Bob Galvin attended a meeting with President Dwight Eisenhower in Washington, D.C., in the spring of 1957. The president urged the businessmen in attendance to increase their imports from Japan. That country was the key to the U.S. position in the Pacific, he said; and it was important to the security of the United States that the Japanese develop a healthy economy and remain in the Western camp.

During the Eisenhower years, U.S. industry enjoyed the fruits of the enormous investments made in technology and capital equipment during the war and afterward. The pent-up demand of the war years unleashed a postwar consumer boom that gave an enormous impetus to American industry. Motorola was typical, with sales going from $23 million in 1946 to $230 million by 1955.[9] U.S. companies had the lowest costs, the highest rates of productivity, the highest quality, and the most advanced technology in virtually every field. It seemed that U.S. industry was destined to lead the world for a long time, if not forever.

In fact, the seeds of later decline were already present in many American attitudes toward industry. The view of a business as being operated primarily for the financial benefit of shareholders gave rise to labor-management relations that were naturally adversarial. This situation led to the creation of strong industry-wide unions rather than enterprise or company unions, as in Japan. The combination of these monopoly unions with strong antitrust laws and the dominance over foreign competitors of American industry generated wage and cost structures that would cause much difficulty later. The reason is easy to understand. With an industry-wide union, the workers at Ford, for instance, could support those at General Motors in an action against GM. Ford and GM, on the other hand, could not band together against the workers. Rather than allow themselves to be picked off, they passed wage costs on to the consumer, and were able to do so for a long time because there were no foreign competitors.

The view of a firm as money machine rather than organism also gave rise to the desire to calibrate and measure performance. During the war, Robert McNamara, later president of Ford Motor Company and secretary of defense, and a group of young analysts known as "whiz kids" developed the use of statistical analysis to evaluate systems. After the war, the nation's business schools were converted one by one to the new religion of "management by the numbers," and generations of MBAs were schooled in its catechisms.

Finally, the overwhelming superiority of the U.S. economic machine gave rise to a dangerous mythology. It became accepted wisdom that the industrial might of the United States was the natural result of national virtues. Americans forgot the omnipresence of the government role during the great wartime investment surge and told themselves that their economic superiority was due mostly to the efforts of private industry. Because they believed success to be the result of inherent virtues, it was an easy jump to the assumption that success would be permanent. It was also easy to ignore economic and industrial matters altogether while pursuing the overriding national concern of containing the Russians.

These developments and attitudes came to have bitter consequences. In 1957, however, the problems were in the future. U.S. industry was confident and beginning major entries into foreign markets, in the form of investment in new plants and equipment overseas and acquisitions of foreign companies. Motorola's first foreign plant was built in Canada in 1958. It was followed by installations in the United Kingdom, France, and Germany in the early 1960s. The motivation for this investment and that of other U.S. companies, as well as the atmosphere in which it took place, are an important part of the picture.

As Galvin's meeting with President Eisenhower indicated, the U.S. government was urging business, as part of the nation's geopolitical strategy, to invest abroad, to transfer American technology, and to import foreign goods. At the same time, U.S. industry saw attractive potential business opportunities overseas. In other words, there was a mix of idealism and self-interest: it seemed possible to do well by cementing the Western alliance and doing good. In that spirit, there was a belief that if a company did business in a country, it should invest in that country and contribute to it. This thinking was best expressed by Thomas B. McCabe, the chairman of Scott Paper Company, who, when asked by me in 1968 why he engaged only in joint ventures abroad, replied that an investor in a foreign country should not try to take a commanding role but should be there to help.

Most U.S. companies at the time did their best to fit into the local overseas scene. Their policy was to hire natives of the country for as many key jobs as possible, with the ultimate aim of having a totally local staff. They sought out local banks and suppliers and bought equipment from local manufacturers. Eventually, many companies transferred some of these local employees to their domestic operations; and some of these people rose to the very top of corporations such as Coca-Cola and Revlon.

In view of later developments and criticism, two factors are worth noting. First, while the U.S. government encouraged its companies to invest abroad, it did not, as Japan later did, develop guidelines or plans for how or where investment should be made; nor did the companies coordinate their investment thinking among themselves. Second, the success of the American managers in creating these multinational enterprises was a singular management achievement. It was they, for example, who demonstrated to Europe the efficacy of pan-European operations and gave meaning to the term multinational corporation. And although they were later berated for being short-term-oriented, they gave the business world a new vision of its future.

It was in this atmosphere that Bob Galvin and others responded to Eisenhower's urging to buy more from Japan. Motorola, which was already buying a few Japanese components, now redoubled its procurement efforts. As a result, Toshiba became a significant supplier. The conditions at the time are interesting to review from today's vantage point. As Galvin explained to me in March of 1987, "Toshiba's early efforts were very fragile. Their quality was not good and their delivery was unreliable. We worked with them and babied them along, however, because we saw long-term potential benefits to the relationship."

While dramatically increasing its procurement from Toshiba and other Japanese sources, Motorola, along with other U.S. companies, began to probe the Japanese market. Because of their higher productivity and superior technology, American sales were growing rapidly in other international markets. With Japan's economy in its high-growth phase, it seemed that attractive opportunities should exist there for U.S. companies. The reception in Japan, however, was politely frigid. Investment was banned. Joint ventures were possible, but licensing of technology to a local producer was preferred and strongly encouraged. Imports were controlled and discouraged. Motorola was told it could sell its two-way radios to one of Japan's newspaper companies, but that would be all. Despite its position at the time as the producer of the lowest-priced television set in the world, the company was prevented from introducing its sets into Japan. I have already noted that lack of effort is often cited as the reason for the relatively poor performance of U.S. businessmen in the Japanese market. And there is some validity in the argument. But it is also true that after being repeatedly rebuffed, many saw little reason to keep knocking on a firmly closed door.

Although Japan became a full member of the General Agreement on Tariffs and Trade in 1965, it nevertheless maintained a wide range of restrictions in its markets. Naohiro Amaya has used a golfing analogy to describe the acquiescence of the United States in these continued restrictions: it was a handicap, he said, designed to enable weaker industries to compete with those of the United States; the acceptance of the restrictions was made possible by the industrial superiority of the United States and its willingness to make economic concessions in pursuit of political and military goals.[10] In concrete terms, the "handicap" meant that Motorola and other companies like it did not receive any benefit from Japan's accession to and apparent acceptance of the liberal trading rules of the GATT. For more than ten years, while its Japanese competitors built strong organizations in the United States, with the encouragement of the U.S. government and industry, Motorola and other American companies were discouraged from entering Japan. Not until after the liberalization of Japan's electronics industry in 1975 was Motorola able to establish a joint venture that eventually became its wholly owned operation in Japan.

Even then, the market was not fully open to it. It was not until 1980 that Motorola was allowed to sell to Nippon Telegraph and Telephone—the same year in which the president of Toshiba presented Robert Galvin with a silver bowl commemorating his company's twenty-five years as a Motorola supplier. Even in 1986, after completion of negotiations to open fully Japan's telecommunications market, Motorola's applications to the Ministry of Post and Telecommunications to provide various telecommunications services in Japan were held up while the ministry attempted to persuade Motorola to enter into joint ventures with several Japanese companies that would significantly reduce its share of the business.

In recent years, there has been a spate of books and articles about U.S. "success" stories in Japan. Companies like IBM, Coca-Cola, Shick, Texas Instruments, and NCR, which have significant sales in Japan, are singled out as examples of what farsighted management and real effort can do. The implication is that because these companies have been successful, others could have been too had they only been smart and energetic enough.[11]

The argument is not wholly without merit. While Japan long banned investment that entailed payment of dividends in dollars to overseas investors, it never prevented the establishment of so-called yen companies. By this device, foreign companies could establish firms in Japan that were based on the yen and that lacked the authorization to pay dividends or otherwise transfer funds out of the country. It was a very risky kind of investment, but a few companies, such as Coca-Cola and General Foods, made it. Galvin admitted to me that he could have done the same, and would had he to do it again. However, he noted that while Coca-Cola has been successful, General Foods has not: "Most of us were not geniuses, and were concerned that, having put money in, we would never get it back. Our concern was not diminished by the cold reception we were getting from the Japanese otherwise." With regard to IBM and Texas Instruments, they achieved entry only on the basis of their strong patent positions and their consequent ability to trade technology for entry.

The word *success*, like *open*, is subject to many interpretations. Today IBM–Japan has annual sales of more than $4 billion, which is large by anyone's measure. However, its market share in Japan is less than that of IBM in any other major market and, in the past few years, has slipped from first to third place, behind Fujitsu and NEC, in the Japanese market. Some observers question whether that is truly a success, particularly in view of IBM's unparalleled financial and technical strengths. The Texas Instruments story is similar. Although it was the world's largest semiconductor producer for years, its market share after twenty years of operations in Japan is less than 5 percent, and it has lost its number-one world ranking to NEC and Fujitsu. While this record is better than any other U.S. semiconductor company, it is not called a success by the tough entrepreneurs in Dallas when they speak privately.

Sometimes the citations of success were actually some of the best evidence of lack thereof, and were even embarrassing. In its issue of 24 August 1987, *U.S. News and World Report* noted the success of Goodyear Tire and Rubber Company, which it said was exporting 500,000 tires per year to Nissan Motor Company in Japan.[12] The explanation that those tires were mounted on cars to be shipped back to the U.S. was offered without apparent recognition of the black humor involved. The fact is that for years the U.S.

government has pressured Japan to buy a few U.S. auto parts to offset in some small way the $25-billion trade deficit in automobiles. A quasi commitment, made in the form of a forecast, to import $300 million of U.S. parts in 1981–82 was never realized. The biggest import was the chemical compound for catalytic converters, hardly an auto part.

Finally, under enormous pressure to do something about the trade deficit, the Japanese decided to buy some tires. But were the tires to be attached to cars for sale in Japan? Not on your life. They were to be shipped right back to the United States. It was a beautiful solution. Japan got credit for the imports, but the product would never have to be used in Japan. To top the story off, the U.S. press called the sale a success, and Goodyear thumped its chest about how hard it had had to work to get the order. In fact, it was not a success. This sale was part of the problem. Here the greatest tire company in the world, with a dominant market share in the world market outside Japan, was boasting of its success because it had been able to sell tires destined for the U.S. market after both it and its government had practically gotten down on their knees and begged Japan for a favor.

The Goodyear attitude illustrated another major part of the problem. When asked how they were doing, virtually all U.S. companies claimed they were doing just wonderfully in Japan. Indeed, it was difficult to understand how the United States could have such a large trade deficit with a country in which its companies were doing so well. In the fall of 1987, the Public Broadcasting System attempted to do a show on the problems of U.S. companies in Japan. I was astonished to find that companies such as Monsanto, Cray Research, IBM, Motorola, and Corning Glass, all of which had asked me for a great deal of help with their problems in Japan, told PBS that there were no problems, and they were doing very well, thank you. What was going on?

The companies were hostages. They knew, and told me so directly, that if they raised their voices too loud, even the little success they had had or hoped for could be taken away from them in many subtle hidden ways by the networks of the Japanese government and industry, and their own government would do little to help. In fact, it was highly likely that their own government would criticize them for not trying hard enough. Better, therefore, to go along in order to get along. In lieu of a U.S. government policy, the Japanese system reached into the United States and disciplined companies there just as it did in Japan. The U.S. companies were more afraid of the Japanese government than of their own.

There are, of course, some exceptions: Coca-Cola, Schick, Fuji–Xerox, and a few others show that, under certain circumstances and with both skill and luck, foreign companies can succeed in the Japanese market. But, on the whole, the U.S. experience in Japan has been very difficult. That the fault has not been entirely or even largely a matter of American bumbling is shown by the fact that the Europeans, the Koreans, the Taiwanese, and others have been no more successful. James Fallows captured the essence of the issue in an article in *The Atlantic* in September 1987. After agreeing with the standard argument that with enough work anything can be sold in Japan, he added:

> The difference is the natural tendency of the system. The United States, putting the consumer's interest first, naturally buys up whatever offers the best value. Japan, putting the producer's interest first, naturally resists importing anything but raw materials. Selling to America is like rolling a ball downhill. Selling to Japan is like fighting against guerillas, or bailing against a siphon, or betting against the house. You can win, but the odds are not on your side.[13]

## JAPAN'S CONQUEST OF TELEVISION

The inability of most U.S. companies to gain a foothold in Japan when they had strong advantages was the first step toward the ultimate hollowing of many of them. The policies of the U.S. government, which encouraged imports and transfer of U.S. technology and capital abroad, were not conceived for the benefit of the long-term strategic position of U.S. industry. They combined with the very opposite policies of Japan to create a situation in which U.S. industry was always the target. The Japanese could launch forays and, if they failed, retreat to their country to prepare another try. The U.S. companies had few opportunities to raid and no sanctuary.

The second step in the hollowing process was the Japanese conquest of key U.S. markets to which this situation led. As Motorola's supply contract with Toshiba indicates, Japanese industrial vitality was already making itself felt in the U.S. in the mid-1950s. By the early 1960s, textiles had become a major item of trade friction and a harbinger of what was to come in steel, autos, semiconductors, and other industries. Of all the Japanese advances into the U.S. market, however, none was so significant or had such later consequences as their conquest of the television industry.

Motorola and other U.S. television manufacturers, such as RCA, General Electric, and Zenith, expanded their production rapidly in the postwar period. For fifteen years they had a technological lead as well as a cost advantage over foreign producers. As a result, they held the domestic market and created one of the major postwar American industries. During this initial growth phase, the Japanese had barely gotten off the ground. Because the Japanese market was effectively closed to them, however, the only way for the U.S. companies to gain any financial return in Japan on their technological lead was to license the technology. Thus, in the early 1950s, RCA and General Electric both licensed monochrome television technology to Japanese producers. In later years, this move was criticized as stupidity, but at the time it was encouraged not only by Japan but by the U.S. government, which placed primacy on keeping Japan in the Western camp, even if that meant making economic concessions.

The licensing had three consequences: it generated short-term earnings; it hastened the closing of the technological gap between U.S. and foreign producers; and it locked the U.S. producers into the position of producing exclusively for domestic demand. Thus, they were precluded from realizing the economies of scale and experiencing learning-curve efficiencies (in most industries, every doubling of cumulative volume yields a cost decline of 20 percent to 30 percent) that would have arisen from volume production for export and that might have sustained their competitive position for a longer period.

In retrospect, 1966 was the critical year for the U.S. television industry. Motorola announced the world's first solid-state color television set. At the same time, while preventing imports from the United States, the Ministry of International Trade and Industry launched one of its promotion programs to develop solid-state color television technology in Japan. Most important, however, the steadily growing flow of Japanese black and white sets into the U.S. became a flood, leading to the complete restructuring of the U.S. industry in such a way as to make it the quintessential example of hollowing.

The U.S. industry responded to the tidal wave of exports from Japan by moving monochrome production offshore and concentrating domestic production on color television, where it still had a lead. By 1972, more than 62 percent of monochrome sets sold in the U.S. were imports; and of these, half were from American overseas subsidiaries. Moreover, even when assembly remained in the United States, the percentage of value-added domestically declined as component and subassembly manufacture was moved abroad. By the end of 1976, imports accounted for about 98 percent of the U.S. market.[14]

The movement to color television provided only a brief respite for the industry. Just as it was beginning its first mass-production runs in 1962, RCA licensed its color television technology to Japan.[15] This was a critical moment. The Japanese had gained confidence from their success with monochrome sets. In a sense, from there on, everything was just a matter of repeating the pattern, which was to get the technology, build up production volume in the protected domestic market, and then flood the U.S. market with aggressively priced products. The Japanese constantly looked for what they called "boom items" to which to apply the process. The dynamism of the Japanese companies and their structure really showed itself for the first time in this period. Thus, although Motorola had been first in 1966 with a prototype, Hitachi was first with a commercial solid-state color television in 1969. By 1970, 90 percent of Japanese color sets were solid state. Motorola abandoned television in the early 1970s; and the two leading U.S. firms, RCA and Zenith, did not offer complete solid-state lines until 1973.[16]

Between 1970 and 1976, the monochrome story was repeated in living color. The Japanese share of the U.S. market went from 17 percent to 45 percent. The number of U.S. producers, which had stood at twenty-seven in 1960, shrank to three (GE, RCA, and Zenith) in 1980; and much of their production was in Asia. Employment in the industry, halved between 1966 and 1970, fell another 34 percent by 1975, as the Japanese share climbed and the Americans once again moved production to Asia.[17] The latest installment of the story occurred in 1986–87. First GE bought RCA and then, a few months later, sold the combined GE–RCA television business to the French firm Thompson CSF. That left Zenith as the only U.S.-owned television maker.

Popular postmortems of this débacle have dwelt upon the advanced technology, quality, low costs, and aggressiveness of the Japanese. They have also noted marketing mistakes by the Americans in not offering sets with smaller screens, along with sluggish product development and the "stupidity" of licensing. These explanations are not incorrect. Elements of all were present. The Japanese did a superb job, and the Americans made some mistakes. But these factors do not begin to constitute a sufficient explanation. Three other important influences led to the hollowing of the U.S. television industry: the policies of U.S. mass merchandisers and distributors, Japanese collusion in trading activity, and U.S. government policies.

The importance of merchandiser and distributor attitudes became apparent in a meeting Bob Galvin told me he had with a U.S. retailer of Motorola sets in the summer of 1964. As Galvin was leaving, he overheard the head of the company say to his son, "Never forget: the power is with the buyer"—and, in that instant, realized that selling television sets was "just like participating in an auction." Despite the years of effort his father and he had spent in cultivating distributors and retailers, they did not put loyalty or other factors above price. And who could criticize them? After all, that was the American way. Businessmen were cowboys, not settlers. The whole purpose of being in business was not just to exist but to make money. Deciding there were better ways for Motorola to make money Galvin prepared to withdraw from the television business as soon as he could do so in such a way as to assure the future employment of the workers involved. In preparation, Motorola created a new brand, Quasar, and gradually structured the television division so that it could be sold or operated independently. It was sold in 1974 to Matsushita.

The influence of the U.S. distribution system, which Galvin was trying to escape, is very great. For a sale to occur, a customer must be able to see the product in a store. No matter how good the quality or how low the price, if the product is not distributed, it will not sell. I have already noted the control manufacturers exercise over distribution in Japan. Even without quotas, tariffs, and other protectionist devices, this factor alone would have been enough to stymie foreign sales in Japan. Motorola and Zenith both tried for years to obtain distribution in Japan, but without success.

In the United States, distribution was wide open. U.S. manufacturers had spent many years and much money in developing distribution networks and training the sales and service people of the mass merchandisers. When they entered the market, the Japanese piggybacked on these, free of charge. U.S. antitrust laws prevented manufacturers from controlling merchandisers and distribution. In addition, Americans did not view business in nationalistic terms. The objective was to make money, not to keep American workers employed or to contribute to a positive trade balance. It was thought proper that the code should be every man for himself. Indeed, the government encouraged the imports. As a result, U.S. mass merchandisers established buying centers in Asia and became the primary engine of import penetration. Ironically, Sears, Roebuck, the company that had helped give Paul Galvin his start, was the leader.

The second factor was the collusion by many of the Japanese companies in controlling prices and distribution. Documents at Japan's Fair Trade Commission confirm that collusive activity occurred from 1955 until at least 1974, and was facilitated by a series of "clubs" and associations. For example, the Tenth Day Group, made up of mid-level managers of the television manufacturers, met on the tenth of each month at the Palace Hotel in Tokyo. It passed recommendations and unresolved problems to the Palace Group of more senior executives, which met at the same hotel. From these meetings, very important matters went to the Okura Group, which met monthly at the prestigious Okura Hotel, under the chairmanship of none other than Konosuke Matsushita.[18]

Export activities were coordinated by the Television Export Council of the Japan Machinery Exporters Association. This council devised a five-company rule, under which each exporter specified five American companies as its exclusive customers. No council member could sell to another member's U.S. customers without prior approval of the council. Transgression of the rule resulted in a fine of one-third the value of the offending shipment.[19]

This council was also used to administer a price check system that was established by the Ministry of International Trade and Industry in the early 1960s in response to U.S.

complaints of dumping. Under the system, companies were supposed to avoid export sales at prices below a floor price established in consultation with MITI. When U.S. companies later complained of collusion and antitrust violations, the Japanese argued that the system was benign and designed to prevent illegal activity as well as complaints. Later investigation, however, showed that the companies sold below the "check prices." Although the agreed prices appeared on all official invoices and U.S. customs documents, the producers made covert kickbacks to U.S. merchandisers, using Hong Kong and Swiss bank accounts. This eventually resulted in a major case of customs fraud against both the Japanese producers and the U.S. retailers in 1976 because the legal tariffs were not being paid.

Of particular interest is the fact that while the price-check system was being thus evaded, the five-company rule was vigorously maintained, ensuring, according to Professor Kozo Yamamura of the University of Washington, that the full impact of the price cutting in the U.S. market would fall only on U.S. producers. Throughout this period, says Yamamura, the retail prices of Japanese television in Japan averaged 50 percent more than comparable sets in the U.S. At one point, this situation resulted in a series of articles in the *Yomiuri Shimbun* (a leading Japanese newspaper) and a nationwide boycott of television sales in Japan.[20] That this occurred despite the extreme docility of the Japanese consumer is a measure of how glaring the situation was.

It must be noted here that retail price differentials between Japan and the United States were somewhat influenced by the multitiered and more controlled Japanese distribution system. Differentials at the factory door were less, although they still existed. While this activity appears predatory in American eyes, the practice of price discrimination was in perfect accord with the dynamics of Japanese competition and the Japanese company.

One result of all these practices was constant litigation. Between 1962 and 1981, twenty unfair trade cases were filed with the U.S. government, which conducted thirty-seven investigations of the television industry.[21] The three cases of greatest importance involved dumping, fraud, and antitrust issues. An antidumping case was filed by the U.S. industry in 1968. Such cases normally take about a year to complete, but this one took three, becoming meanwhile the source of bitter controversy. Finally, in 1971, dumping was found to have taken place, and the Treasury Department began assessing duties. Within a year, however, it stopped, for reasons that have never been fully explained. Some observers suspect it was a quid pro quo for Japan's agreement to limit textile exports at about the same time.

In any case, no further action was taken until 1976. At that point, congressional hearings on the plight of the industry and discovery of the fraudulent kickback scheme merged to create immense political pressure on the Treasury Department, which responded by suddenly directing its customs commissioner to calculate new dumping duties: he arrived at a sum of $400 million.[22] The Japanese strongly objected, and a contentious debate ensued. Inadequacies in the U.S. law made actual calculation of the dumping margins complex and dependent on interpreting data supplied by the defendants. The Customs Service had only a small staff, which the Japanese consciously overwhelmed with literally miles of documentation, much of it conflicting. No one in the United States understood Japanese accounting, and acrimonious debate erupted over the different accounting procedures. At one point, Japanese producers justified lower prices in the United States by saying they used only young workers on U.S.-bound sets, which were therefore of poorer quality than those made by older workers for Japanese use.

The Japanese also retained a number of U.S. lobbyists, including a former deputy U.S. trade representative who received a fee of $300,000. After meeting with these lobbyists and one day before the new assessments were to be mailed, senior Treasury officials directed that they be reduced to only

$46 million. Protests from its own Customs Service led Treasure to reorganize the service and to reassign those who had been pursuing the investigation.[23]

The dumping case was intertwined with the customs fraud case involving illegal kickbacks. U.S. importers such as Sears, Roebuck were potentially subject to as much as $1 billion in civil penalties for fraud, while estimates for the liability of the Japanese for dumping penalties varied from $140 million to $700 million. In December 1979, Treasury tried to persuade Congress to allow it to settle everything for $50 million, saying it was afraid of touching off a trade war with Japan.[24] Congress not only rejected this proposal, but, in its disgust with Treasury, transferred authority for dumping cases to the Commerce Department. In 1980, Commerce announced a settlement, for about $76 million—$66 million for dumping and $10 million for fraud. It had been twelve years since the case began. The penalty amounted to less than one year's kickbacks.

The major antitrust case was filed against the Japanese in 1970, but did not reach summary judgment until 1982, when it was dismissed. Behind the dismissal was the court's decision to bar documents taken from Japanese companies by Japan's Fair Trade Commission because they failed to meet the tests of the federal rules of evidence. In effect, the court ruled for the Japanese after eliminating most of the evidence.[25] The case was appealed and went to the Supreme Court in 1984. The U.S. Justice Department filed an *amicus curiae* (friend of the court) brief with the Court on behalf of the Japanese—an astonishing step. Although all the evidence of Japan's FTC had been barred by the U.S. court, it was well known to the U.S. government that the Japanese companies had in fact colluded. Secretary Baldrige strongly opposed the Justice Department action, but the State Department and Treasury supported it. They were afraid that a ruling against the Japanese would invalidate the legal basis for the voluntary restraint Japan had placed on its auto exports from time to time. In effect, the United States supported unfair trade in order to preserve the agreements that were in part its result.

In response to these developments, the U.S. producers continued to move manufacturing to Taiwan and Mexico. This was facilitated by the U.S. government, which quietly encouraged these countries to create packages of tax holidays and tariff measures designed to entice U.S. investment. The U.S. tax code treated such investment favorably. Moreover in 1963 the tariff schedule was amended to make it more attractive still.[26] New provisions allowed products exported from the United States for adaptation or assembly overseas to be reimported, with duties levied only on the value added overseas. Thus, while U.S. companies faced powerful foreign competitors, the U.S. government did not effectively provide its companies the protection of its trade laws, but did strictly enforce its antitrust laws against them, while providing every encouragement to them to move their operations abroad—as many did, with far-reaching consequences.


## Problems of U.S. Business


### THE FLIGHT OF U.S. TECHNOLOGY

The most serious consequence was a decline in new product development in many U.S. companies, and the subsequent reduction of skills, as I have noted earlier. The best example is the VCR which, although invented in the United States, was developed and first sold by the Japanese. U.S. management was severely criticized for not developing this and other technology that U.S. scientists had invented. It seemed that the United States was as creative as ever, but that its incompetent managers were preventing it from enjoying the fruits of its creativity. Few critics realized that the television experience created a new pattern. The U.S. manufacturers had commercialized monochrome technology and then taken a bad defeat. They had gotten off the floor to come back with the new technology of color television, and again had been badly beaten, partly due to a very unfavorable environment. They were not about to try it a third time with VCRs or anything else. Better to become distributors or move into some other business.

Other industries watched and knew they were subject to the same syndrome. By 1984, it had reached the point where companies were criticized if they tried to manufacture in the United States. A concrete example of what was happening in industry after industry occurred in the summer of 1987. Interlink Electronics is a small venture company in Santa Barbara of which I was a director. Its product is a force-sensitive resistor which is used in a variety of electronic instruments. Interlink's founder invented the product and has patents in the United States and Europe. The patents applied for in Japan had not been issued by that time. Suddenly we found that a prospective Japanese customer, the Roland Company, to whom we had given significant technical data, had asked the Toshiba Silicon Company to make our product, which it was now doing while processing a competing patent application in Japan.

What were we to do? Toshiba Silicon could object to our patent under Japan's procedures and tie us up in litigation for years at heavy expense, which it could bear more easily than we. Meanwhile, it could sell the product in Japan. We could sue to prevent sale in the United States, but that too would entail time and expense we could little afford. After we threatened to make the case a trade issue, Toshiba Silicon expressed an interest in a licensing arrangement. We did not really want such an arrangement, but the superior strength of Toshiba Silicon made it an offer we had to consider. This scenario was played out thousands of times as the long delay in patent issuing and the lack of an effective judicial appeals system in Japan worked to the disadvantage of the United States. The system, and the lack of any U.S. government response to it, siphons off U.S. technology, particularly of small venture firms.

Ultimately, as American companies could not make a return on the products they developed, they tended to stop developing them; and, thus, there was less need for or interest in research. As many universities found it increasingly difficult to interest U.S. companies in their projects, they turned to Japan. In September 1984, *Business Week* reported that the University of Arizona had received $5 million from Toshiba to support digital radiography research after General Electric and other U.S. companies demurred.[27] Georgia Tech formed a partnership with the giant Japanese trading company Nissho Iwai to market its patents. At MIT, Japanese firms endowed nine chairs to the tune of several million dollars. Japanese researchers were sent to work at MIT, and twenty-nine Japanese companies were involved in its industry liaison program. Thus, the last bastion of American industry, its superiority in technology, was being eliminated as the Japanese tapped directly into the scientific source—an outcome that would have been acceptable and even desirable had there been a reciprocal opportunity in Japan, but there was not.

While commentary on these events always involved criticism of U.S. management, coupled with praise for the knowledge-thirsty Japanese, few stopped to think that the Japanese knew they could probably make a return on these new ideas, while the Americans knew that, faced with Japanese competition, they probably could not. This is a critical difference. The purpose of a company is first and foremost to make money.

## SHORT-TERM PROFIT VERSUS LONG-TERM GROWTH

In addition to the difficulty of entering the Japanese market and the unevenness of the battle in the U.S. market, the third major impediment to the ability of the Americans to compete is the financial discipline under which they labor. For example, in the fall of 1985, United Technologies Corporation announced that it was planning to close its Mostek semiconductor division because of substantial losses. The closure was significant for two reasons. On the one hand, because United Technologies is a large, diversified, and vertically integrated company (its components divisions supply parts to divisions making end products), closure was a blow to those who thought that the salvation of the independent U.S. semiconductor makers lay in consolidation with such companies. On the other hand, Japanese companies such as Hitachi, which were about the same size and in many of the same businesses, were also suffering losses in semiconductors but were not closing their divisions.

At the time, there were comments in the United States— as well as in Japan—that this was another example of short-sighted American planning, where a U.S. company was allowing critical technology to slip away in the interest of short-term profitability. But was that really it? I had worked in Japan, and managed Japanese companies. I knew the Japanese are much more risk-averse than U.S. managers. How was it possible that they kept plants open while the Americans closed theirs?

The answer is the environment in which they operate and the performance expected of them. Because the major shareholders in most Japanese companies are other related companies, and investment is made in terms of the long-term strategic survival of the group, the necessary capital is relatively inexpensive, and the risk of investment is reduced by the nature of the group structure. A friendly government is also a help. In the United States, even for a large company like United Technologies, the source of capital is Wall Street, and Wall Street demands performance. If profits sag below expectations, even for a quarter, U.S. companies find that their share prices drop, thus increasing the cost of their capital and their vulnerability to financial raids. A low savings rate means there is a lack of capital in the United States, which causes investors to demand a high return, and produces tremendous pressure for short-term profits. United Technologies, big though it was, faced higher risks in absorbing the losses of its semiconductor division than did Hitachi.

A comparison of NEC and Motorola is revealing in this regard. Superficially they appear to be similar. Both companies are electronics manufacturers, both are in the communications business, and both sell a significant amount to government entities. In 1979, they were of comparable size: Motorola's sales were $2.7 billion, and NEC's were $3.6 billion. Unlike NEC, however, Motorola is a member of no group and faces a government that is at best neutral toward it. Consequently, Motorola's capital is 80 percent equity and 20 percent debt, the reverse of NEC's situation. Between 1979 and 1986, Motorola's profit after tax was between 5 percent and 7 percent of sales; for NEC, the figure was 2 percent to 3 percent. Motorola's return on assets varied from a low of 9.4 percent to a high of 16 percent; NEC's ranged from 4 to 7 percent. On every measure of profitability for asset management, Motorola was nearly twice as good as NEC. In one critical area, however, it was not: NEC's annual growth over this period was about 21 percent; Motorola's, 15 percent. As a result, in 1986 Motorola was a $6 billion company and NEC a $17 billion company.[28] (NEC's figure was also boosted by changes in the exchange rate.)

This was leverage and low risk at work. Despite Motorola's profitability, it was being surpassed by NEC, and found itself under increasing pressure in its radio, semiconductor, and communications businesses. In terms of management performance, Motorola was doing quite well. Its mathematically sustainable growth rate was 12.4 percent, and it was actually growing a bit in excess of that. NEC was slightly below its sustainable rate. So Motorola's management appeared to be doing their job, but its environment demanded profit, while NEC's demanded growth. The result was that

Motorola's long-term ability to compete with NEC was hampered.

When I asked Bob Galvin why he didn't increase his debt, or even take the company private to avoid the financial pressures of Wall Street and the analysts, he told me such debt levels would be too risky for his company, because he did not operate in a Japanese-style environment. If Motorola carried high debt and got into trouble, the bankers would call the debt, and the company could easily go under. Moreover, he added, high debt levels would cause analysts to rate his offerings as speculative and further raise his cost of capital, thus inhibiting the growth the maneuver was meant to foster.

But the pressure is not only from lenders or analysts. A company like Motorola has a pension fund, on which it wants the best possible return. Individual investors put money into mutual funds and other institutions, seeking the maximum possible return. The Securities and Exchange Commission requires quarterly reporting of profits (Japan requires only semi-annual reports). Fund managers are given incentives to maximize their short-term profits. The laws require boards of directors to entertain takeover bids that raise share prices in the short term, even if they could cripple the company in the long run. Our government officials think in the two-year terms of the election cycle. The fact is that we have created a national structure that focuses excessively on the short run. The concept behind this structure—that the company exists only for the short-run benefit of its shareholders—permeates our business and government institutions and asserts itself even when we attempt to reform them.

To my question whether Motorola could survive as a mainly U.S. manufacturer in the long term, Galvin answered yes—but only because, although he does not control the company, he and his family still own a large share, which, along with being the founder's son, gives him unusual strength to resist short-term pressures and take the longer view. Whether other managers in other companies can do the same is more problematic, he thought, and there were limitations even to what a Galvin could do. Even as we spoke, Motorola was beginning a joint venture in which Toshiba would supply it with memory chips, the very kind of semiconductor Motorola had pioneered in developing. Moreover, Galvin could foresee the possibility that in five to ten years, Motorola might have to move a substantial part of its operation overseas, despite his desire not to do so. And today even mighty IBM appears to be abandoning the lower end of the personal computer business, unable to ignore the demand of the U.S. system for short-term performance.

In many respects, the much-vaunted venture capital movement has only added to the problem. While venture capital launches start-ups that are sometimes wildly successful, and some entrepreneurs have made a fortune, it also encourages bright engineers to desert their companies for seemingly greener pastures. This syndrome creates a proliferation of small companies, without financial staying power, which are tempted to sell their technologies for short-term financing; and also robs stronger companies of some of their best talent. It may be good for the venture capitalists, but whether it is all a net plus for the United States in the long term is less clear.

The critical impact of the business environment was most clearly indicated in October 1986 by a report of the National Bureau of Economic Research on the competitive ability of U.S. multinationals.[29] The report showed that, while the share of exports of world manufactured goods accounted for by the United States as a country declined from 17.5 percent in 1966 to only 12.3 percent in 1983, the share of such exports accounted for by U.S. multinational corporations, including their overseas locations, held steady at 17.7 percent during that time. As Bradshaw had said, some of the companies are doing fine. Far from being incompetent, some American managers are doing superlatively something most Japanese companies fear to try: operating from global manufacturing locations with a truly multinational team, including top management personnel. The problem is not so much that U.S. multinational companies cannot compete, but rather that the United States as a country or operating location cannot compete.

## THE DECLINE OF QUALITY AND PRODUCTIVITY

The most obvious problem of the U.S. companies, and one that costs them much credibility, is quality—as shown by the experience of Motorola and the other American semiconductor producers. When the Japanese entered the U.S. market with the 16K DRAM, their quality was distinctly better. And even though the U.S. producers quickly improved theirs, it took a long time to change the public perception of lax management.

The situation is similar with regard to the productivity of labor, perhaps the most stunning example of which was the General Motors–Toyota joint venture in Fremont, California. Prior to the start of the joint venture in 1983, the plant had been run by GM with a rate of absenteeism of 20 percent and 5,000 grievances pending at any one time. GM was eventually forced to close the plant for two years. With its reopening under Toyota management, absenteeism dropped to 2 percent and grievances to virtually zero. In addition, the new plant needed only 2,500 people to do what 5,000 had done previously.[30] Although the fact that the workers had had no work for two years doubtless contributed to the statistics, it was still an impressive performance.

The problem of quality and productivity is the Achilles' heel of U.S. industry. Bob Galvin admits that often U.S. quality is not as good as Japanese. American unions are often blamed, but companies like Motorola are not unionized. Galvin himself attributes some of the problem to differences in the educational level and stability of the two labor forces, but mostly, he says, it is due to the U.S. approach to manufacturing, which concentrates too heavily on high output and reduction of specific costs without considering the entire process. He admits that he and other American executives have learned much from the Japanese and that there is still more to learn.

In this regard, he notes that Motorola moved some operations overseas in the late 1960s, in an effort to reduce labor costs. He is learning now, he says, that the just-in-time manufacturing system of the Japanese not only reduces inventories but also forces manufacturers to study their processes as a system and to understand why they have quality problems while compelling their resolution, because now any defect can stop the whole plant. "When we think in those terms and operate that kind of system," says Galvin, "the search for lower labor costs alone is not necessarily the answer. We have to understand the entire manufacturing system thoroughly." Although there is still room for improvement, Galvin says, "We now know how to get top quality, and we find that, in an increasing number of areas, we are beating Hitachi, Toshiba, and others in direct comparison. So we are improving." As evidence, he notes that as a result of a very high quality rating, Nippon Telegraph and Telephone recently doubled its purchases of Motorola pagers while reducing those from other Japanese suppliers.

Of course, notes Galvin, quality is not something that occurs in a vacuum, but depends on investment and expectations. The short-term financial pressures under which U.S. corporate managers operate tend to make it more difficult for them than for the Japanese to take the measures necessary for top quality. And, of course, investment requires a healthy cash flow, which can be difficult to maintain in the face of the export onslaught.

On the subject of labor and productivity, Marvin Runyon has a unique viewpoint. He spent nearly thirty years running Ford Motor Company plants before taking on the task of establishing Nissan's first assembly plant in the United

States, in Smyrna, Tennessee. A slight man with a shock of white hair and a low-key manner, Runyon is steeped in the lore of the auto business. He has seen everything from both the U.S. and Japanese sides. On a recent tour of the Smyrna plant, he was obviously proud that it is equaling the quality and productivity levels of the home company, proving—as he said—that American workers are as good as any in the world when properly organized and managed.

I pressed him on this point. Could he, I asked, duplicate at Ford what he had done here with Nissan? His response was, "Yes, if you promise me I won't have unreasonable union work rules." I pressed further. What is it exactly about some unions that makes it impossible to do what you have done here? He pointed to a light bulb in the ceiling. "If I have to change that bulb here, I might get a ladder and do it myself or call one of the custodians. If this were Ford, I would have to have an electrician change the bulb and someone else to carry the ladder."

Noting Runyon's blue company uniform and the fact that he ate in the cafeteria along with everyone else, I asked about the management side of the equation. Agreeing that there is a strong effort within Nissan to create a family atmosphere and a sense of identity between worker and company, Runyon stressed the importance of reducing the gap between the shop floor and the executive suite. At the same time, he noted that American workers are more independent and individualistic than the Japanese and cannot be managed in exactly the same way.

Tony DeJesus, head of the UAW local at General Motors' Toyota plant in Fremont, addressed the management issue more bluntly in an interview with *Business Week:* "Here we find the executives make sacrifices before asking concessions from the workers. We had no confidence of this under previous management."[31]

It was Sony's Morita who articulated the final piece of the equation. In September 1986, while discussing with him his plant in San Diego, I asked whether it had the same quality levels as his plants in Japan. He said it did but that to get the quality took more effort. Noting its more diverse nature and generally lower educational level, he said that the U.S. work force was less attuned to and able to use the necessary techniques. Japanese workers, he said, constantly experiment with the allowable margins of error and try to reach optimum productivity. Americans are more passive and willing to accept broader margins. Moreover, Morita said, if a piece is coming down the line close to quitting time, a Japanese worker would finish it even if that meant staying after the quitting bell. The Americans, he said, tend to stop in midstream. The solution to the problem, according to Morita, is for Sony engineers to establish narrower margins for U.S. workers and to give them orders not to begin new pieces just prior to quitting time.

The message seems to be that both U.S. management and labor need to improve and, above all, work together.

## THE ISOLATION OF U.S. BUSINESS

A final factor in the trend of U.S. business to move overseas or into more protected service and financial enterprises is the fact that no one has seemed to care whether it stays in the United States. The press, consumers, and the American government have traditionally had little, if any, sense of identity with American business, which has tended to be seen as a necessary, but somewhat untrustworthy, institution, with a life apart from the rest of the community.

In the television wars, the U.S. press sided with the Japanese and condemned its own industry as protectionist—as it did in the later semiconductor wars, even though the executives in these companies had long been staunch supporters of free trade. The press has never dug too deeply into Japanese attitudes or why U.S. executives who run large multinational enterprises would be supporters of "protectionist" measures. The press has also tended to analyze trade problems solely in terms of the failures of American management as the cause of declining American living standards.[32] There was no mention of the environment, including the media environment, within which management must work.

The public has been just as unsympathetic. The most striking example occurred in the spring of 1987 when President Reagan announced the sanctions against Japan for unfair trade in semiconductors. Without exception, the concern of the man or the woman in the street expressed in press interviews was not for the semiconductor producers or workers, but rather for whether one would still be able to buy a VCR.[33]

At about the same time, when the United States had been pressuring Japan to lower its interest rates in an attempt to stimulate its domestic economy and thereby relieve pressure on the U.S. trade deficit by consuming more of its own products and exporting fewer, I was interviewed on Japanese television. When the anchorman in Tokyo asked what I thought of the fact that Japan was being asked to sacrifice itself for the sake of the U.S. economy, I was stunned into momentary silence. It had never occurred to me that lowering the interest rate or stimulating domestic consumption could be considered a sacrifice—but, of course, in Japan, which identifies with the producer, it can be.

The disengagement of the United States was illustrated in the winter of 1986 when a group of congressmen from Kentucky asked me to brief them before they traveled to Japan. Toyota had just announced it would build an assembly plant in Kentucky, and the congressmen were hoping to attract parts suppliers to the state as well with various incentive schemes. At one point I asked whether they realized that for every Japanese plant that opened in Kentucky, an American one in Michigan was likely to close. Their response was, "We're not the congressmen from Michigan." By contrast, in Japan MITI coordinates the policies of the various provinces to prevent them from bidding against one another for foreign investment.

In the United States, it's every man for himself. There seems to be no concept that we all might be better off if we supported each other. And so U.S. business feels isolated and vulnerable. Japanese products are not always the best, but the environment in Japan gives the producer a chance to improve. In the United States, there are no second chances.

Then again, U.S. business itself has little unity and little understanding of its own situation. In the 1960s, many businessmen criticized the textile industry for being protectionist. In the 1970s, the semiconductor industry criticized the steel and automobile industries for the same thing; and in the 1980s, the computer and software people are making the same criticism of the semiconductor industry.

To remain innovative and independent of the Japanese, the U.S. computer and telecommunications equipment makers need a healthy U.S. semiconductor equipment industry, because the performance of their products depends on the chips they use, and the quality of the chips depends on the equipment used in making them. But the equipment industry cannot be healthy while its customers, the semiconductor companies, are hemorrhaging. Yet when in 1986 the government moved to aid the semiconductor industry by preventing dumping, some members of the electronics industry complained of being cut off from inexpensive Japanese chips.

The U.S.–Japan Businessman's Conference provided further examples of confusion and misunderstanding. This group of top business leaders from both countries meets twice a year. In 1985, its review of Japanese and U.S. industrial policy concluded that Japan has a coordinated and effective industrial policy that makes a major contribution to Japanese success, while the United States has policies that affect industry but no overall industrial policy. These U.S. policies, the report said, are often contradictory and ill coordinated, and tend to retard U.S. progress.[34] At the press conference at the Madison Hotel in Washington, D.C., at which the report was announced, Edson Spencer, the American chairman and the chief executive of Honeywell Corporation, was asked whether it would not be wise for the United States to adopt a more coordinated approach. The response was, "Absolutely not. We in the United States do not believe in government interference in business."

I attended a meeting of this group in Honolulu in February 1986. The attitudes on both sides were fascinating. Several U.S. businessmen warned the Japanese that the United States needs industrial strength to support its national security as well as that of Japan. While there was some truth in this warning, there was also an implicit plea: "Please don't hit us too hard." The obvious message was that these businessmen and their government were not prepared to take the steps necessary to preserve competitive strength. In effect, they were begging the Japanese to prop up the United States.

While some of the Americans thus humbled themselves, the Japanese took a well-coordinated and strong position. They generally denied any problems of transparency or market barriers in Japan. They also pleaded poverty to argue that Japan's trade surpluses are necessary. One speaker noted that Japan's debt is a greater percentage of the gross national product than that of the United States. He neglected, however, to point out that its savings rate is also much higher than the American one, which makes the net burden much less. Another speaker stressed that Japan is not wealthy; and that even if it has a surplus, people do not get to use the money because of cramped living quarters and high prices. Still another speaker argued that there are no distribution problems in Japan. The *keiretsu* do not interfere with distribution of foreign goods, he emphasized.

The Americans let all that pass. No one asked, for example, why, if distribution is not a problem, U.S. soda ash sales are stuck at 220,000 tons per year, when 500,000 could easily be expected, based on economic considerations. The Americans worked hard to assert common interests with the Japanese, and tended to express appreciation for market-opening measures that no one believed would open the Japanese market, in order to establish goodwill and encourage further action by the Japanese side. Some Americans, however, were terribly frustrated by the meeting. Donald Peterson, the chairman of Ford Motor Company, issued a cry of anguish at one point: "I wish someone would tell me that manufacturing is not un-American."

Many executives in corporate America echo that cry. They feel they are putting up a great fight. With weaker financial structures, a less well educated work force, and the world's most open market, they are surviving. The struggle has forced them to move some of their operations overseas. While they have been criticized for this action, in terms of management it has been an achievement, proving that they can integrate and coordinate far-flung operations involving many nationalities. In fact, as the National Bureau of Economic Research noted, many companies have been doing well based on their overseas operations, having found a way to survive that in many respects is quite ingenious.[35]

The problem is that it is difficult to survive as an American company. Men like Peterson and Galvin take pride in their companies and in their country. They want the companies to stay in the country and have done all in their power to keep them there. But in order for them to succeed, the country has to want the companies. There has to be a common bond, a feeling among consumers, workers, businessmen, media gurus, and bureaucrats that ultimately they are all in the same boat.

# 8

# TRADERS OR WARRIORS: THE CONFLICT BETWEEN ECONOMIC AND NATIONAL SECURITY

---

Foreign trade is a war in that each party seeks to extract wealth from the other.
—RIMEI HONDA,
Tokugawa Philosopher, 1744–1821

THE economic environment in which Robert Galvin of Motorola and other U.S. businessmen operate is primarily conditioned by the doctrine of perfect competition and free trade, on the one hand, and by the exigencies of national security, on the other. That the United States has not grappled with the problem of integrating these often-conflicting imperatives, while Japan and other countries have done so, is one of the chief causes of the unfriendliness of the environment and of U.S. decline.

## The Loss of a Critical Industry

The best example of this situation is the machine tool industry, which became the focal point of public attention in the summer of 1987, following an incident in 1986 in which a U.S. hunter submarine in the North Atlantic was zapped by the sonar of a nearby Soviet submarine—something that was not supposed to happen. The U.S. Navy had spent billions of dollars recording the sound signatures of every Soviet sub, and U.S. submarines were supposed to hear the Russians long before they got close enough to bounce sound waves off U.S. hulls. What had happened?

The answer to this question caused a public furor a year later. The Japanese Toshiba Machine Corporation and the Norwegian Kongsberg Corporation had teamed up to sell the Soviets sophisticated machine tools which could be used for milling quiet propellers—in violation of international undertakings and through fraudulent documentation and a circuitous sales route. Although the Japanese government had not known of the scheme ahead of time, its general laxness toward strategic exports (it had a control staff of twenty to thirty compared with the U.S.'s seven hundred) to the Soviets had certainly contributed to a somewhat permissive atmosphere. While serious, it seemed on the surface to be merely another, albeit egregious, case of standard industrial espionage and smuggling. In fact, the story had a rich history and many more complex and interesting aspects.

Machine tools are not usually the stuff of high drama. They do not appear on television, and ordinary people do not buy them. The industry is small: in a good year, sales might reach $6 billion, about 5 percent of General Motors volume. Those sales, however, underpin the entire industrial economy. At the simplest level, machine tools make screws, screwdrivers, nuts and bolts, and the like; at a more sophisticated level, they make the presses, the casters, and the robots that are used in steel, auto, and electronics plants. As the tools that make other tools, machine tools are the building blocks of industry.

The critical importance of this industry has been particularly evident in every war the United States has fought in this century. In the First World War, it was given an A priority, along with battleships and submachine tools—one of the key steps leading up to Pearl Harbor. In the Second World War, Congress authorized expedited procurement of "naval vessels, aircraft, and machine tools."[1] Nevertheless, the lack of tools became a critical bottleneck, for which our troops paid in blood. As a result, in 1948, Congress directed that a national reserve of machine tools for emergency production of critical items be established.[2] Despite this measure, the Korean War again found the country short of essential machine tools; and Congress once again addressed methods of ensuring adequate supply. Among other things, it passed a resolution in 1955 which stated, "We must not depend on foreign factories for our industrial mobilization base."[3]

The United States was not alone in this concern. In planning their industrial structure, the mandarins at the Ministry of International Trade and Industry did not neglect machine tools. In 1956, the Extraordinary Measures Law for the Promotion of Specified Machinery Industries was written by MITI and passed by the Diet. Similar to and a forerunner of the Extraordinary Measures Law for the Promotion of the Electronics Industry of 1957, this new law created a council to oversee the industry and directed MITI to develop and execute the plans to promote it. Passage of the law was not noted in the American press; and the U.S. embassy in Tokyo, preoccupied with more glamorous political issues, paid little attention. Both should have been more observant for this law has continued, in one form or another, for more than thirty years to provide the basis for making Japan's industry pre-eminent.

### THE MACHINE TOOL INDUSTRY IN THE UNITED STATES AND JAPAN

Since skilled craftsmanship has traditionally been the key to success in the machine tool industry of all countries, this has been an ideal industry for entrepreneurial engineers and machinists, who have typically founded small companies based on skill rather than financial strength. The worldwide industry is thus characterized by small, often family-owned, companies. As one of the most cyclical of industries, it is always faced with a critical operating decision. To be able to respond to peak demand with rapid delivery, one would have to maintain a production capacity far in excess of that required when demand drops at the bottom of the business cycle, and thus have a strong financial base. Because machine tool companies typically have not had such a base, they have tended to choose an alternative strategy; at times of peak demand, they have simply backlogged orders and delivered them several months after receipt.

These "boom and bust" tendencies and small scale have combined to create the industry's other distinguishing characteristics: high risk and undercapitalization. It is not an industry at which bankers want to throw money. Consequently, investment and research and development have tended to be limited to what could be done from internal cash flow, a circumstance that has exacerbated the tendency toward backlogging and limited innovative activity.

In 1956, the U.S. and Japanese industries shared these characteristics. In every other way, however, they were quite different. The U.S. industry was the world's largest, with 75,000 workers and $1.3 billion in sales. It was the biggest exporter of machine tools and had the most advanced technology, the highest level of investment per worker, and by far the highest output per worker of the world's tool industries. In short, the U.S. industry was the best.[4]

As the bureaucrats at MITI drafted their promotion law that winter, the task of equaling the U.S. industry must have seemed almost impossible. Japan's 1,500 manufacturers produced barely a quarter of the U.S. volume, and, to do that, needed more than half as many workers, meaning it took more than two Japanese to do the work of one American. One third of Japan's machine tools were imported, and the imported products were less expensive and of better quality than the domestic brands.[5]

Over the next thirty years, both countries took steps to assure themselves of adequate machine tool supply. The United States administered prearrangements for production of certain equipment upon declaration of an emergency. The fourth was the Manufacturing Technology, or MANTECH, program which began in 1949 when the Air Force became interested in improving manufacturing techniques for aerospace equipment. It funded an effort at the Massachusetts Institute of Technology to improve machining which resulted in the development of numerically controlled, or NC, machine tools. By having computers control the movements of machine tools, the developers eliminated the need for human operators, made the tools more precise, and revolutionized the industry. The Air Force transferred this technology to U.S. industry primarily by placing orders for such tools with selected manufacturers and making licenses for manufacture available to them. This action made the technology available to several large defense contractors, but dissemination throughout the industry was not emphasized and was slow because of the financial limitations of the firms and their innate conservatism. The technology was also disseminated abroad, as licenses were offered to foreign manufacturers at reasonable fees. Several Japanese companies were able to obtain the technology.

In addition to these positive moves, the United States took others that created a more difficult environment for the industry. It severely restrained exports of the highest-technology equipment, even to friendly and neutral countries, in order to prevent leakage to the Soviets. This restriction not only created an incentive for foreign countries to develop their own technology, but also prevented the American industry from obtaining volume that would have lowered its costs and generated cash for further technology development. On top of this, the United States actually nurtured the development of the foreign industry to which it had thus given incentive by pursuing the liberal licensing policies already noted. That such foreign industries might be less finicky about selling to the Soviets than was America was not considered. The U.S. government also removed barriers to imported tools in the U.S. market while failing to achieve reciprocal liberalization abroad, especially in Japan, and responding only slowly to complaints of unfair international trade by the U.S. industry.

The Japanese were more thorough. Years of study and experimentation had convinced MITI's analysts that custom production of small lots by many small manufacturers would always result in a system that was undercapitalized, vulnerable to cyclical swings, and thus unable to introduce new technology rapidly. Accordingly, in March 1957, the first basic plan for the industry adopted the objective of reducing costs, improving quality, and raising productivity through centralization of manufacturing. The goal was for certain producers to concentrate on only a few products, thereby increasing their scale of production.

This plan and others that followed over the years were detailed and specific. For 1967, production was targeted at 1.5 billion yen, with an export goal of 250 million yen. The 1971 plan called for 50 percent of production to be numerically controlled tools by 1980. (They just missed, hitting only 49.8 percent.) MITI directed that companies cease producing any item that was less than 5 percent of industry volume and 20 percent of their own volume. The Japan Machine Tool Builders Association established the Manufacturing Share

Deliberation Committee which determined the areas of concentration for each manufacturer. The committee was, in effect, a cartel that operated in one form or another until at least 1983.[6]

This program was supported by a panoply of market-protection measures, coupled with various financial incentives, including the usual special depreciation, reserves for export losses, retirement, and price fluctuations, along with various tax credits. Capital was allocated to the industry through the Japan Development Bank, as well as through the private banking network.

The program that showed the imagination of MITI at its peak, however, was the Bicycle Racing Fund, which later became the focus of many complaints. Capitalizing on the fact that bicycle racing is a popular sport in Japan, MITI wrote a law allowing legal wagering on bicycle races. Passed by the Diet, the law permits Japan's municipalities to organize races and the betting on them. Although most of the money received goes to the municipalities, a portion goes to the Japan Bicycle Rehabilitation Association, which is dedicated to the "promotion of industries related to machines." This organization, like several others such as the Motor Boat Racing Association, is controlled by MITI. Over the past thirty years, the association's budget had totaled over $2 billion (at current rates) and has proven to be a substantial source of off-budget funds for various MITI projects, including the machine tool industry.*[7]

The results of all this were dramatic. By 1986, Japan had become the world's largest producer of machine tools. Japan's investment per worker was nearly double that of the United States, as was its productivity per worker. While the industry had shrunk from 1,000 firms to about 600 in the United States, Japan had rationalized its industry down to only about 250 companies. Fifty percent of Japanese machine

*The Bicycle Racing Fund is an example of why official Japanese statistics on government support of industry are sometimes misleading, the line between what is public and what is private being much more blurred in Japan than in the United States.

tool workers were employed by companies with over 1,000 workers, while the figure for the United States was only about 20 percent.[8]

Most important, Japan absolutely dominated the most advanced and fastest-growing segment of the industry: the numerically controlled machines that had been invented in America. In 1986, it produced three times as many numerically controlled tools as the United States. A single Japanese company, Fujitsu Fanuc, controlled 60 percent of the world market for the control devices.[9] Many numerically controlled tool manufacturers in the United States were dependent on the Japanese for their controls and thus for the technology of their equipment. And the armed forces, which thirty years earlier had insisted on the necessity of not being dependent on foreign machine tools, had largely become so.

The export drives began in 1977, when Japan's share of the U.S. market was negligible. From there the line shot nearly straight up. By 1982, Japanese firms controlled more than a third of the American market and, in the critical area of numerically controlled tools, did about 40 percent of the business.[10] Despite a check price system organized by MITI that established floor prices for exporters in order to avoid charges of dumping, actual Japanese prices were 20 percent to 40 percent below U.S. prices.[11] Sometimes this was accomplished not with a direct price cut but by including in the sale a gift item such as an automobile. In an industry that had been characterized by the system of backlogging of orders, the Japanese kept on hand as much as a year's inventory, making for happy customers who got rapid delivery even at times of peak demand, and enabling the Japanese to make big inroads into the market while the Americans struggled to move orders from backlog to production.

Although the management of American industry was severely criticized for not meeting this challenge, it faced significant difficulties. Carrying such inventories meant that the Japanese were not always profitable. The Americans simply could not afford to take losses as the Japanese could. Beyond that they had other problems. Despite several rounds of liberalization, foreign sales in Japan remained small as countermeasures similar to those in the semiconductor industry were put into effect. The Americans also found their licenses and patents being violated. In one such case, when Houdaille Industries, a major U.S. machine tool manufacturer, was directed by a federal court to send a lawyer to Japan to develop evidence, the Japanese government refused to issue the attorney a visa. Not surprisingly, such actions led to charges that the Japanese were engaging in unfair trade.

## THE HOUDAILLE DECISION

Phil O'Reilly, Houdaille's chief executive officer, is a big blond Irishman with a straightforward manner, a ready grin, and an unpretentious sense of humor. This former football player and U.S. marine was determined to plug the dike against the Japanese flood. He had long thought it unfair that products subsidized by foreign governments nevertheless received the benefits of the American investment-tax credit when bought for installation in American factories. In 1981, he met Richard Copaken, a pastels painter by avocation and one of the hardest-driving international lawyers in Washington. Copaken told O'Reilly that the practice was not only unfair but also illegal. A little-known and never-invoked clause, section 103 of the Revenue Act of 1971, provided that the president could exclude a foreign product from the credit if he determined that the country where the product originated engaged in certain unfair trade activities. O'Reilly immediately retained Copaken, who launched the most comprehensive vivisection of Japanese industrial policy and trade practices undertaken to date.

On 3 May 1982, Houdaille filed a massive 1,000-page petition with the office of the U.S. Trade Representative, carefully summarizing, from the Japanese government's own laws and administrative directives, the record of the machine tool cartel and the loans, subsidies, and other financial incentives given to the industry over the years. The petition also noted the record of protection of the Japanese market and the Japanese efforts to counteract various trade liberalizing measures, and mentioned in this regard that the foreign share of Japan's market never seemed to rise above 10 percent, despite repeated "trade concessions." The petition charged that Japan was illegally subsidizing its industry, tolerating and even encouraging an international cartel, and discriminating against U.S. commerce. Houdaille now asked President Reagan to revoke the tax credit for Japanese machine tools.

Thus began one of the most bitter and divisive internal debates of the Reagan administration. On one side were the proponents of pure free trade. On the other were individuals and agencies who saw a connection between a declining machine tool industry and a weakened national security; and who questioned whether the concept of free trade could successfully coexist with industry-targeting practices like those of Japan.

The first group, who dubbed themselves the "White Hats" —led by the Office of Management and Budget under David Stockman and the Treasury Department under Donald Regan and his deputy, Tim McNamar—included the State Department, the Council of Economic Advisers, the Justice Department, the National Security Council, and the Department of Defense. State, Defense, and the National Security Council were in this group not so much for reasons of economic theory as because they opposed anything that might disturb political and military relations with Japan. The second group, who called themselves the "Realists," was led by U.S. Trade Representative William Brock and Commerce Secretary Malcolm Baldrige, who were under increasing pressure from Congress to do something about Japanese trade practices. They were supported by the Agriculture and Labor departments in favoring a firm approach.

The first arguments were procedural. The law said that a president could retaliate against unfair practices, such as toleration of an "international cartel" that burdens U.S. "commerce." The opponents of the petition said that "commerce" meant only exports, not imports. They argued further that while the Japanese tool builders might constitute a cartel, it was not an international cartel because its members were all Japanese, even if some of them operated in the United States. Finally, they said that many of the acts of which Houdaille complained had taken place in the past; and that the law, because it was written in the present tense, could affect only present practices. Thus the petition should be summarily rejected.[12]

These arguments gave rise to eight months of legal research into the meaning of the word *commerce* and whether a cartel had to have members of more than one nationality to be considered "international." A legal conclusion was never reached: politics made the decision. With the trade deficit soaring and Congress becoming more impatient, the government decided it could not ignore the petition and decided to proceed.

The issues were framed at a cabinet-level meeting on 16 January 1983, chaired by Brock. Of medium height with a youthful shock of wavy, chestnut hair, Brock is the heir of the Brock Candy fortune. Before joining the Reagan administration as the U.S. trade representative, he had served as a senator from Tennessee and as chairman of the Republican Party. Brock had always been and still was a firm internationalist and supporter of free trade. Initially, he had believed that Japan was doing its best to open its markets, but gradually his experience of the frustrations of negotiating with the Japanese had led him to believe that only firmness would induce them to meet their international obligations. As I listened in the back of the room, he made an argument for some kind of action, explaining how Japan protected its home market while providing various export incentives to the machine tool industry. In particular, he called attention to the Bicycle Racing Fund. While Japan claimed that little money had gone to the machine tool industry, it had never been willing to document the figures. Because Japan viewed the industry as critical, it was reasonable to assume that the amounts given to it had been substantial. The Japanese themselves had acknowledged the existence of a cartel that had been formally disbanded only after this case had begun. The cartel consisted entirely of Japanese companies, but it certainly operated outside of Japan and had international effects.

Brock also pointed out that trade-liberalization actions had been offset by various countermeasures, with the result that foreign penetration of the Japanese market remained in the 10-percent range. In contrast, the second largest exporter, Germany, also imported 32 percent of its tools.[13] Brock felt that these policies and actions by the Japanese over a long period had effectively nullified Japan's obligations under the General Agreement on Tariffs and Trade and justified some action by the United States. Brock called for a finding of unfairness to be followed by a negotiated settlement with Japan.

William Niskanen of the Council of Economic Advisers led the rebuttal. Tall and likable, Niskanen is an avid tennis player with a strong faith in the efficacy of free trade. That he has the courage of his convictions was demonstrated in 1979–80 when, as chief economist of Ford Motor Company, he opposed restraints on imports of Japanese cars, restraints that other Ford executives were demanding. This stand probably explained why he had been available to join the Reagan administration. He now argued that the problems of the U.S. industry had nothing to do with the Japanese, but were the result of the recent recession and poor management. Terming Japan's industrial policies nothing more than "hortatory goals," he said that there was no evidence of a causal link between those policies and the substantial penetration of the U.S. market by Japanese industry. Because the cartel had been disbanded in 1982, there was no evidence of any present violation of international agreements. To take action would be protectionism in the extreme, and would hurt U.S. industry by raising the prices of the Japanese machine tools it bought, a result that could harm the economic recovery. Niskanen urged rejection of the petition.

The two positions could not be reconciled. Brock did not achieve consensus at this meeting or at the subsequent meetings that continued into April. In response to a request for more facts made by the representatives from State, the National Security Council, and Defense, two independent studies were undertaken, which concluded that the Japanese industry had a significant lead, and one likely to widen in the future. The studies attributed this lead to Japanese industrial policies, which had resulted in the concentration of production of key tools in a few hands and to a highly focused strategy aimed at dominating key segments of the industry. It stressed that leadership in machine tools had important national security implications.[14] These reports did not change anything. Those opposed to the petition attacked the reports, particularly their analysis of the efficacy of industrial policy. In one sense, they had to attack, for to accept that industrial policy could work would be to undermine the argument for free trade which they supported.

One of the most vociferous critics of the petition was Tim McNamar, the deputy secretary of the treasury, who now emerged as the leader for the opponents. A former banking executive and business consultant, he is a slight, energetic man who sports the perpetual tan of many Californians. Because of his business background, his views carried particular weight on this subject. Copaken realized that if he could turn McNamar, he might win the whole argument. He and O'Reilly thus asked for a special meeting to present all the facts and to try to persuade McNamar of the efficacy of their case.

The meeting took place on 14 March. Representatives of virtually all of the government agencies were there, and none will ever forget it. McNamar, the tanned, coiled, welterweight jogger faced O'Reilly, the big ex-football player across the table. In an echo of Sgt. Joe Friday of the old television serial *Dragnet*, McNamar said all he wanted was the facts, just the facts. One could almost hear the "ma'am" at the end. Where was the cause and effect relationship? Where was the evidence that MITI's goals were more than hortatory? Where was the documentation of specific subsidies? O'Reilly tried to respond but could never get more than two words out before another question was fired. The meeting ended with Copaken sliding a copy of the 1,000-page petition across the table and suggesting McNamar read it to get the facts.

It was also in March that, during a trip to Japan, Ambassador Brock tried a clever maneuver. He had arranged for a White House meeting that did not include Treasury, CEA, or OMB representatives. Here it was agreed that he should tell the Japanese there was a consensus within the cabinet that Japan was being unfair and that the only thing left to discuss was how Japan would limit its exports to the American market. Brock duly told this to the Japanese and elicited offers of a voluntary restraint similar to that in effect in the auto industry. The whole scheme fell apart, however, when he returned. Those who had not attended the White House meeting got wind of it and demanded to know what consensus Brock had in mind. They opposed a voluntary restraint and let both Brock and the Japanese know it. Thus was the rug pulled from under Brock and this particular stratagem.

As time passed and no resolution was reached, the petition began to become a political embarrassment. Finally, Baldrige proposed a last-ditch effort. He directed that a special interdepartmental group be convened under the direction of Wendell Gunn, one of the assistants to the President, as a final attempt to develop a consensus recommendation to the president. The group, of which I was a member as the Commerce Department representative, met on 12 April 1983. After heated repetition of the arguments, the two sides finally agreed that Japan had maintained restraints on imports which were illegal under the General Agreement on Tariffs and Trade until at least 1968 and on foreign investment until at least 1973. It also agreed that MITI was currently setting quantitative objectives for the machine tool industry, providing de facto antitrust immunity, directing collaborative efforts, and providing some level of subsidy.

The group further agreed that the Japanese industry's current activities were probably in contravention of the General Agreement on Tariffs and Trade as well as of U.S. trade law. Despite these points of agreement, Gunn could not get the group to agree on a recommendation. The White Hats would not agree to any finding or negotiation, because they thought to do so would constitute an act of protectionism. Although they acknowledged that as much as $1 billion might have gone to the industry from the Bicycle Racing Fund, they did not think that the actual amounts were nearly that much. They were more inclined to accept the Japanese view that the donations came to only a few thousand dollars, despite the fact that the Japanese offered conflicting data and no supporting documentation.* In keeping with their belief that industrial policy is of little importance, they did not think that measures other than subsidies were worth worrying about. In addition, the great fear of the State Department and the National Security Council was that a positive finding in this case would open the floodgates for similar petitions in other industries, and thereby disturb the harmony of overall relations with Japan, maintenance of which was their top priority.

While the Realists of the Commerce Department and the U.S. Trade Representative's office believed that Japan's practices warranted action under the law, they were not interested so much in punishing Japan as in ensuring the survival of a key U.S. industry. They believed that Japanese actions,

---

*I was later told by MITI officials that the reason for not making the data public was that the funds are actually an off-budget account used by MITI to fund a broad variety of activities. Again, however, no evidence was presented.

coupled with lack of action on the American side, created a particularly disadvantageous environment for U.S. industry, and wanted to alter it. The difficulty was that American law provided no way for them to do so, except by finding Japan to be acting unfairly. Thus, to help their own industry, they were forced to recommend action against Japan.

There was, however, one alternative. Despite the collapse of Brock's earlier effort, the Japanese had continued to indicate a readiness to enter into some voluntary restraint agreement. I am not sure exactly why, but I believe it may have been at least in part because they themselves were not comfortable with the idea that their ultimate defender would not have this critical industry. When it became clear that the ad hoc group could not reach a consensus, the Japanese approaches about the possibility of a voluntary restraint were discussed. Could we agree to negotiate something like that? I asked. Some responded favorably, but again the White Hats were opposed, on the basis that such restraints were in violation of free trade. The unresolved issue was thus passed back to the cabinet.

On the evening of 15 April, members of the cabinet labored for more than two hours in an attempt to reach agreement on a recommendation to the President. The cabinet had reviewed Gunn's report on the proceedings of the special group, which stated that—although Japan and its industries had engaged in, and continued to engage in, activities that would justify action under U.S. and international law—the group could not reach consensus on an action recommendation. Neither could the cabinet members. After lengthy debate, they decided that there was no alternative but to send the dispute to the President for resolution, and a meeting with the President was set for the following Friday, 22 April. All present were sworn to strict secrecy.

Within minutes of the close of the meeting, Kazuhiko Otsuka, a brilliant MITI official in Washington, knew the secret. He had staked himself out at the trade representative's office and, when Brock returned there at about 8:00 P.M., asked whether a decision had been made. When Brock did not respond affirmatively, Otsuka deduced that the answer must be no and that there was still time to unleash a last-minute lobbying effort. He dashed for his embassy and the phone to Tokyo.

On the weekend of 17 April 1983, a message for delivery to the President was flashed from the prime minister in Tokyo to the Japanese embassy in Washington. It instructed the Japanese ambassador to meet with key U.S. officials and express the hope of Prime Minister Yasuhiro Nakasone that his good friend Ron would give favorable consideration to the difficulties of Japan and to his (Nakasone's) own political problems in deciding on what action to take on the Houdaille petition.

On 22 April, the cabinet met in the afternoon with the President in attendance in the White House cabinet room overlooking the Rose Garden. Baldrige made the case for action, arguing that the President should make an official finding of unfairness and direct that negotiations be held to find ways to ameliorate it, but did not call for retaliatory or punitive action. As Baldrige later related the story, it was obvious as soon as he concluded that the decision had already been taken: "I looked behind me to see where the troops were, and found there were none." Brock had obviously gotten the word, because he said little. Then, uncharacteristically, the President announced his decision. Since he usually listens to the cabinet and then makes a decision alone after a meeting, his speaking in the meeting meant the decision had been pre-cooked. A firm believer in free trade, Reagan reiterated his faith and then said that Nakasone was our best friend in Japan and was trying to help the United States by expanding Japan's defense role. Therefore, said the President, he wanted to help Nakasone. He indicated no action on the petition but directed that talks be held to determine whether Japan's industrial policies really had an adverse effect on U.S. trade.

Undoubtedly the President's decision would have been different had he known that at that very moment steps were being taken by a Japanese company that would help turn the tables on U.S. hunter submarines in the North Atlantic; and that these steps were, at least in part, a result of the export-at-all costs mentality that had given rise to the necessity for his decision on Houdaille's petition. But the President did not know. In 1984, following his decision, Houdaille closed its machine tool operations despite a higher rate of productivity than the Japanese average. Other manufacturers of machine tools quickly followed, until the Japanese market share was about 80 percent in important sectors of an industry that Congress had repeatedly called critical.

## The Force of Economic Theory

### CONVERSATIONS WITH ECONOMISTS

U.S. economists of all stripes are bound together in opposition to any firm government response to questionable foreign trade practices regardless of the consequences to U.S. industry. Divided on almost everything else, the supply-siders, the Keynesians, the monetarists, and other breeds can all unite on this, opposing any trade actions except negotiations to open foreign markets. That such negotiations are doomed precisely because of the reluctance to consider alternative actions has not been a consideration. This attitude is not only the legacy of the Depression and the peculiar circumstances of the postwar era but also reflects a focus on consumers that ignores strategic economic objectives as well as other participants in the economy.

Economists are virtually unanimous in their view of the Smoot-Hawley Tariff Act of 1930, which raised tariffs to very high levels on about half of U.S. imports, as a major cause of the Depression—a mistake they are determined never to allow to be repeated. Thus, those Americans and Europeans who led the restructuring of the world economy after the war founded it on the doctrine of free trade, which was institutionalized in the General Agreement on Tariffs and Trade, the International Monetary Fund (IMF), and the Organization for Economic Cooperation and Development (OECD). There the concepts of multilateral trade (trading within an overall multinational framework rather than on the basis of bilateral agreements), most-favored-nation* and national treatment (giving the same treatment to both foreign and domestic companies) were enshrined. All of these agreements and structures were based on the competitive market and comparative advantage theories of the eighteenth- and nineteenth-century economists Adam Smith and David Ricardo and their later elaborators. Joseph Schumpeter was not in fashion (see pages 254–56), and no one even knew any Japanese economists at the time.

The postwar economic structure was also based on some important long-term assumptions. A key one was that the overriding purpose of economic activity is to improve the welfare of consumers in the relatively short term; implicit was the view that economics has little relation to matters of grand strategy. Indeed, U.S. leaders often explicitly said that trade and security matters should be handled separately. Another assumption was that the "national treatment" of the countries that were members of the General Agreement on Tariffs and Trade would be similar. For clearly if there were gross differences the system would be inherently unfair: the most open and liberal society would clearly be at a disadvantage as foreign enterprises would be able to penetrate its markets, while the reverse would not be true. That this problem was recognized was demonstrated by the fact that

---

*Before the Second World War, trade had been on the basis of bilateral arrangements with nations giving better terms to some trading partners than to others; most-favored-nation treatment extends these favorable terms to all partners equally.

GATT members applied different rules to their trade with the Soviet bloc. A third assumption was that under most-favored-nation rules, the major traders would impose similar levels of overall trade restrictions. Again, if they did not, the system could not work. Nations with few trade restrictions would not long accept the argument from those with many that the resulting trade was fair because the restrictions applied to everyone equally.

Finally, looming over all the others, was the key assumption that the U.S. economy was an impregnable rock that would always underpin the system—an assumption that made immaterial the validity or lack thereof of the others. For, in the postwar world, the United States, as Amaya said, gave a handicap: it accepted that, for some time at least, its trading partners would restrict trade in various ways that it did not. It did so in the belief that the handicap would not matter greatly.

The great superiority of U.S. industry and agriculture after the war made it easy to hold this assumption. Although it was largely the result of the destruction of Europe and Japan and the wartime production programs in the United States, Americans came to see their success as the natural outcome of their democratic ways and entrepreneurial skills. For Americans the word *free* means "good." Confident in the superiority of U.S. economic capability, the representatives of labor, management, and agriculture eagerly embraced the doctrine of free trade. As prosperity returned after the war and trade grew, they were confirmed in their faith, so much so that debate on the subject became impossible. To raise questions was only to reveal ignorance or greed, or both.

By the mid-1970s, successive rounds of postwar trade negotiations had removed most U.S. quotas and reduced tariffs to a negligible level. America's faith in free markets and its own superiority induced it to continue to take the lead in attempts to remove nontariff trade barriers also. The U.S. thought that, if it set the example, other countries would follow. Thus, while other countries in fact delayed, the U.S.

market became a huge cornucopia essentially open to anyone who could come and take it. And come they did. First were the Germans, then the Japanese, Taiwanese, the Koreans, and the Hong Kong Chinese, their inexpensive goods welcomed by consumers and economists alike as a great contribution to U.S. welfare.

By the mid-1960s, however, such U.S. industries as textiles, steel, and consumer electronics were beginning to find that the handicap did matter. Aside from consumers, the other major participants in the economy are management and labor. As they found themselves increasingly at a disadvantage from the handicap, they began to file complaints and petitions that questioned the validity of all the assumptions. They pointed out that many countries do not give priority to consumer welfare and often encourage companies to engage in practices that are illegal in the United States, while keeping unions weak and minimum wage laws nonexistent. The social and political structure of these countries make national treatment a meaningless cliché since domestic companies are systematically promoted. Most-favored-nation treatment is also meaningless from countries that are more or less sealed against imports of foreign goods or capital.

Where was the logic, asked the petitioners, in passing antitrust, minimum wage, and union-shop legislation and then allowing imports from countries with none of these to negate the intended benefits? Did it make sense, for example, to allow—even encourage—U.S. firms to establish plants abroad and import goods with fifty-cent-a-day labor while forcing them to pay $3.00 a day in the United States? In fact, wasn't there a certain dishonesty in intervening massively in the free market with such legislation and then refusing to take any action to correct unequal trading circumstances on the basis of free-trade doctrine? And wasn't it just plain dumb, they asked, to accept rivers of goods from countries that remained adamantly closed to our own products?

The response was usually that, no matter what other countries did, the principles of comparative advantage dictated that the United States would be best served by an unrestricted flow of goods. Of course, some American workers and managers might be hurt, said the experts, but consumers would be better off by being able to buy cheaper foreign goods. The economy would actually become more efficient because labor and capital would move out of low-wage, low-tech industry into more productive areas. That argument was both logical and reassuring, but it assumed that there were more productive sectors to which workers could easily shift. Actually, most workers could not easily be retrained; and if they could be, they could not always easily move their families to where the attractive jobs were. The skilled craftsmen of the machine tool industry, for example, could not just pull up stakes and move to Silicon Valley to become semiconductor engineers when Houdaille and other manufacturers closed their doors.

Whenever trade was restrained by such measures as the Japanese self-restraint agreement on automobiles, U.S. economists adduced numbers showing how much was being spent per worker to preserve jobs. Such calculations tended to be extremely simplistic: the price of a new automobile, for instance, would be compared with a price it was assumed the car might have sold for without restraints. The difference was then multiplied by the number of cars sold and divided by the number of jobs thought to have been preserved. The result was always some ridiculous number like $150,000 per job saved, making it appear that the protection was an expensive rip-off of consumers by greedy companies and unions.

There was some validity to the argument, but the exclusive focus on the consumer tended to obscure the other side of the equation. Never calculated was the expense of retraining and moving displaced workers or of unemployment compensation, lost tax revenue, and social costs such as stress-related health care and family and marriage counseling. The fact that workers might not be able to move because of the needs of children and aged parents was likewise ignored. It was also assumed that related industries could easily become suppliers to the foreign producers or to new domestic industries—assumptions not established as facts.

These costs had been easy to ignore when problems appeared to involve only a few industries. But the Houdaille case did not occur in isolation. It was just the biggest and most important of a rapidly building wave of similar situations. While the Houdaille petition was being considered, Boeing complained that the Europeans were unfairly subsidizing the export of airbuses. The semiconductor wars between the United States and Japan had just begun. Corning Glass prepared to file a lawsuit against Sumitomo for patent infringement. And numerous investigations found various foreign companies to be engaged in dumping and other unfair activities in the U.S. market: as the unquantified costs of the activity rose, so did the pressure to do something about it.

In the face of this pressure, economists both inside and outside the government opposed any retaliatory or relief measures. It was ironic that these people, who were for the most part humane and gentle, could be more ruthless than most businessmen. In their application of economic doctrine, they were ardent champions of the consumer but had less concern for workers and producers. I was amazed by their doctrinaire attitude. Having been in international business all my life, with my whole career based on free trade, I supported the concept of trade expansion because I knew the power of trade as a force for peace as well as for economic welfare. But I knew, too, that free trade has more often been honored in the breach; and, more important, that the economic doctrine of Japan and some other countries does not accord with the U.S. view. In particular, I knew that they do not believe that short-term consumer welfare is the purpose of economic activity. The Japanese, as settlers, think of the welfare of all their players.

I often discussed these issues with members of the president's Council of Economic Advisors. One of these conversations took place in 1983 and concerned the company Siemens-Allis, a manufacturer of hydrogenerators—in fact, the last such manufacturer in the United States of these machines that are used to turn water power into electricity. Westinghouse had given up, and GE had moved its operation to Canada, both actions the result of severe price competition from Japanese companies. Siemens-Allis had come to see me to say that, unless something could be done about what it called Japan's collusive and predatory pricing, their company too would have to leave the business.

The Siemens-Allis executives had presented some interesting documentation. Over a period of several years, three Japanese companies—Hitachi, Toshiba, and Fuji Electric—had bid on a number of projects in the United States. There appeared to be a pattern to their bidding: first, one would bid very low, while the others bid high; for a second project, another would come in low; and so forth. The variation in the prices bid within short periods of time could be as much as 200 percent.[15] Siemens-Allis executives said that they could understand that one manufacturer might have had a consistent cost advantage, but not how a company could be the lowest bidder one day and the highest the next on the same equipment.

My friends at the Council of Economic Advisers were unconcerned about these discrepancies, saying they meant that American users were getting cheap generators and that consumers in the United States were probably benefiting by paying lower rates for electricity. The U.S. companies and workers who were displaced could go into other industries where they would be more competitive. If the Japanese then raised prices, the U.S. companies could go back into the business. The council truly did not seem to understand that no businessman in his right mind would consider going back into the business: even if he could reassemble the skilled team and the plant and equipment required, he would face a repetition of the old experience as long as the Japanese had the ability to collude. In fact, there was really no natural economic dynamic that would prevent the Japanese from monopolizing the business. The council was unprepared to deal with this aspect of the issue because it was a market imperfection which their theories and econometric models assumed away.

The discrepancy between theory and practice pointed to another issue also raised by the Houdaille case and by the semiconductor industry's problems: the question of strategic industries. The Japanese argued that, because of their impact on other industries and the development of technology, some industries, such as semiconductors and aerospace, are more important to long-term economic health than others, such as toy manufacturing or travel services. They also saw some industries as providers of more international bargaining power than others. They "targeted" these industries for development, thus tending to create conflict with U.S. industry.

When Brock and Baldrige and other officials suggested that Japanese practices distorted free trade and should be offset or the U.S. might take a page from the Japanese book, the economists at the council and elsewhere demurred. They did not believe in the power of governments to create comparative advantages in such industries. But even if governments could, they said, it would not matter, because there is no evidence that one kind of economic activity is more useful or productive than another. That some industries confer more strategic power than others was not addressed. The relationship of economics to the rest of national life was not part of the theory. Thus, if Japan were better than the United States at producing semiconductors or machine tools, that was nothing to be concerned about. We should buy their chips and concentrate our efforts on other industries for which we were better suited. As one economist put it, "We'll buy semiconductors from them and sell them rock music."

The economists were generally skeptical of business and labor. Whether the U.S. produced shoelaces or computers, or whether U.S. companies produced anything anywhere in the world, was a matter of indifference to them. The burden of proof of unfair trade was always on the U.S. petitioner who was suspected of pleading for illegitimate special interests.

These attitudes were frequently expressed in the Trade Policy Review Group, an interagency body at the undersecretary level, where recommendations are fully aired before going to the cabinet level. In the course of my five years in Washington, numerous complaints were discussed by this group. Never once did I hear an economist or a representative of any economic agency speak in favor of granting relief or of taking action to aid a U.S. industry. They sometimes bowed to political necessity, but never willingly. An ironic case was that of the Harley-Davidson Corporation, the venerable maker of large motorcycles better known among the fraternity of riders as "hogs." By the summer of 1983, Harley, which at one point had been dominant in the U.S. market, was down to a market share of 3 percent to 5 percent and was close to bankruptcy. It did not claim there was any unfair trade; it just asked for relief under section 201 of the trade law which enables temporary protection of industries while they attempt to adjust. It is the international equivalent of the domestic bankruptcy laws. The debate in the review group was long and hot. The lineup was exactly the same as in the case of Houdaille, with the White Hats opposed to granting relief and the Realists inclined to give some, while the Japanese, who held 95 percent of the market, decried rising protectionism in the United States as if they were being threatened with losing the market instead of being held at 95 percent. The fact that the International Trade Commission had voted to recommend relief, and that the concurrent Houdaille case was causing an uproar in the Congress, made it seem politically necessary to give some help to Harley in the form of a five-year tariff increase on big "bikes." Had Houdaille not occurred at the same time it is unlikely Harley would have gotten any help. Within three years, Harley had recovered its health and asked the President to suspend the tariff increase which legally still had two years to run. The President made a triumphal visit to Harley's plant, and his economic advisors called the Harley experiment, which they had vigorously opposed, a victory for Reaganomics.

The incident I remember most clearly occurred in the spring of 1985. The Trade Policy Review Group met to consider possible retaliation against Japan for not opening its telecommunications market. At one point, I suggested that, if we retaliated, we should do so in such a way as to maximize the benefit to the U.S. telecommunications companies. Immediately the undersecretary of state for economic matters, an economist and former professor of Secretary of State George Shultz, objected: "No. We don't want to help American companies too much. They might become too fond of the protection."

This view of U.S. business as a lone rider was in stark contrast to that of the Japanese, who always talked of "our country's industry" or "our companies." When the dollar began to fall in 1985, the Japanese government immediately began to offer low-interest loans to companies affected by the strong yen. When the Japanese petrochemical or paper or other industries fell on hard times, the Japanese government joined in to see what might be done. There was an identity of common interest with the industry. Like the American settlers, they all worked together. The Japanese bureaucrat, along with the Japanese worker, looks upon industry as something that contributes to the welfare of all Japanese, not just shareholders.

Not so in the United States, whose officials do not see their fate as linked to that of U.S. companies. They have faith that the unseen hand will ensure that something will

always be there to produce the wealth. Whether the producer is American or not is a matter of indifference. What
matters is the short-term desires of the consumer.


## U.S. TRADE LAWS AND THEIR UNREALISTIC ASSUMPTIONS

American trade laws as well as the rules of the General
Agreement on Tariffs and Trade reflect these economic
views. Because the assumption is that all market economies
operate within a framework of open societies and open procedures, the primary barriers in such economies are thought
to be overt, identifiable ones, such as tariffs, quotas, and
subsidies. Dumping is seen as a potentially undesirable export of unemployment, but only if it results in injury to industries in the country where the product is being dumped.
The concepts of injury do not include any recognition of the
experience curve or of the fact that a company may be injured by a loss of market share even if it is growing in absolute terms. Thus, only actual financial losses, closure of
factories, and layoffs of workers count as injury.

Because the laws are based on theories that do not acknowledge the concepts of strategic industries and industrial
policy, they do not handle these concepts well. For example,
government subsidies to industry such as the special tax advantages and payments from the Bicycle Racing Fund in the
Houdaille case are clearly seen to be violations of free-trade
doctrine. But the remedy is to calculate the amount of subsidy, divide that by the number of units produced to arrive at
a subsidy per unit, and apply a countervailing duty of that
amount to offset the advantage the subsidy gives the foreign
product when the product is imported. Such a calculation
often produces a ridiculous figure that has no meaning. The
problem is that a quite small subsidy can have a powerful
effect. If someone had walked into the garage where Apple
Computer began in 1976 and offered a subsidy of $50,000, it
might have been the difference between life and death. Ten

years later, when the company was producing thousands of computers, the $50,000 divided by the thousands of units would have yielded a very small, meaningless, and easily payable countervailing duty.

Likewise, the antidumping laws of the United States were not made to deal with industrial strategy in the modern world. Because the assumption of these laws is that dumping is a gift to the consumer, unless severe injury is caused to a domestic industry, the burden of proof is put on the domestic company: first, it must show that dumping is taking place, and then that it has caused severe injury. The procedure is costly and time consuming, and the penalty is not retroactive to the time dumping first occurred, but only to when it is first officially investigated. The result is that dumping is not inhibited. The penalties are seen merely as a cost of doing business. The case of pagers is a concrete example.

The Nippon Telegraph and Telephone monopoly was the only buyer of pagers in Japan in the early 1980s, dividing its procurement between six suppliers, including Matsushita and Motorola. Procurement was not on the basis of an open bidding system. Instead, NTT established a price that in this case was higher than the one Motorola was prepared to bid. So although Motorola was in the Japanese market, it was prevented from aggressively attacking Matsushita because of NTT's policies. Matsushita could, however, attack Motorola in the United States: it slightly altered the pager it sold to NTT, and began selling it in the U.S. market at about half of Motorola's price, which was a fraction of the price to NTT. Although Matsushita was later found to be dumping, as a business decision the strategy made sense.

Before proceeding, Matsushita's thinking might have been as follows:

> Motorola needs to be disciplined for its high-handed attitude in demanding a share of NTT's business. It can't attack us here in Japan. If we attack in the United States, Motorola might not respond. If it doesn't, we'll take the American market, which is

much bigger than the Japanese market. Once we've driven them out, we can raise our prices. In the meantime, the extra volume will drive our costs down, so that eventually we may actually be able to make money at the ridiculous prices we're contemplating. If Motorola responds by cutting its prices, its cash flow will be reduced and its ability to spend on research and development to stay in the game in succeeding rounds will be impaired. Sure, these prices don't help our cash flow either, but initially we'll be selling only a few pagers, while Motorola will have to reduce its prices on an enormous volume of products. Their loss will be great, while ours will be relatively small. Our volume will be growing, thus reducing our costs and raising theirs.

Motorola might initiate an antidumping case but, if so, it will cost them more money and will take more than a year to complete. In that time, we can take a large share of the market, if not the whole market. If we lose the case, the worst that can happen is that we have to raise our prices and post a bond for the dumping duty, which won't be collected because we will have raised our prices. Since we will have gotten a large share of the market in the meantime, we won't be unhappy about raising prices. That will allow us finally to make some money. Even better, we can use the case as an excuse to tell our customers how sorry we are to increase our prices, but the U.S. government is making us do it.

But we might not lose the case. Certainly MITI's offices in New York and Washington will help us. We can call on high-ranking former U.S. officials to lobby for us. The Commerce Department and the U.S. trade representative will be against us, but some of the other agencies think the antidumping laws are protectionist and will oppose any action. In addition, the State Department will want to avoid any friction, and the National Security Council and the Defense Department won't want to endanger possible Japanese participation in the Strategic Defense Initiative over a minor trade dispute. In short, we have nothing to lose and everything to gain.

Aside from the statutes aimed at specific unfair subsidies and predatory pricing activities, there is section 301, the unfair trade law under which the semiconductor industry filed its petition. This law theoretically gives a president power to do almost anything he wants in response to acts of a foreign government that are "unreasonable, unwarranted, or unjustified," and that thereby burden U.S. commerce. Such legislation would appear to be a powerful club, but presidents agonize when they are asked to use it.

There are three major reasons for such reluctance. The first is that, since the statutes do not anticipate anything but a U.S. type of economy, they focus on the removal or alteration of specific current acts of a foreign government. The emphasis is on quantifiable, concrete actions or events that cause serious injury to U.S. interests and on activities that are obviously outside international law or practice. A series of coordinated policies executed over a lengthy period for the purpose of altering the entire international industrial environment is beyond the ken of the law. The theory on which the law is based never contemplated such a possibility.

The second difficulty follows from the first. Because the law assumes the essential righteousness of the Western economic model, it allows for dealing with deviations only in terms of fairness and unfairness. A situation that may be disadvantageous to Americans cannot be addressed except in strident, moralistic terms. To obtain relief, a petitioner must first prove that his foreign competitor is a liar and a cheat. Not surprisingly, when the competitor resides in a friendly foreign country, a president is typically reluctant to brand it because to do so may involve branding the company's government as well.

The third reason is national security policy and the U.S. view of commercial activity as divorced from and secondary to it. Whenever a trade petition comes before a president, it inevitably becomes mixed with all the other aspects of U.S. relations with the country in question. In the case of the Houdaille petition, action would have been seen as an insult by the Japanese. The President wanted Nakasone's support on defense and other projects such as the Strategic Defense Initiative. With the unstable situation in the Philippines, he wanted to be sure of the use of the military bases in Japan. As I have said, Americans are not schooled to think in terms of "economic security," as the Japanese have been. Against that background of concern, an American president almost inevitably finds trade issues less important.

A prime example of how the interplay of American trade theory, trade laws, and security concerns works to the disadvantage of American industry and ultimately of the American economy is that of commercial aircraft. Long the symbol of technological achievement, the American aircraft industry has dominated world markets and production more completely than any other. It is America's leading export industry as well as a generator of new technologies and highly paid jobs for skilled engineers and workers. There can be no doubt that dominance of the aircraft industry is a net plus for the American economy in addition to being important to national security. Nevertheless, the American position is eroding, not because others produce better or cheaper airplanes, but because of the American approach to trade.

America's leading producer, Boeing, is involved in a joint venture with several Japanese companies for development of the next-generation airliner. This was not Boeing's preferred scenario. It would have preferred to develop the plane itself while perhaps using the Japanese as subcontractors, but the current arrangement was agreed upon after the Ministry of International Trade and Industry offered a financial guarantee valued at between $1 billion and $2 billion.[16] This offer was not based on a sudden surge of philanthropic feeling, but was motivated by Japan's desire for technology transfer. Teams of Japanese engineers are now living at Boeing and learning every aspect of aircraft design, development, and marketing as part of Japan's long-term plan for aerospace development. The cooperation inevitably ties Boeing to more Japanese suppliers and displaces existing American ones. For example, since Boeing first started using Japanese contractors in the early 1960s, the percentage of a Boeing jet made in Japan has crept up from zero to 15 percent for the 767. In the next-generation 7J7, it will be 25 percent. Thus, not only is employment transferred to Japan, but so is technology development as well. As in the case of semiconductors, the United States faces the possibility of losing important skills.

I have had long discussions with Boeing executives who, though concerned about this trend, see no alternative. The reason is the European airbus. Heavily subsidized by the European governments, it is sold at very low prices in world markets. Although this is harmful to U.S. aircraft makers, the U.S. government has done little aside from registering ineffectual protests. Thus we have the ultimate irony of the Japanese government subsidizing an American industry upon which our own government has turned its back.

In 1986 and 1987, a large number of airbuses were sold by Airbus Industries to several U.S. airlines at prices that very likely constituted dumping. These sales reduced the numbers of American aircraft produced and thus raised the future costs of the U.S. aircraft manufacturers. This chain of events harmed the long-term trade prospects of the United States by making its largest exporter (the aircraft manufacturers) less competitive. It also meant that some workers who made around $15 per hour would have to find other jobs which probably would pay considerably less. This was so not because European workers were better, but because they received government help.

Yet, in the fall of 1985, when the President created the strike force to act against unfair trade, it declined to act against Airbus. Secretary of State Shultz usually did not attend the strike force meetings, but he did attend the one on the airbus in December 1985. Any action against the airbus, he said, would upset our relations with the Europeans and most especially with the French. This would harm our national security and therefore should not be considered. The question of whether a healthy aircraft industry might also be important to national security was not addressed. There was the implicit assumption that the American industry will always be dominant because it always has been.

Beyond national security, it was also argued that the subsidized airbus planes were a good deal, a kind of gift, for the American airlines buying them. That the gift would contribute to a trade deficit, unemployment for skilled U.S. workers, and a weakening of the dollar, which makes all Americans poorer, was not discussed.

Finally, some officials argued that the aircraft companies are big boys and should file dumping cases if they believe they are being injured by the airbus. While apparently reasonable, this argument ignores the fact that American companies are often hostage to foreign governments. In this case, Boeing and McDonnell Douglas were selling airplanes to, and were engaged in joint ventures with, a number of European entities that were subject to government influence. If they complained openly about European industrial policies, they could be virtually sure of retaliation in other business areas. In lieu of a specific complaint, the United States government saw only the immediate interest of the consumer—an attitude not held in either Europe or Japan.

Thus, in the name of the consumer and national security, the United States created an environment inimical to the interest of its own industries. Ironically, this environment increased its military dependence on foreign suppliers who were less focused on the consumer and did believe in strategic industries. Thus, America's obsession with consumer welfare and the narrow questions of immediate national security served to undermine its long-term national security interests.


## Economic versus National Security


The growing dependence on foreign suppliers led to the sequel to the Houdaille case. While the economic doctrine of the United States does not assign greater significance to one industry over another, its military doctrine does. The continued existence in the United States of certain industries and technologies has long been deemed critical to America's military forces. In particular, reliance on other countries for the most advanced technologies has always been thought to be desirable. That the consequences of pure free-trade doctrine might conflict with the exigencies of military requirements has long been recognized. Thus section 232 of U.S. trade law provides that a president may extend protection to critical industries if their ability to supply national defense needs is likely to be impaired by imports.

## REVISITING THE MACHINE TOOL ISSUE

It was under this clause that, in March 1983, the National Machine Tool Builder's Association, following Houdaille, petitioned the secretary of commerce for protection from Japanese imports. Noting the reluctance of Congress to allow the United States to become dependent on foreign tools, the industry said that it was operating at only 40 percent of capacity and that Japanese imports held 30 percent of the overall market and about 50 percent of the market for the most sophisticated numerically controlled tools.[17] The petition concluded that only drastic action could preserve more than a remnant of the industry. Thus, forty-three years after the U.S. embargo on machine tool exports to Japan that preceded Pearl Harbor, the U.S. industry questioned its own ability to fulfill military requirements as the nation became dependent on Japan.

The Commerce Department launched a year-long interagency investigation. The required form of these investigations is bizarre but important. The question of whether an industry can adequately supply defense needs is asked only in the narrow context of wartime production capability: that is, not whether an industry will be able to continue to invest in research and development and modern equipment so as to keep the nation's defense industry at the cutting edge of technology, but rather whether, if there is a war tomorrow, the industry will have enough capacity to supply the Pentagon's needs.

The scenario that is chosen virtually determines the outcome of the investigation. The supposition of a small war obviously has different consequences than of a large war. Assumptions about allies and their likely capabilities are also crucial. The economists at the Council of Economic Advisers, the Office of Management and Budget, the Treasury Department, and the National Security Council knew before the investigation even started that they did not want to provide any relief to the machine tool industry. Thus the jockeying over determination of the proper scenario was intense. Ultimately, it was assumed that there would be a major war in Europe and a brushfire war in Latin America or Africa, but nothing in Asia. The latter point was critical, because an assumption of war in Asia would call into serious question the possibility of Japan's supplying large amounts of tools.

With the scenario established, the investigation began. It assumed that all the machine tools in the Pentagon's inventories would go into production, despite the fact that prior reports by the Army indicated that most of these tools are obsolete.[18] It was also assumed that many of the tools in use in private industry could be turned to wartime production, and that no additional tools would be required to meet civilian needs during the war. Even with all this, the report indicated insufficient supply potential.

The critical question thus became what levels of supply could be expected from Japan in the event of war. The answer rested on two judgments. Could Japan be relied upon as a supplier, even if intimidated by the Soviet Union? The State Department was responsible for answering that question, and its yes was a foregone conclusion. Then it was the Navy's turn. Could the Navy keep the seaplanes to Japan open under the scenario? No one was surprised when the Navy said yes.

Despite all this, the report the secretary of commerce sent for review to the National Security Council before it went to the President concluded that there were several sectors, including most numerically controlled machine tools, in which the President should provide some relief to the industry. The report led to an acute revelation of dichotomy in U.S. national security doctrine.

The National Security Council is interested primarily in political and military relationships. Aircraft carriers and the Soviets are the big leagues. Trade and industrial economics are strictly bush league. With regard to Japan, the priority is on maintaining harmonious relations in order to preserve U.S. use of Japan's military bases and Japan's support on broader political and military questions. In recent years, great emphasis has been placed on persuading Japan to increase its defense budget. The annual debate in Japan over whether it will be .90 percent or .99 percent of the gross national product is followed closely in Washington (the United States spends 7 percent), and all increases are causes for elaborate expressions of appreciation. Likewise, the United States was grateful when Japan announced it would defend the sealanes up to 1,000 miles from its shores. Beyond that, the United States counts on Japan's support in the United Nations and on its financial assistance to countries like the Philippines. Finally, the United States wanted Japanese participation in the Strategic Defense Initiative and in the proposed space station.

All of these were seen to be national security issues and of greater immediate importance than the condition of the U.S. machine tool industry. This perception, combined with the aversion to any trade restrictions, led the National Security Council to bottle up the report for months. During that time, the Japanese manufacturers increased their share of the numerically controlled tool markets to as much as 85 percent, while U.S. capabilities in key areas of technology withered.

The advent of the strike force in the fall of 1985 provided the mechanism for revisiting the machine tool issue. With the American industry rapidly dying, the Pentagon had begun to turn its attention from ensuring Japan's military cooperation, which had never been in question anyhow, to the defense consequences of nearly complete dependency on foreign machine tool suppliers. It began to share the concerns of the Commerce Department and joined in urging the National Security Council to pass to the President a recommendation for action.

Now a new debate arose. Having opposed any efforts to revitalize the U.S. industry in the past, when it might more easily have been done, many economists now argued that reliance on a technologically inferior, relatively high-cost U.S. industry would only harm user industries. It could also actually reduce American military capabilities. This was the end of a certain line of logic. Initially, it had been argued that the U.S. should do nothing to respond to foreign industrial policies aimed at achieving leadership in key industries. To do so, it was said, would be unwarranted interference in the free market which could actually deter the U.S. industry from becoming more competitive. National security concerns were dismissed as crass protectionism. Later, after the industrial policies had had their intended effect and U.S. industry had lost the lead, it was said that the United States should not respond lest national security be endangered by inefficient U.S. industry.

The President did not accept this logic. Ultimately, the National Security Council did pass the Commerce recommendation to him, and he directed that we negotiate a voluntary restraint agreement with Japan. But this was precisely what the Japanese had offered in 1983. It had been rejected then on the grounds that it would be protectionist. Now it was embraced on grounds that the continued health of the industry was critical to national security.

Eventually it was agreed that the Japanese share would be rolled back to the levels prevailing in 1983, or about 50 percent of the subject markets.[19] However, because many of the American companies had gone out of the business, more than a mere reduction of shipments from Japan would be needed to revive the industry. As with semiconductors, so with machine tools, a structural change was taking place. The status quo ante would not automatically obtain. Because America was not prepared to take the necessary steps to assure revival (that would constitute undesirable government intervention), one result was that Japanese companies moved more of their operations to the United States. While this was a positive step, there was no requirement that they transfer technology to the United States, and the Defense Department remained dependent on Japan for much innovative technology.

Here lay a massive contradiction. For fear of alienating a major ally, and in the name of a doctrine of free trade that did not accept the concepts of strategic industries, we had neglected to act in the Houdaille case. Now, in the name of the same national security, we were saying that there are strategic industries, and were offending our ally by effectively reversing an earlier decision in its favor. Moreover, by acting as we had in the beginning, we weakened our position in the end and became more dependent on others in an industry whose independence we had long ago asserted was fundamental to our national security. The disjuncture between economic doctrine and strategic doctrine led in effect to defeat for both.

The problem was an apparent dichotomy. Promoting or protecting particular strategic industries seemed to run counter to the larger requirements of an efficient economy as defined by prevailing economic theories. Thus it seemed that what might be necessary to maintain vital defense industries could be harmful to the overall economy and thereby in the long term, to defense.

The solution to the puzzle lies in the assumptions on which the economic theories rest. As the eminent economist Paul Krugman of MIT has pointed out, most of the assumptions are invalid.[20] The theories assume that markets are perfectly competitive, meaning that a single producer has no influence on overall levels of production or price. This is true of many agricultural commodities, but not of such things as automobiles or semiconductors or most other traded goods. It is further assumed that economies of scale (bigger plants yield lower costs), experience-curve phenomena (every doubling of production cuts costs 20 percent), and costs of entering or leaving an industry do not exist or are merely unimportant market imperfections. But the fact is that most business activity and most trade negotiations are concerned precisely with these factors. Dealing with them rather than with theoretical, perfectly competitive markets constitutes the main body of economic activity.

Once this is recognized, it becomes apparent that, as Krugman says, there may well be strategic sectors after all. Here the term *strategic* is used broadly to indicate that some industries may contribute more than others, in terms not just of national security but also of pure economic welfare. Thus some American economists have begun to recognize what the Japanese have known all along. This recognition resolves the paradox. If there are industry sectors that are strategic economically as well as militarily, then special promotion of them involves no agonizing choices between defense and economic requirements or between consumers and producers. The problem then becomes one of means rather than ends.

## THE BURDEN OF MILITARY SPENDING

In the little-noted talks on industrial policy following rejection of the Houdaille petition, the Japanese justified their policies of "economic security" by arguing that U.S. defense policies provide the same benefits to the United States—a view also widely accepted in some U.S. military and economic circles. In the later semiconductor debates, several high-ranking officials contended that defense drives technology; and, echoing the Japanese, that U.S. military expenditures are a subsidy that will ensure the U.S. its place as the technological and industrial leader. If, in spite of everything, the United States is not the leader, most observers concluded that inept American management could be the only reason.

There is truth in the "spin-off" concept. It is a fact that some military developments have led to commercially useful products. In a world of no response, this might ensure the technological lead of the United States. But Japan does respond. Whereas the United States does not integrate its economic and strategic doctrines, the Japanese do with their concept of economic security. While the United States is pleased if spin-off gives it certain industrial advantages, it does not aim for them. Indeed, it thinks to do so is wrong. The Japanese, however, see industrial capability as being as important a source of national strength as the Americans think military capability is, and thus focus on developing a friendly, risk-reducing environment for industry. Economic policy is developed to serve industrial ends. So, too, is defense policy, which sees expensive military coproduction as a further source of industrial strength.

The difference is subtle but powerful. Superficially both countries had seemed to take measures to promote their machine tool industries. But those of the Japanese were comprehensive and sustained, while those of the Americans were more narrowly focused and sporadic. Comparison of Japanese and U.S. programs in semiconductor research is also illustrative. In Japan, the Ministry of International Trade and Industry and Nippon Telegraph and Telephone selected several companies to work on government-backed research projects. The government funding was significant but not overwhelmingly large. In addition, however, NTT provided a steady source of procurement which resulted in large profits. The research themes chosen were all aimed specifically at ultimate development of commercially useful products. The companies chosen to participate were those that sold largely to consumer and commercial markets and had both the incentive and the marketing and sales capability to sell such products. These characteristics made it worthwhile for them to put up some of the development money themselves. The projects were organized to ensure the broadest possible dissemination of technology.

In contrast there was the Very High Speed Integrated Circuit project of the Pentagon aimed at developing advanced semiconductors. Some commercially oriented companies were chosen, but many were large defense contractors that had neither the incentive nor the capability to develop and sell commercial products. The research objectives were oriented toward specific defense needs that might or might not have any relevance to commercial activities. Indeed, in some cases, such as the requirement that the semiconductors be highly resistant to radiation, the defense needs conflicted with commercial requirements. Little effort was organized to disseminate whatever technology might result from the project for commercial use.

The interplay of the Japanese and the U.S. approaches inevitably has tended to give Japan the advantage in the development of commercially useful technology. Because the United States does not have an integrated approach or even any concern about it, the broad structure of industry in both countries is beginning to be determined by the Japanese, who do have an integrated approach and a great concern. The most dramatic example of how the two approaches differ and the consequences of the difference is in the area of military technology to Japan under coproduction arrangements. Little consideration is given to the effect of this transfer on the overall industrial strength of the United States. Yet, as the General Accounting Office noted in its report on coproduction mentioned earlier, in Japan the primary motivation is to use that technology to strengthen the overall industrial base. Over time, the result is inevitable.

Far from providing leadership, defense spending and production constitute a tremendous drag on U.S. industrial strength. Comparative statistics show the United States spending about 2.8 percent of gross national product on research and development—not much different from the 2.9 percent of countries like Japan and Germany.[21] In truth, however, about half of U.S. research and development is military.[22] As weapons become more esoteric, more and more of this research and development is insignificant from the commercial point of view. Thus, the United States is really spending relatively much less than its competitors on commercially useful research and development. Furthermore, it transfers military research and development that might have commercial uses to organizations in Japan that are much better organized to exploit it commercially than are U.S. defense contractors.

Likewise, defense procurement is a snare and a delusion. It certainly pumps a great deal of money into the economy, and makes the business of companies such as Lockheed, Rockwell, and General Dynamics handsome indeed. But it is largely nonproductive. The items most of those companies deliver to the Pentagon are expensive, quasi-custom-made machines that do not shore up the productive base of the economy. They do, however, soak up great numbers of the best scientists and engineers who might otherwise be more productively employed. Beyond this, for companies that are not major producers of defense materials, Pentagon business is not attractive. Unlike the case of the Japanese and Nippon Telegraph and Telephone, everything is done on bid and under intense public scrutiny. The companies cannot count on getting the business; and, when they do, it is not always terribly profitable. Robert Galvin pointed out to me that the business Motorola does with the U.S. government is on the whole less profitable than its nongovernment business.

Because neither our economists nor our military men see any strategic importance in the structure of the overall industrial establishment, we are building ever more islands of industry that exist strictly to supply the military. And the military market is not large enough to enable real experience-curve economies. For example, in the early 1960s, defense procurement accounted for well over half the market for semiconductors; in 1987, it constituted less than 10 percent of the market.[23] A manufacturer supplying only the Pentagon would not be selling enough quantity to achieve a competitive cost structure. Moreover, since procurement cycles are so long, weapons often do not embody the latest technology. A semiconductor supplier selling only to the Pentagon would not be making leading-edge chips. Thus, as Norman Augustine urged in the report of the Defense Science Board on semiconductors, in order to maintain a leading-edge capability that would serve the strategic interests of the nation, it is necessary to have a competitive commercial capability. Contrary to the accepted view that defense drives technology, the fact now is that civilian technology drives defense.

Having a leading commercial capability, however, will require a resolution of the contradiction between the economic and the national security imperatives. The United States will have to stop blaming its industrial decline on its "corporate" business and recognize the effect of the business environment and of the policies of other nations. If it proves unable to do that, the sheer mathematics are overwhelming. As Masahiro Sakamoto of Japan's International Trade Institute has noted, in 1983 the United States accounted for 40 percent of the total GNP of itself, Japan, West Germany, France and Great Britain, but carried 57 percent of the defense burden. For Japan, the figures were 14 percent and 3 percent.[24] The United States is spending roughly $300 billion a year on defense. Much of that money is thrown away from a productive point of view, and much of what is potentially useful is transferred to foreign entities better organized to use it. Japan spends one tenth as much, throws little away, and transfers little abroad. Under these circumstances, the continuing relative technological and industrial decline of the United States is inevitable; and in the process, its ability to defend both countries as well as to provide the productive economy necessary to ensure the welfare of its citizens and a stable world environment will greatly diminish.

# 9

# U.S. TRADE NEGOTIATIONS: THE PLAYERS

---

Why not the best?

—ELLIOT RICHARDSON, 1987

THE United States has tried to avoid facing the contradiction between its trade policies and security commitments on the one hand, and its declining economy, on the other, by negotiating over a series of trade problems. Reluctance to admit systemic weaknesses has led to treatment of the problems as unrelated; and despite repeated announcements of negotiating successes, the problems have multiplied in step with the country's accelerating decline, causing ever more frequent negotiations. When they began in the early 1960s, the talks concerned textiles, and the trade deficit was $1 billion. By the end of the Reagan years, the almost continuous talks concerned semiconductors, cars, and finance; and the deficit had soared to nearly $60 billion.[1]

# The U.S. Congress

## THE STRAUSS-USHIBA AGREEMENT (1978)

Congress is the central institution in negotiations between the United States and Japan. Were it not for Congress, it is unlikely that there would be any negotiations at all. All postwar U.S. administrations have been reluctant to press hard for U.S. commercial advantage and have hesitated to enforce U.S. trade law. As in the cases of semiconductors and machine tools, trade problems are always presented to the White House in the context of other seemingly more pressing problems. We want the Japanese to bear more responsibility for defending their sealanes. We want Japan to condemn the Soviets in Afghanistan. We want Japan's support in the Persian Gulf. Invariably, these national security issues are seen as far more important than a few dollars' worth of trade. Thus, denied significant assistance from the executive branch, those injured by important or unfair trade turn to Congress, which—because it cannot help by negotiating directly itself—usually responds to the complaints of its constituents in the only way it can: by introducing bills that threaten to impede the entry of foreign goods into the U.S. market.

The reigning administration normally responds by labeling such measures "protectionist" and hastening to negotiate, not primarily to solve the problems but to give an appearance of progress so that Congress, not really wanting to act beastly to U.S. trading partners, will find an excuse to keep from doing so. The subsequent bow to political reality involves some agreement that limits the growth of, but does not reduce, imports in the sensitive sector while attempting to demonstrate the advantages of free trade by trying to open Japan's markets to competitive U.S. goods. In this way, successive administrations have hoped to demonstrate to Congress that they are doing "something," and to Japan that they are not violating free-trade doctrine any more than political reality necessitates. The game is complex and is played at several levels: sometimes congressional threats are real; sometimes they are merely to frighten reluctant administrations into action; and sometimes an administration asks to be frightened so that it can then point to the danger of congressional action as a negotiating tool.

The pattern of negotiations attained classic form in the late 1970s during the Carter administration. As the trade deficit with Japan rose from $1.7 billion in 1975 to $11.6 in 1978,[2] Congress threatened retaliatory legislation, including an import surcharge on television sets to stop Japan's rout of the U.S. television industry. To forestall this legislation, which he called "protectionist," the U.S. trade representative Robert Strauss, a former chairman of the Democratic National Committee, who often said that while he knew nothing about trade he knew a lot about politics, negotiated agreements with Japan. The first in 1977 was a so-called orderly marketing arrangement under which Japan agreed to limit its TV shipments to the U.S. market. The other, concluded with Japan's ambassador Nobuhiko Ushiba, became known as the Strauss-Ushiba agreement. Under it Japan agreed to provide reciprocal access to its own markets while increasing its imports of manufactured goods and enlarging its strict agricultural quotas. Japan also made "emergency" imports of airplanes and strategic metals in order to dress up its immediate trade statistics, and agreed to stimulate its domestic economy to achieve GNP growth of 7 percent in order to become a locomotive of world economic growth by sucking in imports. In Tokyo, the U.S. ambassador, Mike Mansfield, hailed the agreement as the end of U.S. trade problems with

Japan; and in Washington, Strauss said there was no longer any need for legislation.[3] In response, Congress dropped its bills.

## THE AUTO AGREEMENT (1981)

This pattern repeated itself in early 1981. The flood of Japanese automobiles into the American market in 1979 and 1980, and the unemployment and financial losses it caused, led Congress to threaten a limitation on Japanese automobile imports. This led, in turn, to the first trade agreement of the Reagan administration and to further repetition of the pattern over the next seven years.

Actually, the agreement was a nonagreement. On 1 May 1981, in response to the congressional threat of quota legislation, Japan announced that it would voluntarily restrain its shipments of automobiles to the United States market for the next two years. Establishing the voluntary restraint was Amaya's last act before leaving the Ministry of International Trade and Industry. Indeed, it was later said that the conclusion of the agreement precipitated his departure because, by Japanese custom, as the leader he had to take the blame for an unpopular measure. For his efforts in the negotiation, he was described by some auto magnates in Tokyo as a "running dog" of the Americans. In fact, he deserved a medal for an outstanding act of industrial statesmanship in a drama that can only be compared to Grand Kabuki.

The Reagan administration was caught on the horns of a dilemma. An even stronger adherent of free trade than previous administrations, it did not want to violate its own doctrine with a protectionist quota at the very beginning of its term. At the same time, it faced the real possibility that Congress might override a veto. There was also the political factor of large numbers of unemployed auto workers, many of whom had voted Republican. A limitation of shipments by

Japan was desirable both politically, and, although not a major consideration, for the long-term viability of the U.S. industry. Thus, how to obtain such a limitation without imposing it or asking for it became the question of the hour— as Amaya knew (he was now vice minister for international affairs at MITI).

For him, the long-term position of the Japanese auto industry was the primary consideration, and in that interest he was prepared to be flexible regarding free-trade doctrine. If Congress were to impose quotas, it would determine how many cars Japan could sell in the U.S market, under what conditions, and for how long. Moreover, if the Americans were smart, they would impose tariffs and take for themselves the excess profits that would accrue as prices on Japanese cars rose in response to the limited supply. On the other hand, if Japan were voluntarily to limit the shipments, the amounts, duration, and conditions would all be subject to negotiation and thus be much more under Japan's control. Moreover, the benefit of the price increase would accrue to Japan, which would also acquire a lever—namely, the possibility of dropping the restraint in future negotiation with the United States. Finally, MITI would administer the program, and its authority would be enhanced as it defended the national interest.

An intricate minuet ensued. Knowing that the administration wanted a restraint but was reluctant for doctrinal reasons to ask, MITI noted that voluntary restraints had been used in the past. The administration let it be known, in early 1981, that it would not object if Japan proposed such a measure now. Japan began to suggest possible figures for the level of restraint. Eventually, a deal was made for a quota of 1.67 million cars per year. Japan, with its pragmatic approach to free trade, kept the initiative and the money; and the United States was able to maintain the fiction of being a free-trader without having to be one. The irony was that maintenance of the fiction depended on a Japanese industrial policy and on a MITI authority which the United States alternately objected to and denied. The U.S. government could not tell companies how many cars to import or export, and had always said MITI should not or did not have that power either. But now that was precisely the authority that the United States government relied upon to save it from a painful dilemma.

As in past cases, the uproar in Congress in 1981 was only partly due to the impact of imports. It was also part of a growing belief throughout the country that Japanese trade was unfair. Japan had never come close to the 7-percent growth promised by Strauss and Ushiba, many problems that had been reported as solved still were active, and bitterness toward Japan continued to grow as its markets remained impenetrable and complaints of unfair trade piled up in Washington. Like all administrations before it, the Reagan administration was concerned but adamantly opposed to any retaliatory action, and typically launched a major effort to mollify both Congress and the public by returning once again to the task of persuading Japan to open its markets. The first step was to develop an agenda.


## The Management of Trade in the United States


### THE OFFICE OF TRADE REPRESENTATIVE

The manner in which agenda for trade negotiations are developed is a result of this country's trade organization, which both reflects and creates its uncertainty on international economic issues. In principle, the Office of the U.S. Trade Representative is responsible for developing trade policy and for carrying on all trade negotiations. Organized as part of the executive office of the president, its approximately 150-member staff is charged with coordinating the other departments of the government to arrive at policies and negotiating positions. It also administers some, but not all, of the laws dealing with unfair trade.

This office was originally created in 1962 for the purpose of leading the U.S. effort in the Kennedy round of multilateral tariff-cutting negotiations that were aimed at further opening international markets. Tariffs were then thought to be the chief barriers to trade, and the idea was to reduce them on an overall reciprocal basis. In lieu of a policy to promote key industries through exporting, U.S. tariff-cutting strategy became a matter of balancing competing interest. Should we give up something on baseballs in order to get something on beef, and, of course, the everpresent foreign policy concerns had to be weighed.

The Office of the U.S. Trade Representative was thus created to be the coordinator, to be a lean and mean élite unit that would cut across the government and respond quickly to the needs of U.S. commercial interests. While there is much to be said for this kind of organization for multilateral tariff negotiations, such negotiations have by now been largely completed. Today most negotiations no longer involve horse trading over tariffs and are no longer multilateral. As a result, the implicit weakness of the coordinating concept has become increasingly evident.

The trade representative coordinates by chairing a series of interdepartmental committees, culminating in a cabinet-level committee that passes recommendations to the president. The concern for ensuring that all possible interests are considered in making any trade policy means that virtually every agency of the government sits on these committees. This procedure puts strong emphasis on consensus. Unanimity is not required, but major efforts are made to accommodate dissenting agencies. The inevitable result is that trade policy proposals tend to be watered down because most of the departments involved have their primary interest outside of trade.

The contrast with other policy areas is stark. For example, the Treasury Department is the sole determinant and negotiator of U.S. international financial policies. Although the exchange rate is one of the most important influences on U.S. trade, no representatives of the departments of Commerce or Agriculture, or the Office of the U.S. Trade Representative attend those negotiations. Moreover, when the president holds economic summit meetings, the U.S. trade representative and the secretaries of commerce and agriculture do not attend. Rather, the president is accompanied by his secretary of state and his secretary of the treasury.

So also in matters of antitrust and national security. Coproduction arrangements have resulted in enormous technology transfers, but the U.S. Trade Representative has not been involved. Other national security policies have affected trade in innumerable ways, but the U.S. Trade Representative and the Commerce Department are not included in National Security Council deliberations. The fact that the only participants are those directly involved means that defense issues do not become cluttered with secondary concerns and are, in effect, elevated by being made exclusive. Implicit in the idea of trade policy as merely a matter of coordinating many bureaucratic interests is the belief that it is secondary. In effect, the agenda becomes a residual. Hence, U.S. trade policy seems always to result in calls for broad negotiations aimed at an undefined opening of foreign markets. That is the only action on which full agreement can be reached.

The development of a comprehensive trade policy agenda is made more difficult by the dispersion of authority over the various elements that would have to be contained in it. Thus, although the U.S. Trade Representative is responsible for developing trade policy, the Commerce Department is responsible for administering much of it. For example, anti-dumping and anti-subsidy laws, a much-used and potentially powerful tool of trade policy, give rise to some of the most important trade negotiations, as in the case of semiconductors. Because Commerce administers these laws, it often becomes the de facto negotiator as a result of its legal authority and expertise.

Commerce also staffs the commercial sections of U.S. embassies, licenses exports and high-technology goods, recommends to the president which industries should be protected for purposes of national security, and promotes U.S. exports. In effect, Commerce controls many of the tools a truly integrated trade strategy requires. But it does not have all the tools, for while it is supposed to promote U.S. exports, the Export-Import Bank, which provides financing for such exports, and the Overseas Private Investment Corporation, which insures investments, are separate entities. The Department of Agriculture has its own foreign service, and airline negotiations are handled by the departments of State and Transportation.

As a result, there is little real coordination. Individual negotiations and issues may be reviewed by all and sundry, but a truly comprehensive approach that brings to bear all the tools and bits of leverage of the U.S. government is simply impossible, because of the splintering of responsibility and the limited coordinator role of the U.S. Trade Representative. Instead, there are frequent turf battles as each agency tries to make its own trade policy. Enormous amounts of time and energy are consumed in maneuvering among the various agencies, which palpably affects negotiations. As noted in the case of semiconductors, some of the hesitation to support Baldrige's proposed dumping case arose out of the reluctance of officials at the Office of the U.S. Trade Representative to see Commerce play a larger role. Such fencing is unseemly and destructive—and also inevitable, under the circumstances.

This turf situation seriously weakens us in negotiations because the Japanese and others know they can play on the division between U.S. agencies to divide and conquer. An appeal to the State Department not to allow some pressing trade issue to rend the fabric of the overall relationship will always be met with sympathy. The ability to lead can effectively be denied to the trade representative by a clear demonstration, on the part of foreign governments, of a preference for dealing with the Commerce Department or vice versa. By dispersing authority, the United States creates many channels and thereby gives Japan the ability to pick the one it prefers. In their desire to lead, U.S. agencies may compete to retain the favor of the Japanese, each trying to be more reasonable than the other. A prime example was the case of Nippon Telegraph and Telephone discussed earlier. Under the so-called NTT agreement, NTT had theoretically opened its procurement to foreign bidders in 1981. By the time the agreement was up for renewal in 1983, however, little actual procurement had taken place— partly because of the normal time required to establish relations with new suppliers, but also partly because of continued resistance to such procurement (it was NTT's former chairman Tokuji Akikusa who said, in 1982, that the only things NTT could buy from abroad would be telephone poles and buckets and mops).[4] In negotiating renewal, the trade representative took a hard line and pressed for a concrete purchase target. To the amazement of many in Washington, the usually hawkish Commerce Department opposed this policy. But NTT was not surprised. It had carefully cultivated Commerce officials in an attempt to separate them from their brethren in the Trade Representative's Office.

While the Japanese also have turf battles—some on a far greater scale than ours owing to the greater power of their ministries—in most negotiations they are much more united than we, because of the greater scope of their ministries and the fact that for them there is no overriding national security concern. When we negotiate on an industrial matter, for example, the Japanese negotiator is not an interagency delegation but MITI, which unites under one roof the responsibilities we divide among Commerce, the trade representative, and other agencies. And whereas we treat trade as secondary to national security, for MITI trade is national security.

Thus the opportunity for us to divide and conquer is much less. For example, while I might negotiate on semiconductor issues for the U.S. side, NASA would handle talks on the space station, and the Pentagon would lead in talks on co-production or dual-use technology. But in Japan it was all MITI. Thus, in every case the Japanese negotiator had a broader view and access to more levers than the Americans.

Conflicts among U.S. agencies reflect the disarray of Congress and the confusion of U.S. thinking about trade. At least seven committees of Congress have some kind of trade oversight authority, and many others get into the act from time to time. Congress, lacking any concept of trade as part of an integrated economic policy aimed at ensuring long-term American prosperity and power, thus organizes itself to deal with the parts, not with the whole. One committee writes a law assigning responsibility for trade promotion to Commerce, while another gives trade policy authority to the U.S. Trade Representative. No effort is made to link the two.

Congress also constantly reaffirms the secondary status of trade. All of the unfair trade laws, which it is forever threatening to toughen, allow the president the discretion to ignore them if he determines that their application might harm the national security interests of the United States. Because almost anything can be so construed, this position virtually guarantees that the laws will rarely be applied. Thus does Congress ensure that successive administrations cannot and will not develop an agenda that responds satisfactorily to its demands that they do something about the trade problem.

CIVIL SERVANTS: THE MAKERS OF TRADE POLICY

Not only is the U.S. side bedeviled by division, it is also handicapped in the personnel department. While the Japanese mandarins are selected and operate as an élite corps of professionals, the U.S. team consists of a very different kind of official who prepares for the game in a very different way.

The difference was illustrated by a question posed to me in 1983. "What do you mean by administrative guidance?" asked a newly appointed assistant secretary of commerce who would be an important U.S. trade negotiator. I had been briefing him for most of the morning and it had been heavy going. A pleasant person who had had modest success on Wall Street, he had no international experience, little knowledge of trade, and none of Japan, our most important trading partner. Moreover, he told me he was really only stopping over at Commerce until something more interesting turned up at the Treasury. His powerful connections in the White House soon took him first to the Treasury and then to the White House as a trade expert. It was from that position that he was later to respond to the plea of the lobbyists for Japan's semiconductor industry by trying to order Commerce to withdraw the Federal Register notification of the U.S. dumping case of 256K RAMs.

Like the Japanese ministries, the departments of the U.S. government are all staffed by career civil servants. Unlike Japan, however, in the United States the top four levels of roughly three thousand positions tend to go to outsiders appointed because of their political connections to the president or his party. While theoretically this hallowed tradition allows the president to bring in talented individuals who will faithfully execute his policies, in practice the system has serious weaknesses with regard to international negotiations.

First, the average tenure of office is only about two years. Between 1981 and 1988, for example, the Commerce Department had four assistant secretaries for trade development. Because even a talented person needs some time to learn the ropes, this means that U.S. officials are always in training. Such a situation generally has obvious drawbacks, but it is particularly disadvantageous in international negotiations when there are professionals on the other side.

The implications for internal communication, esprit de corps, and coordination are also obvious. Even if they are geniuses, the men and women who come to these positions usually are strangers to each other. The splintering of authority that creates the conditions for turf battles tends to put them in situations of competition with the other departments of government; and as a result of the selection process, this competition is not usually leavened by long association or friendship. I have often seen officials of one department fail to brief those of another department, or leak stories to the press, or attempt to bar a talented official from another department from a delegation, all in an effort not to surpass opponents but to gain supremacy in the U.S. policy-making process. The tendency toward internal competition is exacerbated by the limited tenure of office. Officials, knowing they will be in positions only a short time, are understandably eager to obtain visibility quickly in order to enhance credentials for the switch in the near future to private industry or practice.

Institutional memory is another casualty. The Japanese have taken advantage of this weakness to sell U.S. negotiators the same horse many times over. They know that if an issue is drawn out long enough the U.S. players will change, allowing the Japanese to offer the old proposals once more. It was because of this lack of continuity that few on the U.S. side remembered that Strauss-Ushiba had already supposedly solved many of the problems still being discussed as late as 1988. Our agenda in Tokyo was new only to the U.S. negotiators.

The ignorance and divisions on the U.S. side give rise to one of the favorite tactics of the Japanese, which is to zero in immediately on a new official and try to isolate him from his more experienced colleagues and subordinates. In one major negotiation in which I was involved, the leader of the U.S. team had been on the job for only about two months. Formerly the head of a major corporation, he was completely unfamiliar with the issues and with the Japanese, but prided himself on his skills as a negotiator. Suddenly the head of the Japanese delegation, who had been negotiating on the problems before us for years, suggested that the room be cleared of everyone except the American leader, himself, and another Japanese official who was acting as the interpreter. The American accepted and put himself at a disadvantage in terms of knowledge of the issues, number of people, and language. The very fact of his success in another career would not let him admit that he was out of his depth here. Nothing concrete resulted from this incident, but the American had signaled to the Japanese that he was a prime candidate for future individual wooing. They were sure to begin telling him and others what a great negotiator he was, complimenting him on his amazing understanding of Japan.

Every American negotiator knows that the Japanese operate as a unit with a long memory, and that everything one says and does will be stored in that memory bank for possible use against one later. The American also knows that the constant turnover in personnel on the U.S. side leaves no memory bank, and that colleagues may just as readily desert one as support one. Thus, while the American has little to hope for or to fear from his or her own side, the reverse is not true—a situation that exerts a kind of subtle discipline on the U.S. negotiators and makes them more cautious.

Even with excellent appointees, the U.S. system has certain disadvantages, and all appointees are not excellent. Many are political operatives or donors whom the White House needs to reward for past services. Because of their political connections, they are often virtually unaccountable. Their lack of knowledge makes them insecure and suspicious of those who are knowledgeable in the field, most particularly the career civil servants for whom they can and often do make life miserable by dint of their control over performance evaluations. They tend to love sycophants. Most of all, they provide an embarrassing contrast to their Japanese counterparts in terms of both knowledge of the issues and commitment to a program.

The career civil servants are the unsung heroes of the trade negotiations. Some, like Maureen Smith, director of the Japan office of the Commerce Department, and Donald

Abelson of the Office of the U.S. Trade Representative, are the only sources of institutional memory. After nearly twenty years in government, they have participated in virtually every kind of trade negotiation. Others like them have worked long hours with great skill and devotion for small rewards. Unfortunately, however, the rapid turnover at the top of the departments means that the leaders have little time for the training and development of officials in the career service. Even the best appointees simply have no incentive to do so: after all, they must focus on what they are going to do when they leave government two years hence. The result of all these factors is that, in trade negotiations with Japan, the United States is outclassed. Its negotiators nearly always face a better-staffed, better-trained, and better-organized opponent. That they will not be successful is almost inevitable.

## PRESS AND PUBLIC RELATIONS

The skill differential is particularly evident and significant in the area of public relations. The presentation of their story through the press, lectures, and seminars is something to which the Japanese devote a great deal of effort. Most Japanese officials who deal with the United States are fluent in English; and some—such as the consul general in New York, Hidetoshi Ukawa—are colloquial in it. The Japanese assiduously follow all commentary on them in the U.S. press and often make rebuttals. Ukawa appeared with me on the television program *Adam Smith's Money World* in December 1985; and he and other Japanese diplomats are regular visitors on U.S. interview shows. In addition, they frequently lecture at American universities and participate in meetings attended by the American power élite. Indeed, in a real way the Japanese are part of this élite, wheeling and dealing in Washington just as domestic interest groups do. Thus in 1984 several

Japanese officials attended the U.S. political party conventions as observers.

Japan's ministries are also unrivaled in the energy and sophistication with which they support Japanese business overseas. The Japan External Trade Organization has large staffs in major cities throughout the world. In addition, Japanese consular and embassy officials are well attuned to the needs of its industrial establishment and are constantly on the lookout for useful information. One of the best examples of creative intelligence gathering came to light recently at the University of California in Berkeley, when several Japanese graduate students reported to Professor Chalmers Johnson that they had been asked by Japanese consular officials in San Francisco to provide reports on developments in biotechnology at the university.[5]

Japanese companies that become involved in legal scrapes in the United States can always count on assistance from Japanese government officials. Dumping complaints are usually brought by one private company against another. The United States government does not advise its companies in such circumstances, but the Japanese government does. In any dumping, patent infringement, or other trade case involving Japanese companies, MITI will coordinate the counterstrategy, including the selection and overall direction of appropriate lawyers and lobbyists. MITI's willingness to help encourages Japanese industry to keep it informed, which in turn becomes a subtle but important source of influence and power both domestically and vis-à-vis the generally less well informed American officials. That knowledge is power is much better understood by Japan's mandarins than by U.S. political appointees.

An endless stream of slick magazines and quasi-official periodicals is sent gratis to influential people in the U.S. Obviously well coordinated, they all seem to say the same things at the same time. Japanese corporations, which do not typically make donations to universities or charities in Japan, are encouraged to do so in the United States. Nearly every

U.S. university and think tank with even a small interest in Japan is a recipient of Japanese funds. The subtle effect of this practice is readily apparent: with a few exceptions, the research and publications of these institutions tend to avoid any criticism of Japan. On one occasion, I was even told by a senior official of a Washington think tank that it might avoid appointing critics of Japan to its staff in view of the source of its funds. This did not mean that their Japanese donors put any strings on their donations. I am sure they did not. Rather, it was a form of self-censorship, which, of course, was much better from the Japanese point of view.

Ivan Hall, veteran observer of Japan currently teaching at Keio University in Tokyo, refers to this phenomenon as an aspect of the "mutual understanding industry."[6] He notes that one of the enduring assumptions about the relationship between the United States and Japan is that the problems that characterize it are primarily due to U.S. ignorance of Japan. To change this assumption, both governments have funded and encouraged the development of a national net-work of Japan-America societies aimed at broadening under-standing of Japan in the United States. The result, says Hall, is a powerful lobby that includes a majority of the important commentators on both sides who have a vested interest in perpetuating the assumption. This works in Japan's interest because it spares Japan from having to deal with its own faults. Japan can blame everything on U.S. misunderstand-ing, and count on many well-placed Americans to agree while they smugly lament the woeful ignorance of their un-washed countrymen; by so doing, the latter claim to be among the "happy few" who are cognoscenti. It is in the interest of U.S. experts to do so because it creates well-funded employment.

The problem, as Hall says, is that there is nothing mutual about an understanding that consists primarily of explaining to Americans how misinformed and stupid they are. There are few America-Japan societies in Japan and hardly any

American studies programs in Japanese universities. In fact, it was long illegal for foreign professors to have full faculty status in Japan; though it has recently been made legal, most universities still put foreign professors on temporary contracts. In some cases, professors who had been teaching for more than ten years at a certain institution were told they would have to leave.[7]

The reason that those experts who wring their hands over U.S. ignorance do not stand up for American professors in Japan, or otherwise comment on Japanese misperceptions, was explained by Dr. Glen Fukushima of the Office of the U.S. Trade Representative in a speech to the American Chamber of Commerce in Tokyo in September 1985: "If you are a foreigner who is too critical of Japan, your sources of information, funding, or friends dry up."[8] Hall agrees: "Japan's groups with their all or nothing emotional bonding cannot accommodate dissent."[9] This became evident in the early winter of 1987 when the Dutch journalist Karel van Wolferen's mildly critical article "The Japan Problem" appeared in *Foreign Affairs*.[10] A twenty-year resident and observer of Japan, van Wolferen was subjected to a broadside of personal criticism from the leading political and media figures in Japan as his article became the focus of discussion on prime-time television. By way of contrast, it was just a little after this, in the summer of 1987, that the dean of a leading American graduate school told an audience at International University in Niigata that a major source of the trade problem is Commerce Department bureaucrats who are interested in using the issue to further their careers.[11]

The effort to maintain a favorable image also extends to monitoring the statements of U.S. officials. No matter when or where I gave a speech during my tenure at the Commerce Department, I could count on hearing some comment about it from the Japanese embassy. They would praise me when I said nice things or voice disappointment when I was critical. There was nothing wrong with their doing so, and at least I knew they were interested, but it was also a subtle kind of pressure aimed at encouraging me to be as favorable as possible in my public utterances.*

A more unpleasant aspect of this situation is the tendency of the Japanese, because of their emphasis on personal relations, to create heroes and villains. The discussion of trade issues in Japan is always personalized. If there is a problem, Japanese officials tend to look for the U.S. official who they think is causing it. He or she soon acquires a "hawk" label and through the Japanese press becomes an instant villain to all of Japan.

I had a personal experience of this kind in the spring of 1982 when I accompanied Vice President George Bush on a Far Eastern visit. I had been interviewed by *Nihon Keizai* before leaving the United States. As I left Air Force Two at Tokyo's Haneda airport, a reporter snapped my picture, which appeared the next morning on the front page. Although the story purported to be a biographical sketch, most of the facts were incorrect, as was the conclusion that I was the culprit responsible for the trade tensions between Japan and the United States. Nevertheless, even today Japanese will often refer to that story upon being introduced to me. This is a difficulty that Japanese officials usually do not have to contend with in the United States.

U.S. negotiators simply cannot do the same things in reverse. Only about 10 percent of the U.S. embassy staff in Tokyo speaks any Japanese at all, and only one or two are truly fluent in it. The officers assigned to China or Russia must have language capability; but in Japan it can be an outright disadvantage because superiors who do not speak Japanese are sometimes uncomfortable with subordinates who do. As a result, U.S. officials do not appear on Japanese talk shows or at universities and usually cannot even speak to—

*An example of the lengths to which the Japanese sometimes go: Mike Benefiel is a mid-level Commerce Department official who is fluent in Japanese and lived there for ten years; on 10 October 1986, he gave a speech in Mississippi; the Japanese consul general who attended objected to his remarks and later wrote to the conference organizers, criticizing them for having had a speaker who was anti-Japan.

let alone, socialize with—Japan's power élite. Moreover, most U.S. officials don't even try to play the public relations game in Japan for fear of being accused of interfering in Japan's internal affairs. And in any case, Japan's society provides many fewer chances for foreigners to participate. U.S. groups discussing Japan always want to hear the Japanese view. This is less true in Japan. As a result, the U.S. story rarely gets told in Japan, and U.S. actions often seem irrational and even vindictive to the Japanese public.

## LOBBYING AND LOBBYISTS

Beyond attempting to create a favorable overall environment, the Japanese put great emphasis on directly influencing the U.S. government, and thus making an enormous effort at many levels. For example, in 1984 the Japanese government issued a study entitled *The Role of Congressional Staff in U.S. Policy Decision Making*, an analysis of the career patterns of more than thirty thousand congressional staffers and their role in policy making.[12] Later in 1986, U.S. officials discovered in MITI's budget proposal for the year an item for conducting a "grass roots campaign" in the United States apparently aimed at influencing members of Congress.

In addition, there are the efforts of private industry. Companies like Sony assign important executives to more or less full-time lobbying activities, while *Keidanren* (the federation of Japanese big business) is very active even at the state level. In the 1970s, many states, led by California, passed unitary tax bills that provided for taxing corporations operating in the state on their worldwide sales in an effort to prevent tax avoidance through intracompany pricing. *Keidanren*, encouraged by the U.S. government, sent wave upon wave of executives to lobby state legislatures and to threaten withholding of investment in their states if they did not change the law. Most of the laws were eventually repealed. Had U.S. businessmen tried the same in reverse they would have been roundly condemned for interfering in Japan's internal affairs.

The transparency of the American system facilitates this activity. The drafting of legislation and the internal debate and compromising that takes place in a closed process within the ministries in Japan takes place in full view in the Congress of the United States. Here testimony is taken in open session, and the final drafting or "mark up" of bills takes place in public. The Japanese are full players in this game because their companies in the United States are legally U.S. citizens. As a result, they are well informed in advance of likely developments in the United States and are thus able to organize opposition if necessary.

Furthermore, with the possible exception of the Israelis, the Japanese are unexcelled in the big leagues of classic high-roller Washington lobbying. A common step for high U.S. government officials is from government to a Washington law or lobbying firm. According to data released in 1985 by the Justice Department, 182 of these firms were then officially registered as working for Japanese interests and received a total of nearly $23 million for their efforts.[13] It is also estimated that there are about 200 unregistered lobbyists for the Japanese; and that total spending is in the neighborhood of $50 million, while some estimates go as high as $200 million.[14]

This money is used to retain a blue-ribbon list of former U.S. officials. During the textile wars of the late 1950s, the Japanese firms retained former presidential candidate Thomas Dewey to represent them. Since then, it has become common for Japanese interests to retain former high-ranking U.S. officials or their firms after they leave office. Some of the most prominent have included former Senator Edward Brooks, former Senate Foreign Relations Committee Chairman Frank Church, former C.I.A. Director William Colby, former National Security Advisor Richard Allen, former U.S. Trade Representative and Democratic Party Chairman Robert

Strauss, and former U.S. Trade Representative William Eberle. In addition, a large proportion of officials at the second and third levels in the U.S. trade agencies are eventually retained by Japanese interests. In fact, a corporate executive recently complained to me that it was difficult to find a law firm in Washington to represent his case because all the law firms were working for Japanese companies.

Some of the activity involved was illustrated in a *Washington Post* report, on 22 August 1987, that Frank Fahrenkopf, head of the Republican National Committee, was also representing Toyota in arranging meetings with top Commerce department officials.[15] But Japanese lobbying skill was most effectively demonstrated in 1987 when Congress threatened to bar imports of Toshiba products in retaliation for the shipment to Russia of the submarine propeller milling machines by one of its subsidiaries. Major customers were mobilized to testify on Toshiba's behalf, as well as thousands of its employees in the United States. At the same time, the list of lobbyists retained by Toshiba read like a who's who of Washington: James Jones, former assistant to President Lyndon Johnson and former congressman from Oklahoma; Michael Barnes, former Maryland congressman; William Walker, former deputy U.S. trade representative; and Leonard Garment, former White House counsel under President Nixon. In connection with related developments, Nippon Electric Company also retained Charles Manatt, former chairman of the Democratic National Committee; and the Japanese trading company C. Itoh retained Roderick Hills, former chairman of the Securities and Exchange Commission and a former boss of then national security adviser Frank Carlucci.[16]

Another example at about the same time was that of Global USA, Inc., a well-connected Washington lobbying firm. Global represents several major Japanese companies including Fanuc, Komatsu, and Kyocera.[17] In the summer of 1987, Global added a new client, the federation of Japanese construction companies, which comprised the *dango* preventing foreign bidding on most contracts for the new Osaka airport. The fee of $225,000 was twice the amount of the engineering consulting contract finally awarded to the Bechtel Corporation as a result of U.S. pressure.[18]

Sometimes, as in the Toshiba case, Japanese firms retain consultants independently, but often the Japanese government is involved. The Japanese embassy paid more than $200,000 to the firm of Gray & Company to handle public relations for the trip to the United States in 1985 of Susumu Nikaido, a key Japanese political leader.[19] One of the firm's vice presidents is Admiral Daniel Murphy, former chief of staff to Vice President George Bush. The semiconductor case was another example in which the Japanese government actually chose the lobbyists, although in this instance the semiconductor companies paid the bills.

Getting to the right person at the right time is the classic skill of the lobbyist—a skill that those representing the Japanese use often and well. For example, in the winter of 1986, the U.S. government prepared to retaliate against Japan's restrictions on imports of aluminum. On 26 February 1986, word was passed that the White House would approve an action recommendation. Last-minute lobbying removed the item from the agenda the next day.

Even more important than intervention, however, is analysis and anticipation. The splintering of authority in the United States means that decisions are made within a context of constantly shifting alliances among the various players. Knowing who is backing whom for what is critical information for purposes of devising counterstrategies, especially in gauging the true intent of Congress. Well-connected lobbyists and their own coordinating skills often give the Japanese a better picture of what is happening in the United States government than most U.S. participants have.

Another element is more subtle but very powerful. Because of their political activity and personal ties, the lobbyists often have better access to the White House and to important appointed officials than do subordinates in their own departments. Subordinates are thus often forced to cope with superiors who hold views that have already been influenced by lobbyists. In this indirect way, the Japanese are able to participate in the development of U.S. strategy.

The possibility of being retained by the Japanese in the future may also influence how officials deal with issues while in office. It is well known in Washington that working for the Japanese puts one on the path to riches. Throughout 1986 and 1987, one of the major issues in trade talks was opening Japan's market for automobile parts. Robert Watkins, deputy assistant secretary of commerce for automotive affairs, consistently argued against a firm U.S. approach. In October 1987, the *Washington Post* reported that Watkins had written a letter to Japan's automobile companies proposing that they hire him to represent them in Washington.[20] Although Watkins resigned from his high position as a result of this exposure, this is an example come to light of a game that is sometimes played far more subtly at even higher levels and for much higher stakes.

Congressional hearings provide another means of entry for the Japanese. Many experts who testify before Congress on proposed trade legislation are former trade officials or political operatives now retained by Japanese interests. Congress calls on them because of their previous positions and presumed expertise, but there is clearly the potential for their testimony to be influenced by existing client relationships. Further, because hearings are open, the Japanese can listen as U.S. strategy is discussed. In one recent hearing where I testified on how to handle an approaching negotiation, the head of the Japanese delegation was in the audience listening.

Appointments are also an area of possible subtle influence. The White House usually seeks advice from political operatives who are also lobbyists on appointments to key positions. Thus, in the case of trade appointments, the Japanese may, through their lobbyists, influence the choice of those with whom they will negotiate in the future. In addition, they may also be able to shape the agenda. The U.S. Trade

Representative is formally advised on his agenda and tactics by the Advisory Committee on Trade Negotiations, a group of representatives from private industry. Lobbyists for the Japanese have served on this committee.

Of course, U.S. companies have their own lobbyists, sometimes the same ones as the Japanese, who engage in the same efforts and use the same tactics, all in keeping with the hallowed tradition of U.S. interest-group politics. And the lobbyists are sometimes helpful in facilitating communication and enabling each side accurately to interpret the signals of the other. The inevitable question is whether there is anything wrong with lobbying for the Japanese.

It is a difficult question, and the answer depends on how the issue is perceived. A prominent lobbyist once explained to me that foreign interests have a right to their day in court and there is no doubt that this is true. On the other hand, a prominent Japanese businessman confided to me that Washington is just like Jakarta: "You just have to find out who to pay off." Whatever the rights or wrongs, there is no doubt that the interplay of the American and Japanese systems puts U.S. negotiators on the defensive. While the Japanese can penetrate the U.S. system, the reverse is much more difficult because former Japanese officials do not usually become lobbyists for foreign interests. They don't have to, because, as noted earlier, their ministries see to it that they are placed in a good position with a good salary. Thus the Japanese are participants in the American debate, but the Japanese debate is exclusive. The battle always takes place on American ground.

## Boundaries of Negotiation

At the center of the debate and jockeying are the more or less constant negotiations, which take place within the context of certain basic assumptions and attitudes. The fundamental viewpoint of the Japanese was described to me by a Japanese embassy official in the fall of 1985. The United States, he said, is like an old lion. It may be graying and losing its teeth, but it can still be dangerous. Therefore it is important to watch the lion carefully and avoid running in front of him when he is aroused. Thus the Japanese are constantly watching and probing and taking the temperature of the lion. In the course of a negotiating session he openly told the U.S. team that Japan would never allow its trade deficit to balloon as the United States had. The fact is that the Japanese cannot believe that the Americans can continue to live by an economic doctrine which, in Japanese eyes, has been close to disastrous for the United States. They, therefore, watch carefully for any signs of U.S. change. Finally, the Japanese view Americans with a certain incomprehension. As one embassy official told me, "There is no government in Washington; it is just a bunch of interests."

The basic view governing U.S. actions is that Japan is not only one of America's best friends, but that it shares U.S. thinking about economics and trade. The governing assumption of the U.S. side is that Japan shares its view of the world and of economics, and that the purpose of negotiation is to clear up misunderstandings while working toward common goals. However, this is not a unanimous view. The attitude and motives of the key U.S. players are as follows:

## CONGRESS

Congress wants to protect the interests of its constituents and desires that they be treated fairly in world trade. At the same time, it believes in free trade and fears being labeled protectionist. At bottom, it is afraid of its own strength and tends to accept any new trade agreement on even the start of negotiations as a reason not to act to defend U.S. commercial interests. The classic way to handle a congressional threat is to begin a negotiation and then argue that Congress should not act because doing so might harm the negotiation.

## U.S. TRADE REPRESENTATIVE

The Office of U.S. Trade Representative leads much of the actual negotiation. It tends to want to be tough in defense of U.S. commercial interests, but as a coordinator it must often mute its own beliefs in order to be the honest broker. Its staff does not believe Japan shares U.S. economic principles, but the Office is compelled by the ruling assumption to act as if it does. It is frequently in turf battles with other agencies and is handicapped by lack of staff support. While it supports free trade, it is not doctrinaire.

## COMMERCE DEPARTMENT

Commerce shares most of the view of the U.S. Trade Representative's office and, having no need to coordinate, is an even stronger champion of U.S. business interests. Also a nondoctrinaire supporter of free trade, Commerce is frequently involved in bureaucratic competition with the trade representative.

## STATE DEPARTMENT

State sees itself as the primary defender of the overall friendly relationship with Japan. It knows nothing of industry and little of economics and believes that these issues are secondary to political and military concerns. State thinks the trade problems are mostly the fault of the United States and particularly of lazy U.S. businessmen. It often works with the Japanese to "control the crazies" in the U.S. government (that is, Commerce, the U.S. Trade Representative and the Congress) and is sometimes a conduit of confidential information to Japan. It is a more or less doctrinaire supporter of free-trade theory and believes the United States must try to change Japanese thinking.

## U.S. EMBASSY, TOKYO

Run by the State Department, the U.S. embassy in Tokyo is even more supportive of Japanese positions than is the department. Because Japanese-language officers do not have a bright future in the foreign service, there are not many; and a large percentage of the embassy staff knows little of Japan. There is great emphasis on positive reporting. Officers who write cables at all critical of Japan often have difficulty getting them cleared by superiors and those who are constantly critical find themselves assigned elsewhere. Neither the ambassador nor most of his staff see penetration of the Japanese market as an important matter. For years as the trade deficit grew, the ambassador blocked assignment of extra commercial officers to Tokyo. The embassy always opposes any firm attitude toward Japan.

## NATIONAL SECURITY COUNCIL STAFF

The staff of the National Security Council is an outpost of the State Department in the White House on these issues.

## DEFENSE DEPARTMENT

The main concern of the schizophrenic Department of Defense is usually to maintain a harmonious military relationship, but increasingly it fears loss of U.S. technological leadership. The department is generally not pro-business.

## TREASURY DEPARTMENT

The Department of the Treasury tends to take a high theoretical approach to trade issues with Japan except where financial matters are concerned. Here it can be very tough in protecting U.S. banking interests, but generally prefers to negotiate over free-trade procedures.

## COUNCIL OF ECONOMIC ADVISERS

Totally doctrinaire on economics, the Council of Economic Advisers always wants to negotiate for free trade, but is never prepared to react when it cannot be obtained.

## AGRICULTURE DEPARTMENT

The closest thing to an American MITI, the Department of Agriculture has a comprehensive agricultural policy as MITI has an industrial policy, and is aggressive in defending the interests of U.S. farmers. It is not at all theoretical about economics. Its strength causes U.S. negotiators to overemphasize minor farm issues.

## CENTRAL INTELLIGENCE AGENCY

Of all the agencies in Washington, the Central Intelligence Agency had perhaps the clearest, most comprehensive view of Japan. Its analyses and forecasts were usually borne out by events. It did not believe that Japan shared U.S. economic views, and foresaw that neither devaluation of the dollar nor stimulation of Japan's economy would resolve U.S.-Japan trade problems. It particularly feared growing U.S. technological dependence and urged vigorous support of U.S. industry. Its reports were largely ignored. Often a new study of a subject already thoroughly covered would be requested of the C.I.A. by State or the National Security Council. This was seen as an effective delaying tactic.

# 10

# U.S. TRADE
# NEGOTIATIONS:
# AN INSIDER'S REPORT

---

Free trade is the hypocrisy of the export interest; the clever device of the climber who kicks the ladder away when he has attained the summit of greatness.
—CHARLES P. KINDLEBERGER, economist

THE first meeting of the Reagan administration to discuss options for opening the Japanese market was called in the fall of 1981 at the Office of the U.S. Trade Representative. I had just joined the administration as a trade negotiator, and this was my introduction to Washington.

## SETTING THE AGENDA IN WASHINGTON (1981)

The long list of attendees was already an omen of the likelihood of success, the size of a meeting in Washington being usually in inverse proportion to its importance. (When the subject is arms negotiations with the Soviets, only a few agencies are invited to attend; when the issue is trade with Japan, it is an open house.) Like most meetings of its kind, this one was called on short notice. I was to learn that this, as well as the fact that briefing papers were often not distributed until the meeting actually began, was the result not so much of poor management as of overwork. Contrary to popular belief, officials at the upper levels of the U.S. government carry a tremendous workload. Secretary of Commerce Baldrige once told me that being a corporate chief executive was a snap compared to being secretary of commerce. Because of the press of business, usually only an hour would be devoted to an issue before the next interdepartmental meeting on another topic began. Superficial discussion and superficial agendas were the result.

Although billed as a strategy session, this meeting at the Office of the U.S. Trade Representative on the Japan agenda produced little discussion of strategy and no comment on objectives. While it was understood that our objective was to open the Japanese market, we did not address what was meant by *open*, whether it was realistic to believe we could open the market, and whether if we got what we wanted, the trade deficit would decline. Even less consideration was given to the likely Japanese response to certain initiatives. And no consideration was given to the staple issue of all negotiations: how to use a judicious mixture of carrots and sticks to achieve the objective.

Of the two approaches discussed, one had been suggested by Etienne Davignon, the commissioner for trade of the European Economic Community (Common Market), during a recent trip to Tokyo, where he had called on the Japanese to establish an overall target for imports of manufactured goods. The motivation for his request lay in the fact that Japan's imports of manufactured goods were about the same as those of Switzerland, a country with about 5 percent of Japan's population.[1] In fact, Japan's manufactured goods industries showed a strange profile. Germany, for instance, was at once a large importer and an exporter of machine tools, automobiles, and other machinery, as were the other industrial countries, except Japan. Whenever Japan had a strong exporting industry, imports in that industry were likely to be close to zero.[2] Davignon had concluded this was because the structure of Japanese industry tended to reject imports. To correct Japan's surpluses, he therefore urged the structural solution of an import target.

Although some in our meeting suggested that the United States should join with the Europeans in this approach, the idea was quickly dismissed. The Council of Economic Advisers, the Office of Management and Budget, and the Treasury Department all said the proposal violated free-trade principles, while the State Department and National Security Council said that we should not risk harming our good relationship with Japan by "ganging up with the Europeans." The favored alternative was to attack specific, identifiable barriers to trade—on the assumption that if trade did not flow where Western theory said it should, there must be some identifiable hindrance that, if removed, would result in new sales.

There was no systematic analysis of which U.S. industries had the best opportunities in Japan or of which Japanese barriers were most significant in terms of potential U.S. sales. Each agency came to the meeting with a list of barriers that had come to its attention either through past negotiation or through the complaints of various companies and their lobbyists. These were now added to the agenda. It became clear that the Office of the U.S. Trade Representative was primarily a coordinator. Its limited staff and its need to obtain the cooperation of the other departments and agencies prevented it from doing more than superficial analytical work or from taking a position much different from the majority view. It thus had a great tendency to take whatever lists were available and run off to negotiate. A few examples will give the flavor of the agenda thus compiled:

1. Import Quotas. Because of the political power of its

farmers, Japan maintained twenty-two quotas on agricultural goods, such as rice, oranges, and beef, despite the fact that Japanese prices were five times higher than world levels and that the quotas had been illegal under international agreements for years.

2. Certification and Standards. It was lack of the proper safety certification seals that had kept U.S. baseball bats out of Japan, as noted earlier. Equipment shipped to Japan was often taken apart and reassembled before being given customs clearance because Japan did not accept U.S. safety standards or test data.

3. Tobacco Monopoly. As a result of high tariffs and distribution that was limited to 20,000 of 250,000 possible outlets, U.S companies had a market share of less than 2 percent. In the free market of Hong Kong, they had about 40 percent.

4. Restrictions of Lawyers. U.S. lawyers were virtually barred from Japan. For example, for a U.S. lawyer to meet in Japan with a client for whom he was doing work in the United States, he had to present an invitation from his client to obtain a visa.

The list went on. All were legitimate problems and worthy of attention, but few got to the heart of the real problem of penetrating the Japanese market or of dealing with the causes of the growing U.S. hostility toward Japan. Even as we debated, Japan's semiconductor industry was rapidly overtaking ours in the RAM market, and its paper industry had just formed an importer's association, which included most of its producers, for the purpose of "avoiding confusion in the marketplace" if imports should increase. A recession cartel was being considered for Japan's petrochemical industry and its government-funded research centers continued to postpone purchases of supercomputers until a Japanese model was available. Yet none of these issues was on the list, although they were more significant for U.S. exports and the health of U.S. industry than many items that were on the list.

As our delegation prepared to depart for Tokyo, it occurred to me suddenly that many of the items on our agenda had supposedly been resolved back in 1978 in the Strauss-Ushiba agreement.

## TALKS IN TOKYO (1981)

In addition to an inadequate agenda and splintered trade organization, the United States is also handicapped by the venue of most talks. About 80 percent of trade negotiations between the United States and Japan take place in Tokyo, partly because the Japanese know the value of the home field and partly because U.S. negotiators tend to equate movement with progress. The flight from Washington to Tokyo's Narita airport takes sixteen hours. Once there, the visitor finds that Japan's fabled long-range planning does not always work. The airfield is sixty miles from downtown. Depending on traffic, it can take from one and a half to three hours to get to a hotel and a much-needed bed.

On our mission to open the Japanese market in the fall of 1981, however, I learned that U.S. negotiators do not rest. I had just stepped into the shower when the phone rang. The Okura Hotel, which is where all U.S. negotiators stay in Tokyo, is thoughtful in this regard, providing a phone next to the shower. It was a MITI official inviting me to dinner. Brilliant, I thought, as I made an excuse. He knows I'm dog-tired, but he thinks maybe he can get me to accept so that he can ply me in a weakened state. Just then the phone rang again. It was the U.S. embassy, informing me there would be a delegation meeting in two hours. Apparently our leaders also preferred us in a weakened state.

U.S. trade negotiators are the last bastion of macho. Ready to travel anywhere at the drop of a hat, they neither slumber nor sleep. For a trip as long as the one to Tokyo, they are entitled to a rest day. To take it, however, would be the sure mark of a wimp. Late-night delegation meetings, followed by calls in the wee hours to Washington, become a syndrome. In time, I became convinced that one reason we tended to do poorly in negotiations was that we were always half asleep.

The leaders of a new delegation in town always begin their work with a courtesy call on the U.S. ambassador. Mike Mansfield had long been one of my political heroes. A legend in his own time, he has a reputation as an expert on the Far East, where he served with U.S. forces as a young man. From there he had gone on to be a coal miner, college professor, U.S. senator, Senate majority leader, and finally U.S. ambassador to Japan. Now, in about fifteen minutes, speaking without notes, the octogenarian ambassador summarized the situation concisely as we carefully listened for some guidance or strategic insight. Noting that the trade deficit of about $10 billion was too large, Mansfield nevertheless said that he was particularly worried about the noises from Congress. Although he had hailed the Strauss-Ushiba agreement as the final solution to the U.S.–Japan problem, he now urged us to understand that the Japanese needed more time to open their markets. We needed to be firm but not unreasonable, he said, and at all costs we had to stop any protectionist action by Congress, which he appeared to see as the real source of the problem.

With this statement, Mansfield, who is revered by the Japanese, put David MacDonald, the deputy U.S. trade representative who was leading our delegation, in a difficult position. Aside from the threat of Congress, he had no carrot with which to tempt and no stick with which to frighten the Japanese. His task was essentially to obtain trade concessions on the basis of his handshake and electric smile. Prior to coming to Japan, MacDonald had made a few firm statements both to reflect the strong feeling of Congress, to which he ultimately had to answer, and to give himself a little bargaining leverage. Now Mansfield was cautioning him to cool it a bit. MacDonald thanked the ambassador for his help, and we were left to catch the embassy van to the Kasumigaseki area of Tokyo where Japan's ministries are located.

After leaving the ambassador, we went to the Foreign Ministry, where we were greeted by the glare of television lights. In Tokyo, this would be the lead story on the television evening news. In Washington, it would not even appear in the newspapers.

Over the next five years, I would come to know our meeting room well. It has a side for visitors with one row of chairs at the table for principals and two rows of backup chairs for the rest of the delegation. We did not need them. Americans believe in being "lean and mean." We had only one backup for each of our nine principals. Not so the Japanese. The home-team side of the room was filled with at least 150 officials. The size of Japanese delegations became a joke among U.S. negotiators. But the laugh was really on us. Those backup officials would one day be sitting at the negotiating table. Now they were learning; and while they learned, they kept their principals supplied with every possible statistic and bit of information. On our side, few would even be in the government in three years, and because we were not concerned with quantifiable objectives, we had little need of data or of the people who gathered it.

The Japanese were always amazed by our lack of data and analysis. Once an official of the Economic Planning Agency asked how we created our agendas. His agency, he said, had carefully studied the competitiveness of various U.S. industries, and in his opinion there were much better issues for the U.S. to pursue than the ones on its list. I invited him to our next delegation meeting.

The magnitude of MacDonald's task became apparent soon after the meeting began. He opened with a speech that warned of a poisoning of relations between the United States and Japan unless the unfairness issue was resolved. Haggling over barriers one by one, he contended, was not a productive approach, and he called on the Japanese to take affirmative actions to ensure broader foreign participation in their economy. He emphasized that—regardless of the reasons for it—the fact that Japanese companies could buy seats on the New York Stock Exchange, acquire U.S. companies, and ship cars and other goods to the U.S. market without the necessity of customs inspections, while the reverse was not possible for U.S. companies in Japan, was bound to lead to trouble.

Of course, we immediately fell to haggling, spending the rest of the morning reading each side's talking points. In standard negotiating form, the Americans would read one of their issue papers, such as on the soda ash cartel, and ask for removal of the offending barriers (in this case, the cartel). The Japanese would respond by saying that the Americans were suffering from misperception. There was no cartel, they would insist, and blame the problem on the poor quality of U.S. ash and a lack of sales effort. This was not a negotiation. It was a ritual.

Although Japanese officials professed devotion to free trade and open markets, their style was to give as little as possible at the very last possible minute and then only under the maximum pressure. Although we were not asking for anything we hadn't already given them, it was clear that most of our requests struck directly at the power of the mandarins across the table, and they were not going to give it up for a theory called free trade. There was also a deeper issue, which I came to call the "black ship mentality." The Japanese press always casts its bureaucrats in the role of defending the sacred islands from invasion. Trade is seen both by the Japanese public and its officials as a zero-sum game;* and while the necessity of keeping the U.S. market open imposes on them the need to use the free-trade rhetoric of the West, no Japanese bureaucrat who values his reputation can think of making a concession until he has demonstrated publicly that there is absolutely no alternative. The ban on imports of bull semen is a good example. Potential imports could not have been more than $5 million; hardly anyone in Japan would have been affected. Nevertheless, we were read a treatise on

*In a zero-sum game, for one side to win, the other has to lose: a no-win option.

how Japan's entire livestock pool might be threatened by lifting the ban. The hierarchical dynamic of Japan creates great pressure to maintain everyone in his assigned place. The legitimacy of the élite derives from its ability to prevent disturbance in the structure. If it cannot do that, there is no need for an élite. Thus, it cannot accede to change except under duress. This characteristic creates a negotiating style that, after a time, itself became a major factor in the trade tensions. Japan always gave too little too late, and U.S. negotiators increasingly balked at engaging in the charade of mutual negotiations to open markets that the Japanese not only had no intention of opening but could not open even if they so desired. Economists and commentators on the outside often criticized the U.S. team for being too harsh. But when we added representatives from the President's Council of Economic Advisers to our team, they quickly became the toughest of the tough.

After a break for lunch, the afternoon session was a repeat of the morning ritual except that it was now the turn of the Japanese to voice their dissatisfactions with the United States. While this procedure—followed religiously in all such sessions—seemed to be only fair play (Americans are quick to accept any proposal in the name of fair play), in fact it was a clever maneuver that subtly changed the whole basis of the discussion. Japan already had an enormous trade surplus. The whole purpose of the talks was to open the Japanese market, not the U.S. market. In discussing trade barriers in the United States, we implicitly acquiesced in the impression that the two countries were equally difficult to penetrate. The purpose thus shifted from opening Japan to mutual opening, and the United States found itself on the defensive trying to explain why it did not import even more than it did so that its trade deficit could be larger.

A striking example in this session concerned a bid Fujitsu had lost to supply a large part of the new optical fiber trunk line AT&T was constructing between Washington and Boston. Fujitsu complained that even though it was the low bidder, it had lost because of political pressure to buy American. In fact, Fujitsu was essentially correct. Yet it seemed unreasonable that the United States should have to explain itself on the matter to a country that had systematically excluded American optical fiber makers from its market for years. It seemed even more unreasonable in view of the fact that Fujitsu had won other bids in the United States while no U.S. company had ever even been allowed to bid in Japan. I was assigned to respond, and Japan's explanations for why its markets are so difficult to penetrate provided me with a ready line. I pointed out that price is only one consideration; there are also quality, delivery, and service, which apparently AT&T thought could be better supplied by a domestic supplier.

These meetings always end with two separate press conferences, the reason for which became clear to me the next morning while reading the *Nihon Keizai* over breakfast. The paper reported that the United States had presented a number of demands that were based on misunderstandings; but that the Japanese had explained the true situation, and the Americans were now satisfied. This was the story the Japanese side wanted to present. It gave the Japanese public the impression that their mandarins had everything under control and were keeping the uninformed foreigners at bay.

I rushed to the U.S. embassy and asked whether the ambassador knew about the article and whether we were going to issue a counter statement. I was told that few embassy officials were aware of the story because it had not yet been translated. Further, I was advised that a counter statement was unlikely because this news item was standard operating procedure and there was little reason for concern. Over the years, I was to find that the Japanese nearly always had the upper hand in propaganda. Their ministry press clubs are a potent weapon.

DEVISING A U.S. STRATEGY (1982)

The question of what the United States wanted had been posed by the LDP leader Esaki when he presented his package of ninety-nine market-opening measures to Baldrige in January 1982 (see pages 187–92). In the spring of 1982, it was posed again within the U.S. administration. The trade deficit was continuing toward the stratosphere as the Japanese advanced rapidly in semiconductors, machine tools, and other high-technology industries. Congress was reacting by threatening to pass Senator John Danforth's reciprocity bill. Although all it really did was ask Japan to carry out the commitments of the Strauss-Ushiba agreement, this bill was tagged as "protectionist" because it provided for possible sanctions against Japanese imports if negotiations did not produce reciprocal treatment in a reasonable time.

In response, new Japan strategy sessions were called within the administration. Secretary of Commerce Baldrige and Undersecretary Olmer directed that the Commerce Department develop a comprehensive plan as an alternative to the old list of issues. This proposal, which focused on results, was based on the belief that some actual sales in Japan would do more to calm angry members of Congress than any ad hoc removal of barriers. It pointed out, as the European leader Davignon had done earlier, that Japan had built an exporting economy by consciously pursuing import-substitution policies (trying to replace imports with domestic goods) which had now become part of the fabric of its economy. The only way to obtain change was for Japan to begin consciously to restructure. It therefore argued that the United States should systematically analyze its industries to determine in which areas a negotiating success would have a significant impact.

The proposal also suggested a judicious use of carrot and stick, recommending that the administration stop urging Japan to act solely out of concern for congressional displeasure. The administration should express its own displeasure and indicate that it was prepared to act on its own, if necessary. Further, the proposal called for coordination of U.S. policy toward Japan: for example, that coproduction negotiations should be coordinated with trade negotiations, as should overtures from NASA to the Japanese for their participation in space projects; and that the involvement of Japanese scientists in research at the National Institutes of Health (there were then more than three hundred Japanese in residence)[3] should be reviewed in light of restrictions on U.S. companies participating in Japanese government research projects.

At this time, too, Baldrige wrote a long letter to the MITI minister Shintaro Abe, explaining in detail what he wanted. He emphasized that, while such steps as reduction of specific tariffs were always welcome, they were not the heart of the matter. The key, said Baldrige, is equal treatment: "We want you to give Americans the same opportunities we give Japanese."

There was no response to the letter, and at two cabinet-level meetings the response to the proposed strategy was negative. The Council of Economic Advisers and the Treasury said it violated free-trade principles, and the State Department said there could be no linkage of threats. Another factor at work was protection of turf. Such a coordinated strategy would impinge on the freedom of action of several departments. No one wanted to have his authority diminished. It was thus decided that the administration should fight the proposed reciprocity legislation while, in another round of negotiation, urging the Japanese to be more forthcoming. Thus, in March 1982, a few months after the declaration of victory by the Japanese electronics industry in the *Scientific American* (see chapter 2) and shortly before the filing of the Houdaille machine tool case (see chapter 8), we were on our way back to Tokyo for further discussion of beef, oranges, tobacco, lawyers, soda ash, and other items on a list that still did not focus on larger issues.

## GAINING LEVERAGE IN TOKYO (1982)

In Tokyo, we met again with Ambassador Mansfield before beginning talks at the Foreign Ministry. The threatening noises from Congress had become much louder as the deficit mounted sharply toward $16 billion and with the Esaki package's poor reception in Washington. The embassy was now well and truly worried. Its staff felt the atmosphere was overheating, and the ambassador urged us to cool the rhetoric and to work things out quietly. MacDonald again thanked him for his help, and we proceeded to repeat the old ritual which produced the old results. With no progress in sight, MacDonald used the only leverage he had: the threat that unless Japan made some concessions, Congress would pass protectionist legislation. This threat, the perennial club of all U.S. negotiators, had long ago lost credibility. But with no alternative, there was always the remote chance that Congress would actually do something.

It was a demeaning way to have to negotiate. MacDonald and other top officials were testifying in Washington against the proposed legislation. The President had said he would veto it. To persuade the Japanese to make concessions, we had to try to frighten them by suggesting that, despite our best efforts, we might not be able to restrain the Congress. Implicitly we were linking ourselves in common cause with the Japanese and creating a false sense that free-traders on both sides were fighting against the black hats in Congress. The negotiation thus changed direction: originally a matter of U.S. government requests, it became one of mutually calibrating just how much action would be necessary to keep Congress leashed. Instead of a negotiator, the U.S. trade team became an adviser to the government of Japan on how to handle the U.S. Congress.

This tendency reached a climax in the spring of 1987 when the U.S. trade representative openly orchestrated efforts by representatives of Japan and other foreign governments to lobby against trade legislation opposed by the administration. It had become so normal that no one lifted an eyebrow; yet no other government in the world would consider mobilizing foreign interests against its own legislature.

THE ISSUE OF BARRIERS

The reluctance of the U.S. government to take a firm stand and the difficulty of devising a comprehensive agenda were to some extent a reflection of an ambivalence with regard to the possible result. One of the enduring debates of the trade dispute between the United States and Japan has been what would happen if all barriers were lifted. The Japanese and most U.S. economists claimed very little. In 1981, when the deficit was in the range of $10 billion to $16 billion, it was commonly asserted by these experts that lifting all barriers would result only in an additional $1 billion to $2 billion of U.S. exports. In 1985, as the deficit soared and it was pointed out that lifting restrictions on tobacco sales alone would cover the $1-billion-to-$2-billion figure, the estimate was revised to $8 billion to $10 billion.[4] By then, however, the deficit was heading for $60 billion. Elaborate econometric manipulations, in studies often funded at least in part by Japanese interests, were used in an attempt to demonstrate that Japan's trade balance and pattern was just what anyone with a modicum of intelligence would expect it to be. The implication at all times was that trade barriers are not really important, and that the U.S. government is acting the bully in harassing Japan about them.

Our agenda both reflected and fed this argument. Because it was the easy thing to do and conformed to the classic model of Western economics, we focused on removing the traditional barriers of tariffs, quotas, and standards, rather than the effects of recession cartels, industry targeting, and the like. It was probably true that if we had gotten everything we asked for in terms of the lifting of traditional barriers, exports would have been increased by only a few billion dollars. But the real issue involved the assumptions behind the debate and the definition of *barrier*. In a brilliant piece of econometric analysis, Bela Balassa of Johns Hopkins University has found previous studies inadequate because they are based on faulty assumptions. His work established that Japan's trade pattern is atypical, skewed by structural factors and attitudes that act as barriers. For example, between 1975 and 1983, while the average import-penetration ratio for manufactured goods rose from 7 to 10.3 in the United States and from 24 percent to 35 percent in Germany and similarly in France and Italy, it rose only from 4.9 percent to 5.3 percent in Japan.[5]

Analyses by the Department of Commerce were not nearly as sophisticated as Balassa's work. Nevertheless, an internal estimate by Commerce done in 1982 when the deficit was approaching $19 billion, showed a potential for more than $20 billion of additional sales, assuming that U.S. products achieved a market share in Japan similar to what they had achieved in other major markets.[6] Soda ash provided a good example. There was no tariff or formal quota; as noted previously, an informal cartel operated to keep U.S. exports at 60,000 tons annually, until they surged in the wake of the orders that the cartel cease and desist. Nevertheless, the econometric models had assumed no barriers in soda ash and had explained lack of sales in terms of distance and other macroeconomic factors.

It is not entirely true to say that we overlooked the influence of nontraditional barriers in our negotiations. As already noted, one result of the Houdaille petition was a yearlong industrial policy dialogue in which we debated the effect of such barriers on trade. When it was over, the U.S. team wrote a report, yet to be published, that concluded that Japan's industrial policies and structures were indeed responsible for major impediments to imports. The logical inference to be made from this report was that our negotiating agenda would have to be drastically changed. However, the grip of conventional thinking was too strong. The real objective of most U.S. negotiators was not to get results but to mollify Congress by demonstrating action. Since they expected little, they were not prepared to use comprehensive, firm methods and, of course, obtained little.

## THE "FISH AND CHIPS" POLICY (1982)

As our talks in Tokyo continued, the potential of an approach that includes leverage was being demonstrated in the North Pacific, as was the inadequacy of the economic models. None of the models foresaw much potential for exports of U.S. fish to Japan. Then in the spring of 1982, the United States restricted Japan's fishing rights in Alaskan waters. Under the Fisheries Management Act of 1980, the United States allocates, on a quarterly basis, quotas for the catch of foreign fishermen in U.S. waters. In passing the act, Congress stated that its purpose was to build up the U.S. fishing fleet (our version of industrial policy). To accomplish this aim, the Commerce Department, which administers the program, followed what it called a policy of "fish and chips." It withheld the allocations for Japan until Japan agreed to buy a certain amount of fish from American boats. It thereby provided a guaranteed market and encouraged the Americans to take the risk of expanding their fleets. It was MITI come to American shores, and it worked. Each year, after arduous negotiation, Japan agreed to increase the amount of fish it bought from the Americans, and even agreed to import processed products from the United States.

The irony, of course, was that while the United States was using industrial policy to build its fishing fleet, it deemed such policies as inappropriate and ineffective for high-technology industries. Thus while the Japanese government actively promoted the semiconductor and other industries, the U.S. government literally went fishing.

## TRADE NEGOTIATIONS AND THE SUMMIT CONFERENCE (SUMMER 1982)

Of course, angling was only an avocation. Any larger lessons it offered were ignored in the spring of 1982 as both governments concentrated on cooperating to stop Danforth's reciprocity legislation in Congress. The prescience of Amaya now came into play. The Japanese believed that while the Americans spent all their time talking about open markets, what they really cared about was protecting ailing industries, such as the automobile industry. In March 1982, they announced the extension of the voluntary restraint on auto exports for another year at the same level as the past year. Had the U.S. side originally imposed the quota instead of suggesting and then accepting Japan's offer of the voluntary restraint agreement in 1981, the Japanese would not now have been able to use this announcement as a tool to relieve trade tension without granting an iota of increased access to their market.

Then, just before the summit of free-world leaders at Versailles in May 1982, a second package was presented. Again the numbers were impressive: there were tariff cuts on 198 industrial products and on 17 agricultural products. The cuts, announced in percentages, went up to 50 percent on some items. But the tariffs were already very low. No one would sell more of the affected products because of the reduced tariffs.[7] Fifty percent of nothing is still nothing.

Distribution of tobacco was also to be expanded from 20,000 outlets to 70,000, out of a possible 250,000. However, the prohibitive tariff remained. The aluminum baseball bat case was solved for the second time, and Japan repeated the commitment of the old Strauss-Ushiba agreement that foreign producers would be allowed to participate in standards-setting procedures. Finally, Japan agreed to support the U.S. administration in its call for a new multilateral round of negotiations to open international service industry markets, a major objective of the administration because of the strong belief that the future of the U.S. economy lay in the service industries.

This package was assessed by our trade negotiators as not responsive to U.S. requests because it ignored most of the key items on the American list. But there was a summit coming up and a protectionist Congress to be tamed. The Japanese representatives pointed out that even if we were not totally satisfied, we ought to express appreciation for the effort. Otherwise, they said, those who were trying to open the market in Japan would become discouraged and stop trying. This was a very shrewd move, for the Americans were asked not to bless the package, but only to thank the Japanese for trying. How could the U.S. side be so churlish as not to thank Japan for its effort? And yet, once you have thanked someone, it is difficult to criticize him. Moreover, it created the appearance of Japan's doing the United States a favor rather than merely fulfilling old obligations.

With the State Department and the National Security Council emphasizing the need for a harmonious summit, the decision was taken to go ahead with expressions of appreciation. Accordingly, Baldrige and Brock, trying not to gag, said that this package would be very helpful if implemented. It was light praise, but the reciprocity bills died in the summer as Congress heaved a sigh of relief.

THE RON–YASU RELATIONSHIP (1982–83)

Summits are always planned to leave a warm afterglow. Thus, trade tensions eased in the summer of 1982 in the wake of the Western leaders meeting at Versailles. By September, however, monthly trips by the negotiators to Tokyo were leading to a conviction that the implementation of which Brock and Baldrige had spoken was not taking place. In October, the U.S. trade representative delivered to Congress a comprehensive report that compiled Japan's trade barriers and that, for the first time in a U.S. government document, identified as potential barriers industrial policy and the *keiretsu* structure of Japanese industry. Pressure from Congress again began to build, and administration officials warned the Japanese that they might no longer be able to oppose restrictive legislation unless Japan further opened its markets.

At this juncture, in November 1982, Yasuhiro Nakasone became Japan's prime minister. One of his first acts was to visit the United States. When a head of government goes visiting, he takes a gift package along, and this trip was no exception. The new package, in response to the old U.S. list of requests, included more tariff cuts, promises further to streamline import procedures (by now they should have looked like bullet trains), and a commitment to change certain standards laws. It also solved the aluminum bat case for the third time. Again, though all were useful measures, none was likely to change the overall circumstances very much; and while they were being offered, Japan was preparing to renew its depressed industries law enabling legal cartels, had just told us that its companies could not buy American satellites, and maintained its rigid protection of agriculture. This was also the time of the first semiconductor agreement in which Japan could only agree to "seek to ensure" equal market opportunities.

President Reagan, however, took a liking to Nakasone, and what became known as the "Ron–Yasu relationship" was launched. A fundamental responsibility of any Japanese prime minister is to handle the Americans. That the Japanese thought Reagan and Nakasone were on a first-name basis was political gold for the latter. It also meant that the American side expressed appreciation for another package, and that criticism was muted.

After rejecting the Houdaille petition, partly in response to Nakasone's plea in April 1983, the President prepared to go to Japan in October. There ensued a battle for his ear. Brock and Baldrige wanted the President to press hard for resolution of trade problems, but they were opposed by the rest of the cabinet. Differences flared in the briefing of the President. Olmer noted that the deficit was now approaching $20 billion, and that Japan's refusal to buy U.S. satellites or to respond to other U.S. requests indicated the need for the

President to take a firm approach. Secretary of State Shultz objected. He argued that our overall relations with Japan had never been better, that Nakasone was the best hope we had in Japan, and that the President should nurture the relationship. That argument carried the day.

After arriving in Japan, the President received another package that streamlined import procedures one more time and cut more tariffs. (These packages always contained tariff cuts because tariffs were no longer significant barriers; they were thus a painless way to make the numbers look good.) In a carryover from the Carter era, the Japanese also reiterated their commitment to stimulate their economy, thereby trying to make it an engine of world growth. The automobile card was played again, as Japan indicated it would continue restraining exports for a fourth year; and finally, Japan indicated that it would begin gradually to open financial markets. It was also at this time that the second semiconductor agreement was hailed as the final solution for opening Japan's market.

In the interest of nurturing the Ron–Yasu tie, the package was also greeted enthusiastically by the United States government—despite the fact that, even as it was being delivered, legislation was being drafted in Japan that would virtually ban foreign companies from its telecommunications market and undermine the software advantage of American computer companies. After this, American trade policy came to be strongly influenced by how it would affect Nakasone. When he faced an election, a frequent occurrence in Japan, the word went out to U.S. trade officials to take it easy. On his side, Nakasone pressured and cajoled his bureaucracy to be more forthcoming and to develop more packages. Some observers on the U.S. side wondered whether he was as frustrated as they were.

## U.S. TASK FORCE (1983–84)

Upon his return from Japan in the fall of 1983, President Reagan directed Vice President Bush to follow up on the trade matters he had discussed with Nakasone. The vice president formed a special advisory task force, of which I was a member. The timing was fortunate. The steady presentation of market-opening packages by Japan had been accompanied by other major developments. It was in 1982 that the incident occurred in which Hitachi and Mitsubishi Electric were caught trying illegally to obtain proprietary IBM software. At about the same time, Fujitsu was also found to be infringing IBM's software copyrights.

This was a major blow to the Japanese computer industry and its sponsor, the Ministry of International Trade and Industry. The strategy of building hardware compatible to IBM's and trying to piggyback on its software had backfired, and the Japanese industry's boasts of being able to surpass the old nemesis, IBM, looked hollow. MITI responded immediately by drafting a bill to change Japan's copyright laws as they pertained to computer software. The existing law, administered by the Ministry of Education, provided protection for fifty years and included no registration or licensing requirements. MITI's proposed special new law would apply only to computer software (not to books and music) and would limit copyright protection to fifteen years, require registration, and provide for compulsory licensing at MITI's direction.

This was one of MITI's most sophisticated and daring industrial policy stratagems. The Japanese had equaled U.S. computer hardware, but they still lagged in software. In one fell swoop at virtually no cost, MITI's new bill would have made it possible to force U.S companies to license the software that gave them their edge. The move was so clever that many in the U.S. government totally missed its significance. They could not believe that Japan would declare war on the U.S. computer industry, and tried to ignore the move as an arcane matter for specialists. But eventually a U.S. embassy officer reported a conversation with the source who was also a highly placed MITI official at the time, on why MITI was making this move. He quoted the source as saying: "We don't believe our computer companies can catch up with IBM because the software disadvantage is too great." We will never know why he made this admission, contradicting as it did MITI's official line. In any case, it showed that nearly thirty years after the industrial structure council had targeted IBM, the drive to catch up persisted, and it moved the U.S. government to act.

Nor was the drive limited to computers. At the very same time, the bill to deregulate Japan's telecommunications industry and transform Nippon Telegraph and Telephone from a government monopoly into a private company was being prepared by the Ministry of Posts and Telecommunications. Through its Washington office, MPT had been dismayed to observe deregulation and the breakup of AT&T. How can the Americans willfully take measures bound to put them at a disadvantage in international trade? the MPT officials wondered. There was to be none of that for Japan. It was commonly acknowledged that the U.S. telecommunications industry was more advanced than Japan's, particularly in software-based areas such as value-added networks (airline reservations and credit-card verification systems are examples of VANs). To ensure that Japan's weakness would not result in domination of the market by the dreaded foreigners, the new draft bill provided that total foreign equity in any Japanese telecommunication enterprise could not exceed 20 percent. It further provided for strict licensing of VANs as a means of regulating who could enter the market.

Thus did Japan act to nullify U.S. advantages in what it had identified as two of the critical industries for the twenty-first century. These were steps of great importance. If Japan succeeded, it could well repeat in these fields the story of steel, automobiles, and consumer electronics. No one should have been surprised: MITI and MPT were only pursuing the goals and policies they had always pursued. But these measures were in addition to Japan's continued refusal to allow procurement of U.S. satellites, to its continued protection of agricultural markets such as beef and oranges, and to the continued lack of reciprocity in product certification and testing procedures. The gap between these acts and the words of the prime minister in his market-opening packages was a shock to official Washington, again disproving the contention that industrial policy no longer has significance in Japan.

These issues thus became the core of Vice President Bush's agenda. His mission was to end in May 1984 with a visit to Tokyo. Knowing the Japanese would desire such a trip as a sign of success, the task force agreed in December 1983 that unless satisfaction was gained on all the items on the agenda, the vice president would not indulge in a charade of success by traveling to Tokyo.

The task force got off to a slow start as the State Department and the U.S. Trade Representative's office, in response to the well-organized farm lobby, focused on beef and oranges which had a total trade value of less than $500 million. In response to requests for information on the status of the software and telecommunications bills, the Japanese government said that it could not discuss draft bills until they were submitted to the Diet—when of course their passage would be a foregone conclusion. Here was the great disadvantage of the United States. Under reverse circumstances, Japan would long since have known the contents of any similar U.S. bill and would have mobilized lobbyists against it. We, on the other hand, were becoming informed at the eleventh hour. While the bureaucracy stalled, I traveled to Tokyo in February 1984, and quickly concluded that both the software bill of MITI and the telecommunications bill of MPT were well on their way to becoming law. Both bills had strong support in industry and among leaders of the Liberal Democratic Party. If the United States did not act quickly, it would soon suffer major blows to its industrial leadership. But it was not yet too late because I found that the support was not unanimous. Because the Ministry of Education (MOE) administers the copyright laws, MITI's software bill infringed on its turf, not entirely pleasing MOE which was opposing MITI by developing its own bill.

The real battle, however, was between those old antagonists, MITI and MPT. For years, MITI had played *kentei* (clever younger brother) to MPT's *gukei* (foolish older brother). But communications technology had now given MPT a chance to avenge the humiliation. If MPT wrote the legislation governing telecommunications in a particular way, it could extend its administrative guidance authority into the whole information industry field. Conversely, if the telecommunications field were to become completely deregulated, MITI's existing authority over the information industries would allow it to expand its power into telecommunications transmission areas as well. The stage was thus set for a bruising battle between the two ministries as they continued their one-hundred-year-old struggle for domination over each other. With MITI supporting a completely open telecommunications market and MPT striving for maximum regulatory authority, each ministry turned for support to its political and business constituency.

MITI's strength is in the major electronics companies and industry associations, over which it has administrative authority. Usually nearly invincible, this base had a peculiar vulnerability in this case. Because Japanese technology was inferior to that of the United States, an unregulated, open market raised the possibility that IBM and AT&T would take large market shares. It was to co-opt the MITI base, by playing on this vulnerability, that MPT had introduced the 20-percent equity limitation on foreign participation in the telecommunications business. The maneuver succeeded to some extent, and MPT received much support from big business. MITI, however, was not without resources. Konaga, who had earlier explained industrial policy to us, had just been named vice minister because, some said, of his strong influence with key politicians. Both ministries also needed a public argument. That of MPT was national security. Through its press club, it raised the specter of the "black ships" and an invasion of foreign capital, with IBM and AT&T taking over Japan's entire telecommunications industry—or, as MPT said, the central nervous system of the country. MITI countered by pointing to the threat of a rise of U.S. protectionism if Japan closed its markets.

MOE is less of a powerhouse than the other two ministries, but Japan is signatory to two international copyright conventions which MITI's bill might have violated. In addition, the Commerce Department and the U.S. Trade Representative's office had by now aroused Congress, which was threatening to lift copyright protection in the U.S. market for Japanese software if the MITI bill passed. Thus MOE turned MITI's own argument against it by also pointing to the possibility of American protectionism. It must be emphasized that neither of the ministries was primarily concerned with U.S. views, but each tried to use them for its own purposes.

Out of this maneuvering came an invitation for me and other U.S. negotiators to testify before the LDP committee, chaired by Yoshiro Hayashi, on international economic problems. The request was the first of its kind. No foreigner had ever before given testimony in Japan's legislative process. I did not entirely understand what combination of interests lay behind the invitation, but it presented a rare opportunity for the United States to participate in the Japanese debate as the Japanese do in the United States.

Upon returning to Washington in mid-February, I was surprised to find opposition to accepting the invitation. The State Department feared that acceptance would constitute unwarranted meddling in Japan's internal affairs. More important, the U.S. Trade Representative's office objected, maintaining that we should wait to see whether the bills passed before responding and that we should rely on normal trade-negotiation channels. Passage of the bills would be a clear demonstration of Japanese protectionism and would enable the United States to strike back vigorously, it was argued. The controversy showed vividly how the turf battles that inevitably arose out of our fragmented trade organization truly threatened U.S. economic interests. Indeed, the whole episode demonstrated the chance nature of U.S. trade policy as well as the extremely uncertain environment in which the U.S. industry operates.

With legislation pending in Japan that could cripple two of America's most important industries, the U.S. government had become aware of the full danger only as a result of reporting from Tokyo by William Finan, the Commerce Department economist, who had earlier predicted the decline of U.S. high-technology industries and was now in Tokyo only by chance, Olmer and I having sent him to follow up on the second semiconductor agreement. The U.S. embassy had neglected to report on these developments earlier, out of either ignorance or a desire to avoid more trade friction. Now fully informed of the situation, the U.S. Trade Representative's office opposed accepting the Japanese invitation largely because it would enhance the Commerce Department's negotiating role (Commerce was also guilty of similar attitudes). Normally the trade representative's opposition would have prevailed, but Vice President Bush's assignment to follow up on the President's visit happened to coincide with the invitation. When informed by Commerce Secretary Baldrige, to whom he was close, that the bills in Japan would probably pass in some form disadvantageous to the United States unless we intervened directly and immediately, Bush directed Assistant Trade Representative James Murphy and me to go to Japan at once and do whatever was necessary to stop passage.

We began our mission the week of 6 March 1984 with a meeting at Keidanren (the federation of Japanese big business), which just the previous week had issued a ringing declaration in support of free trade by calling on Japan's leaders to abandon its protection of agriculture. We had asked for the meeting in the hope that we could elicit this same kind of support for free trade in value-added networks and other telecommunications businesses, as well as for strong copyrights for software.

The response was disappointing. Without dissent, Japanese business leaders told us that they could not support an open market in telecommunications services. The United States, they explained, had "giant sumo wrestler companies" like AT&T (then being dismantled) and IBM, while Japan had only small, "baby" companies. The "babies" cannot wrestle with the "giant sumo wrestlers," they argued. "First they need to grow up and then later we can open the market and they can wrestle." Their attitude was no different regarding software. Some spoke of the monopoly of IBM, then number two in Japan's market, and the desirability of bringing about more competition in the computer field. I was shocked. Japanese businessmen whose companies owed their prosperity and even their existence to the American market said nothing. Men who spent fortunes retaining lobbyists to prevent any restriction on their business in the United States, who inveighed regularly against the danger of U.S. protectionism, and who constantly criticized U.S. management for lack of effort, remained silent. Even worse, some of the most prominent actually directed their lobbyists to convince Washington that it had once again misunderstood.

With no support from Japan's free-traders, Murphy and I lobbied the key ministries and politicians ourselves. We met in the morning with officials at MOE to see how we could help each other, after which we met with MITI to oppose its bill and to discuss how we could jointly oppose the MPT bill. Later still, we visited MPT and did the reverse. We met with all the key politicians. I particularly remember our meeting with Shin Kanemaru, a major power behind the throne in Japanese politics and a member of the so-called telecom *zoku*, or "tribe" (a term the Japanese use to describe those who are knowledgeable and influential in an area). Kanemaru, a seventy-year-old Japanese version of the Godfather with a grizzled crew cut and large gnarled hands, was a key supporter of the MPT. While aides paid him respectful attention and young ladies scurried to serve the coffee, he listened quietly to our requests and assured us that he would see to it that everything would come out all right. All right for whom? I wondered, as I left his office in the Diet building.

The high point of the trip was the testimony we gave before Hayashi's subcommittee, which would have an important influence on the final decision to be made in the ruling Liberal Democratic Party. We urged the many Diet members and officials who attended to reject the MITI and MPT bills in the name of the free trade to which they constantly vowed devotion. They, in turn, expressed great concern for national security. Repeating the theme that telecommunications is the nervous system of the country, they asked if we really expected them to allow its potential domination by foreigners. We pointed out that telecommunications services are an open market in the United States, which is as concerned about national security as Japan. Again the monopoly power of IBM with regard to software was mentioned. It was clear that many Diet members had an obsessive fear of foreign capital, and that national security meant keeping big U.S. companies out of the market.

It was at this point that I realized how skewed the whole trade discussion is. The debate is always carried on in terms of the threat of rising protectionism in the United States. Yet the U.S. Congress, in its most protectionist moments, had never in recent memory considered anything as restrictive as the bills Japan was considering. Of the many U.S. congressmen and senators I knew personally who were constantly castigated as protectionists in the press, none had ever expressed chauvinistic sentiments as strong as those expressed in Japan during the last several days. The whole structure of the dialogue seemed to be based on the assumption that free trade means that the United States market should be open regardless of the situation elsewhere.

In our continuing campaign, Murphy and I tried to seize the initiative. In a first for U.S. officials, we challenged the ability of the Japanese ministries to mold public opinion through their influence on the press. We avoided press conferences but gave private exclusive interviews every day. Our objective was to try to have our story presented in some detail in a major paper each day.

It soon became clear that jurisdiction was MITI's main objective. It was willing to be flexible and could, it said, extend the term of protection from fifteen years to longer if that would satisfy us. MITI was prepared to make many concessions if we would agree to the idea of protecting software under a new kind of law that would give MITI jurisdiction. We resisted, knowing that once MITI had the turf it could always write another law or ordinance. Substantively, MITI's argument was that software is like any other mass-produced product and should therefore be protected under a law similar to patent law rather than copyright law, which covers books, music, and works of art. We argued instead that like a book or a musical score, software is a unique expression of ideas perfectly suited to copyright protection. The difference was critical. Patents are more difficult to obtain than copyrights because patents require a unique concept while copyrights require only unique expression, and MITI's law included compulsory licensing while copyright did not. Our support greatly strengthened the position of MOE, and the momentum turned against MITI.

Our negotiations with MPT centered on two provisions. We wanted complete removal of foreign equity restrictions on telecommunications services businesses as well as removal of the licensing requirement for entering the value-added network business. We feared the classical Japanese strategy of multilayered defense. Getting rid of the equity restriction was no use if entry into the market could be controlled via a discretionary licensing procedure administered by the very people who were proposing an equity restriction.

In early March 1984, we were invited to a secret meeting at the new Otani Hotel with one of the key politicians in the telecommunications reorganization. Enjoining strict secrecy,

Ryutaro Hashimoto, resplendent in a green leather suit, dramatically offered a compromise. It would be difficult, he said, but he thought he could guarantee to remove any equity restriction and to do away with the licensing procedure if we would agree to a registration system for one type of value-added network and a notification system for another. This was classic Japanese negotiation: give up the outer wall if the opponent will agree not to attack the inner one. We said we would gladly accept the removal of the equity restriction but would have to consult Washington on the registration idea because it appeared to be a licensing procedure by another name.

Both the software and the telecommunications issues hung in the balance for several weeks after our return to Washington. MITI marshaled its troops and launched an all-out effort to stop MPT at the last moment. MPT accused it of selling out to the Americans and of being agents of national dishonor. In Washington there was confusion. Registration "just for statistical purposes" did not sound so bad to some. Many did not understand that in the hands of a Japanese official any required documentation can become an excuse for giving guidance. In addition, the State Department was urging compromise. We had gotten rid of the equity restriction, and that sounded like success. Washington began to waver. As MITI felt its ally weakening, I began receiving frantic calls from high MITI officials, urging me to make the Americans stand their ground. Didn't U.S. officials understand, they asked, that the real control was the bureaucratic procedures and not the equity restriction?

At the same time, MITI was also making a last-ditch effort to save the software bill that our lobbying efforts, coupled with MOE's activities, had endangered. Ultimately, however, MITI was not able to get enough support and withdrew the bill. While this was good news, it was not a complete victory for the United States because, fearing our own lack of institutional memory and continuity, Murphy and I had insisted on a commitment that such a bill would not be introduced in the future—a commitment we did not get. MITI knew the advantage of being able to fight another day.

As attention shifted to telecommunications, the Japanese embassy in Washington got into the act. A key member of the vice president's staff said, in a conversation with the Japanese embassy's economic counselor, that the United States would not have a problem with registration, if that were indeed all it was. He made it clear that the United States would oppose any procedure that required permission to go into business, not understanding that in Japan registration usually means permission. The counselor's cable to Tokyo was leaked to the press just when the deliberations among the key politicians and officials were at their height. Was the foreign ministry teaming up with MPT against MITI? We will never know, but the leak broke the dam. It seemed to signal that the Americans would accept some restriction. My telephone rang all night with calls from MITI urging me to get a counter statement out of the U.S. government. Several key Japanese political figures called me to verify the American position. Along with several other U.S. officials, I insisted that the American position remained unchanged. But the damage was done. The bill went forward without equity restrictions but with registration and notification systems.

The negotiation was hailed as a victory in the United States, and Murphy and I were congratulated for our tactics. But on the evening of 4 April 1984, MPT held a victory party on the eleventh floor of its headquarters building next to the MITI building. It was not victory over the United States they were celebrating, however—that was incidental; the victory was over MITI.[8]

Two other events at this time had an important bearing on later ones. The agreement opening NTT's buying to foreign bidders was renewed, and Nakasone announced that Japanese defense spending might exceed 1 percent of GNP in the future. NTT illustrated the phenomenon of the long yes. Although it accepted foreign bids, its buying of imports remained at about 2 percent to 3 percent of its total. Both announcements were praised in Washington where the vice president was considering the results of his follow-up mission.

In late April, a meeting was held in the vice president's office to review the progress of his follow-up mission and to decide whether he should signal U.S. satisfaction with Japanese efforts by visiting Tokyo. Intensive debate ensued, with Commerce and the Trade Representative's Office, united again, saying no and pointing to the original decision not to go unless we got all of our requests. We felt we had only half a loaf on software and telecommunication. In addition, although Japan had agreed that private companies could buy U.S. satellites, government entities still could not. Some enlargement of the quotas on beef and oranges had been offered, but the amounts were small. The State Department, however, urged the necessity of the trip by arguing that we should not harm our overall relationship with Japan by being tough on trade.

We were at an impasse, as it appeared that those opposing the trip might be in the majority. Suddenly a key member of the National Security Council staff, who had carefully nurtured the "Ron–Yasu" relationship and would later become a high-ranking State Department official, slapped the arm of his chair. "We must have those bases. Now that's the bottom line," he insisted. He meant that with Viet Nam's Cam Ranh Bay in Soviet hands and the status of U.S. bases in the Philippines shaky, Japan offered the only secure bases for U.S. forces beyond Hawaii. No one knowledgeable about Japan believed for an instant that the Japanese would ask us to leave. But the NSC staffer raised the specter of the United States being driven back to Hawaii to override the trade-based objection to the trip. The majority swung behind him, and the vice president went to Tokyo in early May. The pressure had been relieved once again. In fairness, the vice president's mission had been more successful than others.

A NEW STRATEGY: MARKET-ORIENTED/SECTOR-SPECIFIC (1984–85)

By the end of 1984, however, the deficit was soaring to $34 billion, the agreement for Japan to transfer dual-use technology to the United States had not yet resulted in transfers, prices of semiconductors were beginning to nosedive, the necessary transmitting wave-length assignment for the satellite NTT had finally bought was being denied by MPT, and Congress was again threatening action. To head it off, Nakasone again asked for a meeting with the President, and it was set for Los Angeles on 2 January 1985. Preparation for it provided the occasion for the next round in the debate over process versus results.

The Commerce Department and the U.S. Trade Representative proposed that the President suggest that Nakasone develop a plan and set a target for imports. Their proposal was backed up by several arguments: We have been negotiating with Japan to open its markets since the days of Townsend Harris and have little to show for it. We cannot identify all the barriers in Japan and, if we could, we could not get them all removed. This whole negotiating process is destructive, driving us constantly to accuse the Japanese of being unfair. It corrodes the very relationship we have been trying to preserve by avoiding serious action on the trade problem. The Japanese really do not share our understanding of an open market, but they are the world's greatest planners and pragmatists. If instead of constantly threatening them with the wolf of Congress, we tell them that we, the administration, want something specific, we can negotiate concrete results. Moreover, we will have a better relationship.

This proposal was opposed by the other departments because it was said to violate free-trade principles. Through intensive negotiation, Treasury had just obtained a Japanese commitment to open financial markets. Not recognizing that Japan's financial industry wanted liberalization because it needed more places in which to invest the cash it was accumulating, Treasury attributed the agreement to its own negotiating style. It now proposed similar talks in other areas. The idea was to choose a few key industrial sectors in which the United States was competitive and to conduct intensive, high-level negotiations to remove every barrier in that industry, including *keiretsu* ties, recession cartels, and other industrial policies.

Commerce objected, pointing out that, in effect, we were proposing nothing short of a complete restructuring of Japanese society. We would not send missionaries of God to Japan, it said. Why should we send those of economics? But the other departments agreed with Treasury, and we settled on the Market Oriented Sector Specific (M.O.S.S.—"more of the same stuff"?) strategy. The President proposed, and Nakasone accepted, intensive talks in telecommunications, electronics, forest products, and medical equipment and pharmaceuticals. Undersecretary of Commerce Olmer was selected to head the telecommunications talks, and I became the day-to-day negotiator.

That telecommunications was again a major issue was evidence of the realization of earlier fears. By January 1985, it was clear that the registration and notification requirements of the new law were going to make the telecommunications services business a strictly controlled one. In addition, testing and certification of imported equipment was to be done by a new institute funded and staffed by the Japanese telecommunications equipment manufacturers which would refuse to accept foreign test data and retained elaborate technical requirements (such as voice-quality standards for telephones) that had been used in the past to keep foreign goods out. This meant that compared with the United States, which accepts foreign test data and allows any equipment that does not cause harm to the telecommunications network to be attached to it, the Japanese market would remain relatively closed despite our earlier declaration of success in opening it.

Our protestations on these points over the past six months had fallen on deaf ears, but the new M.O.S.S. talks gave us a way of attacking them. The first meetings took place in Tokyo in January 1985. Moriya Koyama, the vice minister of MPT and the lead negotiator for the Japanese, had first come to prominence in 1979 and 1980, when, as chief secretary, he had represented MPT in an inquiry into a smuggling incident by the head of Japan's International Telephone & Telegraph company. His noncommittal performance in press conferences had then earned him the nickname Endless Tape.[9] He was now placed in an even more difficult position as the full weight of the U.S. frustration with the trade deficit crashed down upon him.

Our objective was to obtain an environment similar to that in the United States with regard to telecommunications enterprises, equipment standards, and certification. The difficulty and emotion involved is best illustrated by three incidents. First, in a press interview, the MPT minister Megumu Sato warned that this was not the Occupation and that Japan is a sovereign nation that can determine its own policies.[10] The second incident was a discussion I had with a Diet member and later foreign minister, Tadashi Kuranari, a true friend of the United States. Noting that they treated U.S. and Japanese companies alike, he asked why Americans feared that Japanese bureaucrats might be unfair. He stressed that there was no discrimination. I agreed but noted that U.S. bureaucrats treat Japanese companies more liberally than do Japanese bureaucrats. National treatment can effectively be unfair if it is unbalanced.

The third incident involved voice-quality standards. The fact that Japan required them, as opposed to the "no harm to the network" standard of the United States, became one of the major sticking points in the negotiations. At one point, a high MPT official said, "If we got rid of the standards, our market might be flooded by cheap, poor-quality telephones from Korea and Singapore. People would blame us for the poor quality." I thought this was self-serving, but later the same day I asked the opinion of a longtime Japanese friend who had no connection to the issue. "Oh yes," he said, "we would not want the market flooded with low-quality telephones, even if they were inexpensive." He agreed that MPT had the responsibility to make decisions that in the United States would be left to the consumer. There was the whole trade problem in one sentence. The philosophies of the two countries regarding the relationships of citizens to government are simply entirely different.

Under enormous pressure, with the U.S. Senate voting 92 to 0 to demand an open market in Japan, Koyama eventually agreed to most of the U.S. requests, but not to changing the voice quality and other technical standards. Facing an angry Congress in late March, cabinet-level officials met to consider possible retaliation measures against Japan if it did not agree to a telecommunications market as open as that of the United States. The result of the meeting was a decision to send Gaston Sigur, a senior National Security Council staff member, and Lionel Olmer to Tokyo on an emergency presidential mission to confer with Nakasone, Sigur's longtime acquaintance.

Sigur and Olmer went to Tokyo over the weekend on a special air force jet. On Sunday, 31 March 1985, the world was treated to the spectacle of the Japanese prime minister meeting two senior representatives of the President of the United States on an urgent basis to discuss the voice quality of Japanese telephones. Nakasone gave them a commitment to review the matter over the next sixty days. Olmer and Sigur returned the next day to Washington and immediately released a statement saying the negotiations had been successful. Olmer told Congress that the Japanese market was as open as that of the United States, and Congress once again backed away from tough legislation.

Shortly afterward, it became apparent that Olmer's statement had been premature. It turned out that the requirements we had just negotiated away for other equipment still existed for radio equipment, which was governed by another law called the "radio wave law." So the talks started again. By January 1986, we had eventually negotiated all the procedures so that they more or less mirrored those of the United States. Now it was my turn to report progress in opening the Japanese market. I had mixed feelings. We had made a better effort than any U.S. negotiators before us. The Japanese market was more open than in the past, and U.S. companies were already making sales that would previously have been impossible. By concentrating on concrete goals, we had had a measure of success. But the market was not open as Americans understand the term, and it never would be. This was demonstrated over the next year as the foreign companies trying to enter Japanese paging, car-telephone, and international-cable businesses were directed by MPT to delay their applications while it attempted to create consortia of companies acceptable to it. Many in the United States saw this as unfair and not in accord with the agreements. But the problem was not one of ethics. It was rather that the Japanese were marching to a different drummer.

It was this march to a different drummer, and the U.S. failure to recognize it, that led to the criticism of Japan that came to be known as "Japan bashing." The constant repetition of the negotiating cycle with minimal results could lead only to frustration. Many supporters of Japan and of free trade saw the criticism as an attempt to make Japan a scapegoat for the failure of the United States. There was certainly some truth in this view, but there was a tendency on the part of those who took it to apply the pejorative "Japan basher" rather liberally to anyone who voiced dissatisfaction with Japanese policies. In time, the label became a demagogic tool. To label someone a "basher" was to discredit him or her and automatically to cut off discussion.

This situation was particularly pernicious for U.S. negotiators. The very nature of their task made it necessary to criticize Japanese policies and to threaten dire consequences, particularly because the U.S. approach called for negotiating over procedures rather than quantifiable goals, and rejected the idea of the use of leverage. U.S. negotiators were forced to talk loud precisely because they carried a small stick. They faced the alternative of doing their job and being labeled "Japan bashers" and "protectionists" for their trouble, or of merely going through the motions and collaborating with the Japanese in an effort to keep Congress quiet.

The irony was that it was precisely the procedural, issue-by-issue approach favored by those who saw themselves as friends of Japan that called forth the harsh criticism, as the problem continued to grow despite repeated solutions. The real friends of Japan were, in fact, those who attempted to attain concrete goals and who insisted on treating the Japanese as adults rather than as protégés. That this was not widely recognized doomed the two countries to repeating the process.

# PART IV

# *A Look toward the Future*

# 11

# WAKING UP

We're driving down a dark road with no headlights.
—MAKOTO UTSUMI, Ministry of Finance official

IF we become a kind of fourth-world country with all our assets owned abroad, won't our political, economic, and even leisure decisions tend to be made abroad? What are the hazards of becoming a colonial territory again? Or are we entering a new era of economics which tends to break down national boundaries, customs, and allegiances?

## The Situation Today

For more than forty years, a combination of complex dynamics has been leading both countries to ponder these questions (specifically posed by the writer Fletcher Knebel in the winter of 1987, in an interview in the *Washington Post*).[1] Under the leadership of its élite bureaucracy, Japan's homogeneous, group-oriented society has striven to improve its standard of living and to avoid dependence on or intrusion by outsiders. It has done so by rejecting Western assumptions and theories and by focusing all of its enormous energy on building an industrial structure with comparative advantage and bargaining power. This strategy, operating within an international environment of great advantage to Japan, has produced an industrial establishment of unparalleled efficiency which has conquered world markets but also engendered great resentment.

The success of Japan's machine has been greatly facilitated by the nature of U.S. society and the policies and responsibilities of its government. Because this country was built to assimilate outsiders, its society and its markets have been easy to penetrate. Secure in its postwar industrial superiority, the United States has undertaken to preserve the world from the Communist menace by providing defense and by trying to enrich those in its camp. It has run its economy primarily for the short-term benefit of the consumer and to stimulate the economic development of its allies with little heed for the relationship of economic power to national security. It has indulged in excessive consumption and paid little or no attention to the environment within which its businesses have to operate. When they have performed poorly, analysts have blamed management, while the government has pursued trade policies that have only worsened the environment, founded as they are on total misperceptions of the nature, the objectives, and the policies of Japan.

Because most economists and commentators have tended to blame America's decline almost entirely on the strong dollar and the enormous budget deficits of the Reagan years, it is important to re-emphasize here that by 1981—before the dollar was strong or the deficits had an effect on Japan—the result was clear. Not only did the Japanese electronics industry declare victory, but the Nikko Research Center issued a report stating that Japanese industries had overwhelmed most of their U.S. counterparts. It predicted that Japan would stage "a direct frontal challenge to compete with America" which would lead to further bilateral strains.[2]

While not the root cause of U.S. problems, the folly of the strong dollar and the budget deficits of the 1980s did greatly hasten the fulfillment of the Nikko prophecy. Within a few years, the United States lost positions of industrial and financial strength nurtured over the previous century.

As a result of the hollowing of its industry, the United States no longer makes hundreds of products, ranging from ceramic semiconductor packages to bicycle tires to VCRs. Consequently, even though in 1985 most economists predicted that the trade problem would resolve itself if the dollar fell from 240 yen to 200 yen, the actual fall to 125 yen, by the end of 1987, barely stabilized the deficit with Japan at $60 billion. It was not possible to buy American at any price. Moreover, the survival-minded Japanese companies have chosen to hang on to market share rather than raise prices in the U.S. market; and in Japan, the nearly 50-percent fall in the value of the dollar has led to only a 10–15-percent jump in imports from the United States. The composition of the trade has made the United States look ever more like a developing country. It imports high-technology goods and capital from Japan and, aside from airplanes and some mainframe computers and parts, exports to it mostly commodities, such as logs and soybeans, and unfinished manufactured goods.

The most recent example of the widening U.S. lag is high definition television, which uses twice the current number of lines to create a television picture with definition similar to that of a 35mm photo. High definition television is the next wave of television technology. While plans are already well advanced for its introduction in Europe and Japan by 1991, there is nothing beyond research activity in the U.S. The Europeans and Japanese are locked in a struggle over which will dictate the all-important definition of standards and protocols, for whoever does will have taken a long step toward dominating the industry. There are not even any Americans involved in this struggle. The United States is not present at the table of power.

The terms of trade have moved against the United States so that it has to export more cheap commodities just to continue to buy a fixed amount of goods it can no longer produce. Some commentators, such as James Fallows of the *Atlantic*, argue that it will not be possible to change the pattern while continuing to adhere to free-trade doctrine.[3]

Today, however, the trade question is no longer the main point. Clearly, there is some value of the dollar at which it will become prohibitive to buy any foreign goods. Already breakfast in a good hotel in Tokyo is going for $40.00, and Americans accustomed to going first class are looking for cheaper accommodations. Extreme devaluation could ultimately reverse the trade deficit, but by then the United States might be a very poor country. Bangladesh does not have a trade deficit either. The weak dollar, which was supposed to, but did not, make Japanese exports much more expensive, has made U.S. assets less so. With the great pile of dollars earned from their exports, the Japanese and others are now acquiring these assets at lightning speed. In 1986 alone, $6 billion of Japanese money went into U.S. real estate, including the Exxon, the ABC, and the Tiffany buildings in Manhattan.[4] By 1987, it was estimated that nearly half the office space in downtown Los Angeles was in Japanese hands, and it was predicted that Japan would be the dominant force in U.S. real estate in the future. Shigeru Kobayashi, the founder of the Shuwa Corporation, stated that "the United States has the charm [he meant inexpensiveness] of a developing country." In the same year, investment in American companies skyrocketed as $10 billion from Japan helped to power Wall Street and one investment bank after another announced it was selling part of itself to Japanese interests. (Of course few U.S. companies were able to buy into Japanese companies.) And this is just the beginning. *Nihon Keizai* predicted in 1987 that Japan's net foreign assets, which had been $11.5 billion in 1980 and $180 billion in 1986, would climb to $853 billion in 1995; and that most of that investment would come to the United States, which would go further into debt to the tune of $400 billion.[5]

## A COLONY-IN-THE-MAKING: THE UNITED STATES

Most analysts have seen the Japanese investment in positive terms, claiming that it will be like U.S. investment in Europe after the war and revitalize American industry. Others, like Knebel, have wondered. Living in Honolulu, he has observed that Japanese tourists arrive on Japan Airlines, take Japanese tour buses downtown to Japanese-owned hotels, and dine at Japanese-owned restaurants. In San Francisco, this practice is known as the "closed circle"; and local travel companies have brought suit on antitrust grounds.

In April 1987, the *Chicago Tribune* addressed the problem in a series of articles on Japanese investment in the United States.[6] The first article, focusing on the new Toyota plant in Georgetown, Kentucky, pointed out that the construction company building the plant was the Japanese Ohbayashi Gumi Corporation. The suppliers were also Japanese, mostly those that are part of Toyota's *keiretsu* in Japan. Nearby, Topy Industries planned to make wheels to supply the new factory, while Hitachi was also building a plant close by; and just down the road, Trinity (Japanese despite the name) was setting up its painting facility. Meanwhile, the financing was being done by the Mitsui Bank, which is affiliated with Toyota in the Mitsui Group.

According to the article, this pattern of vertical investment is being used to reinforce an already strong market position by transferring the domestic *keiretsu* system to the United States. It differs greatly from the pattern of U.S. investment in Europe or of European investment in the United States, whose purpose was to gain market entry by acquiring or developing local ties. In particular, U.S. investment tends to seek market entry through full-line manufacturing and substantial technology transfer, while Japanese investment has so far tended to be in assembly plants with key technology being held at home. Another key difference is the fact that between Europe and the United States, there has been a mutual investment flow; while with Japan, it is largely a one-way street. U.S. companies or real estate are sold to Japanese, but the opposite rarely occurs. And it is this nonreciprocation that is at the heart of the questions about Japanese investment.

The article concluded that Japan is building a separate economy in the United States, one that, in addition to its vertical nature, is characterized by a young, nonunion work force, generous subsidization by local and state governments that compete with one another to attract it, and use of the most modern plant and equipment, financed at very low rates by Japanese banks and state industrial revenue bonds. Thus, this new Japan–U.S. economy will have a potentially tremendous competitive advantage over the older U.S.–U.S. economy. Estimating that for each job created in a Japanese factory in the United States, more than two are lost at a competing U.S.-owned factory, the *Tribune* said that the benefits normally associated with investment might be more limited in the case of Japanese investment because of the tendency of the Japanese to run a closed system.

In addition to its vertical nature, Japanese investment is also characterized by a sense of national purpose and the coordination of views and investment plans—as was revealed in a meeting held at Keidanren in September 1986, which included Akio Morita of Sony, Hiroshi Kurosawa of the Industrial Bank of Japan, Masataku Okuma, president of Nissan Motors, and Takushin Yamamoto, the president of Fujitsu.[7] Convened for the purpose of discussing the form and extent of Japanese investment in the United States, the meeting was not at all sinister. Indeed, the concern of the participants for the health of the United States was touching, as was their sensitivity to the potential dangers of creating too large a Japanese presence too rapidly.

It was the implicit that was arresting. First, the fact of the meeting itself: no similar group of U.S. executives ever meets to consider investment strategy in Japan. Second was the complete confidence displayed in their own ability to surpass U.S. industry. It seemed completely natural to them that they should be meeting to discuss not if, but how they would expand in the U.S. market. Morita best summarized their view of the United States. Recounting that a U.S. banker had recently told him that there should be no concern over the transfer of U.S. manufacturing operations overseas, Morita predicted that the United States will no longer be an industrial country if it continues to think like that. Yamamoto emphasized that "U.S. companies have not been able to beat Japan up to now because they don't understand Japanese competition." Okuma agreed, but cautioned that "in the United States, we must avoid a bloodletting competition as in Japan." While suggesting that "the strong should walk on tiptoes," Yamamoto urged that a study be made on joint ventures in the United States.

The Ministry of International Trade and Industry was also considering these questions. A high-level official told me, in the fall of 1987, that several government-industry commissions were studying how to structure Japanese overseas investment. (The Japanese preoccupation with structure persists even when it concerns overseas industry.) As another MITI official told me, "We may take industrial policy to America." Again, nothing sinister was implied; but, clearly, the plans of the Japanese will be drawn with their own interests in mind. The men at MITI and Keidanren may walk on tiptoe, but they will not plan to stub their toes as they consider how to rebuild the United States. These discussions were further signs that the United States is rapidly passing economic hegemony to Japan. As it does, some analysts speak glibly of the negotiating leverage in the hands of the

United States because of the Japanese need for its market. But the American need for Japanese money is much more powerful. As *Business Week* noted, in its issue of 16 November 1987, the decline of America into debtor status may keep a lid on export growth even if the dollar continues to fall. It is difficult for Washington to pressure Japan while running cup in hand to Tokyo at each monthly bond auction. Said *Business Week*, "You don't argue much with your banker, especially if he is also your landlord and employer."[8]

The political effect is already dramatic. In a meeting I attended in early 1987 in Nashville, Tennessee, Governor Lamar Alexander said he had been to Tokyo more often than to Washington during the past four years: "That's where we can get some real help."[9] Later, Governor Martha Layne Collins of Kentucky said that during one of her trips to Japan, fourteen other governors had been there as well.[10] At the same time, Senator James Sasser of Tennessee pointed out that Nissan had supported his opponent in recent elections, warning that the Japanese can punish U.S. politicians who take positions the Japanese don't like.[11] The Republican leader in the House of Representatives, Robert Michel, noted that the Japanese and other foreign investors could get concessions that were unavailable to U.S. companies.[12] Also in early 1987, the economist C. Fred Bergsten summarized the situation (and seemed to answer Knebel's questions) by saying that the United States is indeed becoming vulnerable to Japanese decision making on both foreign policy as well as economic issues.[13]

The truth of this became more evident as the year progressed. In the summer of 1987, the Komori Printing Machinery Company approached AM International, Inc., with a joint venture proposal that would have given Komori control of AM's Harris Graphics Division.[14] AM declined the offer, but in the fall Komori returned with additional joint-venture proposals while informing AM that it, Komori, was accumulating AM stock and already owned nearly 7 percent of it. In November, AM announced that it would begin negotiating joint arrangements between Harris and Komori. There was speculation that use of such tactics by Japanese companies would increase in the future. At this same time there was much talk in Tokyo of the need to "talk back to America." One article said Japan must become more independent of the United States in order to do so.[15] In another, the Bank of Japan adviser Teruhiko Mano pointedly noted that, "if we wish, we can shift those assets into gold or other merchandise."[16]

This, the natural result of decline, would not be remarkable except that the United States continues to bear the heavy military responsibility of the traditional hegemonic power. This is surely the first time in history that a territory in the process of being colonized has actually paid for the right to defend the colonizer. It is an unnatural situation filled with potential tension and danger, and suspicion of betrayal.

## THE DOUBLE-EDGED SWORD OF SUCCESS: JAPAN

Japan's situation, too, is strange. Despite its trade surpluses, its domination of many key industries, and its ranking now above the United States in per-capita gross national product, Japan's citizens do not have the amenities enjoyed by those of other wealthy nations. The fact is that while Japan is rich, the Japanese are not. Sanae Yoshimura, a Tokyo housewife interviewed by the *Wall Street Journal* in September 1987, complained, "We live in small houses and we can't own land because it is so expensive. It isn't easy to take a vacation."[17]

The average Japanese dwelling is less than half the size of the average dwelling in the United States. A two-bedroom condominium an hour and a half by train from Tokyo costs nearly $600,000. To buy it, a Japanese couple must make a down payment of about 30 percent and borrow from six to ten times their annual income on the understanding that repayment will be completed by their children.[18] Moreover, interest payments on a mortgage are not tax deductible. Most Japanese work at least two Saturdays per month and take less than a week of vacation. When they do take time off, the opportunities for recreation and leisure are limited because of the lack of facilities. New applicants to the Tokyo Lawn Tennis Club, for instance, face a forty-year waiting period; and golf club memberships have become investment vehicles, selling for as much as $3 million.[19]

On weekends and holidays, family outings become nightmares as roads to resort areas are clogged with traffic. Several years ago, I drove to the seaside resort of Kamakura on a Saturday. Although the town is sixty miles from Tokyo, it took six hours to get there and seven to return (and there were no construction delays). Such odysseys are not uncommon for Tokyo citizens in search of recreation. Nor is shopping much fun when prices for television sets, cameras, and other goods are higher in Japan than for the same goods in New York or Hong Kong.

Land and a stubborn insistence on maintaining the status quo are at the heart of the matter. Protection of some of the world's highest-cost agriculture has resulted in half of Japan's scarce land being reserved for rice growing, while the 94 percent of Japanese who are not farmers make do on the other half. In addition, Japan's tax system discourages land sales, while building regulations severely restrain highrise offices and apartments. The result is both the world's highest food prices—rice sells at five to ten times the world market price—and its highest land prices, which continue to soar as the few plots available are bid up. A square foot of prime downtown commercial land in Tokyo now goes for $40,000 compared with $1,200 for Washington, D.C.; and the entire real estate value of Japan is twice that of the United States, a country twenty-five times its size.[20] Furthermore, legal restrictions aimed at protecting thousands of small "mom and pop" retail shops severely limit the number of large retail outlets. This situation, in turn, creates the need

for a multitiered distribution system which adds to the cost
of everything sold.

The *keiretsu* system does for stock prices what the agriculture and tax systems do for the value of land. Since most
shares are held in related hands and never trade, those that
do are bid up to stratospheric levels. The average price-to-
earnings ratio of a share on the Tokyo Stock Exchange is over
60, while that on the New York Stock Exchange is only about
20.[21] The bidding up of land and share prices is being fueled
by the liquidity resulting from Japan's huge trade surpluses,
which also fuel investment in U.S. bonds and assets.

If this bubble bursts, the consequences could lead to a
world depression. In any case, resentment piles up over
what Kenichi Ohmae calls Japan's double standard of
preaching free trade while slowly opening its home markets
and practicing economic nationalism.[22] Thus is Japan without
joy at the moment of its greatest triumph.


THE DILEMMA


As the United States declines, it is increasingly faced with
the choice between maintaining its support of noninterven-
tionist free-trade policies and of ensuring the continued
health of important industries. We do not want to abandon
free trade or begin targeting development of strategic industries, but we also are uneasy about the loss of technological
leadership. We look with dismay at the example of Great
Britain and draw uncomfortable comparisons as we think
about the years to come. Indeed, the U.S. position could be
worse than Great Britain's, for Japan is, by its own admission, neither able nor willing to assume the U.S. mantle of
leadership. Thus, America faces the possibility of having to
bear an unbearable burden, and is pressed to find a solution.

According to current U.S. doctrine and law, deviations
from free trade can be justified only on the basis of national
security or the unfair activities of others. Grounded in the

universalist assumption that other market economies are based on the same principles as that of the United States, this nation does not provide a pragmatic way of handling deviations. Thus, as Japan's success, based on a very different economic doctrine, expands, the United States is increasingly driven to shield its industry for national security purposes, while accusing Japan of being unfair and demanding that it save the United States from its own folly by opening its market and stimulating consumption in an economy built not to consume. Few realize that this reaction to Japan's challenge is nothing more than an anguished cry: "Please be like us!"

Caught in their own dilemma, the Japanese have derived great benefit from the international trading system based on the universalist U.S. concepts; yet these policies and practices are in many respects at odds with the system's assumptions. To some extent, Japan's success has been derived from the ability to use the international system without conforming to it or accepting its burdens. When Japan's economy was relatively small, this anomaly did not matter; but as Japan and the United States have traded places, the system has become more strained and now threatens to collapse under the weight of the contradictions. This would be a disaster for Japan. On the other hand, to change long-standing policies and basic social assumptions is extremely difficult and may be seen as an even worse disaster.

At stake is nothing less than Japan's definition of itself. As Peter Drucker pointed out in a recent article, for over a hundred years Japan's policies have aimed at putting it in the modern world without being part of it.[23] Japan's perception of itself as unique dictates that it be somewhat apart in order to remain genuinely Japanese. But the steps necessary to overcome its mounting problems require greater integration.

Unwilling to face this dilemma, the Japanese look for an alternative. Just as the easy way out for the United States is to accuse the Japanese of being unfair, so for the Japanese it is to accuse the United States of not trying hard enough—

really the same admonition as that of the Americans, "Please be like us!" This request is a dead end for both countries. It can only continue to result in rising mutual recrimination as the problem grows, while neither country pays attention to its real causes. Both countries must face up to difficult decisions.

## A Prescription for the Future: The United States

The United States must, first, decide both that something needs to be done and that it is legitimate to act. As the country has declined, it has become fashionable in some circles to ask rhetorically whether it is necessary for the United States to be number one in everything. The manner of the asking always indicates that only a fool or a hopeless chauvinist would answer in any way but no. While it may no longer be possible for the United States to be number one in everything, we are not required to connive at our own demise.

Technological and industrial leadership confer both wealth and power. The entire structure of the free world is founded on the assumption of U.S. leadership. Even if it were willing, Japan's sense of being apart would prevent it from filling America's shoes. But the United States cannot lead the free world or remain a society of opportunity in a state of continuing decline and dependency. To keep its promise to itself and to the world, the United States must remain wealthy and powerful. None are more aware of this than Japanese leaders like Amaya, who expressed his view to me in the fall of 1987 that there is no substitute for U.S. leadership. He— like Konaga, Morita, and other Japanese leaders—have agreed wholeheartedly with me that the United States must act to halt its decline. Some Japan experts believe that this argument, too, is in Japan's interest since, as long as America bears the burden of leadership, Japan avoids it. But halting the U.S. decline should not mean replaying the same old game.

The first act must be to cut the U.S. budget deficit and increase savings. As long as huge U.S. borrowing needs exist, all other concerns will pale into insignificance as the imbalance distorts the world economy. The way to restore a balanced situation is to combine increased taxes on consumption, such as a tax on gasoline and a value-added tax, with cuts in the major areas of expenditure—defense and entitlements. Indexation of social security and government pensions must be revised. Many senior citizens do not need social security at all, and it is obscene for retired generals to receive more in retirement compensation than active-duty generals are paid. Above all, savings must be stimulated. Consumer credit rules should be tightened by banning home-equity consumer loans and tax deduction of mortgages on second homes, and a compensation system based on bonuses related to company performance should be considered. Interest on some portion of savings should be tax free, while profits should be taxed no more than once. But having said all this, we must recognize that, while getting our own fiscal house in order is a prerequisite for anything else, such action will not suffice by itself to restore U.S. vitality. The problems are many and deep-seated, and we must deal with all of them.

One of the first things we must do is to stop blaming everything on the incompetence and greed of our business executives. Of course, legitimate criticism is always in order, but we must recognize that even our very best managers will have difficulty if the environment in which we place them is unfriendly. We live in a world of competitive nation states that do not always share our values or economic assumptions. Survival, long-term power position, and national pride all enter the equations involved in economic decision making. So long as they do, the playing field cannot be level. Each player will seek to shape it to his own advantage; and those who, out of principle or ignorance, are oblivious to its configuration will find the lines drawn by others.

The arguments in the United States over industrial policy are mostly beside the point. It must be recognized that micro- and macro-economic policies are inextricably intertwined. The fact is that continued American power is critical for world peace, prosperity, and stability. And power cannot be sustained without a leading capability in a wide number of industries. Those industries cannot survive in a manner useful to the support of American power on the basis of selling solely or primarily to the military. The industrial structure that undergirds American power must be competitive in world commercial markets. The contradiction between the demands of world leadership, and the lack of government concern for the composition of the economy that supports that leadership, must be resolved if American power is to be sustained. The solution is to recognize that, in a world of imperfect markets, leadership in key industries confers economic as well as strategic benefits. Thus, for example, having the world's leading aircraft industry not only enhances U.S. military power but also produces a wage and profit level not possible with industries such as fast-food services.

The real question is what kind of environment we want to create for our economy. At issue is not pure free trade or total protectionism—we never have had and never will have either one; but rather what combination of free and managed trade we will have. It is not a matter of whether the U.S. government intervenes in the economy—it does and will intervene, massively; but whether it will do so in a way that helps or hurts. Some commentators argue that we cannot copy the Japanese. Of course not, but there is a difference between copying and learning from others. We must learn what we can from Japan to make our own system work better.

The most critical point is priority. As in Japan, maintaining the industrial, technological, and financial strength of the country must be at the top of the national agenda. The next president must see issues of trade and industrial leadership as worthy of the same attention as arms negotiation, because if he cannot maintain America's economic might, he will eventually have no arms over which to negotiate.

## SETTING NEW PRIORITIES

In practice, this aim will require a substantial reordering of structures and procedures. For instance, while at the moment most papers on economic issues that go to the president are reviewed by the National Security Council, and council staffers sit on all interagency economic-affairs committees, the reverse is not the case. Pentagon programs that have massive impact on American R&D directions, and direct the efforts of thousands of scientists, are never reviewed by the economic or trade-policy groups in terms of their effect on the competitive structure of the U.S. economy. The same holds true for the Justice Department. The breakup of AT&T and the complete restructuring of the U.S. telecommunications industry was done on the basis of an antitrust suit and under the direction of a federal judge whose only prior knowledge of telecommunications was that required to dial a telephone. The decision was never reviewed by the trade agencies of the U.S. government with regard to its potential impact on trade. As a result, breakup and restructuring opened the U.S. market to foreign manufacturers without a reciprocal opening of their markets. The prohibition of manufacturing by the Baby Bells meant that if they did not want to buy equipment from AT&T, in lieu of any other U.S. producers, they had to import foreign equipment and that led to a massive overnight deficit in U.S. telecommunications trade.

To make the United States able to compete, such matters as these must be reviewed from the perspective of their likely competitive impact. Members of the key economic agencies should have the opportunity to participate in and review initiatives of the Pentagon, the Justice Department, and other agencies that will have an impact on U.S. economic and industrial leadership. Just as the national security and political angles of all decisions going to the president are reviewed, so should the competitive economic angle be reviewed. All presidential decision papers should carry a statement regarding the potential impact of a decision on U.S. economic and industrial leadership.

In 1984, the report of the Japan–U.S. Businessmen's Conference on U.S. and Japanese industrial policies found that the U.S. government administers many policies affecting industry, but that most of these are uncoordinated and contradictory and therefore unproductive over all.[24] For example, it is not a criticism of the "fish and chips" program of the Commerce Department (see chapter 10) to point out that, while we were engaged in promoting development of the fishing industry, we refrained from any action to assist the more critical semiconductor or machine tool industries. Yet at the same time, we budgeted billions of dollars for a space station, whose objectives were fuzzy at best.

Nearly everyone agrees on the importance of high technology to the future of the United States. Yet the enormous resources expended on it by the government are only haphazardly directed at improving America's competitive capability. NASA spends about $10 billion a year on rockets that don't fly and on other space projects that have limited commercial or even scientific potential. The national laboratories at Livermore, California, Los Alamos, New Mexico, and Sandia at Albuquerque, New Mexico, are priceless national assets; no other country has anything to match them. Yet they have little orientation toward the transfer of interesting technology to industry for commercial purposes. Nor are their international relationships at all coordinated with U.S. trade initiatives. Thus, as noted earlier in chapter 5, in 1982 and 1983, while U.S. negotiators were pressing Japan to open its market to U.S. supercomputers, Lawrence Livermore Laboratories was helping the Japanese test their new designs.

Then, of course, there is the Pentagon. Its Advanced Research Projects Agency (ARPA) is one of the primary supporters of important advanced research in the country. Its work in the past has created whole new industries such as artificial intelligence, time sharing, and networking. Now, however, it is being focused on narrower military objectives such as battlefield management systems and expert systems for use by fighter pilots. Moreover, as the Pentagon spends to develop technology, on the one hand, it is often contracting to transfer it abroad through coproduction programs on the other. At the same time, for reasons of national security, it often opposes the export of products containing even obsolete technology, thereby harming the competitive capability of many American companies who lose the sales to Japanese companies using technology that originated in the United States. The upshot is that the United States gets very little bang from its R&D bucks. It not only spends less than its competitors on commercial research and development as a percentage of gross national product, but gets less out of what it spends.*

We must strive for a more rational organization of our R&D programs. The Pentagon often justifies programs by speaking of possible commercial spin-off, and when we get it, we hail the results. The country would be much better served if, rather than waiting for spin-off, we organized consciously to develop technology for civilian use and to maximize its benefits for Americans.

In addition to the Sematech project for regaining semiconductor leadership (see pages 175–76), a step in the right direction has been taken in the case of superconductivity—a step that broke into the headlines in early 1987 after announcement of dramatic advances by Swiss and U.S. labora-

---

*U.S. spending on civilian research and development is 1.6 percent of GNP, versus Japan's 2.9 percent.[25]

tories. Able to carry electricity without the resistance of normal conductors such as copper, superconductors could enable computers to run much faster, home appliances to use virtually no power, and cables to carry electricity around the globe. In the past, superconductivity has been possible only at temperatures close to absolute zero. The advances indicated that superconductivity might soon be possible at room temperature. Announcements of the breakthrough were followed immediately by press reports of Japanese efforts to create government-sponsored R&D consortia. The *Wall Street Journal* reported frenetic efforts in Tokyo to match the United States and to push ahead in commercialization.[26] These activities were accompanied by the usual efforts to build Japanese public consensus behind the project. The standard American pattern would have been to ignore the Japanese activity while funding some military effort in superconductivity and hoping for spin-off; and eventually, when we had an exotic weapon and the Japanese were well on the way to taking the lion's share of commercial markets, we would have dispatched a team of negotiators to tell the Japanese that their project was unfair and to plead with them to control both it and the industrial structure it had spawned.

This time, however, spurred by fears of precisely such a scenario, President Reagan announced a new program aimed at ensuring that the United States gain the commercial fruit of this new technology.[27] Under this program, the Pentagon will increase research expenditures, "quick start" grants will be available for commercial applications, antitrust laws will be relaxed to permit joint production ventures, and the Freedom of Information Act will be suspended so that valuable technology in government labs does not have to be released to the U.S. subsidiaries of foreign firms. In addition, the plan calls for creation of an industry advisory group and of research centers by the departments of Commerce and Energy as well as by NASA.

As announced, the project is inadequate (in the fall of

1987, the National Academy of Science called for a more ambitious ten-year effort with funding of $100 million in the
initial year) and the Pentagon, which has all the wrong incentives for commercial projects, is the wrong godfather.[28]
Nevertheless, this program along with Sematech (which has
similar weaknesses), is a milestone. By reversing the administration's own arguments against government intervention,
it establishes the legitimacy of cooperation between government and business to reach specific industrial goals. It asserts that because we know superconductivity is a key
technology promising great economic benefits, and because
our power as a nation rests on industrial and economic
strength, we should not balk at enhancing it just as we
would not balk at developing weapons technology. And if
this logic holds for superconductivity or semiconductors, it
should hold for other areas as well. A systematic approach is
the only logical conclusion.

The question, then, is what criteria we will use to choose
projects and industries for promotion. In a grudging editorial
in October 1987 in support of the Sematech project as a lesser
evil than protectionism, the *Washington Post* sufficiently over-
came its longtime aversion to government cooperation with
industry to offer three excellent suggestions: the industry
should be crucial, it should be able to draw up its own research agenda, and it should contribute half the cost.[29] That
is a good start. We know that there are some industries and
technologies critical to our national defense. To the extent
that the health of these sectors rests on commercial markets,
we have a stake in ensuring the ability of U.S. companies to
compete. In addition, some of the criteria of the Japanese
may be useful. Knowledge-intensive industries promise the
creation of whole new fields that improve skills and justify
high remuneration. Industries that are characterized by rapid
growth and high elasticity of demand, and affect many other
industries, contribute disproportionately to economic growth
and productivity: it is clearly better to encourage them than,

for example, the real estate industry, which has been favored for many years.

Promotion does not necessarily mean subsidy. Broad dissemination of technology, reduction of risk, consistency, and steadiness of purpose are the key elements of a successful promotion policy. For example, it has been estimated that the counterfeiting of U.S. high-technology products cost American workers 750,000 jobs in 1987.[30] If U.S. patents or copyrights are being violated, U.S. companies should not have to prove that they are being injured to obtain redress: the very act of violation should be considered injurious as it is in purely domestic cases. Moreover, companies, especially small ones, should not have to face crippling legal fees to protect their property. The U.S. government should actively intervene to prevent theft of intellectual property. Effective legislation in this regard and enforcement of it would cost very little but would be worth billions to U.S. industry. In the same way, a review of the AT&T breakup from a trade point of view would have cost nothing but might have enabled us to arrange for much better negotiating leverage to open foreign telecommunications markets than we now have. A review of military co-production programs would cost virtually nothing but could prevent the giveaway of priceless technology. Thus, the key is not subsidy but thought. Once we know the areas of importance, we can systematically review the government's current activities to ensure that they are coordinated and provide maximum support.

To do the thinking, the staffing of government agencies dealing with industry and trade must be improved, possibly by development of a cadre of industry, finance, and trade experts akin to the military and foreign services. While the current U.S. and Foreign Commercial Service suggests the concept, it is not presently adequate to the task. This service runs the domestic district offices of the Commerce Department and is also in charge of commercial activities at all U.S.

embassies and consulates. It is not adequate because its scope is confined to export promotion, and its staff reflects years of bureaucratic neglect. It could, however, serve as the basis for development of an élite service with the broad purpose of conducting a strategic economic policy. Like Foreign Service officers of the State Department or military officers, its members might work at various times on congressional staffs, at the National Security Council, and at the Pentagon, State Department, Treasury, or Federal Reserve Board.

An important task of such a service would be dissemination of technology, which is much slower in the United States than in Japan. In years past, we successfully established land-grant colleges and an agricultural extension service to develop and disseminate agricultural technology. The United States should now consider adopting the same techniques in industry and create a mechanism that would push technology into broad commercial uses as rapidly as possible.

The personnel for this kind of service should be the very best. The U.S. government operates the military academies and ROTC programs that educate young men and women at public expense in order to ensure adequate staffing for the armed forces. On the assumption that our industry is as important as our armed forces, why shouldn't we have programs that educate people for service in areas of government dealing with it? Presently, when the bidding for MBA graduates at the nation's business schools takes place, neither the Commerce Department nor other government agencies are there. And if we recruit top people, we must give them opportunities. The political appointees who now mostly fill the upper levels of the government agencies should be limited in number in order to develop and retain skilled professionals who will provide continuity and institutional memory. No more than half the jobs in the top four tiers of these departments should go to appointees.

To formulate and administer such programs and policies, a directing and coordinating mechanism will be necessary. There has been much discussion in recent years about a U.S.

Department of International Trade and Industry (DITI) to oppose Japan's MITI. In 1983 and 1984, Baldrige tried to bring about a merger of Commerce with the Office of the U.S. Trade Representative and failed. The problem is that specific bureaucratic proposals tend to founder on the shoals of vested interests both in the bureaucracy and in the Congress. In fact, specific bureaucratic form does not matter; of the many that could be successful, all will have the same elements.

First, there has to be someone in charge. Whether a secretary of the Treasury, a U.S. trade representative, a secretary of Commerce, or someone in a new position does not matter, but whoever it is must clearly be the president's man in this area. Second, the person in charge must have at his or her command a body that has clout and can hold its own in Washington's political and bureaucratic battles. It could be a large department or something smaller like the National Security Council staff, but it must have power and must be involved in the flow of decision papers to the president. Third, it must not be the Defense Department, which would immediately skew the whole idea. The danger is that, in lieu of any active policy, Defense automatically inherits responsibility in this area—as, for example, it already has in the case of Sematech and superconductivity. Fourth, the effort must tie together many of the activities of the departments of Treasury, Commerce, Defense, Energy, and Justice, the Office of the U.S. Trade Representative, the Export Import Bank, the national laboratories, and NASA. And tying them together means that whoever is in charge must have a call on the resources of these agencies and be in a position to give them direction. Finally, this would be greatly facilitated if Congress would restructure its committee organizations in parallel.

## TRADE POLICY AND NEGOTIATIONS

As for the matter of trade, the first step in improving U.S. policies is development of a comprehensive agenda in which trade and domestic programs mesh. Rather than being determined by today's batch of complaints, the trade agenda ought to be based on the overall interests and priorities of the United States. If, by using the criteria I have noted earlier, we have identified those industrial, financial, and commercial areas of most importance to us, then they will become the basis of our trade agenda. This is not to say that we should ignore legitimate complaints—in any case, our laws would not allow us to do so; but that we will not spend all of our time on issues of relatively minor import.

Our negotiations should always be for results. To negotiate over the procedures of a foreign culture in hopes of obtaining an undefined "open" market is to court failure and frustration. We can negotiate to alter a revision in a law. We can negotiate to prevent a law from passing. We can negotiate a market share or a specific amount of sales or a sliding scale. We can negotiate anything identifiable and concrete. We cannot negotiate philosophy or perceptions and should not try to do so.

We should never send our negotiators abroad without sticks and carrots. We cannot always count on their charisma to be as effective abroad as it is at home. We should stop forcing them to make a bogeyman of the Congress. Our negotiators should have a significant agenda composed of concrete objectives. To attain them, they have to be able to make credible threats. We would not think of sending our arms negotiators to talks without bargaining chips. Neither should we do so in the case of trade negotiators.

Presidents of both parties have argued that their discretion for retaliation in trade matters should not be removed. They say they need flexibility for the sake of national security. As long as national security is seen apart from and more important than trade, we will always do poorly in trade. There will always be a Strategic Defense Initiative or a political interest that we do not want to endanger for the sake of some seemingly minor trade case. In fact, the president would have more real discretion if retaliation were compulsory for certain trade activities because then our trading partners would know they had to negotiate. Now they know they do not.

To deal with this and other problems, Congress must do three things. First, it must coordinate itself. The executive branch responds to the fiefdoms in Congress and cannot be truly coordinated if Congress is not. Second, it must begin to envision trade as an integral part of American economic and national security policy and must move away from the moralistic fair-unfair paradigm to a more practical and inclusive position. Finally, it must stop the hypocrisy of demanding action while continuing to write laws containing national security loopholes that ensure no action.

If these changes could be accomplished, our trade organization would operate more smoothly. Even so, it needs to be overhauled. Trade policy, negotiation, promotion, and finance are all naturally linked. They need to become more administratively integrated as well. Negotiators for the United States must be able to sit at the bargaining table with a complete hand of cards. The openness and decentralization of the United States makes it vulnerable to coordinated, goal-oriented activity by outsiders. We must try to be as coordinated as our competitors.

In this regard, we should also protect ourselves from manipulation by foreign interests. Their lobbying is different from that of domestic interests because, while enjoying the benefits of the U.S. system, they do not bear many of its burdens, and their goals can often be attained only at the overall expense of the United States. Foreign interests have a right to legitimate representation by their diplomats and to fair treatment under U.S. law. But they should not be permitted to buy influence or to intimidate or tempt U.S. officials. There should not be even the hint of a possibility that U.S. officials could enrich themselves later by trimming their sails to foreign winds while in office.

## LEARNING TO COMPETE WITH JAPAN

The United States and Japan are fated to be closely linked. Our task is to find a way to integrate Japan's economy with our own and that of the world without being overwhelmed by it. Having gotten our own house in order, we should move quickly to undertake comprehensive talks with Japan. If it ever was, the General Agreement on Tariffs and Trade is no longer an adequate basis on which to do business with Japan. The entire framework of our relationship and the assumptions on which it rests are no longer appropriate. We must develop a new structure based on comprehensive guidelines that cover the whole relationship—military, political, and economic. Talks should include members of Congress and Japan's key political leaders as well as executive branch officials of both governments.

For the United States, the first step is to discard the belief that the Japanese market is like that of the United States, and that it can be opened and made to operate similarly if only the Japanese will stop being unfair. The mentality of the Japanese and the structure of their society and economy exist. Neither fair nor unfair, they need to be handled as they are, with a clear understanding of their likely effects. It is counterproductive to continue to act the missionary toward Japan in the matter of trade and economics. We must get away from the stereotyped free-trade versus protectionist debate. There is an approach that falls in between. If there were not, we would not engage in much trading. The United States cannot be and should not attempt to be a protected island. Neither, however, should it stand by and watch its industries disappear because of the industrial aspirations of Japan and other nations.

Our talks with Japan must be realistic, based on an assessment of the actual situation in several industries in both countries. For some of these talks, we might consider the international airline negotiations as a model. International airline service is not conducted on the basis of free trade because, except for those in the United States, most airlines are regulated and many are state-owned. In most countries the airline is a symbol of the nation, and the decision to operate it is a matter of national sovereignty, not of consumer economics. For that reason, it would be useless to try to negotiate free trade in this area, and the United States does not. It conducts extensive and profitable trade in airline services—by negotiating deals on the basis of reciprocity. We give $x$ number of flights a week to Japan, and they give us $x$ number of flights in return. It is not an open market; but within the reciprocal framework, a great deal of competition does take place.

Another interesting example is banking. The United States has been pressing for more open financial markets as it has deregulated over the past several years. But when Japanese and other banks quickly gained major positions in the U.S. market because lower capital requirements abroad resulted in lower costs, the Treasury reacted immediately. It did not call for free trade or consumer rights. Instead, recognizing that banking is a key industry, it undertook negotiation to create a "level playing field" by persuading foreign banks to increase capital reserves. In effect, the Treasury moved to give limited protection of U.S. banks by creating an equitable framework for competition. Imagine the outcry against protectionism had we demanded that Japan's semiconductor companies saddle themselves with the same cost of capital as the U.S. companies. But what is the difference? It is only that the Treasury thinks banking has a national significance that semiconductors lack. It is prepared to "let the semiconductor industry go if it can't hack it," but not the banking industry.

In Japan and in other nations, as I have said, industries such as semiconductors, satellites, fiber optics, computers, and aircraft have the same significance as airlines, banks, and agriculture. The element of nationalism is important in these industries, and we cannot expect completely open markets because they are really nonnegotiable. In addition to these industries that are national champions, there are others in which we know foreign penetration will be almost impossible for structural and social reasons. The Japanese automobile companies, for example, are unlikely to import substantial amounts of parts. Again, demanding an open market and leveling accusations of unfairness will only lead to frustration.

In those instances in which realistic analysis of the situation leads us to conclude that truly free trade is unlikely, we should bargain as we do in airline or banking negotiations, attempting to create structures that retain large elements of competition but that do not make our industries hostage to the national sovereignty policies of other nations. To the possible objection that this course will bog us down in endless, unwieldy bilateral negotiations, the reply is that we already are so bogged down—except that now the talks are so rancorous as to be all but unmanageable. We are constantly forced into bilateral negotiations as a result of political pressures and legal cases when the problems are acute and almost unsolvable. But most of these situations are foreseeable: for example, since we will almost certainly have trade problems in industrial ceramics, aircraft, financial services, and biotechnology in the future, we would be wise to deal with them now in the early stages.

From now on, investment decisions will probably be more important to the shape of our future than standard trade activities, although the two are closely linked. There will be enormous Japanese investment in the United States over the next twenty years. We can obtain great benefit from it, but we also face the dangers Knebel suggested. We must devise policies to obtain the benefits and avoid the dangers. The first step is knowledge. At the moment, the Japanese government is better informed about Japanese investment in the United States and vice versa than is the U.S. government. We need some system of prior notification. Rather than pressuring a Fujitsu to disgorge a Fairchild after the fact, we should have a mechanism for consultation before the fact. The structure of Japanese investment in the United States should not be determined solely by MITI, Keidanren, and spasms at the Pentagon.

Beyond this, our consultations with Japan should include guidelines for investment. If we know, as we should, that certain industries and technologies are critical to us, it would be prudent to guide Japanese investment in those areas in such a way as to enhance and not lose our capabilities. For instance, it might be that in some areas joint ventures rather than wholly-owned operations should be encouraged. Japanese investors, such as Honda Motors who anticipate working with U.S. suppliers and transferring technology and skills to them, should be more welcome than others who plan only low-value assembly operations, or who plan to bring their *keiretsu* with them. We should ensure that, as a result of the investment, the skills of our workers will be improved, and that we will learn everything the Japanese have to teach.

Technology is the key to our future. We are a creative nation with an unrivaled basic technology infrastructure. Our continued investment in it can only be justified, however, if we get some eventual commercial return on all the technological advances to which it gives rise. We must not be indifferent to the flow of technology, giving away—for little or for the achievement of temporary political gain—that which took much to create. Foreign countries that benefit from the use of our publicly funded technology infrastructure should be required to make some investment in it, and the flow of technology in key areas should be monitored. We should insist on actual concrete access to foreign technology in a way that is equivalent to that granted in the United States.

For example, about 330 Japanese scientists participate in biotechnology research at the National Institutes of Health each year under U.S. government-funded programs.[31] There is no such program in reverse: for one thing Japan doesn't have an NIH; and Japanese companies are not doing much bio-tech research in government-supported programs, and it is scientists from these companies who come to work at NIH. The United States should insist on sending its own researchers to participate in programs at the companies that send scientists to work in U.S. programs. At a minimum, the United States should insist on full flowback of any Japanese technology in these programs. It is ridiculous and demeaning for the United States to have to beg for access to technology from a nation that owes much of its success to the ready availability at low cost of American technology. The means of establishing an equitable balance in the flow should be a major part of the comprehensive discussions.

Another concept that must be confronted is that of national treatment. This pillar of the international trading system works against the United States. While the idea that each country treats foreign firms as it treats its own sounds fair and equal, in practice the most open, liberal society is always at a disadvantage. For example, the semiconductor agreement, calling for Japan to grant "full national treatment" to United States companies, will not help, because Japan metes out different treatment among its own companies. Thus, U.S. companies have always been treated like third-class Japanese companies. What is really needed is an agreed-upon code of treatment that will apply equally in both countries and be readily understood by all. The banking regulations previously mentioned may be a prelude to this outcome.

Last, but far from least, is the matter of bearing the public costs of the free-world system. It is no longer acceptable or healthy for the United States to bear the major part of these costs while Japan bears hardly any. The present situation creates resentment in the United States at Japan's free ride and a continuing feeling of inferiority in Japan—a feeling that is transmuted into resentment at what is perceived to be U.S. bullying. The two countries must operate as true equals. This delicate issue must be faced directly. Japan's offer in October 1987 to defray some of the costs of the U.S. Persian Gulf patrol was a welcome step. But—while it ameliorated somewhat the ridiculous spectacle of the United States guarding waters from which it gets virtually no oil while Japan, which depends on the gulf for most of its oil, bore none of the cost—the amount, $10 million, is really only symbolic.

It would be more generous for Japan to pay the whole cost and also to pick up the full tab for U.S. forces stationed in Japan. Indeed, Japan might consider assuming half the cost of total U.S. defense efforts in Asia while greatly increasing its aid and lending to less developed countries and international institutions. With a $2-trillion economy, a 5-percent contribution of $100 billion annually (compared with today's $20 billion to $30 billion) toward the public costs of maintaining the free-world system does not seem unreasonable.

STRENGTHENING BUSINESS

The single greatest weakness of U.S. industry in competing with Japan is lack not of management effort but rather of financial staying power. Our capital is both too expensive and too impatient. Reducing the budget deficit would help. Beyond that, the United States must create more capital by stimulating a higher savings rate. Important positive steps would be, as I have suggested, to eliminate all taxes on consumption, and halt subsidization of corporate takeovers by allowing interest on the borrowed funds involved to be deducted from taxes.

Patient capital should be encouraged through rules on corporate takeovers that are much more restrictive, as well as through high taxation of short-term capital gains. Other methods might be examined, such as the creation of different classes of shares with voting rights restricted only to those that entail long holding periods. Restrictions on banks holding major equity positions in companies might be relaxed. The Securities and Exchange Commission might also switch reporting requirements from a quarterly to an annual basis; and the whole system of financial analysis of companies should be reviewed, with more emphasis on nonfinancial factors. High debt should not always be seen as risky, and low debt as safe: the reverse is sometimes the case. It is silly to give a triple-A bond rating to a typical unleveraged, blue-chip U.S. company if it is in a slugging match with a major highly leveraged Japanese company. The Japanese will normally win.

The two great adversarial relationships in the United States must become cooperative. The United States cannot succeed if industry and government maintain their traditional mutual suspicion and hostility. Elevation of the priority of economic and industrial matters would go a long way toward encouraging better relations. In particular, antitrust law should be reviewed and overhauled in light of international realities. Recently, for example, there has been discussion of a link between Airbus Industrie and the McDonnell Douglas Corporation. Current antitrust law would allow such a merger, but would prevent a similar one between McDonnell Douglas and Boeing. Yet from the overall U.S. viewpoint, the latter possibility would be more advantageous. Beyond new antitrust rules, creation of an industry advisory council to work closely with whatever government structure for promoting U.S. economic and industrial leadership emerges will be necessary.

The United States also cannot win if its labor-management relationships remain strained and uncooperative. Steps to create a closer identification of interests between labor and management must be taken. The essential bargain has to be job security for wage and work-rule flexibility. This is the Japanese bargain, and it has proven very effective. Both strikes and layoffs should be made more difficult, while compensation should be tied significantly to the productivity and success of the company. Constant training and retraining should be encouraged. The government should develop guidelines and actively promote a change in the whole structure of labor relations aimed at forcing more dialogue and less confrontation. U.S. policy should promote shared interests between companies and their employees. The presumption of a naturally adversarial relationship must be removed. Companies and employees should see that they have a stake

in each other, and any barriers in the way of this understanding should be removed through, if necessary, revisions
of U.S. labor law.

U.S. business and business schools must take a hard look
at their values and what they teach about the purpose of
business. Is it to maximize shareholder values? That can only
lead to short-term financial legerdemain. Or is it to create
wealth by improving productivity and developing technology? That can only be done by organizations that focus on
something other than the price of their shares.

Finally it is true that U.S. business must try harder. It must
hire people knowledgeable about Japan. It must train its best
people in the Japanese language; and just as Akio Morita
moved his family to live in the United States in the 1950s, so
top U.S. executives must spend time in Japan. We must establish the personal relationships which count in Japan and
come to know its system as well as it knows ours.

U.S. business must learn to think in terms of industrial
and commercial statecraft, and be capable of maneuvering in
Tokyo as well as in Washington. For he who writes the rules
will control the game.

## A Prescription for the Future: Japan

And what of Japan? The very policies and practices that have
succeeded so dramatically now seem to threaten the fruits of
that success, as real-estate and stock-market speculation
mounts domestically and resentment grows abroad. How
can Japan escape from the cul-de-sac of national pride that
avoids facing these problems by blaming them on the leth-
argy of others?

The world today stands at the brink of a depression that

could equal or surpass that of the 1930s. The huge U.S. trade deficits that have powered world economic growth cannot continue. At some point, the United States must run a trade surplus, which will mean a swing in its accounts of roughly $200 billion. If the world economy is not to come to a grinding halt, other countries must pick up this slack. With the world's second largest economy, Japan is the prime candidate: hence, the incessant demands from Washington that Japan stimulate its domestic economy. Although it is unlikely that it will be able to do so sufficiently to make a significant dent in the U.S. trade deficit, the potential is great. While its per-capita gross national product is now larger than that of the United States, per-capita ownership of cars, telephones, television sets, and similar items is about half that of the U.S. Thus, the great irony: while the Japanese view U.S. requests as excessive and discuss them in terms of gloom, doom, and sacrifice, the United States mainly requires only that Japan improve the material standard of living of its citizens. In effect, the world stands at the precipice in large part because of the stubborn insistence of the Japanese on protecting the traditional way of life of its farmers, small shopkeepers, and exporters. The double irony is that for Japan to improve its standard of living, there will have to be revolutionary changes. Japan's great strength has been its absolute confidence that it can always be more austere and rigorous than others: now it must try to be less so.

## LAND REFORM

Japan needs to carry out a second land reform. When houses have only three or four small rooms, there is no need or space for several telephones or television sets. When it takes six hours to drive sixty miles on a Sunday outing, the last thing anyone desires is a new car, particularly when membership in a golf or tennis club to which one might drive has a forty-year waiting list and a $3 million membership fee. Land reform will require political reform. Drawn when most of the population was rural, Japan's electoral districts have never been revised, so that the political influence of farmers is greatly disproportionate to their numbers. These districts should be revised in line with supreme-court directives; and at the same time, public financing of political campaigns and stricter regulations on political contributions by special interest groups should be considered. With the power of such interests reduced, Japan should drop protection of its agricultural markets as well as its subsidies to agriculture. At the same time, tax and land-usage rules, which discourage sale of land for other than agricultural purposes, should be changed; and industrial plants should be moved out of central Tokyo, while building codes are revised to allow more high-rise apartments. Japan might even reconsider the right-to-sunlight rules which have blocked high-rise construction in many areas.

## HELPING THE CONSUMER

Japan should begin to look upon housing as a strategic industry like the computer or semiconductor industries. Programs to allow home purchases with small down payments, tax deduction of mortgage interest, and other subsidies to housing should be considered. Money saved from dropping agricultural subsidies could be used for this purpose. The restrictions on building large retail stores should be dropped in order to simplify the labyrinthine distribution system; and at the same time, the control major manufacturers exert over the system should be loosened by giving much greater power along with a larger budget and staff to Japan's Fair Trade Commission. Private damage suits or a similar provision for appealing on antitrust grounds should also be permitted.

TRADE AND INVESTMENT

In regard to trade and investment, Japan must become a major international market. This means not only that Japan must import more, but also that the imports must not be controlled by Japanese companies. There must be a growing foreign presence in the Japanese market. Since this won't happen naturally, Japan should consider affirmative-action policies. In carrying out industry structure planning, Japan should consciously plan for foreign participants. The Japanese government should work with its companies to establish targets for procurement of foreign goods. In particular, large exporters like the auto companies should be required to develop significant foreign suppliers. At the same time, acquisition of Japanese companies by foreign investors should be encouraged; and in its overseas investment, Japan should emphasize joint ventures and construction of integrated manufacturing instead of assembly plants. Manufacturers should be discouraged from taking their traditional suppliers with them.

SHARING IN THE FREE WORLD

Japan must bear more of the cost of maintaining the free-world system. Its aid and military expenditures total less than 2 percent of gross national product, compared with the United States's of around 8 percent: 5 percent ($100 billion) is, as I have suggested, a reasonable target for Japan.

Finally, Japan must be *of* the modern world as well as in it. A change in the attitudes that keep Japan apart, and engender resentment among other nations, is essential. First, the emphasis of the Japanese on their racial purity and their own uniqueness should be reduced. As the author Kenichi Ohmae has noted, Japan is not racially pure; and while it is unique, so is the United States.[32] Every nation is, by definition, unique. It would greatly enhance Japan's ability to deal with others if it could grasp this reality. A good symbolic step would be to change the signs at Narita Airport, where passport inspection is now done for Japanese and "aliens." Perhaps aliens could be changed to "non-Japanese," just as the Europeans provide for European Economic Community and non-EEC passport holders. Second, Japan's schools and media must drop the "small island nation with no natural resources" incantation, which is simply not relevant. Finally, the tendency to see everything in terms of "us versus them" must be altered. Pursued long enough, it becomes a self-fulfilling prophecy.

*Kokusaika* (internationalization) has become a watchword in Tokyo recently. Everyone in Japan believes it is essential. But does Japan understand what it means? *Kokusaika* means that Japan no longer fingerprints foreign residents. That maybe 10 percent to 20 percent of office space in Tokyo is in foreign hands. That thousands of foreign students attend Japanese universities. That a major Japanese firm has a foreign president. And that a major Japanese bank or company is acquired by foreign interests. *Kokusaika* means being less exclusive. Can Japan do it?

## Conclusion: Hanging Together

At the conclusion of its analysis of the decline of the United States—after citing reduced investment, short-term views, adversarial labor-management relations, and several other points—the 1981 Nikko report commented: "There are many unfavorable factors rooted deeply in American society, such as the declining work ethic, increases in crime, deterioration of education as well as of social discipline and order. It is

vitally essential that this fact is well recognized and understood to its root."[33]

So it is. All the nostrums and policy changes will avail little
if the values and attitudes underlying them are flawed.
Seven years in Washington have taught me many things.
One of the most important is that the spirit of the Founding
Fathers is very much alive today. Their desire to ensure lib-
erty has driven the United States for two hundred years and
probably always will. Freedom, the rights of the individual,
and equal opportunity are the bedrock on which this country
is built. They are great values, and we should never consider
abandoning them. But any philosophy can be taken to excess. In its obsession with the rights of the individual, the
United States has lost sight of another early value. We have
embraced the myth of the cowboy so completely that we
have forgotten that most of us are descendants of settlers,
whether they were earlier colonizers of the east and west or
later immigrants settling in the cities.

A country in which government and consumers perceive
no stake in the success or the failures of producers, in which
producers and workers perceive few common interests and
few mutual obligations, which pays young corporate takeover artists twenty to thirty times what it pays veteran
teachers, and which most often settles disputes in a court of
law, is a country in trouble. No amount of policy tinkering
will help it if the fundamental values are absent. The United
States is being tested now as it has been tested only a few
times before in its history. Again, the question is whether
"that nation or any nation so conceived and so dedicated can
long endure." The United States must decide once more
what kind of nation it wants to be and what role it wishes to
play. Will it be "every man for himself," or "all for one and
one for all"?

The motto of our country *E Pluribus Unum* (out of many,
one) needs to be reaffirmed. The Founding Fathers saw lib-
erty as possible only in the framework of a community that
recognizes duties and obligations as well as rights. The

United States has been a beacon of hope to the oppressed throughout its history. The refugees of the world do not flock to other shores but come here, because we offer hope and a fair chance. But we can offer it only if we remain strong, and we can remain strong only if we affirm our stake in each other. Benjamin Franklin said it best at the very beginning: "We must all hang together, or assuredly, we shall all hang separately."[34]

# NOTES

Introduction to the Paperback Edition

1. Akio Morita and Shintaro Ishihara, *A Japan That Can Say No* (New York: Kodansha, 1989).

2. Richard J. Samuels and Benjamin C. Whipple, "Defense Production and Industrial Development: The Case of Japanese Aircraft," unpublished paper, Massachusetts Institute of Technology, 1988, p. 12.

3. O. R. Hall and R. E. Johnson, "Transfers of United States Aerospace Technology to Japan," in R. Vernon, ed., *The Technology Factor in International Trade*, (New York: National Bureau of Economic Research, 1970), pp. 305–63, as cited in ibid., p. 9.

4. "Japanese Airlines Try, Try Again," *The Economist*, 8 April 1989, p. 72.

5. Ichiro Akashi, "On One Trillion Yen FSX Business," *Seikai Orai*, August 1987, pp. 38–45.

6. Shunji Taoka, "Oreta? Nichibei Yuko no Tsubasa," *Aera*, 23 May 1989, p. 30.

7. "F-1 to Serve Three More Years, Making Domestic Development in Time for FS-X," *The Wing Newsletter*, 12 December 1984, p. 1.

8. James Auer, interview with author, 24 June 1989.

9. Gregg Rubinstein, interview with author, 15 June 1989.

10. Casper Weinberger, press conference reported in *Nihon Keizai Shimbun*, 5 May 1986, p. 3.

11. Kazuhisa Ogawa, "Home Production of FSX Will Save the Crisis of Japan," *Seikai Orai*, November 1986, pp. 48–62.

12. Gerald Sullivan, interview with author, 16 June 1989.

13. Reported to the author in an interview with a former Defense Department official who prefers to remain unnamed.

14. Stephen Kreider Yoder, "Japan Picks General Dynamics Fighter," *Asian Wall Street Journal*, 22 October 1987, p. 3, as cited in Richard P. Lawless and Therese Shaheen, "Airplanes and Airports: The Subtle Skill of Japanese Protectionism," *SAIS Review* 8 (Winter-Spring 1988): 111.

15. "Draft U.S.-Japan FS-X MOU," memorandum from Deputy Undersecretary of Defense Stephen D. Bryen to Undersecretary of Defense for Policy, 19 January 1988.

16. "This Is the Secret Memo for Japan-U.S. Semiconductor Agreement," *Bungei Shunju*, May 1988, pp. 124–37.

17. "Little Old Agreement on F-16," *Newsweek*, 30 January 1989, p. 34.

18. Clyde Prestowitz, "Giving Japan a Handout," *Washington Post*, 29 January 1989, p. D1.

19. Reported to the author by three State Department officials who wish to remain unnamed.

20. Reported to the author by Kevin Kearns, 29 June 1989.

21. "Japan's FSX Fighter: Technology and Competitive Impact of Development Options," Technology and Industrial Competitiveness Division, C.I.A., 3 March 1989.

22. "Japanese Airliners Try, Try Again," p. 72.

23. This is the language of the oral statement and exchange of letters of 28 April 1989 between Secretary of State James Baker and Japanese Ambassador Nobuo Matsunaga.

24. "Japan's Aircraft Strategy," *Japan Economic Journal*, 28 April 1989.

25. "Japanese Quest for U.S. Market Share," *ENR*, 3 March 1988, p. 30.

26. Mike Sesit and James White, "Japanese Firms Have Yen for U.S. High-Tech Investment Skills," *Wall Street Journal*, 11 July 1989, p. C1.

27. "Tutoring Japanese on Takeovers," *New York Times*, 23 May 1989, p. D1.

28. Simon Pyuwer, "Invisible Hands & Secret Plans," *Business Tokyo*, November 1988, p. 35.

29. "Japan Is Buying Its Way into U.S. University Labs," *Business Week*, 24 September 1984, p. 72.

30. "Is the U.S. Selling Its High-Tech Soul to Japan?" *Business Week*, 26 June 1989, p. 97.

31. "Why Tokyo's Stock Market Is Still Soaring After All These Years." *Business Week*, 25 July 1988, p. 56.

32. Pyuwer, "Invisible Hands & Secret Plans," p. 35.

33. William Kresnak. "Foreign Investment in Isles Debated," *Honolulu Advertiser*, 8 August 1989, p. A3.

34. Norman J. Glickman and Douglas P. Woodward, *The New Competitors* (New York: Basic Books, 1989), ch. 5.

35. "Foreign Investment: Growing Japanese Presence in the U.S. Auto Industry," General Accounting Office, March 1988.

36. "Impact on Employment of Japanese Transplants," United Auto Workers, 1988.

37. Glickman and Woodward, *The New Competitors*, p. 131.

38. "Third Survey of Japanese Overseas Subsidiaries," Ministry of International Trade and Industry, 1988.

39. Douglas Frantz and Catherine Collins, *Selling Out* (Chicago: Contemporary Books, 1989), p. 303.

40. Robert Reich, "Japan Inc., U.S.A.," *New Republic*, 26 November 1984, p. 19.

41. Michael S. Flynn, Sean McAlinden, and David S. Andrea, "The U.S.-Japan Bilateral 1993 Auto Trade Deficit," unpublished report, Office for Study of Automotive Transport, University of Michigan, June 1989.

## Chapter 1. The End of the American Century

1. Theodore White, "The Danger from Japan," *New York Times Magazine*, 28 July 1985, p. 19.

2. Dennis Healey, quoted in "Wake Up America," *Business Week*, 16 November 1987, p. 170.

3. François Froment—Meurice, ibid., p. 170.

4. Albert Bressand, "Chaos: Strategic Tool," *The International Economy*, November 1987, p. 44.

5. National Academy of Engineering, *Strengthening U.S. Engineering Through International Cooperation: Some Recommendations for Action* (Washington, D.C.: National Academy Press, 1987).

6. *New York Times*, 7 November 1986, p. D11.

7. *Moody's Bank and Finance Manual*, 1982 (New York: Moody's Investors Service, 1982), p. 1:a2.

8. *Moody's Bank and Finance Manual*, 1987 (New York: Moody's Investors Service, 1982), p. 1:a2.

9. "Florio Warns Foreign Bank Holdings in U.S. Poses Problem for Economy," news release from Congressman James J. Florio, U.S. House of Representatives, 11 March 1987 (photocopy).

10. "BIS Says Japan Has Passed the U.S. in Share of International Banking," *Wall Street Journal*, 31 January 1986, p. 25.

11. "Japan on Wall Street," *Business Week*, 7 September 1987, p. 85.

12. "Japanese to Invest in Bank of America," *Washington Post*, 27 August 1987, p. E1.

13. First Manhattan Consulting Group analysis, May 1987.

14. Office of Japan, International Trade Administration, Department of Commerce.

15. Ministry of International Trade and Industry, *The Vision of MITI Policies in the 1980s* (Tokyo: MITI, March 1980), p. 1.

16. Nikko Research Center, *Japan's Cooperation for the Revitalization of American Industry* (Tokyo: Nikko Research Center, 1981), pp. 1, 9.

17. Interview with Frank Vargo, economist at U.S. Department of Commerce, International Trade Administration, June 1987.

18. U.S. Department of Commerce, International Trade Administration, "An Assessment of U.S. Competitiveness in High Technology Industries" (Washington, D.C., February 1983).

19. Frank Vargo, International Trade Administration, Department of Commerce.

20. Robert Bennett, "Economists Caution on Risks in Continued Drop of Dollar," *New York Times*, 28 November 1987, p. 1.

21. "Can America Compete?" *Business Week*, special survey, 20 April 1987, pp. 45–49.

22. *Business Week*, 16 November 1987, p. 165.

23. Richard Koo, quoted in Edwin A. Finn, Jr., "In Japan We (Must) Trust," *Forbes*, 21 September 1987, p. 34.

24. Bruce Nussbaum, "And Now the Bill Comes Due," *Business Week*, 16 November 1987, pp. 160–63.

25. Mayahoshi Hotta, quoted in Steven Schlossstein, *Trade War* (New York: Congdon & Weed, 1984), p. 104.

## Chapter 2. Losing the Chips: The Semiconductor Industry

1. U.S. Department of Defense, Office of the Undersecretary of Defense for Acquisition, *Report on Semiconductor Dependency*, prepared by the Defense Science Board Task Force (Washington, D.C., February 1987), pp. 1–10.

2. Marie Anchordoguy, "The State and the Market: Industrial Policy Towards Japan's Computer Industry," Ph.D. dissertation, Harvard University, 1986, pp. 68–69.

3. Ibid., p. 72.

4. "American IC Manufacturers Moving for Investments in Japan," *Nihon Keizai*, 27 March 1971.

5. Anchordoguy, "The State and the Market," p. 91.

6. "IBM Is a Tiger Turned Loose in a Field," *Bungei Shunju Zasshi*, September 1982, pp. 94–105.

7. "Tension Mounts from Planned U.S. Entry into IC Industry," *Japan Economic Journal*, 27 April 1971.

8. "Texas Instruments Poses Threat to IC Makers," *Japan Economic Journal*, 4 January 1972, p. 11.

9. Japan Electronic Industry Development Association, *Monthly Report of the Electronics Industry* 18 (January 1976).

10. Verner et al., *The Effect of Government Targeting on World Semiconductor Competition* (Cupertino, Calif.: Semiconductor Industry Association, 1983), pp. 72–73.

11. "Plunging into IC Liberalization" (translated by Semiconductor Industry Association), *Nippon Kogyo*, 12 December 1974.

12. Gene A. Gregory and Akio Etori, "Japanese Technology Today," *Scientific American*, October 1981, pp. 15–46.

13. Semiconductor Industry Association, *The U.S. Crisis in Microelectronics* (San Jose, Calif.: Semiconductor Industry Association, 1987), appendix A, exhibit II-6.

14. "Semiconductor Firms Are Slated to Make Capital Expenditures of About Y140 Billion," *Nihon Keizai*, 6 May 1980, p. 6.

15. Verner, Liipfert, Bernhard, McPherson & Hand, *The Effect of Government Targeting*, p. 37.

16. U.S. Department of Defense, *Report on Semiconductor Dependency,* p. 46.

17. Ibid., p. 57.

18. Verner, Liipfert, Bernhard, McPherson, & Hand, *The Effect of Government Targeting,* p. 58.

19. Ibid., p. 59.

20. Ibid., p. 40.

21. Ibid., p. 43.

22. "Pushing for Leadership in the World Market," *Business Week,* 14 December 1981, p. 61.

23. Dan Morgan, "Battling to Innovate and Emulate: Intel vs. Nippon Electric," *Washington Post,* 2 May 1983, p. 1.

24. U.S. Department of Commerce, "Agreement of the High Technology Working Group on Semiconductors," Office of Japan, International Trade Administration (Washington, D.C., November 1982).

25. U.S. Department of Commerce, "Second Agreement of the High Technology Working Group in Semiconductors," Office of Japan, ITA (Washington, D.C., December 1983).

26. U.S. Department of Defense, *Report on Semiconductor Dependency,* p. 20.

27. Ibid., p. 74.

28. Regis McKenna, Inc., *ECONS, Republished Graphics on Economy, Trade and Issues Affecting Technology Industries* (Palo Alto, Calif., 18 December 1986).

29. Mark Potts, "U.S. Chip Industry's Gloomy Future," *Washington Post,* 10 May 1987, p. H1.

30. *Petition of the Semiconductor Industry Association Pursuant to Section 301 of the Trade Act of 1974, as amended, for relief from the effects of industrial targeting practices of the government of Japan* (San Jose, Calif., Semiconductor Industry Association, June 1985).

31. "Semiconductor Makers Resigned to Sharp Drops in Profit," *Nihon Keizai,* 30 July 1985, p. 5.

32. William F. Finan and Chris B. Amundsen, "An Analysis of the Effects of Targeting on the Competitiveness of the U.S. Semiconductor Industry," a study prepared for the Office of the U.S. Special Trade Representative, the Department of Commerce, and the Department of Labor (Washington, D.C.: Quick Finan & Associates, 1985 [photocopy]).

33. William F. Finan and Chris B. Amundsen, "Report on Estimating U.S. Market Share in Japan," a report to the SIA (Washington, D.C.: Quick Finan & Associates, 8 November 1985 [photocopy]).

34. U.S. Department of Commerce, Import Administration, "Preliminary Finding of Dumping: Japanese EPROMS," 51 *Federal Register* 9087, 17 March 1986; and "Preliminary Finding of Dumping: Japanese 256K DRAMs," 51 *Federal Register* 9475, 19 March 1986.

35. U.S. House of Representatives Resolution 4800, *Congressional Record,* 21 May 1986.

36. Office of the U.S. Trade Representative, Arrangement between the Government of Japan and the Government of the United States of America concerning Trade (Washington, D.C., 2 September 1986 [photocopy]).

37. White House announcement on semiconductor sanctions, 27 March 1987.

38. Quick Finan & Associates, "Forces for Change in Semiconductors," multi-client study (Washington, D.C., 24 September 1986 [photocopy]).

## Chapter 3. Perception Gap: "Unfair" Trade and "Open" Markets

1. U.S. Department of Commerce, International Trade Administration, "Market Access Indicator," April 1987 (photocopy).

2. *Yearbook of U.S.–Japan Economic Relations 1982* (Washington, D.C.: Japan Economic Institute of America, 1983), p. 47.

3. Todanabu Tsunoda, *The Japanese Brain* (1978).

4. Shinji Ito, "Nakasone Apologizes to U.S. over Controversial Remarks," *Japan Times*, 27 September 1986, p. 1.

5. Lafcadio Hearn, *Japan: An Interpretation* (Tokyo: Charles E. Tuttle, 1970), pp. 168–69.

6. See Takeo Doi, *The Anatomy of Dependence* (Tokyo: Kodansha, 1986); Jared Taylor, *Shadows of the Rising Sun* (New York: William Morrow, 1983); and Chi Nakane, *The Vertical Society* (Tokyo: Kodansha, 1967).

7. Ellen Frost, *For Richer, For Poorer* (New York: Council of Foreign Relations, 1987), p. 26.

8. U.S. State Department, Office of Refugee Affairs, September 1987.

9. Shumpei Kumon, address given at the Woodrow Wilson Center, Washington, D.C., 21 June 1987.

10. E. S. Browning, "Unhappy Returns: After Living Abroad, Japanese Find It Hard to Adjust Back Home," *Wall Street Journal*, 6 May 1986, p. 1.

11. "Japan's Farmers Try to Beef Up Quantity and Quality," *Nihon Keizai*, 3 April 1984, p. 7.

12. "Hong Kong Appeals to Japan for More Trade," *Journal of Commerce*, 13 December 1984, p. 5a.

13. Commission of the European Communities, "Revised List of Requests to the Japanese Authorities" (Brussels: European Economic Community, April 1984 [photocopy]).

14. "Tokyo's Protectionism: Time to Fight Back," *Singapore Monitor*, 18 January 1985, p. 15.

15. "ASEAN's Trading Relationship with Japan and Australia Requires Review," *Japan Economic Journal*, 5 June 1984, p. 24.

16. Herbert Cochran, interview with author, September 1986.

## Chapter 4. The Mandarins: Japan's Powerful Ministries

1. Richard Samuels, *The Business of the Japanese State: Energy Markets in Comparative and Historical Perspective* (Ithaca: Cornell University Press, 1987), p. 224; and a memorandum from Samuels to the author, 29 June 1985.

2. "We've Nothing More to Say to Japan but 'Open the Door,'" *Los Angeles Times*, 31 March 1985.

3. Chalmers Johnson, *MITI and the Japanese Miracle* (Stanford: Stanford University Press, 1982), p. 37.

4. E. Herbert Norman, *Origins of the Modern Japanese State: Selected Writings of E. H. Norman*, ed. John W. Dower (New York: Pantheon, 1975), p. 225.

5. Ibid., pp. 232–33.

6. Ibid., pp. 234–42.

7. Chalmers Johnson, "MITI, MPT, and the Telecom Wars" (Berkeley Roundtable on the International Economy, working paper no. 21, University of California, Berkeley, 11 September 1986 [photocopy]), p. 15.

8. Ibid., p. 16.

9. Johnson, *MITI and the Japanese Miracle*, pp. 98–110.

10. Ibid., p. 132.

11. Ibid., pp. 118, 169, 172, 309.

12. Ibid., pp. 173–74.

13. Ibid., pp. 194–95.

14. Ibid., p. 210.

15. Bruce R. Scott, John W. Rosenblum, and Audrey T. Sproat, *Case Studies in Political Economy* (Boston: Harvard Business School, 1980), p. 190.

16. Covington & Burling, *Petition to the President of the United States through the Office of the United States Trade Representative for the Exercise of Presidential Discretion Authorized by Section 103 of the Revenue Act of 1971* (Washington, D.C.: Houdaille Industries, 1982), p. 112.

17. Norman, *Origins of the Modern Japanese State*, p. 457.

18. Johnson, "MITI, MPT, and the Telecom Wars," p. 22.

19. Ibid., p. 45.

20. Ibid., p. 33.

21. Hans Baerwald, *Party Politics in Japan* (Boston: Allen & Unwin, 1986), pp. 12–33.

Chapter 5. Mandarin Strategies: Japan's Industrial Policy

1. *Business Week*, 9 August 1982, p. 42.

2. Ministry of International Trade and Industry, "Note on U.S. Industry Related Policies," Industrial Policy Dialogue, Tokyo, 12 September 1983 (photocopy).

3. Ministry of International Trade and Industry, *The Vision of MITI Policies in the 1980s*, p. 15.

4. Hiroya Veno, quoted in Marie Anchordoguy, "The State and the Market: Industrial Policy Towards Japan's Computer Industry," Ph.D. dissertation, Harvard University, 1986, p. 21.

5. Organization for Economic Cooperation and Development, *Japan Economic Survey* (Paris: OECD, July 1984), pp. 84, 88.

6. National Science Board, *Science Indicators 1986* (Washington, D.C.: National Science Board, 1987), p. 192.

7. Joseph A. Schumpeter, *Capitalism, Socialism, and Democracy,* 3rd ed. (New York: Harper & Brothers, 1950), p. 84.

8. Ibid., p. 84.

9. Bruce R. Scott and Peter Fuchs, "Japan as No. 1," case study (Boston: Harvard Business School, 1986).

10. Miyohei Shinohara, *Industrial Growth, Trade, and Dynamic Patterns in the Japanese Economy* (Tokyo: University of Tokyo Press, 1982), pp. 21–57.

11. Long Term Credit Bank, *Annual Report 1981,* Tokyo, 1982.

12. For more discussion, see *The Yearbook of U.S.–Japan Economic Relations* (Washington, D.C.: Japan Economic Institute of America, 1979–80).

13. International Trade Commission ruling on Fiber Optics, Corning Glass Corp. *v.* Sumitomo (18 April 1985 [photocopy]).

14. Stuart Auerbach, "U.S.–Japan Trade Cable Released by Rep. Dingell," *Washington Post,* 28 April 1987, p. C1.

15. Michael Dickey of Cray Research, interview with author, April 1987.

16. Space Activities Commission, "Outline of Japan's Space Development Policy," unofficial translation, rev. ed., 23 February 1984 (Tokyo: Space Activities Commission [photocopy]), p. 7.

17. Ministry of International Trade and Industry, *Report of the Aircraft Machinery Industries Council* (Tokyo: MITI, April 1985), p. 5.

18. Comptroller General of the United States, *U.S. Military Coproduction Programs Assist Japan in Developing Its Civil Aircraft Industry.* Report to the Chairman, Subcommittee on Trade, Committee on Ways and Means, U.S. Congress, House of Representatives (Washington, D.C.: General Accounting Office, 1982), p. ii.

19. Ibid., pp. 19–21, and Dan Morgan, "Is It Sharing Know-How or Selling the Store?" *Washington Post,* 4 May 1983, p. 1.

20. Morgan, "Is It Sharing Know-How or Selling the Store?," p. 24.

21. *Japan Metal Bulletin,* 6 October 1977, cited in Verner, Liipfert, Bernhard, McPherson & Hand, *Japanese Government Promotion of the Steel Industry: Three Decades of Industrial Policy.* Study prepared for U.S. Steel Corporation and Bethlehem Steel Corporation (Cupertino, Calif.: Semiconductor Industry Association, 1983), p. 39.

22. *Japan Metal Bulletin,* 25 August 1979, cited in Verner et al., *Japanese Government Promotion of the Steel Industry,* p. 17.

23. "Fair Trade Commission Investigates Steel Price Hikes," *Japan Economic Journal,* 11 May 1982.

24. *Nihon Keizai,* 7 January 1981, cited in Verner et al., *Japanese Government Promotion of the Steel Industry,* p. 34.

25. "Papermakers Engage in Joint Activity," *Japan Economic Journal,* 10 September 1981, p. 4.

26. Industrial Structure Council, *Japan's Petrochemical Industry in the 1980s* (Tokyo: Ministry of International Trade and Industry, 1981), p. 4.

27. See Richard J. Samuels, "Industrial Destructuring of the Japanese Aluminum Industry," *Pacific Affairs* 56 (Fall 1983): 498.

28. Frank Upham, "Legal Framework of Structurally Depressed Industry Policy," mimeographed paper, Boston College Law School, 1983, p. 12.

29. See OECD Report on Positive Adjustment of Mature Industries (Paris: Organization for Economic Cooperation and Development, 1982).

30. Yoshizo Ikeda, "How Tokyo Can Regain Its Credibility," *New York Times*, 23 October 1983, p. 2.

## Chapter 6. *Kaisha:* Doing Business in Japan

1. Terutomo Ozawa, "Japan's Industrial Groups," *Michigan State University Business Topics* 28 (Autumn 1980): 34.

2. Dodwell Marketing Consultants, *Industrial Groups of Japan* (Tokyo, 1987).

3. *Nippon Electric Company (NEC) Yuka Shoken* (Japanese version of Securities Exchange Commission 10K Report) (Tokyo: Ministry of Finance, 1983).

4. Ozawa, "Japan's Industrial Groups," p. 38.

5. Bruce R. Scott, John W. Rosenblum, and Audrey T. Sproat, *Case Studies in Political Economy* (Boston: Harvard Business School, 1980), pp. 229–30.

6. I gathered this story from interviews with executives of Cray, Nissan, and Japanese government officials, September 1986.

7. *Technocrat* (Tokyo, March 1975).

8. Department of Commerce, "Soda Ash Analysis," November 1981 (photocopy). See also soda ash reports done by Thomas Howell of Dewey Ballantine, Washington, D.C., 1986–87.

9. Japan Fair Trade Commission, "Soda Ash Investigation," August 1982–March 1983 (photocopy).

10. John Andrews, president of the American National Soda Ash Corporation, interview with author, September 1986.

11. Kozo Yamamura and Gary Saxonhouse, eds., *Law and Trade Issues of the Japanese Economy* (Seattle: University of Washington Press, 1986), p. 241.

12. James C. Abegglen and George Stalk, Jr., *Kaisha: The Japanese Corporation* (New York: Basic Books, 1985), pp. 176–77.

13. *NEC Yuka Shoken* (Japanese version of SEC 10K Report) (Tokyo: Ministry of Finance, 1985).

14. Ibid.

15. U.S. Department of Defense, *Report on Semiconductor Dependency*, p. 59.

16. Semiconductor Industry Association, "Performance of the U.S. Semiconductor Industry, 1975 to 1985" (Cupertino, Calif.: Semiconductor Industry Association, 1986), p. 16 (photocopy).

17. Ibid.

18. *Nomura Investment Report* (Tokyo: Nomura Research, Inc., March 1987), p. 7.

19. George Hatsopoulos, *High Cost of Capital: Handicap of American Industry* (Washington, D.C.: American Business Conference, 1983), p. 3.

20. Figures from interviews with senior NEC officials, Spring 1987.

21. *NEC Yuka Shoken*, 1983.

22. Interviews with MITI officials, September 1986.

23. Abegglen and Stalk, *Kaisha: The Japanese Corporation*, p. 74.

24. Semiconductor Industry Association, *The U.S. Crisis in Microelectronics* (San Jose: Semiconductor Industry Association, 1987), p. 25.

25. Abegglen and Stalk, *Kaisha: The Japanese Corporation,* p. 121.

26. Ibid., p. 124.

27. Ibid., p. 127.

28. Ibid., p. 124.

29. U.S. Department of Defense, *Report on Semiconductor Dependency,* p. 56.

30. Abegglen and Stalk, *Kaisha: The Japanese Corporation,* p. 143.

31. Japanese Technology Evaluation Program, *Panel Report* (LaJolla, Calif.: Science Applications International Corporation, June 1985).

32. *NEC Yuka Shoken,* 1985.

33. Ibid.

34. Naohiro Amaya, *Seisui no Sentaku* (Tokyo: PHP Research Center), p. 26.

35. "IBM: The Untruth of the Black Ship Uproar," *Nihon Keizai,* 12 December 1985, p. 6.

36. *Nihon Keizai,* 1 August 1978 cited in Verner, Liipfert, Bernhard, McPherson & Hand, *The Effect of Government Targeting,* p. 17.

37. "The Tightest of Closed Shops," *Far Eastern Economic Review,* June 1987, p. 71.

38. Ibid., p. 71.

39. Steven P. Galante, "Japanese Have Another Trade Barrier: They Favor Business With Japanese," *Wall Street Journal,* 12 April 1984, p. 36.

## Chapter 7. Every Man for Himself: Doing Business in the United States

1. Jean Jacques Servan-Schreiber, *The American Challenge,* trans. Ronald Steel (New York: Atheneum, 1968).

2. "The Hollow Corporation," *Business Week,* 3 March 1986, p. 56.

3. Robert Z. Lawrence, *Can America Compete?* (Washington, D.C.: Brookings Institution, 1984).

4. Lewis H. Young, "Technology Going East," *New York Times,* 10 August 1986, sec. 4, p. 2.

5. Bud Newman, "Brock Scolds 'Turkey' Management," *Washington Post,* 16 June 1987, p. C2.

6. David Halberstam, *The Reckoning* (New York: William Morrow, 1986).

7. Harry M. Petrakis, *The Founder's Touch* (New York: McGraw-Hill, 1965), p. 136.

8. Motorola, *Annual Report 1986.*

9. Ibid.

10. Naohiro Amaya, *Seisui no Sentaku* (Tokyo: PHP Research Center), p. 41.

11. See Robert Christopher, *Second to None.*

12. "How to Beat Japan," *U.S. News and World Report,* 24 August 1987, p. 44.

13. James Fallows, "Playing by Different Rules," *The Atlantic*, September 1987, p. 26.

14. Harvard Business School, *Zenith Radio Corporation v. The United States: 1977* (Boston: HBS Case Services, Harvard Business School, 1978), p. 27.

15. John Zysman and Laura Tyson, eds., *American Industry in International Competition* (Ithaca: Cornell University Press, 1983), p. 117.

16. Ibid., p. 118.

17. Harvard Business School, *Zenith Radio Corporation v. The United States: 1977*, p. 27.

18. Marvin J. Wolf, *The Japanese Conspiracy* (New York: Empire Books, 1983), pp. 22–61. See also Kozo Yamamura and Gary Saxonhouse, *Law and Trade Issues of the Japanese Economy* (Seattle: University of Washington Press, 1986), pp. 238–70.

19. Yamamura and Saxonhouse, *Law and Trade Issues*, p. 259.

20. Ibid., p. 256.

21. Ibid., p. 263.

22. Harvard Business School, *Zenith Radio Corporation vs. The United States: 1977*, p. 5.

23. Ibid., pp. 8–9.

24. Ibid., pp. 9–10.

25. See Yamamura and Saxonhouse, *Law and Trade Issues*, pp. 238–70.

26. Zysman and Tyson, *American Industry in International Competition*, p. 115.

27. *Business Week*, September 1984.

28. Motorola *Annual Reports* and *NEC's Yuka Shoken*.

29. Robert Lipsey and Irving Kravis, *The Competitiveness and Comparative Advantage of U.S. Multinationals, 1957–83*, working paper 2051 (Cambridge, Mass.: National Bureau of Economic Research, 1987).

30. "Can America Compete?" *Business Week*, 20 April 1987, p. 45.

31. "Japan, U.S.A.," *Business Week*, 14 July 1986, p. 49.

32. "Japan, U.S.A.," *Business Week*, p. 45.

33. ABC News Broadcast, 28 March 1987.

34. Advisory Council on Japan–U.S. Economic Relations, *Understanding the Industrial Policies and Practices of Japan and the United States: A Business Perspective* (Washington, D.C.: Advisory Council on Japan–U.S. Economic Relations, July 1984), p. 3.

35. Lipsey and Kravis, *The Competitiveness and Comparative Advantage of U.S. Multinationals*, p. 8.

## Chapter 8. Traders or Warriors: The Conflict between Economic and National Security

1. Covington & Burling, *Petition Under the National Security Clause, Section 232 of the Trade Expansion Act of 1962 (19 U.S.C. 1862), For Adjustment of Imports of Machine Tools*, submitted by National Tool Builders Association, Washington, March 1983, p. 76.

2. Ibid., p. 68.

3. Ibid., p. 41.

4. Department of Commerce, "Comparison of the U.S. and Japan Machine Tool Industries," June 1982, p. 10 (photocopy).

5. Ibid.

6. Covington & Burling, *Petition to the President of the United States through the Office of the U.S. Trade Representative for the Exercise of Presidential Discretion Authorized by Section 301 of the Revenue Act of 1971*, submitted by Houdaille Industries, Washington, D.C., 3 May 1982, pp. 55, 76, 81.

7. Covington & Burling, *Comments by the Petitioner*, 31 July 1982, Washington, D.C., p. 10.

8. National Academy of Engineering, *The Competitive States of the U.S. Machine Tool Industry*, Washington, D.C., 1983, p. 21; see also Japan Machine Tool Builders Association Annual Reports, Tokyo.

9. National Machine Tool Builders Association, "Statistics and Analysis," McLean, Va., March 1983 (photocopy).

10. Covington & Burling, *Houdaille Petition*, pp. 123–36.

11. Ibid., pp. 160–65.

12. See section 103, U.S. Revenue Act of 1971, 26 U.S.C., Para. 48 (a)(7)(D).

13. Department of Commerce, Houdaille Petition Machine Tool Analysis, February 1983 (photocopy).

14. Cravath, Swaine & Moore, *Computer-Aided Manufacturing: The Japanese Challenge*, comments submitted to the U.S. International Trade Commission in Investigation no. 332-149 under 19 U.S.C. 1332 (b), Washington, D.C., 1982, p. 3; see also U.S. Department of Commerce, *U.S. Competitiveness in High Technology Industries*, Washington, D.C., February 1983.

15. Reports on bidding results supplied by Siemens Allis, 21 June 1983.

16. Presentation by Boeing Corporation to the Department of Commerce, March 1984.

17. Covington & Burling, *Petition Under the National Security Clause, Section 232 of the Trade Expansion Act of 1962*, p. 138.

18. Cravath, Swaine & Moore, *Computer-Aided Manufacturing*, p. 3.

19. White House press release, 16 December 1986.

20. Paul R. Krugman, ed., *Strategic Trade Policy and the New International Economics* (Cambridge, Mass.: Massachusetts Institute of Technology Press, 1987), pp. 12–15.

21. "Military Spending and Industrial Performance," *New York Times*, 11 November 1986.

22. David H. Brandin and Michael A. Harrison, *The Technology War* (New York: John Wiley, 1987), p. 130.

23. U.S. Department of Defense, *Report on Semiconductor Dependency*, p. 49.

24. Tom Wicker, "How We Got There," *New York Times*, 16 November 1987, p. A19.

## Chapter 9. U.S. Trade Negotiations: The Players

1. Bureau of the Census, *U.S. Merchandise Trade, 1986* (Washington, D.C.: Department of Commerce, 1986), p. 3.

2. Ibid.

3. See *Yearbook of U.S.–Japan Economic Relations, 1978*, p. 52.

4. *Business Week*, 9 August 1982, p. 42, cited in Verner, Liipfert, Bernhard, McPherson & Hand, *The Effect of Government Targeting on World Semiconductor Competition* (Cupertino, Calif.: Semiconductor Industry Association, 1983), p. 85.

5. Chalmers Johnson, interview with author, February 1987.

6. Ivan Hall, "How Mutual Understanding Keeps Japan Closed," unpublished manuscript (Tokyo: Keio University, June 1987), p. 10.

7. *Wall Street Journal*, 6 July 1987, editorial page.

8. Glen S. Fukushima, "The U.S–Japan Trade Conflict: A View from Washington," *Bulletin of the International House* 6 (Spring 1986): 7.

9. Hall, "How Mutual Understanding Keeps Japan Closed," p. 10.

10. Karel van Wolferen, "The Japan Problem," *Foreign Affairs*, Spring 1987.

11. "Nichi-bei Tomo Ni Kosu o Kiri Kaeru Toki" ("Time for Japan and America to Change Course"), *Japan Press Club Bulletin* (Tokyo), 9 June 1987, p. 2.

12. National Institute for Research Advancement, *The Role of Congressional Staff in U.S. Policy Decision Making* (Tokyo: National Institute for Research Advancement, June 1984).

13. *Report of the Attorney General on Administration of the Foreign Agents Registration Act, 1985* (Washington, D.C.: Department of Justice).

14. David Osborne, "Lobbying for Japan, Inc," *New York Times Magazine*, 4 December 1983, p. 131.

15. Thomas B. Edsall, "GOP Chairman Helped Clients Contact Government Officials," *Washington Post*, 22 August 1987, p. A2d.

16. Stuart Auerbach, "Japan Tries to Blunt Toshiba Scandal," *Washington Post*, 3 September 1987, p. B1.

17. Edward T. Pound and David Rogers, "Savvy Lobbyists Gain Clout in Washington for Foreign Clients," *Wall Street Journal*, 14 July 1986, p. 1.

18. *Report of the Attorney General on Administration of the Foreign Agents Registration Act, 1985*.

19. Pound and Rogers, "Savvy Lobbyists," p. 1.

20. James Rowley, "U.S. Trade Official Asked Japanese Car Makers for Job," *Washington Post*, 6 October 1987, p. D3.

## Chapter 10. U.S. Trade Negotiations: An Insider's Report

1. United Nations, *Commodity Trade Statistics. Statistical Papers*, Series A (New York: United Nations, 1983).

2. For more discussion, see Bruce R. Scott and George C. Lodge, eds., *U.S. Competitiveness in the World Economy* (Boston: Harvard Business School Press, 1985), pp. 75–91.

3. Interview with National Institutes of Health personnel office, July 1982.

4. C. Fred Bergsten and William R. Cline, *The United States–Japan Economic Problem* (Washington, D.C.: Institute for International Economics, 1985), p. 124.

5. Bela Balassa, "Japan's Trade Policies," paper presented at the conference on "Free Trade in the World Economy towards an Opening of Markets," Institute of World Economics, Kiel, Germany, 24–26 June 1986, p. 11.

6. U.S. Department of Commerce, Japan Office estimates, 1983 (photocopy).

7. For details of package, see *Yearbook of U.S.–Japan Economic Relations, 1982*, p. 50.

8. James Rowley, "U.S. Trade Official Asked Japanese Car Makers for Job," *Washington Post*, 6 October 1987, p. D3.

9. Chalmers Johnson, "MITI, MPT, and the Telecom Wars" (Berkeley Roundtable on the International Economy, working paper no. 21, University of California, Berkeley, 11 September 1986 [photocopy]), p. 23.

10. *Nihon Keizai*, 16 March 1985.

## Chapter 11. Waking Up

1. Hobart Rowen, "Japan Has a Yen for U.S. Property," *Washington Post*, 25 January 1987, p. K1.

2. Nikko Research Center, *Japan's Cooperation for the Revitalization of American Industry* (Tokyo: Nikko Research Center, 1981), p. 1.

3. James Fallows, "Playing by Different Rules," *Atlantic Monthly*, September 1987, p. 29.

4. First Manhattan Consulting Group analysis, May 1987.

5. "Japan's Future Foreign Investment," *Nihon Keizai*, 13 January 1987, p. 5.

6. Robert Kearns, "Japan-America, Inc.," *Chicago Tribune*, 15 April 1987, p. 1.

7. Originally in *Keidanren Geppo* (in Japanese), September 1986, pp. 2–25, translated in *Japan Report* (Springfield, Va.: Foreign Broadcast Information Service, 3 February 1987), pp. 30–31.

8. Bruce Nussbaum, "And Now the Bill Comes Due," *Business Week*, 16 November 1987, p. 161.

9. Lamar Alexander speech, January 1987, Nashville, Tennessee.

10. Martha Layne Collins, on *Adam Smith's Money World*, 2 March 1987.

11. Martin Tolchin, "Foreign Investment in U.S. Mutes Trade Debate," *New York Times*, 8 February 1987.

12. Ibid.

13. C. Fred Bergsten, on *Adam Smith's Money World*, 2 March 1987.

14. Michael R. Sesit and Judith Valente, "Komori's Pact with A.M. Inter-

national Shows New Muscle of Japanese Firms," *Wall Street Journal,* 23 November 1987, p. 8.

15. Masahiko Ishizuka, "Japan Weighs Its Proper Distance from the U.S.," *Japan Economic Journal,* 17 October 1987, p. 27.

16. Teruhiko Mano, quoted in "Wake Up America," *Business Week,* 16 November 1987, p. 170.

17. Kathryn Graven, "Japanese Housewives Grow More Resentful of Executive Spouses," *Wall Street Journal,* 30 September 1987, p. 1.

18. Kenichi Ohmae, "If They Fall, So Will Our Stock Markets," *New York Times,* 11 October 1987, p. 3.

19. Fallows, "Playing by Different Rules," p. 29.

20. Margaret Shapiro, "Tokyo's Land Madness: $12 Million Condos or Two-Hour Commutes," *Washington Post,* 20 September 1987, p. A33.

21. Fallows, "Playing by Different Rules," 29.

22. Kenichi Ohmae, *Beyond National Borders* (Homewood, Ill.: Dow Jones-Irwin, 1987), p. 9.

23. Peter F. Drucker, "Japan's Choices," *Foreign Affairs* 65 (Summer 1987): 923–41.

24. Advisory Council on Japan–U.S. Economic Relations, *Understanding the Industrial Policies and Practices of Japan and the U.S.,* July 1984, p. 4.

25. National Science Board, *Science Indicators 1986,* p. 192.

26. Stephen K. Yoder, "Racing to Commercialize Superconductors," *Wall Street Journal,* 20 March 1987, p. 4.

27. Kathy Sawyer, "Commercializing Superconductors," *Washington Post,* 29 July 1987, p. A3.

28. National Academy of Sciences, *Report on Superconductivity* (Washington, D.C.: National Academy of Sciences, October 1987), p. 6.

29. "Who Pays for High Tech?" *Washington Post,* 21 September 1987, p. A14.

30. David H. Brandin and Michael A. Harrison, *The Technology War* (New York: John Wiley, 1987), p. 61.

31. Testimony of Undersecretary of Commerce Bruce Smart before the Subcommittee on Science and Technology, U.S. Senate Finance Committee, 15 October 1987.

32. Ohmae, *Beyond National Borders,* p. 67.

33. Nikko Research Center, *Japan's Cooperation,* p. 5.

34. Benjamin Franklin, cited in John Bartlett, *Familiar Quotations* (Boston: Little Brown and Company, 1980), p. 348.

# BIBLIOGRAPHY

Abegglen, James C., and George Stalk, Jr. 1985. *Kaisha: The Japanese Corporation*. New York: Basic Books.

Advisory Council on Japan–U.S. Economic Relations. 1984. *High Technology Position Papers*. Washington, D.C.: Advisory Council on Japan–U.S. Economic Relations.

———. 1984 *The Trade Effects of Japan's Industrial Policies: An American Business Perspective*. Washington, D.C.: Advisory Council on Japan–U.S. Economic Relations.

———. 1984. *Understanding the Industrial Policies and Practices of Japan and the United States—A Business Perspective*. Japan–U.S. Businessmen's Conference Joint Study. Washington, D.C.: Advisory Council on Japan–U.S. Economic Relations.

Amaya, Naohiro. 1984. *Seisui no Sentaku* (Choosing Rising or Falling). Tokyo: PHP Research Center.

American Chamber of Commerce in Japan. 1980. *U.S. Manufacturing Investment in Japan: White Paper*. Tokyo: Radio Press.

Anchordoguy, Marie. 1986. "The State and the Market: Industrial Policy Towards Japan's Computer Industry." Ph.D. dissertation, Harvard University.

Baerwald, Hans. 1986. *Party Politics in Japan*. Boston: Allen & Unwin.

Balassa, Bela. 1986. "Japan's Trade Policies." Paper presented at conference on Free Trade in the World Economy towards an Opening of Markets, Institute of World Economics, 24–26 June, Kiel, West Germany.

Baranson, Jack. 1981. *The Japanese Challenge to U.S. Industry*. Lexington, Mass.: Lexington Books.

Benedict, Ruth. [1946]. 1974. *The Chrysanthemum and the Sword*. Reprint. New York: New American Library.

Bergsten, C. Fred, and William R. Cline. 1985. *The United States–Japan Economic Problem.* Washington, D.C.: Institute for International Economics.

Bloom, Justin L. 1984. *Japan's Ministry of International Trade and Industry as a Policy Instrument in the Development of Information Technology.* Cambridge, Mass.: Harvard University Program on Information Resources Policy, Center for Information Policy Research.

Botkin, James W., Dan Dimancescu, and Ray Stata. 1982. *Global Stakes: The Future of High Technology in America.* Cambridge: Ballinger.

Brandin, David H., and Michael A. Harrison. 1986. *The Technology War.* New York: John Wiley.

Brandin, David, et al. 1984. *Japanese Technology Evaluation Program Panel Report on Computer Science in Japan.* LaJolla, Calif.: Science Applications International Corporation.

Bressand, Albert. 1987. "Chaos: Strategic Tool." *The International Economy,* November, p. 44.

Brown, Warren. 1986 "Q & A: Kenneth Iverson." *Washington Post,* 3 August, p. F4.

Bureau of the Census. 1986. *U.S. Merchandise Trade, 1986.* Washington, D.C.: Department of Commerce.

*Business Week* Team, Bruce Nussbaum, Edward M. Mervosh, Jack Kramer, Lenny Glynn, Lewis Beman, William Wolman, and Lewis H. Young. 1980. *The Decline of U.S. Power.* Boston: Houghton Mifflin.

"Can America Compete?" 1987. *Business Week,* 20 April, pp. 44–69.

Cannon, Lou, and Stuart Auerbach. 1987. "Stop 'Hemming and Hawing' on Trade, Reagan bids Japan, Also Warning Hill." *Washington Post,* 28 April, p. A4.

Christopher, Robert C. 1986. *Second to None.* New York: Crown.

Cohen, Stephen D. 1985. *Uneasy Partnership.* Cambridge, Mass.: Ballinger.

Cohen, Stephen D., and John Zysman. 1987. *Manufacturing Matters.* New York: Basic Books.

Commission of the European Communities. 1984. "Revised List of Requests to the Japanese Authorities." April. Brussels. Photocopy.

Comptroller General of the United States. 1982. *U.S. Military Coproduction Programs Assist Japan in Developing Its Civil Aircraft Industry.* Report to the Chairman, Subcommittee on Trade, Committee on Ways and Means, U.S. Congress, House of Representatives. Washington, D.C.: Government Accounting Office.

*Computer White Paper 1986 Edition.* 1986. Trans. John McWilliams. Tokyo: Japan Information Processing Development Center.

Covington & Burling. 1982. *Comments by the Petitioner.* Washington, D.C.: Houdaille Industries.

——. 1982. *Petition to the President of the United States through the Office of the United States Trade Representative for the Exercise of Presidential Discretion Authorized by Section 103 of the Revenue Act of 1971.* Washington, D.C.: Houdaille Industries.

——. 1983. *Petition Under the National Security Clause, Section 232 of the Trade Expansion Act of 1962 (19 U.S.C. 1962), for Adjustment of Imports of Machine*

*Tools.* Submitted by the National Tool Builders Association. Washington, D.C.

Crandall, Robert W. 1981. *The U.S. Steel Industry in Recurrent Crisis.* Washington, D.C.: The Brookings Institution.

Cravath, Swaine & Moore, 1982. *Computer-Aided Manufacturing: The Japanese Challenge.* Washington, D.C.: Cravath, Swaine & Moore. 1982.

Davidson, William Harley. 1984. *The Amazing Race.* New York: John Wiley.

Dewey, Ballantine, Bushby, Palmer & Wood. 1985. "Brief of the Semiconductor Industry Association before the Section 301 Committee, Office of the United States Trade Representative." 22 October, Washington, D.C. Photocopy.

Dodwell Marketing Consultants. 1987. *Industrial Groupings in Japan.* rev. ed. Tokyo: Dodwell.

Doi, Takeo, M.D. 1986. *The Anatomy of Dependence.* Trans. John Bester. Originally published as *Amae no kozo* (Tokyo: Kobundo, 1971). Tokyo: Kodansha.

Drifte, Reinhard. 1986. *Arms Production in Japan.* Boulder, Colo.: Westview Press.

Drucker, Peter F. 1987. "Japan's Choices." *Foreign Affairs* (Summer).

Edsall, Thomas B. 1987. "GOP Chairman Helps Clients Contact Government Officials." *Washington Post,* 22 August, p. A2.

Electronics International Corporation. 1986. *Electronics in the World—Europe/United States/Japan.* New York: E.I.C.

Fallows, James. 1987. "Playing by Different Rules." *Atlantic Monthly,* September, pp. 22–32.

Fields, George. 1983. *From Bonsai to Levi's.* New York: Macmillan.

Finan, William F., and Chris B. Amundsen. 1985. "An Analysis of the Effects of Targeting on the Competitiveness of the U.S. Semiconductor Industry." A study prepared for the Office of the United States Special Trade Representative, the Department of Commerce and the Department of Labor. Washington, D.C.: Quick Finan & Associates. Photocopy.

——. 1985. "Report on Estimating U.S. Market Share in Japan." Report to the Semiconductor Industry Association. November. Washington, D.C.: Quick Finan & Associates. Photocopy.

Finan, William F., Perry D. Quick, and Karen M. Sandberg. 1986. "The U.S. Trade Position in High Technology: 1980–1986." A Report Prepared for the Joint Economic Committee of the U.S. Congress. October. Photocopy.

Finn, Edwin A., Jr. 1987. "In Japan We (Must) Trust." *Forbes,* 21 September, p. 34.

Frost, Ellen. 1987. *For Richer, For Poorer.* New York: Council on Foreign Relations.

Fukushima, Glen S. 1986. "The U.S.–Japan Trade Conflict: A View from Washington." *Bulletin of the International House* 6 (2): 7.

"Future Direct U.S. Investment Discussed." 1987. Translated. (Originally in Japanese, in *Keidanren GEPPO,* September 1986, pp. 2–25.) Springfield, Va.: Foreign Broadcast Information Service, 3 February, pp. 30–49.

Galante, Steven P. 1984. "Japanese Have Another Trade Barrier: They Favor

Business with Japanese." *Wall Street Journal,* 12 April, p. 36.

Gibney, Frank. 1979. *Japan: The Fragile Super Power.* Rev. ed. Tokyo: Charles E. Tuttle.

*Global Competition: The New Reality.* 1985. The Report of the President's Commission on Industrial Competitiveness. 2 vols. Washington, D.C.: Superintendent of Documents.

Graves, Harold M., et al. 1984. *Changes in the U.S. Telecommunications Industry and the Impact on U.S. Telecommunications Trade.* Report to the Committee on Finance, U.S. Senate, on Investigation no. 332-172, under Section 332 of the Tariff Act of 1930. Washington, D.C.: U.S. International Trade Commission Publication 1542.

Gregory, Gene A., and Akio Etori. 1981. "Japanese Technology Today." *Scientific American,* October, pp. 45–46.

Gresser, Julian. 1984. *Partners in Prosperity.* New York: McGraw-Hill.

Halberstam, David. 1986. *The Reckoning.* New York: William Morrow.

Hall, Ivan. 1987. "How Mutual Understanding Keeps Japan Closed." Keio Univ., Tokyo, June. Unpublished manuscript.

Harvard Business School. 1978. *Zenith Radio Corporation v. the United States: 1977.* Boston: HBS Case Services, Harvard Business School.

Hatsopoulos, George. 1983. *High Cost of Capital: Handicap of American Industry.* Washington, D.C.: American Business Conference.

Hatter, Victoria L. 1985. *U.S. High Technology Trade and Competitiveness Staff Report.* Prepared by the Office of Trade and Investment Analysis, U.S. Department of Commerce, International Trade Administration. Washington, D.C.

Hearn, Lafcadio. 1970. *Japan: An Interpretation.* Tokyo: Charles E. Tuttle.

Hofheinz, Roy, Jr., and Kent E. Calder. 1982. *The Eastasia Edge.* New York: Basic Books.

"The Hollow Corporation." 1986. *Business Week,* 3 March.

"Hong Kong Appeals to Japan for More Trade." 1984. *Journal of Commerce,* 13 December, p. 5a.

"How to Beat Japan." 1987. *U.S. News and World Report,* 24 August 1987, p. 44. ──

Hufbauer, Gary Clyde, Diane T. Berliner, and Kimberly Ann Elliott. 1986. *Trade Protection in the United States: 31 Case Studies.* Washington, D.C.: Institute for International Economics.

Hufbauer, Gary Clyde, and Howard F. Rosen. 1986. "Trade Policy for Troubled Industries." *Policy Analyses in International Economics,* Series 15. Washington, D.C.: Institute for International Economics.

Hufbauer, Gary Clyde, and Jeffrey J. Schott. 1985. "Trading for Growth: The Next Round of Trade Negotiations." *Policy Analyses in International Economics.* Washington, D.C.: Institute for International Economics.

Ishizuka, Masahiko. 1987. "Japan Weighs Its Proper Distance from the U.S." *Japan Economic Journal,* 17 October, p. 27.

Japan Electronic Industry Development Association. 1976. *Monthly Report of the Electronics Industry* 18 (January 1976).

*Japanese Government Policy for the Computer Industry.* 1979. Tokyo: Japan Electronic Computer Corporation.

*Japanese Laws, Government and Industry Documents, and Press Reports Relating to Japan's Promotion of Its Semiconductor Industry, 1967–83.* 1983. Cupertino, Calif.: Semiconductor Industry Association.

Japanese Technology Evaluation Program. 1985. *Panel Report.* La Jolla, Calif.: Science Applications International Corporation.

Japan Fair Trade Commission. 1983. "Soda Ash Investigation." March. Tokyo: Photocopy.

Japan Information Processing Development Center. 1985. *Present Situation of Information Processing in Japan.* Tokyo: JIPDEC.

"Japan on Wall Street." 1987. *Business Week,* 7 September, p. 85.

"Japan's Strategy for the '80s." 1981. *Business Week,* 14 December, pp. 39–120.

Johnson, Chalmers, ed. 1984. *The Industrial Policy Debate.* San Francisco: Institute for Contemporary Studies Press.

———. 1982. *MITI and the Japanese Miracle.* Stanford: Stanford University Press.

———. 1986. "MITI, MPT, and the Telecom Wars." Berkeley Roundtable on the International Economy Working Paper no. 21. Berkeley: Roundtable on the International Economy, 11 September, University of California.

Kearns, Robert. 1987. "Japan–America Inc." *Chicago Tribune,* 15 April, sec. 7, pp. 1, 7.

Krugman, Paul R., ed. 1987. *Strategic Trade Policy and the New International Economics.* Cambridge, Mass.: Massachusetts Institute of Technology Press.

Lawrence, Robert Z. 1984. *Can America Compete?* Washington, D.C.: Brookings Institution.

Lazlo, John J., Jr. 1985. *The Japanese Semiconductor Industry.* San Francisco: Hambrecht & Quist.

Lincoln, Edward J. 1984. *Japan's Industrial Policies.* Washington, D.C.: Japan Economic Institute of America.

Lipsey, Robert, and Irving Kravis. 1987. *The Competitiveness and Comparative Advantage of U.S. Multinationals, 1957–83.* Working Paper no. 2051. Cambridge, Mass.: National Bureau of Economic Research.

Long Term Credit Bank. 1981. *Annual Report.* Tokyo.

Magaziner, Ira C., and Robert B. Reich. 1982. *Minding America's Business.* New York: Harcourt Brace Jovanovich.

Marris, Stephen. 1985. "Deficits and the Dollar: The World Economy at Risk." *Policy Analyses in International Economics,* Series 14. Washington, D.C.: Institute for International Economics.

McCraw, Thomas K., ed. 1986. *America Versus Japan.* Boston: Harvard Business School Press.

McKenna, Regis. 1986 *ECONS, Republished Graphics on Economy, Trade and Issues Affecting Technology Industries.* Palo Alto: McKenna.

Ministry of Finance, Japan. *NEC Yuka Shoken 1980–85.* Tokyo.

Ministry of International Trade and Industry, Japan. 1983. "Note on U.S. Industry-Related Policies." *Industrial Policy Dialogue,* 12 September. Photocopy.

———. 1985. *Report of the Aircraft Machinery Industries Council.* Tokyo: MITI.

——. 1980. *The Vision of MITI Policies in the 1980s.* Tokyo: MITI.

——. 1984. *White Paper on International Trade 1984.* Tokyo: MITI.

——. 1985. *White Paper on International Trade 1985.* Tokyo: MITI.

——. 1981. Industrial Structure Council. *Japan's Petrochemical Industry in the 1980s.* Tokyo: MITI.

Monsanto Electronic Materials Company. 1985. "Japanese Barriers to U.S. Silicon Imports." 22 July. Photocopy.

Moody's Investors Service. 1982. *Moody's Bank and Finance Manual 1982.* New York: Moody's Investors Service.

——. 1987. *Moody's Bank and Finance Manual 1987.* New York: Moody's Investors Service.

Motorola Corporation. 1986. *Annual Report 1986.* Schaumburg, Illinois: Motorola Corporation.

Nakamura, Takafusa. 1981. *The Postwar Japanese Economy.* Trans. Jacqueline Kaminski. Tokyo: University of Tokyo Press. Originally published as *Nihon Keizai: Sono Seicho to Kozo,* 2nd ed. (Tokyo: University of Tokyo Press, 1980).

Nakane, Chi. 1967. *The Vertical Society.* Tokyo: Kodansha.

Nanto, Dick K., et al. 1985. *Japan's Economy and Trade with the United States.* Selected papers submitted to the Subcommittee on Economic Goals and Intergovernmental Policy, Joint Economic Committee, U.S. Congress. Washington, D.C.

National Academy of Engineering. 1983. *The Competitive Status of the U.S. Machine Tool Industry.* Washington, D.C.: National Academy Press.

——. 1987. *Strengthening U.S. Engineering Through International Cooperation: Some Recommendations for Action.* Washington, D.C.: National Academy Press.

National Academy of Science. 1987. *Report on Superconductivity.* Washington, D.C.: National Academy of Science.

National Institute for Research Advancement. 1984. *The Role of Congressional Staff in U.S. Policy Decision Making.* Tokyo: National Institute for Research Advancement.

National Machine Tool Builders Association. 1983. "Statistics and Analysis." NMTBA, McLean, Va. Photocopy.

National Science Board. 1987. *Science Indicators 1986.* Washington, D.C.: National Science Board.

"Nichi-bei Tomo Ni Kosu o Kiri Kaeru Toki" (Time for Japan and America to Change Course). 1987. *Japan Press Club Bulletin,* 9 June, p. 2.

Nikko Research Center. 1981. *Japan's Cooperation for the Revitalization of American Industry.* Tokyo: Nikko Research Center.

Nomura Research, Inc. 1987. *Nomura Investment Report.* Tokyo: Nomura Research, Inc.

Norman, E. Herbert. 1975. *Origins of the Modern Japanese State: Selected Writings of E. H. Norman.* Ed. John W. Dower. New York: Pantheon, 1975.

Nussbaum, Bruce. 1987. "And Now the Bill Comes Due." *Business Week,* 16 November, pp. 160–63.

Office of the U.S. Trade Representative. 1986. "Arrangement between the Government of Japan and the Government of the United States of America concerning Trade." Washington, D.C., 2 September. Photocopy.

Ohmae, Kenichi. 1987. *Beyond National Borders*. Homewood, Ill.: Dow Jones–Irwin.

Organization for Economic Cooperation and Development. 1984. *Japan Economic Survey*. Paris: OECD.

Ozawa, Terutomo. 1980. "Japan's Industrial Groups." *Michigan State University Business Topics* 28 (4): 33–40.

Panel on Advanced Technology Competition and the Industrialized Allies. 1983. *International Competition in Advanced Technology: Decisions for America*. Washington: National Academy Press.

Patrick, Hugh T., and Ryuichiro Tachi, eds. 1986. *Japan and the United States Today*. New York: Center on Japanese Economy and Business.

Pennar, Karen. 1987. "The New Economy: Say Hello to the Lean Years." *Business Week*, 16 November, pp. 164–66.

Pepper, Thomas, Merit E. Janow, and Jimmy W. Wheeler. 1985. *The Competition: Dealing with Japan*. New York: Praeger.

Perry, John Curtis. 1980. *Beneath the Eagle's Wings: Americans in Occupied Japan*. New York: Dodd, Mead.

Petrakis, Harry M. 1965. *The Founder's Touch*. New York: McGraw-Hill.

Program on U.S.–Japan Relations. Center for International Affairs. 1983. *U.S.–Japan Relations: New Attitudes for a New Era*. Cambridge, Mass.: Harvard University, 1983.

Public Law 84, 1978. ("Kijoho") *Extraordinary Measures Law for Development of Specific Machinery and Information Industries*. July, Tokyo.

"Pushing for Leadership in the World Market." 1981. *Business Week*, 14 December, p. 61.

Reischauer, Edwin O. 1981. *Japan: The Story of a Nation*. 3rd ed. Tokyo: Charles E. Tuttle.

*Report of the Japan–United States Economic Relations Group*. 1981. Tokyo: Japan–U.S. Economic Relations Group.

Rosecrance, Richard. 1986. *The Rise of the Trading State*. New York: Basic Books.

Samuels, Richard. 1987. *The Business of the Japanese State: Energy Markets in Comparative and Historical Perspective*. Ithaca: Cornell University Press.

———. 1983. "Industrial Destructuring of the Japanese Aluminum Industry." *Pacific Affairs* 56 (3): 498.

Sansom, George. 1963. *A History of Japan 1615–1867*. Stanford: Stanford University Press.

Schlossstein, Steven. 1984. *Trade War*. New York: Congdon & Weed.

Schumpeter, Joseph A. 1950. *Capitalism, Socialism, and Democracy*. 3rd ed. New York: Harper and Brothers.

Science and Technology Agency. 1981. *1981 White Paper*. Tokyo.

Scott, Bruce R., John W. Rosenblum, and Audrey T. Sproat. 1980. *Case Studies in Political Economy*. Boston: Harvard Business School, Division of Research.

Scott, Bruce R., and George C. Lodge, eds. 1985. *U.S. Competitiveness in the World Economy*. Boston: Harvard Business School Press.

Semiconductor Industry Association. 1985. "Briefing Materials on Semiconductor Trade with Japan for MOSS Electronics Negotiating Team." April. Photocopy.

———. 1981. *The International Microelectronic Challenge.* Cupertino, Calif.: Semiconductor Industry Association.

———. 1985. "Japanese Market Barriers in Microelectronics." Memorandum in Support of a Petition Pursuant to Section 101 of the Trade Act of 1974, as amended. Cupertino, Calif.: SIA. Photocopy.

———. 1985. *Japanese Protection and Promotion of the Semiconductor Industry.* Cupertino, Calif.: SIA.

———. 1986. "Performance of the U.S. Semiconductor Industry, 1975 to 1985." Cupertino, Calif.: SIA. Photocopy.

———. 1983. *Petition of the Semiconductor Industry Association before the Section 301 Committee, Office of the United States Trade Representative.* Cupertino, Calif.: SIA.

———. 1985. *Petition of the Semiconductor Industry Association Pursuant to Section 301 of the Trade Act of 1974, as amended, for relief from the effects of industrial targeting practices of the government of Japan.* San Jose, Calif.: SIA.

———. 1987. *The U.S. Crisis in Microelectronics.* San Jose, Calif.: SIA.

*Semiconductor Trade and Japanese Targeting.* 1985. Hearing before the Subcommittee on International Finance and Monetary Policy. Washington, D.C., 30 July.

Sesit, Michael R., and Judith Valente. 1987. "Komori's Pact with A.M. International Shows New Muscle of Japanese Firms." *Wall Street Journal,* 23 November, p. 8.

Shinohara, Miyohei. 1982. *Industrial Growth, Trade, and Dynamic Patterns in the Japanese Economy.* Tokyo: University of Tokyo Press.

Smith, Adam. 1987. "Money World" television broadcast, 2 March.

Space Activities Commission. 1984. "Outline of Japan's Space Development Policy." 23 February. Photocopy.

Statler, Oliver. 1963. *The Black Ship Scroll.* Tokyo: John Weatherhill.

———. 1969. *Shimoda Story.* Tokyo: Charles E. Tuttle.

Suomela, John W., et al. 1983. *Foreign Industrial Targeting and Its Effects on U.S. Industries, Phase 1: Japan.* Report to the Subcommittee on Trade, Committee on Ways and Means, U.S. House of Representatives. Washington, D.C.: U.S. International Trade Commission Publication 1437.

Tanaka, Ritger, & Middleton. 1985. *Reply Brief of the Electronics Industries Association of Japan before the Office of the United States Trade Representative.* Washington, D.C. November.

Taylor, Jared. 1983. *Shadows of the Rising Sun.* New York: William Morrow.

"The Tightest of Closed Shops." 1987. *Far Eastern Economic Review,* June, p. 71.

Tyson, Laura, and John Zysman, eds. 1983. *American Industry in International Competition.* Ithaca, N.Y.: Cornell University Press.

United Nations. 1983. *United Nations Commodity Trade Statistics. Statistical Papers.* Series A. New York: United Nations.

U.S. Congress, Office of Technology Assessment. 1983. *International Competitiveness in Electronics.* Washington, D.C.

U.S. Department of Commerce, International Trade Administration. 1983.

*An Assessment of U.S. Competitiveness in High Technology Industries.* Washington, D.C.

———. 1983. *High Technology Industries: Economic Indicators.* Washington, D.C.

———. 1987. "Market Access Indicator." Washington, D.C. April. Photocopy.

———. Office of Japan, International Trade Administration. 1982. "Agreement of the High Technology Working Group on Semiconductors." Washington, D.C. November. Photocopy.

———. 1982. "Comparison of the U.S. and Japan Machine Tool Industries." Washington, D.C. June. Photocopy.

———. 1983. "Houdaille Petition Machine Tool Analysis." February. Photocopy.

———. 1983. "Second Agreement of the High Technology Working Group on Semiconductors." Washington, D.C. December. Photocopy.

———. 1981. "Soda Ash Analysis." Washington, D.C. November. Photocopy.

———. Office of Telecommunications. 1984. *A Competitiveness Assessment of the U.S. Fiber Optics Industry.* Washington, D.C.: U.S. Government Printing Office.

———. 1986. *United States Trade: Performance in 1985 and Outlook.* Washington, D.C.: U.S. Government Printing Office.

———. 1985. *1985 U.S. Industrial Outlook.* Washington, D.C.: U.S. Government Printing Office.

U.S. Department of Defense, Office of the Undersecretary of Defense for Acquisition. 1987. *Report on Semiconductor Dependency.* Prepared by the Defense Science Board Task Force. Washington, D.C. February.

———. Office of the Undersecretary of Defense for Research and Engineering. 1984. *Report of Defense Science Board Task Force on Industry-to-Industry International Armaments Cooperation, Phase II-Japan.* Washington, D.C.

U.S. Department of Justice. 1977–1985. *Foreign Agents Registration Reports.* Washington, D.C.: Department of Justice.

———. 1986. *Report of the Attorney General on Administration of the Foreign Agents Registration Act, 1985.* Washington, D.C.: Department of Justice.

U.S. General Accounting Office. 1983. *Assessment of Bilateral Telecommunications Agreements with Japan.* Washington, D.C.

———. 1982. *Industrial Policy: Case Studies in the Japanese Experience.* Report to the Chairman, Joint Economic Committee, U.S. Congress. Washington, D.C. October.

U.S.–Japan Advisory Commission. 1984. *Challenges and Opportunities in United States–Japan Relations.* A Report Submitted to the President of the United States and the Prime Minister of Japan by the United States–Japan Advisory Commission. Washington, D.C.: Office of Public Communication, Department of State.

U.S.–Japan Trade Study Group. 1984. *Progress Report 1984.* Tokyo: U.S.–Japan Trade Study Group.

"U.S. Military Coproduction Programs Assist Japan in Developing Its Civil Aircraft Industry." 1982. Report to the Chairman, Subcommittee on Trade, Committee on Ways and Means, U.S. Congress, House of Representatives. Washington, D.C. March.

Upham, Frank. 1983. "Legal Framework of Structurally Depressed Industry

Policy." Mimeographed paper. Boston College Law School.

van Wolferen, Karel. 1987. "The Japan Problem." *Foreign Affairs* (Spring).

Verner, Liipfert, Bernhard, and McPherson & Hand. 1983. *The Effect of Government Targeting on World Semiconductor Competition.* Cupertino, Calif.: Semiconductor Industry Association.

———. 1983. "Japanese Government Promotion of the Steel Industry: Three Decades of Industrial Policy." Study prepared for U.S. Steel Corporation and Bethlehem Steel Corporation. Washington, D.C. July. Photocopy.

Vogel, Ezra F. 1979. *Japan as Number One.* New York: Harper & Row.

"Wake Up America." 1987. *Business Week,* 16 November, p. 170.

White, Theodore. 1985. "The Danger from Japan." *New York Times Magazine,* 28 July, p. 19.

Wicker, Tom. 1987. "How We Got There." *New York Times,* 16 November, p. A19.

Wolf, Marvin J. 1983. *The Japanese Conspiracy.* New York: Empire Books.

Yamamura, Kozo, ed. 1982. *Policy and Trade Issues of the Japanese Economy.* Seattle: University of Washington Press.

———, and Gary Saxonhouse, eds. 1986. *Law and Trade Issues of the Japanese Economy.* Seattle: University of Washington Press.

———, and Jeanette Van Den Berg. "Japan's Rapid Growth on Trial: The Television Case." In *Law and Trade Issues of the Japanese Economy,* edited by K. Yamamura and G. Saxonhouse. Seattle: University of Washington Press, 1986.

*Yearbook of U.S.–Japan Economic Relations 1978.* 1979. Washington, D.C.: U.S.–Japan Trade Council.

*Yearbook of U.S.–Japan Economic Relations 1979.* 1980. Washington, D.C.: U.S.–Japan Trade Council.

*Yearbook of U.S.–Japan Economic Relations in 1981.* 1982. Washington, D.C.: Japan Economic Institute of America.

*Yearbook of U.S.–Japan Economic Relations in 1982.* 1983. Washington, D.C.: Japan Economic Institute of America.

Zysman, John, and Stephen S. Cohen. 1983. "Double or Nothing: Open Trade and Competitive Industry." *Foreign Affairs* 61 (Summer): 1113–39.

———, and Laura Tyson, eds. 1983. *American Industry in International Competition.* Ithaca: Cornell University Press.

# INDEX